THE
MICHELIN
GUIDE

CALIFORNIA
FROM WINE COUNTRY TO SAN DIEGO

MICHELIN

CONTENTS

DEAR READER,

We are thrilled to announce the launch of our very first MICHELIN guide to California. As part of our meticulous and highly confidential evaluation process, our inspectors are expertly trained food industry professionals who remain anonymous and consumer driven to provide extensive choices to accommodate your comfort, tastes and budget, as well as to accurately reflect the rich culinary diversity this great state has to offer.

Our inspectors dine as "regular" customers to experience the same level of service and cuisine as every other guest. For this debut edition, we have applied our global criteria to reflect some of the more current and diverse elements in California's dining scene, which in turn has seen some distinctive advancements. Besides our famous Stars and Bib Gourmands, some of these developments can be found in each neighborhood introduction, complete with photography depicting our favored choices.

Our company's founders, Édouard and André Michelin, published the first MICHELIN guide in 1900, to provide motorists with useful information about where they could service and repair their cars as well as find a good quality meal. In 1926, the star-rating system was introduced, whereby outstanding establishments are awarded for excellence in cuisine. Over the decades we have made many new enhancements to the Guides, and the local team here in California eagerly carries on these traditions.

As we take consumer feedback seriously, please feel free to contact us via email at: michelin.guides@michelin.com. You may also follow our Inspectors on Twitter (@MichelinGuideCA) and Instagram (@michelininspectors) as they chow their way around the Golden State. We thank you for your patronage and truly hope that the MICHELIN guide will remain your preferred reference to California's restaurants.

A TASTE OF CALIFORNIA

Fringed by the mighty Pacific Ocean, California is the very picture of natural beauty thanks to its sunny beaches, verdant landscapes and soaring mountains. But beyond this familiar milieu, there are a host of other experiences, wonders and attractions to be had. Having achieved its independence after the Mexican-American war and following the Gold Rush shortly thereafter, the Sunshine State saw an influx of new settlers, and continues to do so today. Vast acres of farmland led to its impressive agricultural boom; today, California is a top producer of dairy products, poultry, vegetables, berries and nuts. It is also home to myriad other industries, including technology and entertainment, thereby sealing its standing as an economic powerhouse.

Given its geographical assets, the state's farms and local markets bulge with nature's bounty that makes for an enticing canvas to which local chefs apply their creativity and personality. Whether that inspiration comes from south of the border, across the Pacific or is influenced by the Mediterranean, California's cuisine is ingredient-focused, respectful of the seasons and never bound by convention.

The vineyards of Napa Valley and Sonoma County thrive in this temperate and dry climate, and together account for a majority of the nation's most acclaimed wines. Here, producers of boutique pours and global heavy-hitters rub shoulders. In fact, a number of California labels have become prized possessions for oenophiles across the world.

Sacramento—the state's capital—is revered as one of the most historic towns on the left coast. This central valley city boasts iconic structures and acre upon acre of gorgeous greenery. Here, farming communities reside amidst quaint towns and historic government buildings, thereby making it one of the more unique urban centers around.

With its towering redwood trees and steep cliffs plunging into the Pacific, magnificent Marin County beguiles with ravishing views and rustic charm. Of course, waters off this coast offer exceptional hunting ground for seafood galore—all of which may be enjoyed at restaurants nearby.

Then cross the Golden Gate Bridge to arrive at famously free-spirited San Francisco. From its deeply complex history and pioneering architecture to its culinary significance, this glorious city is one of the nation's most well-tread destinations. While iconic sights draw tourists from all over the map, it's the Bay Area's beatnik spirit, socio-political activism and surfeit of food and drink that is most alluring.

Journey farther along the coast to the historic cities of Monterey and Santa Barbara to discover reminders of the state's Spanish Colonial past, as well as celebrated attractions dotting the drive all the way down to the City of Angels. Los Angeles is a sprawling metropolis and a veritable hub of art and entertainment, retail therapy and groundbreaking dining. Eating your way around LA is a sheer thrill—dig into nostalgic favorites in Hollywood, sizzling barbecue in Koreatown, tempting taquerias, food trucks aplenty and some of the country's most enticing Chinese dining in San Gabriel Valley.

Then venture on to realize the California of your dreams—by way of Orange County. Complete with a tropical vibe, delicious waterfront dining and sun-kissed surfers, this region is the very epitome of beachy luxury.

Speaking of striking surrounds, there is an impressive variety also located along California's second most populous county of San Diego. Settled along the southwestern tip, this sun-soaked city bursting with energy and personality also swarms with historic and artistic attractions as well as an abundance of culinary options.

EATING IN CALIFORNIA

WINE COUNTRY

SACRAMENTO

MARIN

SAN FRANCISCO

EAST BAY

PENINSULA

SOUTH BAY

MONTEREY

Total Number of Restaurants

Starred Restaurants ❀

LOS ANGELES

SANTA BARBARA

ORANGE COUNTY

SAN DIEGO

THE MICHELIN GUIDE'S COMMITMENTS

Whether they are in Japan, the USA, China or Europe, our inspectors apply the same criteria to judge the quality of each and every establishment that they visit. The MICHELIN guide commands a **worldwide reputation** thanks to the commitments we make to our readers—and we reiterate these below:

Our inspectors make **anonymous visits** to restaurants to gauge the quality of cuisine offered to the everyday customer. They pay their own bill and make no indication of their presence. These visits are supplemented by comprehensive monitoring of information—our readers' comments are one valuable source, and are always taken into consideration.

Our choice of establishments is a completely **independent** one, made for the benefit of our readers alone. Decisions are discussed by the inspectors and editor, with the most important considered at the global level. Inclusion in the Guide is always free of charge.

The Guide offers a **selection** of the best restaurants in each category of comfort and price. A recommendation in the Guide is an honor in itself, and defines the establishment among the "best of the best."

All practical information, the classifications, and awards are revised and updated every year to ensure the most **reliable information** possible.

The standards and criteria for the classifications are the same in all countries covered by the MICHELIN guides. Our system is used worldwide and easy to apply when selecting a restaurant.

As part of Michelin's ongoing commitment to improving **travel and mobility**, we do everything possible to make vacations and eating out a pleasure.

THE MICHELIN GUIDE'S SYMBOLS

Michelin inspectors are experts at finding the best restaurants and invite you to explore the diversity of the gastronomic universe. As well as evaluating a restaurant's cooking, we also consider its décor, the service and the ambience - in other words, the all-round culinary experience.

Two keywords help you make your choice more quickly: red for the type of cuisine, gold for the atmosphere.

Mexican • Taqueria

FACILITIES & SERVICES

	Notable wine list
	Notable cocktail list
	Notable beer list
	Notable sake list
	Wheelchair accessible
	Outdoor dining
	Private dining room
	Breakfast
	Brunch
	Dim sum
	Valet parking
	Cash only

AVERAGE PRICES

	Under $25
$$	$25 to $50
$$$	$50 to $75
$$$$	Over $75

STARS

Our famous one ❀, two ❀❀ and three ❀❀❀ stars
identify establishments serving the highest quality
cuisine – taking into account the quality of ingredients,
the mastery of techniques and flavors, the levels of
creativity and, of course, consistency.

❀❀❀   Exceptional cuisine, worth a special journey

❀❀   Excellent cuisine, worth a detour

❀   High quality cooking, worth a stop

BIB GOURMAND

Inspectors' favorites for good value.

MICHELIN PLATE

Good cooking.
Fresh ingredients, capably
prepared: simply a good meal.

WINE COUNTRY

WINE COUNTRY

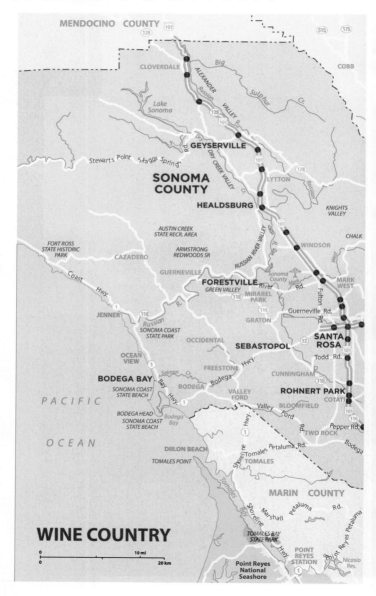

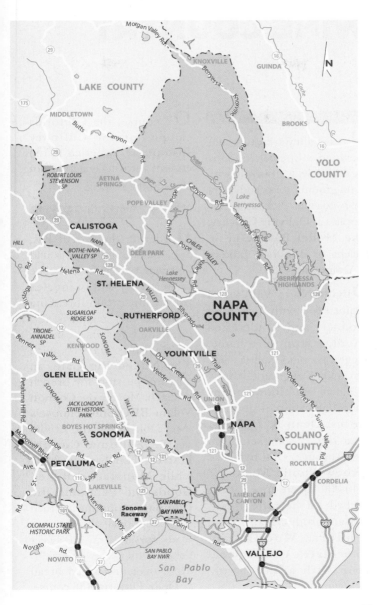

EATING IN...
WINE COUNTRY

NAPA VALLEY

Napa Valley's culture has spawned a special kind of food and wine tourism with tasting rooms, tours and farm-fresh cuisine. Pick up picnic supplies at **Oakville Grocery**, **The Model Bakery** in St. Helena or **Bouchon Bakery** in Yountville.

Olivier Napa Valley is a quaint shop with local food products and handcrafted goodies from Provence. Megawatt personalities like Thomas Keller and Cindy Pawlcyn rub elbows at the flagship location of gourmet grocer, **Dean & DeLuca**, or at farmers' markets from May through October. The **Oxbow Public Market** is a 40,000-square-foot facility packed to the rafters with artisan products and food vendors. **Woodhouse Chocolates** is a regional shop with a nationwide following.

Of course, the California campus of the **Culinary Institute of America (CIA)** ensures a striking lineup of hot chefs in the making.

SONOMA COUNTY

Bordering the North Bay, Sonoma County boasts around 76 miles of Pacific coastline with over 400 wineries producing groundbreaking varietals. This region is also cherished for its culinary destinations starting with **The Naked Pig Café**, an amazing pit-stop for brunch or lunch. Moving on, **Cochon Volant BBQ Smokehouse's** 'cue took home the crown at the **Sonoma County Harvest Fair** back in 2010, while **Moustache Baked Goods** and **Petaluma Pie Company** continue to turn out exceptional, all-American treats for an army of sweet fiends. Others may choose to drool over just-baked bread at **Della Fattoria**. Of course,

some of the best oysters can be found off the Sonoma coast from **Tomales Bay Oyster Company** and **The Marshall Store**, to **Hog Island Oyster Co**. There is so much more than just mollusks to be relished in this part of town, so start your day right with a serious breakfast at **Dierk's Parkside Café**. Here "Gompa's Pancake Breakfast," which includes two eggs, bacon, ham or sausage, is a hearty revelation. Similarly, comfort food is the name of the game at local sensation, **Bear Republic Brewing Company**. This is a family-owned Healdsburg hot spot favored for unique, award-winning brews and tours (by appointment only). Afterwards, stop by for a scoop or slice from **Noble Folk Ice Cream & Pie Bar.** Not far behind, top-notch IPAs are all the rage at **Lagunitas Brewing Company**—a taproom for the Petaluma-based brewery. Serious home gardeners scour the shelves of **Petaluma Seed Bank**, just down the street from its former location.

NAPA VALLEY

AD HOC ⅏○
American • Rustic

 ♿ 🏠 ≈

If you've ever wondered how Thomas Keller cooks at home, Ad Hoc is your best bet. The most casual of Chef Keller's restaurants, it offers accessible fare served family style in a bright and inviting wood-paneled room. Waits are inevitable without a reservation, but the engaging staff keep things hopping. The dining room feels like a country home, with that iconic blue awning and a sign that reads "for temporary relief from hunger."

The food is worth the wait and while dishes may sound simple, the crafting is not—come every other Monday for the outstanding fried chicken. A salad of sautéed red bliss potatoes tossed in Sriracha aïoli is beyond par; and even the humble cheese course dazzles. Generous portions may warrant sharing chocolate mousse for dessert.

▧ 6476 Washington St. (bet. California Dr. & Oak Circle), Yountville
℘ (707) 944-2487 — **WEB:** www.adhocrestaurant.com
▧ Lunch Sun Dinner Thu – Mon   **PRICE: $$$**

ANGÈLE ⅏○
French • Rustic

 ♿ 🏠

Quietly set on the banks of the Napa River, this airy charmer is the perfect place to while away a warm afternoon—complete with a charming vibe, attentive staff, spacious outdoor patio and alluring Edith Piaf soundtrack. No need to shy away on a cooler day either as the rustic interior, with its wood A-frame ceiling and polished concrete floors, is equally compelling.

Order a glass of a local white and savor the bistro food inflected with Californian flavor, from a classic steak tartare tossed with minced capers and horseradish to chicken pot pie layered with pearl onions and maitake mushrooms in a smooth velouté that would do any Frenchman proud. Finish with caramelized banana gratin, heaped with crisp streusel and a big scoop of vanilla ice cream.

▧ 540 Main St. (at 5th St.), Napa
℘ (707) 252-8115 — **WEB:** www.angelerestaurant.com
▧ Lunch & dinner daily   **PRICE: $$**

ARCHETYPE 🍴○
American · Elegant

♿ 🚻 🛋

Even by the standards of luxuriously appointed Napa Valley restaurants, Archetype is quite the looker. Blending farmhouse comfort with luxurious modern touches, it's just as glamorous for an evening meal by the fireplace as it is for brunch on the covered, screened-in patio strewn with climbing yellow rose bushes.

During the day, the menu focuses on comfort food like velvety artichoke soup with parmesan foam and flaky cheddar biscuits with sausage gravy. At night, things get more ambitious with such satisfying plates as oak-grilled duck breast with scallion pancakes and gochujang; or curry-braised red snapper with crab dumplings. There are also plenty of fun theme nights for locals—from fish taco Thursdays to fried chicken and waffle Sundays.

▪ 1429 Main St. (bet. Adams & Pine Sts.), St. Helena
📞 (707) 968-9200 — **WEB:** www.archetypenapa.com
▪ Lunch & dinner Thu – Mon   **PRICE: $$**

BISTRO JEANTY 🍴○
French · Bistro

♿ 🚻

Napa transforms into the French countryside via a meal at Bistro Jeanty, which serves rib-sticking favorites like coq au vin, boeuf Bourguignon and a sinfully rich milk-fed veal chop with chanterelle mushrooms and Camembert sauce. But California's lighter side is here, too: a salad of silken smoked trout and frisée is garden-fresh, and daily specials highlight the best in local produce.

The classic bistro accoutrements (yellow walls, wooden tables, framed retro posters) are present and accounted for, but there's an element of quirky fun here as well—from the flower-bedecked bicycle out front to the porcelain hens and hogs that dot the dining room. Like the flaky, caramelized and unmissable tarte Tatin, this is a gorgeous update on a classic.

▪ 6510 Washington St. (at Mulberry St.), Yountville
📞 (707) 944-0103 — **WEB:** www.bistrojeanty.com
▪ Lunch & dinner daily   **PRICE: $$$**

AUBERGE DU SOLEIL ✿

Californian • Luxury

This is one of the first restaurants to elevate the Napa Valley to greatness. For over a decade, Chef Robert Curry has been ensuring its legacy with cooking that is the very definition of Californian cuisine: global flavors expressed through local and seasonal ingredients. The kitchen's work is as impressive as the setting, although it is during brunch or lunch when the creations truly come to life. Everything seems just a bit more beautiful from this extraordinary perch, overlooking the vineyards and mountains. Those terrace tables have some of the best views around.

Meals may be inspired by the comforting flavors of Sacramento Delta asparagus soup bobbing with lobster bits lurking at the bowl's base. Then Kurobuta pork chop set atop a red wine-Meyer lemon sauce is cooked to a perfect blush and served alongside intensely charred rapini for refreshing bitterness. A warm pineapple tart surrounded by a swirl of salted caramel makes for a sweet, savory and deliciously fruity bite.

Servers are stylish, polite and manage to refill your glass after each sip, without seeming intrusive. Their wine list is one of the most notable in the valley and proudly showcases local growers.

■ 180 Rutherford Hill Rd. (off the Silverado Trail), Rutherford
✆ (707) 967-3111 — **WEB:** www.aubergedusoleil.com
■ Lunch & dinner daily   **PRICE: $$$$**

BOTTEGA ⅏○
Italian • Elegant

 ♿ 🛖 🍽️

Michael Chiarello is one of the original celebrity chefs, and his higher-end Napa Valley outpost draws fans from around the globe. Hopefuls are indeed likely to see him in the kitchen, drizzling olive oil on plates of creamy, almost liquid-fresh burrata and marinated mushrooms; or pouring persimmon purée across thick slices of yellowfin tuna crudo. Even the wine list features his house blends, which pair delightfully with pastas like the whole-wheat tagliarini tossed in a pitch-perfect Bolognese.

Large and boisterous, Bottega's autumn-hued dining room welcomes crowds with comfy banquettes and terra-cotta accents. One will also find lovely outdoor seating by the firepit.

A well-made tiramisu and espresso offer a fine Italiano end to the festivities.

▨ 6525 Washington St. (near Yount St.), Yountville
✆ (707) 945-1050 — **WEB:** www.botteganapavalley.com
▨ Lunch Tue – Sun Dinner nightly   **PRICE: $$**

BRIX ⅏○
Californian • Elegant

 🎉 ♿ 🛖 🍽️ ☎

This roadside treat overlooking the Mayacamas Mountains is almost as lauded for its 16-acre produce garden (which provides many of the ingredients seen on your plate) and vineyard, as it is for its ultra-seasonal and eclectic-Californian cuisine. Dishes are wide-ranging and often refined as verified by ricotta gnocchi cooked to a gentle gold in rosemary-browned butter with squash, plump Medjool dates and almonds; or saffron and orange salmon that arrives firm and pink with quail eggs, dill aïoli and potato salad. An extensive Sunday brunch buffet highlights offerings from the wood-fired oven and charcoal grill.

The interior feels like a mountain ranch with its stone walls, fireplaces and chandeliers cleverly crafted from cutlery. Service is finely tuned.

▨ 7377 St. Helena Hwy. (at Washington St.), Napa
✆ (707) 944-2749 — **WEB:** www.brix.com
▨ Lunch & dinner daily   **PRICE: $$$**

BOUCHON ✤
French • Bistro

♿ 🪑 🍽

Timeless French food is recreated with great regard for quality and technique at Thomas Keller's exuberant bistro, set down the street from his iconic The French Laundry. Complete with lush potted plants, shimmering brass accents and enormous mirrors, this dining room is the spitting image of Parisian chic. A theatrical crowd uplifts the space with conviviality, and every lavish banquette or stool at the bustling bar is full. Always.

Thanks to the house bakery next door, the bread here is ace, so grab an extra hunk of the supremely fresh and crusty pain d'epi to slather with butter. The menu lists well-executed classics, including that beloved platter of escargot, each coated with intensely flavorful and rich garlic-parsley butter and crowned by addictive little toques of flaky puff pastry. Moving on, braised lamb demonstrates the power of rustic French cooking, set over polenta with grilled young leeks and carrots.

Desserts are quite literally the icing on the cake and often the very definition of decadence. Even the humble pie is elevated here, to be served as an almond-spiced pear, glazed with juice and set over a tiny round of puff pastry matched with rich vanilla ice cream.

■ 6534 Washington St. (at Yount St.), Yountville
✆ (707) 944-8037 — **WEB:** www.thomaskeller.com
■ Lunch & dinner daily   **PRICE: $$$**

CA'MOMI OSTERIA

Italian • Rustic

This stand-alone spot aims to promote buon gusto with its "heartcrafted" food (as indicated in a sign above the bar). Expansive and airy, complete with exposed brick and wooden beams, this space is abuzz with pizzaioli turning out Neapolitan pies from the wood-burning oven (note that the counter opposite the fire is the best seat in the house).

The massive menu is inspired by every region of Italy and may feature crispy Piemontese sunchoke chips dusted with salt and fried parsley, as well as Tuscan spinach-ricotta gnudi floating in a rich and creamy butter-and-sage sauce. Save room at the end of your meal for those delicious Campanian angioletti, which is basically fried pizza dough packed with that beloved combination of chocolate and hazelnut.

▪ 1141 1st St. (bet. Coombs & Main Sts.), Napa

✆ (707) 224-6664 — **WEB:** www.camomiosteria.com

▪ Lunch Fri – Sun Dinner Tue – Sun   **PRICE: $$**

CHARLIE PALMER STEAK NAPA ⅋○

Steakhouse • Elegant

Chef Charlie Palmer may have only recently brought his eponymous steakhouse to the boutique Archer Hotel in downtown Napa, but it already fits seamlessly into these environs and feels like it's been here forever. Service is superb, as you would expect of any restaurant in this chain. The sleek interior features dark woods, stone columns and tables that are on the small side for a steakhouse. The kitchen focuses on classic fare, such as freshly shucked oysters, Caesar salad with fried quail eggs and steaks with a choice of standout sauces, particularly the béarnaise. Non-traditional offerings include sweet pea ravioli or a rack of lamb.

After dinner, head to the rooftop, where a bar and expansive lounge with fireplaces attract long weekend lines.

▪ 1260 1st St. (at Napa Town Center), Napa

✆ (707) 819-2500 — **WEB:** www.charliepalmersteak.com

▪ Lunch & dinner daily   **PRICE: $$$$**

THE CHARTER OAK 🍴

Californian • Rustic

Courtesy of The Restaurant at Meadowood's team, this approachable retreat is already highly regarded and rightly applauded as a Napa mainstay. It presents a rustic method to dining that centers on hearth-roasted food, and the beautifully restored room's design and large tables seem to promote sharing platters of roasted beef ribs or broccolini.

Their garden's bounty is on full display in a simple, but beautiful bowl of just-plucked veggies, bettered with a swipe of the savory fermented soy dip. The hearth is indeed the heart of this kitchen, and everything from mains to sides bears traces of the flames. Smashed then grilled into little coins, the potato tostones have a terrific char and smoky flavor—enhanced by the caramel quality of brown butter.

▨ 1050 Charter Oak Ave. (off St. Helena Hwy.), St. Helena
℘ (707) 302-6996 — **WEB:** www.thecharteroak.com
▨ Lunch & dinner daily   PRICE: $$$

CICCIO 😷

Italian • Trattoria

A pleasant contrast to the sleek new spots around town, Ciccio's country-style curtains and slatted front porch are a ticket to another era (and a hot ticket at that, since tables are hard to come by). Its location inside a wood-framed 1916-era grocery could pass as some John Wayne film set, but Ciccio is more of a spaghetti Western, thanks to the focused Italian-influenced menu revolving around pastas and pizzas. Highlights include the feathery ricotta dumplings in a homey veal and pork Sunday red sauce. Spicy mortadella, fiery cherry peppers and creamy fontina are a winning trio atop crispy pizza, but don't miss the signature sponge cake, soaked in citrus liqueur.

The wine list is a delight, as those behind this operation also own Altamura winery.

▨ 6770 Washington St. (bet. Madison & Pedroni Sts.), Yountville
℘ (707) 945-1000 — **WEB:** www.ciccionapavalley.com
▨ Dinner Wed – Sun   PRICE: $$

COMPLINE 🍴○

American · *Trendy*

♨ ♿ ☂

This cool wine bar clearly takes pride in the mastery of its sommelier by pouring a lengthy and thoughtful array of wines from the world over. At the same time, Compline serves a focused menu of appealingly hearty food that pairs well with this list. Find a perch at the bar so you can chat with the staff about their vast selection, but tables in the dining room or patio are just as pleasant.

Savor a glass of champagne with duck fat fries—to whet the appetite—before perusing the menu. Juicy half-pound burgers on brioche are a great way to get going here, especially when layered with Gruyère and mushrooms. Less casual items feature a Liberty Farms duck breast or rustic hanger steak.

Keep an eye on the calendar for themed tasting events and seminars.

▦ 1300 First St. (at Napa Town Center), Napa
℘ (707) 492-8150 — **WEB:** www.complinewine.com
▦ Lunch & dinner daily   **PRICE: $$$**

COOK ST. HELENA 😊

Italian · *Neighborhood*

It's true—solid cooking and sane prices can be hard to come by—but this Italian haven located on St. Helena's main drag appears to have mastered that formula. The cozy space has two seating options: a gleaming marble counter up front, as well as tables that stretch from front to back (the ones up front are lighter, airier and preferable).

The food is thoughtful and refined with a daily rotating risotto, house-stretched mozzarella and burrata and glorious pastas like ricotta fazzoletti with a deeply flavored Bolognese. Grilled octopus salad with potatoes, olives and tomato dressing is boosted by prime ingredients and careful seasoning. The wine list tempts at dinner, but Bloody Marys are all the rage at brunch, served at Cook Tavern next door.

▦ 1310 Main St. (bet. Adams St. & Hunt Ave.), St. Helena
℘ (707) 963-7088 — **WEB:** www.cooksthelena.com
▦ Lunch Mon – Sat Dinner nightly   **PRICE: $$**

EVANGELINE ¶○

American · Rustic

& ⌂ ☒

Jazzy New Orleans flair infuses every inch of this Southern charmer, which adds just a hint of spice to the easy Californian vibe of quaint Calistoga. A trellised garden patio (a must-visit on a warm day) blooms with fragrant jasmine, while the cozy indoor dining room provides an intimate retreat, complete with midnight-blue banquettes.

A collection of French bistro- Californian- and Cajun-inspired dishes abound on the approachable menu. Rich, creamy duck rillettes arrive with toasted baguette and red pepper jelly. Shrimp étouffée is spicy and complex, its thick, dark roux coating a heap of fluffy white rice. And melt-in-your-mouth tarte Tatin slathered with locally made Three Twins vanilla ice cream is as good as any beignet.

▨ 1226 Washington St. (bet. 1st St. & Lincoln Ave.), Calistoga
℘ (707) 341-3131 — **WEB:** www.evangelinenapa.com
▨ Lunch Sat – Sun Dinner nightly   **PRICE: $$**

FARMSTEAD ☻

Californian · Rustic

& ⌂ ☒

For a down-home (but still Napa-chic) alternative to the Cal-Ital wine country grind, follow your nose to this Long Meadow Ranch-owned farmhouse, whose intoxicating smoker is parked right in the front yard. The cathedral ceiling, old-school country music and boisterous locals give Farmstead a permanent buzz; for quieter dining, hit the front terrace.

Dishes are laden with ranch-grown products (from veggies to olive oil), utilized in outstanding preparations like wood-grilled artichoke with sauce gribiche, meatballs with caramelized onions and tomato marmalade or a smoked chicken sandwich with avocado, sweet onion rings and a side of herb-fried potatoes. Try the ranch's own wine, or splurge on a fancy bottle at a shockingly reasonable markup.

▨ 738 Main St. (at Charter Oak Ave.), St. Helena
℘ (707) 963-9181 — **WEB:** www.longmeadowranch.com
▨ Lunch & dinner daily   **PRICE: $$**

GOOSE & GANDER

American • Chic

With its mountain-lodge feel, this clubby retreat has been a favorite among Napa Valley diners since its bygone days as the Martini House. Those classic libations may have long since made way for more elaborate concoctions, but this gander retains all the charm of the goose—as well as the recipe for its justly famous mushroom soup, which could win over even the staunchest foe of fungi.

Elsewhere on the menu, you'll find hearty dishes like fettuccini carbonara, a bone marrow-topped burger and fried chicken sandwich with charred jalapeño aïoli as well as delicious duck-fat fries. Whether you're soaking up summer on the spacious patio or relaxing by the fireplace in the cavernous downstairs bar, you'll quickly feel at home here.

■ 1245 Spring St. (at Oak Ave.), St. Helena
℘ (707) 967-8779 — **WEB:** www.goosegander.com
■ Lunch & dinner daily   PRICE: $$

GRACE'S TABLE 😊

International • Family

Around the world in four courses without ever leaving the wine country? It's possible at this bright and beloved downtown Napa space that balances fun with excellence. Only here can a top-notch tamale filled with chipotle-pulled pork, green chile and black beans be followed by cassoulet that would do any Frenchman proud—thanks to its decadent mélange of butter beans, duck confit and two kinds of sausage.

With Italian and American staples in the mix as well, it might sound too eclectic for one meal, but Grace's Table earns its name with charming service and a thoughtful, well-priced wine list to bridge any gaps between cuisines. Regardless, make sure you don't miss the satiny, ganache-layered devil's food chocolate cake—a slice is big enough to split.

■ 1400 2nd St. (at Franklin St.), Napa
℘ (707) 226-6200 — **WEB:** www.gracestable.net
■ Lunch & dinner daily   PRICE: $$

THE FRENCH LAUNDRY ✿✿✿

Contemporary • Elegant

Over 20 years old and topping every foodie's bucket list, Thomas Keller's legendary destination still doesn't miss a beat. The cuisine, staff and state-of-the-art kitchen embedded with the chef's renowned sense of purpose and functionality continue to remain at their pinnacle. In fact this may be known as the greatest cooking space in America, as every aspect of the setting is carefully determined—from the counter height to the flowing lines of the ceiling. It's a meeting point of the past, present and future.

Chef Keller continues to pair incredibly classic French techniques with wildly fresh ingredients in a setting that is a perfect storm of restaurant greatness—we should all be so lucky to score a reservation here in our lifetime. Choose from two seasonal tasting menus, including a vegetarian option. Both feature products from boutique purveyors. Dinners may highlight signature oysters with white sturgeon caviar in a warm sabayon studded with tapioca pearls, or Scottish sea trout with avocado mousse and a sorrel- and sesame-miso vinaigrette.

Located along a winding road, The French Laundry is the very picture of bucolic charm with ivy creeping up its stone façade and a tastefully decorated dining room.

■ 6640 Washington St. (at Creek St.), Yountville
☎ (707) 944-2380 — **WEB:** www.thomaskeller.com
■ Lunch Fri – Sun Dinner nightly   **PRICE: $$$$**

GRAN ELÉCTRICA 😊

Mexican · Colorful

 ♿ 🏠 🍸

Welcome to Mexico by way of Brooklyn (home to the original location) right in the heart of Napa. Gran Eléctrica is already a neighborhood hit—particularly during happy hour. Servers are always welcoming and ensure a steady meal. Inside this breezy space, find a long bar stocked with mezcal and tequila as well as floor-to-ceiling windows that practically open onto the sidewalk. The massive outdoor patio is just as popular.

Over in the kitchen, tacos, tostadas and larger plates are all made with great care and top ingredients. Be sure to try the ceviche tostada, a starter filled with clean, bright flavors and lime-cured shrimp. Red snapper mojo de ajo is another high point, sautéed in a garlicky red sauce of chile morita, lemon and a bit of paprika heat.

◼ 1313 Main St. (bet. Caymus & Clinton Sts.), Napa
℘ (707) 258-1313 — **WEB:** www.granelectrica.com
◼ Dinner nightly   **PRICE: $$**

HARVEST TABLE 🍴

Californian · Neighborhood

 ♿ 🏠 🍸 🖐

The Harvest Inn is a culinary destination thanks to the thriving presence of Harvest Table. Its Californian menu relies on local purveyors and the inn's own gardens for ingredients. Guests are encouraged to tour these grounds before or after meals. The space is simple and appealingly rustic thanks in part to the large fireplace. Two covered patios offer a comfy perch to enjoy the natural beauty of the inn.

Dark wood tables can be seen groaning under the weight of such enjoyable items as smoked Mt. Lassen trout with Meyer lemon gel. Scallops are then set atop savory cauliflower florets and sweet red grapes for a delightful balance in flavors; while a tropical fruit panna cotta with mango and roasted cashew praline is relished at the end.

◼ 1 Main St. (bet. Lewelling Ln. & Sulphur Springs Ave.), St. Helena
℘ (707) 967-4695 — **WEB:** www.harvesttablenapa.com
◼ Lunch Wed – Sun Dinner Tue – Sun   **PRICE: $$$**

KENZO ❀

Japanese • Minimalist

❀ 🍶 ♿ ⬚

Kenzo Tsujimoto made his fortune developing thrilling video games like Resident Evil and Street Fighter, but his Napa Valley temple of traditional Japanese cuisine is a place to hit pause and wash away worldly cares. Designed by Tsujimoto's wife, Natsuko, this 25-seat arena is spare and minimal, incorporating traditional woods, maple trees and river rocks to create a peaceful sanctuary.

Though Kenzo offers a handful of tables, the best seats are at the lengthy counter, where diners can chat with the chefs and watch their meal being prepared firsthand. The kaiseki experience is beautifully composed, elegantly paced and may feature such exquisite presentations as the seasonal hassun—unveiling poached eggplant in dashi and seared Sonoma duck breast. Other courses have included straw-smoked Hokkaido scallop sashimi with jidori egg yolk sauce; Wagyu beef tenderloin with a reduction of the estate's own Bordeaux-style blend; and the chef's selection of Edomae-style sushi.

There is an outstanding variety of sake showcased here, but savvy diners may want to sample Kenzo Estate's own California-grown wines, which are available by the flight. If on offer, the sauvignon blanc, is highly recommended.

■ 1339 Pearl St. (at Franklin St.), Napa
✆ (707) 294-2049 — **WEB:** www.kenzonapa.com
■ Dinner Tue – Sun   **PRICE: $$$$**

LA CALENDA

Mexican · *Family*

Thomas Keller has brought his magic touch to Mexican food, offering all the impeccable sourcing and technique of The French Laundry at a weeknight price point. Unsurprisingly, everyone wants in; and with no reservations offered, waits for a table can easily run over an hour. The excellent house margaritas help make the time go by a little faster.

Chef de cuisine Kaelin Ulrich Trilling is a Oaxaca native, and you'll know it after sampling his complex mole negro spooned over tender chicken enchiladas. Perfectly caramelized pork al pastor, roasted on a traditional spit in the center of the kitchen, then arrives atop blistered blue corn tortillas. No table should go without that little taste of heaven that is Chef Keller's vanilla bean-flecked flan.

■ 6518 Washington St. (at Yount St.), Yountville
☏ (833) 682-8226 — **WEB:** www.lacalendamex.com
■ Dinner nightly   **PRICE: $$**

MICHAEL WARRING 🍴

Contemporary · *Simple*

Vallejo isn't the first place that springs to mind when you think elevated cuisine, but a seat at this reputed dining counter will have you feeling like you stepped into an episode of Chef's Table. The space itself is simple and intimate, furnished with a handful of tables and seven seats overlooking the kitchen, so book your spot in advance. It's a laid-back scene, where the focus remains squarely on the food.

Chef Warring, who hails from Napa's esteemed Auberge du Soleil, spins his well-honed skill and technique on pristine seasonal products, and the results are enticing. Think of ocean trout crudo with shaved hearts of palm and kohlrabi microgreens; or perfectly seared sous vide ribeye with sautéed maitake mushrooms.

■ 8300 Bennington Ct. (at Hiddenbrooke Pkwy.), Vallejo
☏ (707) 655-4808 — **WEB:** www.michaelwarring.com
■ Dinner Wed – Sun   **PRICE: $$$$**

LA TOQUE ✿
Contemporary • Elegant

You'll want to tip your own toque in appreciation after a meal at this downtown fine-dining lair in the Westin Verasa Napa, which blends a serious approach to cuisine and service that has just enough cheek to keep things lively.

La Toque may display an oversized inflatable chef's hat hanging above its walkway, but the interior is the soul of modern sophistication, with leather-topped tables, a fireplace and an extensive wine list— proffered on an iPad. The cadre of staff is notable, and the well-trained, knowledgeable waiters always appear to be in sync with the celebratory crowd.

Choose from a four- or five-course à la carte, beginning with exquisite canapés like perfectly seasoned tuna tartare or clams with apple vinaigrette. Thin slices of beef loin carpaccio are lightly smoked, then artfully presented to resemble a flower, topped with creamy tuna sauce, sautéed wild mushrooms and dried tomato. Intense Lebanese spices come to life in the wonderfully tender braised squid with dates, almonds, cauliflower and a spoonful of thick Greek yogurt. Desserts, like the butter-crunch cake with apple, underscore the glamorous and delicious character of the restaurant itself.

■ 1314 McKinstry St. (at Soscol Ave.), Napa
✆ (707) 257-5157 — **WEB:** www.latoque.com
■ Dinner nightly   **PRICE: $$$$**

MIMINASHI ‖◯

Japanese • Minimalist

&

Izakaya fare gets Californian flair at this downtown Napa site, which has a distinctive and minimalist look inspired by several trips to Japan. A buzzy crowd of locals fills the wooden booths and tables, while an arrow-shaped bar is a major draw for solo diners.

A variety of skewered chicken parts grilled over the white-hot binchotan are the highlight of the menu—imagine the likes of succulent and smoky chicken thighs, or springy tsukune in an umami-rich tare glaze. A handful of seats at the narrow counter allow guests to chat with the grill cook. The rest of the menu emphasizes local produce, including rice and noodle bowls stuffed with seasonal vegetables; crunchy sweet corn fritters with Kewpie mayo; as well as gingery pan-fried chicken gyoza.

■ 821 Coombs St. (bet. 2nd & 3rd Sts.), Napa
℘ (707) 254-9464 — **WEB:** www.miminashi.com
■ Dinner nightly   PRICE: $$

MUSTARDS GRILL ‖◯

American • Neighborhood

⅋ &

At Cindy Pawlcyn's iconic roadhouse, it's a joy to eat your greens. Lettuces are freshly plucked from the restaurant's bountiful garden boxes and tossed with tasty dressings including a shallot- and Dijon mustard-spiked Banyuls vinaigrette. The fish of the day may unveil grilled halibut sauced with oxtail reduction and plated with silken leeks, fingerling potatoes and baby carrots. But, save room as this is not the place to skip dessert, and the lemon-lime tart capped with brown sugar meringue that is fittingly described on the menu as "ridiculously tall," doesn't disappoint.

It should come as no surprise that there's usually a wait for a table here. But no matter; use the time to take a stroll on the grounds for a preview of what the kitchen has in store.

■ 7399 St. Helena Hwy. (at Hwy. 29), Yountville
℘ (707) 944-2424 — **WEB:** www.mustardsgrill.com
■ Lunch & dinner daily   PRICE: $$$

OENOTRI 😊

Italian • *Trattoria*

There's no sweeter greeting than the aroma of wood smoke that beckons diners into this downtown standout. And with its Neapolitan pizza oven, sunny textiles and exposed brick, Oenotri—from an ancient Italian word for "wine cultivator"—looks as good as it smells.

Chef/owner Tyler Rodde imbues the cooking of Southern Italy with a dash of Californian spirit. From the pasta to the herbs, nearly everything is made from scratch or from the garden. Bountiful salads top every table, but those seeking meatier eats should start with the charcuterie, cured in-house. Options change seasonally, but pizza is a must. Torchio, or torch-shaped pasta, with diced roasted winter squash, toasted pine nuts, fried sage and a drizzle of brown butter is a close second.

▢ 1425 1st St. (bet. Franklin & School Sts.), Napa
☏ (707) 252-1022 — **WEB:** www.oenotri.com
▢ Lunch Sat – Sun Dinner nightly   **PRICE: $$**

PRESS ⅋○

Steakhouse • *Elegant*

The classic steakhouse gets a wine country twist at this standby, where the G&Ts are designed to specifications and the dry-aged USDA Prime steaks hold equal standing with the "vegetable cocktail"—a stunning edible still life of local produce. But indulgence is still the name of the game, from a take on the classic wedge salad made with local Point Reyes blue cheese to a decadent mashed potato pancake.

With a bucolic location off Highway 29, Press combines traditional dark wood, cozy booths and a flickering fireplace with lofty and soaring ceilings. The well-to-do crowd marvels at decorative wonders like a massive ceramic clock sourced from a bygone New York train station, all the while sipping full-bodied Napa reds that pair perfectly with the rich food.

▢ 587 St. Helena Hwy. (bet. Inglewood Ave. & Lewelling Ln.), St. Helena
☏ (707) 967-0550 — **WEB:** www.pressnapavalley.com
▢ Dinner Wed – Mon   **PRICE: $$$$**

REDD WOOD 😳
Italian • *Trendy*

 ♿ ☂ 🖥

Napa Valley's answer to the hip Cal-Ital hot spots of San Francisco, Redd Wood boasts an edgy indie soundtrack and a parade of bearded, tattooed waiters. But unlike some cityside establishments, the waitstaff here is personable and enthusiastic, and there's plenty of breathing room (including a private area that's popular for events).

Artisan pizzas are the main attraction of this kitchen and sometimes simplest is best—like the fresh mozzarella, basil and tomato. Another topped with pancetta, asiago, taleggio and black garlic is equally enticing. But, don't let that limit your choices. The house-cured salumi, fresh pastas and appealing antipasti are also winners—just be sure to save some room for their outstanding toffee cannoli dessert.

■ 6755 Washington St. (bet. Madison & Pedroni Sts.), Yountville
☎ (707) 299-5030 — **WEB:** www.redd-wood.com
■ Lunch & dinner daily   **PRICE: $$**

RUTHERFORD GRILL 🍴
American • *Chic*

 ♿ ☂

As the crowds filter out of neighboring Beaulieu Vineyard and other Highway 29 wineries, they head straight to this upscale chain, which boasts long lines at even the earliest hours. Kudos to the amiable host staff for handling them smoothly. The dark wood interior is clubby yet accommodating, and a large patio offers drinks for waiting diners.

Every portion here can easily serve two, beginning with a seasonal vegetable platter boasting buttery Brussels sprouts, a wild rice salad and braised red cabbage. For those looking to stave off tasting-induced hangovers, the steak and enchilada platter is the ticket with plenty of juicy tri-tip, yellow and red escabeche sauce and a poached egg. A wedge of classic banana cream pie delivers the knockout punch.

■ 1180 Rutherford Rd. (at Hwy. 29), Rutherford
☎ (707) 963-1792 — **WEB:** www.hillstone.com
■ Lunch & dinner daily   **PRICE: $$**

THE RESTAURANT AT MEADOWOOD ✿ ✿ ✿

Contemporary · Luxury

With its elusive balance of rustic luxury, this is the kind of property that will floor you with its understated beauty. Everything about it exudes California-style wealth and comfort, from those cottages dotting the verdant Napa hills to the front lounge's stone fireplace. Beyond this, the dining room resembles a sophisticated barn of sorts, decked with polished stone tables, wood columns and bucolic splendor.

All of this makes for an elegant backdrop for romantic evenings or family celebrations, as long as everyone is willing to splurge. Servers are impeccable, professional and know how to keep their guests happy and at ease.

The magic of Chef Christopher Kostow and team lies in their ability to take just-picked produce and create dishes that are the very essence of laid-back luxury. Vichyssoise, with fermented potatoes and leeks and house-made buttermilk, is an absolute work of art, but wait, there's more. The pine cone—a giant one beautifully plated with greenery—hides a seductive chocolate cream within. Garnished with tiny slivers of crystallized baby pine cones cooked in honey, it's pure genius.

■ 900 Meadowood Ln. (off Silverado Trail), St. Helena
✆ (707) 967-1205 —
WEB: www.therestaurantatmeadowood.com
■ Dinner Tue – Sat   **PRICE: $$$$**

SAM'S SOCIAL CLUB 🍴

American • Elegant

 ♿ 🚻 🛋

Lauded as the main restaurant for the Indian Springs resort, Sam's Social Club is a supremely beloved destination, thanks in large part to its Spanish colonial look and soothing, bucolic vibe. Named for resort founder Samuel Brannan, this Mission Revival dining room boasts lofty ceilings, plush couches, bright murals and a big patio complete with a geyser-fed water feature.

The unpretentious atmosphere extends to the plates, like grilled octopus endowed with a peppy romesco sauce and crispy new potatoes. Specials may include pan-seared duck served with bright green broccoli rabe and sweetly acidic piquillo. Tourists have already caught on: you'll find them happily sharing bottles of wine and digging into plates of strawberry-rhubarb crisp.

 ▨ 1712 Lincoln Ave. (at Indian Springs Resort), Calistoga
 📞 (707) 942-4969 — **WEB:** www.samssocialclub.com
 ▨ Lunch & dinner daily   **PRICE: $$**

SOLBAR 🍴

Californian • Contemporary décor

 🍸 ♿ 🚻 📺 🛋 🧼

It may take a few twists and turns around the palatial Solage Calistoga resort to locate this bijou, but once inside, you'll find a romantic dining room decked out with banquettes and a contemporary fireplace.

The cuisine may be proudly Californian, but the kitchen is well-versed in classic techniques, as evidenced by dishes such as the octopus with Ibérico ham reduction. Dainty and tender faro gnocchetti with a briny-sweet asparagus and clam velouté, coupled with the fett'unta's crispy crust and soft crumb is spot on with an appealing balance of flavors and texture. Eureka lemon and blackberry croccante, with its thin layers of pastry tucked with blood orange gelée, pistachio and Satsuma mandarin sorbet, is a lovely finale.

 ▨ 755 Silverado Trail (at Rosedale Rd.), Calistoga
 📞 (707) 226-0860 — **WEB:** solage.aubergeresorts.com
 ▨ Lunch & dinner daily   **PRICE: $$$**

ZUZU ¶○
Spanish • Rustic

&

This Mediterranean-inspired cutie was dishing out small plates long before it was cool, and its rustic bi-level space still draws a steady crowd of local regulars. Upstairs, long picnic tables are ideal for those who come with a crowd. Spanish-style tile floors, a pressed-tin ceiling and honey-colored walls give Zuzu an enchanting old-world vibe, setting the scene for sharing the more than two-dozen tapas, both frio and caliente.

They include the fantastic shrimp ceviche with bright cara cara oranges, chili oil and shaved red onions; plump Gulf coast shrimp with a smoky pimento sauce; and fried Tolenas Ranch quail over rich, smoky Rancho Gordo posole.

For similar cuisine in a more modern atmosphere, sister restaurant La Taberna is also worth a visit.

▨ 829 Main St. (bet. 2nd & 3rd Sts.), Napa
✆ (707) 224-8555 — **WEB:** www.zuzunapa.com
▨ Lunch Mon – Fri Dinner nightly   **PRICE: $$**

Look for the symbol 🛏
for a brilliant breakfast to
start your day off right.

SONOMA COUNTY

BACKYARD 😊
Californian · Family

 ♿   🏠   🛋

Savvy locals flock to this out-of-the-way charmer, where reasonable prices and an approachable menu draw a crowd of regulars—many of whom have their taste buds set on the famed fried chicken. Thanks to Backyard's husband-and-wife team, you'll feel as though you're in a private home, and the patio looks like a real backyard, complete with picnic tables and a tree strung with lights.

Dishes rotate seasonally, but you might find a tender grilled calamari salad with blood oranges and pickled sunchokes; or creamy house-made pasta à la carbonara with black trumpet mushrooms and smoky bacon. Don't miss the velvety chocolate pudding with salted caramel.

With doughnuts accompanied by apple-persimmon butter and eggs benedict atop biscuits, brunch is a hit.

◼ 6566 Front St. (bet. 1st & 2nd Sts.), Forestville
✆ (707) 820-8445 — **WEB:** www.backyardforestville.com
◼ Lunch & dinner Thu – Mon   **PRICE: $$**

BARNDIVA 🍴
Californian · Elegant

 ⚅   🍸   ♿   🏠   🛋

Pristine ingredients are the real stars at this decidedly un-diva-like restaurant, where the only thing barn-like is the soaring ceiling.

From goat cheese croquettes and Alaskan halibut served with a spring pea risotto to a giant macaron the size of a pancake (that makes an equally big impression), their dishes show wonderful finesse and abundant creativity, yet never sacrifice balance or technique.

With a thoughtfully constructed cocktail menu boasting an array of spirits, herbs and infusions, Barndiva offers lots to explore off the plate. Witty decorative touches like two-story green velvet curtains and a wall hanging made of wood shoe stretchers only add to the fun. And for post-meal perusing, there's even an art gallery located right next door.

◼ 231 Center St. (bet. Matheson & Mills Sts.), Healdsburg
✆ (707) 431-0100 — **WEB:** www.barndiva.com
◼ Lunch & dinner Wed – Sun   **PRICE: $$$**

BRAVAS
Spanish • Cozy

"Jamón in" says the cheeky neon sign at this lively tapas bar, set in a former home full of sunny accents and 1970s psychedelic posters. While there's a small bar inside, most visitors make a beeline to the huge backyard with its outdoor porch and garden. Thanks to a welcoming cocktail-party vibe, this is the kind of place where big groups of tourists and locals can be found in abundance.

Whether you like your tapas traditional or with a little added flair, there's plenty to sample and share, from plancha-seared sea scallops with creamy romesco to a classic tortilla Española. Lighter appetites will enjoy the chilled tuna belly salad packed with crisp fennel and buttery green olives—it's practically made for washing down with a glass of cava-spiked sangria.

420 Center St. (bet. North & Piper Sts.), Healdsburg
(707) 433-7700 — **WEB:** www.starkrestaurants.com
Lunch & dinner daily   PRICE: $$

CAFE LA HAYE
Californian • Neighborhood

For years, Cafe La Haye has been a standby off the square in downtown Sonoma. One bite of its luscious burrata, surrounded by Early Girl tomatoes and crispy squash blossoms in the summer, or vinaigrette-dressed pea shoots in spring, proves it hasn't aged a day. The small, modern space is still charming, with large windows and lots of mirrors. Stunning local artwork for sale decorates the walls.

The food spans cultural influences, including a delicate risotto with pine nuts in a cauliflower broth, or soy-sesame glazed halibut atop whipped potatoes and braised kale. A postage stamp-sized bar pours glasses of Sonoma chardonnay and cabernet, perfect with rich strozzapreti tossed with braised pork ragù, Grana Padano and toasted breadcrumbs.

140 E. Napa St. (bet. 1st & 2nd Sts.), Sonoma
(707) 935-5994 — **WEB:** www.cafelahaye.com
Dinner Tue – Sat   PRICE: $$

UNITED

A STAR ALLIANCE MEMBER ✦

To be more California, we'd have to put avocado on our schedule.

Flying to the most destinations within California.

fly California's global airline

CHALKBOARD 😊

American • *Elegant*

 ♿ ✵

Located in the luxury boutique Hotel Les Mars, Chalkboard is a surprisingly laid-back boîte, with a casual vibe and a buzzing bar that offers a refreshing counterpoint to a day of wine tasting. The dining room's low vaulted ceilings and marble tables might feel a touch austere if not for the rustic wooden chairs, open kitchen and warm, easygoing service. Sip a little wine as you nosh on sweet, tender pork belly biscuits in the cozy backyard.

The menu of small plates spans every cuisine and appetite. Be sure to sample at least one of the homemade pastas: bucatini with pepperoni and Meyer lemon is fresh and delightful. English peas with truffled chevre, mint, potatoes and pickled red onions are a tasty, and visually appealing, celebration of spring.

■ 29 North St. (bet. Foss St. & Healdsburg Ave.), Healdsburg
☞ (707) 473-8030 — **WEB:** www.chalkboardhealdsburg.com
■ Lunch Sat – Sun Dinner nightly   **PRICE: $$**

DIAVOLA 😊

Italian • *Trattoria*

 ♿ ☂

Its home in downtown Geyserville may look like the Wild West, but this devilishly good Italian restaurant can hold its own with any city slicker. Festooned with statues of saints, boar tusks and stacks of cookbooks, it has a playful yet smart vibe.

Excellent pizzas, like the signature combo of spicy meatballs, red peppers, provolone, pine nuts and raisins, are the reason why crowds pack this spot. And top-notch house ingredients like salumi, lardo and cured olives elevate each and every dish. But, that's not to count out their exquisite pastas, including linguine tossed with baby octopus, bone marrow, zucchini and bottarga. Desserts, like the chocolate pistachio semifreddo paired with a perfectly pulled Blue Bottle espresso, are yet another treat.

■ 21021 Geyserville Ave. (at Hwy. 128), Geyserville
☞ (707) 814-0111 — **WEB:** www.diavolapizzeria.com
■ Lunch & dinner daily   **PRICE: $$**

DRY CREEK KITCHEN 🍴

American • Elegant

Attached to the sleek Hotel Healdsburg, find this upscale haunt of famed Chef Charlie Palmer. The wine list beams with Sonoma pride, and each month highlights top vintners from the region. The vaulted room is airy and refined, with white tablecloths and windows overlooking the downtown square. This kitchen may serve American classics, but each has a unique edge, making the five-course tasting a major draw. Indulge in gnocchi with a succulent lamb ragù, black garlic purée and watercress for a bit of pungent fun. The pastry chef's talent is formidable, resulting in beautifully delicate lemon tarts with pistachio sable or strawberry mousse buried under its own unique world of toppings.

If you're lucky, textbook canelé will arrive as a grand finale.

▪ 317 Healdsburg Ave. (bet. Matheson & Plaza Sts.), Healdsburg
✆ (707) 431-0330 — **WEB:** www.drycreekkitchen.com
▪ Dinner nightly   **PRICE: $$$**

EL MOLINO CENTRAL 😊

Mexican • Taqueria

Lovers of regional Mexican food will swoon for this laid-back charmer, which offers full-throttle fare made with quality ingredients. The colorful little building has a strange layout (order at the counter, then pass through the kitchen to dine on the patio), but it still draws a large following—expect to chat with fellow diners hungry for intel on the day's best dishes.

Entrées shift with the seasons, but the preparations are always expert: try the halibut ceviche with house-made chips or the red mole tamales chockablock with chicken and just a touch of masa. The Bohemia beer-battered fish tacos featuring handmade tortillas are a must, as are the addictive poblano-tomatillo nachos verdes. Of course, spice fans can't get enough of the crispy chilaquiles.

▪ 11 Central Ave. (at Sonoma Hwy.), Sonoma
✆ (707) 939-1010 — **WEB:** www.elmolinocentral.com
▪ Lunch & dinner daily   **PRICE:** 🍪

FARMHOUSE INN & RESTAURANT ✿

Californian • Rustic

❀ &

Urbanites seeking an escape from the fray head to this charming inn, nestled in a quiet, woodsy corner of Sonoma, for fine cooking, upscale accommodations or both. Dinner guests will find themselves charmed by the dining room's soothing colors, rustic-elegant décor, crackling fireplace and numerous intimate nooks—including an enclosed patio.

The protein-centric menu reads like an ode to California's purveyors, and a focus on seasonality is in keeping with the area's ethos. Unsurprisingly, the results are often rewarding: succulent, perfectly balanced heirloom tomatoes are twirled with crunchy seaweed, briny clams and mirin dressing, while flaky halibut arrives atop a richly flavored fennel-tomato beurre blanc, dotted with corn and huitlacoche pudding. The signature "rabbit, rabbit, rabbit" showcases the kitchen's creativity, bringing together a confit rabbit leg, an applewood-smoked bacon-wrapped loin and a minuscule rack of chops rounded out with Yukon Gold potatoes and a whole grain mustard-cream sauce.

Pair your meal with a bottle from the impressive list of local and European wines. Then complete the seduction with an airy soufflé concealing a treasure of Blenheim apricot preserves.

◾ 7871 River Rd. (at Wohler Rd.), Forestville
℘ (707) 887-3300 — **WEB:** www.farmhouseinn.com
◾ Dinner Thu – Mon   **PRICE: $$$$**

GLEN ELLEN STAR 😊

Californian • Neighborhood

&

The country charm of this quaint cottage belies the level of culinary chops that will impress even a hardened city slicker. With knotty pine tables, well-worn plank floors and a wood-burning oven, the space is delightful. A perch at the chef's counter affords a great view of the action.

Here, Chef Ari Weiswasser showcases his signature style via the use of Mediterranean and Middle Eastern ingredients. Imagine wood-roasted asparagus with lavash crackers and shaved radish over a tangy hen egg emulsion; or chicken cooked under a brick with coconut curry and sticky rice. Daily pizzas like the tomato-cream pie with Turkish chilies are also a thrill. Save room for house-made ice cream in flavors like vanilla maple Bourbon, salted peanut butter or peach verbena.

■ 13648 Arnold Dr. (at Warm Springs Rd.), Glen Ellen
☎ (707) 343-1384 — **WEB:** www.glenellenstar.com
■ Dinner nightly   **PRICE: $$**

HANA 🍴

Japanese • Simple

🍶 &

Rohnert Park denizens continue their love affair with this spacious gem featuring semi-private nooks and a lounge. Tucked in a hotel plaza next to the 101, Hana is run by affable Chef/owner Ken Tominaga, who sees to his guests' every whim. For the full experience, park it at the bar where the obliging staff can steer you through the best offerings of the day. Top quality fish flown in from Japan (ask for the daily specials), traditional sushi and small plates are the secret to their success, though mains like pan-seared pork loin with ginger-soy jus also hit the spot.

The omakase is a fine way to go—six pieces of nigiri, which may include toro, hamachi belly, kampachi, tai, halibut with ponzu sauce or sardine sprinkled with Hawaiian lava salt.

■ 101 Golf Course Dr. (at Roberts Lake Rd.), Rohnert Park
☎ (707) 586-0270 — **WEB:** www.hanajapanese.com
■ Lunch Mon – Sat Dinner nightly   **PRICE: $$**

HARBOR HOUSE
Californian • Elegant

You'll drive along winding roads past sloping vineyards, apple orchards and sun-dappled redwood trees before arriving at this serene sanctuary set atop a cliff overlooking the Pacific Ocean. The historic property dates to 1916 but reopened in 2018 following a renovation infusing it with a laid-back luxury. The redwood-clad dining room's picture windows frame postcard-perfect views of the gardens and crashing waves; a fireplace adds to the already inviting ambience. Aside from its Instagram-ready good looks, it's a dining destination thanks to Chef Matthew Kammerer's distinctive cuisine.

Great care is paid to details here, from employing local woods to smoke and grill as well as fish caught right off the coast, to house-made sea salt and vinegars. Savor the fresh tuna, aged for eight days and brushed with salted plum paste, jalapeño and okra for a riot of flavors. Sea urchin custard is at once delicate and intense, while tender abalone in a briny broth renders diners speechless. This kitchen's deftness with vegetables is particularly noteworthy; the sweet potato with savory miso and hemp seed is a revelation.

Perhaps most surprising is the price—impressive value for a meal of this caliber.

■ 5600 CA-1 (at the Harbor House Inn), Elk
𝒫 (800) 720-7474 — **WEB:** www.theharborhouseinn.com
■ Dinner Thu – Mon   **PRICE: $$$$**

JOHN ASH & CO. 🍴○
Californian • Elegant

A pioneer in farm-to-table dining, this stalwart in the Vintners Inn (owned by Ferrari-Carano) is 35+ years strong and still serving the region's best, much of it grown in the on-site gardens. The rustic Front Room is a popular happy-hour spot with its menu of bar snacks, while the Tuscan-inspired dining room boasts plush booths, a stone fireplace and Italian landscapes on the walls.

Chef Tom Schmidt has broadened the restaurant's focus, incorporating Latin touches like a halibut ceviche with aji amarillo and creamy sweet potato. But there are still indulgent classics aplenty, like the dry-aged beef filet, cooked to a buttery medium rare and accompanied by decadent Point Reyes blue cheese-mashed potatoes, or even the rich chocolate truffle cake for dessert.

■ 4330 Barnes Rd. (off River Rd.), Santa Rosa
☎ (707) 527-7687 — **WEB:** www.vintnersinn.com
■ Dinner nightly   PRICE: $$$

MONTI'S 🍴○
American • Family

With the scent of wood smoke hanging in the air, it seems impossible to resist ordering the day's offering hot off the rotisserie. Those smoked prime ribs or pomegranate-glazed pork ribs do not disappoint either. But the oak-roasted chicken is a perennial favorite and deserves a visit on its own. Succulent auburn skin, seasoned flesh, heirloom carrots, smashed fingerling potatoes and crisped pancetta render this dish a thing of beauty. End your meal over baby lettuces with Point Reyes blue cheese and candied walnuts; or butterscotch pudding for lip-smacking comfort food—Monti's-style.

Set within Santa Rosa's Montgomery Village, this is your quintessential wine country hangout, dressed with rustic tables and centered around a roaring fireplace—natch.

■ 714 Village Court (at Sonoma Ave.), Santa Rosa
☎ (707) 568-4404 — **WEB:** www.starkrestaurants.com
■ Lunch & dinner daily   PRICE: $$

MADRONA MANOR ✾

Contemporary • *Historic*

This romantic Victorian mansion is the unexpected home of a forward-looking kitchen. It's the kind of place that makes one want to dress up—at least a little bit—to fully engage in the art of dining. Arrive early to enjoy a sunset drink out on the terrace. You can either stay there to dine, or head inside to settle into one of several timelessly elegant dining rooms cloaked in sleek marble, plush silk and old-world grandeur.

The showmanship here extends to the artistic, often theatrical plates that make the most of herbs and flowers to create novel and very focused flavors throughout the carte. Tasting menus begin with a smoked egg amuse-bouche whereby a smoke-filled cloche unveils a delicate eggshell filled with a feather-light sabayon and watercress purée that looks and tastes of magic. The kitchen is also particularly adept with raw vegetables, as may be found in the roasted quail that is cut and served with olive oil-fried chard and onion soubise.

A green profiterole stuffed with apple mousse leads to a "morning breakfast dessert" of Turkish figs, apple sorbet, thin and crunchy melba toast as well as a host of garnishes like chocolate, jelly, raisins and corn caramels.

▪ 1001 Westside Rd. (at Dry Creek Rd.), Healdsburg
✆ (707) 433-4231 — **WEB:** www.madronamanor.com
▪ Dinner Wed – Sun   **PRICE: $$$$**

RAMEN GAIJIN 😊

Japanese • Rustic

 ♿ ⛩

"Gaijin" is the none-too-polite Japanese term for a foreigner, but the American chefs of this noodle joint clearly take pride in their outsider status, fusing local ingredients with traditional technique. It's surely one of the best bowls of ramen around, and you can smell the soup before you're even past the front door.

The best seats are at the counter, where you can chat with the chef as he assembles bowls of light, fresh shoyu ramen filled with thick house-made rye noodles and caramelized pork belly chashu. Appetizers are also notable, like the karaage: crunchy-coated, tender chicken thighs with miso ranch. Desserts, such as the black-sesame ice cream over miso-salted caramel, matcha meringue and coconut flakes, mix sweet and savory for the win.

◼ 6948 Sebastopol Ave. (bet. Main St. & Petaluma Ave.), Sebastopol

☏ (707) 827-3609 — **WEB:** www.ramengaijin.com

◼ Lunch & dinner Tue – Sat   **PRICE: $$**

RISIBISI 😊

Italian • Cozy

 ♿ ⛩ 🍽

Though it's named for a comforting dish of rice and peas, Risibisi's seafood-heavy take on Italian cuisine is a bit more sophisticated. This kitchen excels at both land and sea. Meaty highlights include the fork-tender, delicate braised pork and ricotta meatballs and the winning crispy duck confit salad with bittersweet arugula. All of the pastas are made in house and desserts entice with house-made tiramisu and cannoli with bits of candied fruit, caramel and strawberry sauce vying for your attention.

A makeshift picture gallery constructed out of salvaged Tuscan chestnut window frames, wine barrels and wagon wheels brings character to this inviting brick-walled dining room. A back patio offers views of the Petaluma river and old train tracks.

◼ 154 Petaluma Blvd. N.

(bet. Washington St. & Western Ave.), Petaluma

☏ (707) 766-7600 — **WEB:** www.risibisirestaurant.com

◼ Lunch & dinner daily   **PRICE: $$**

RUSTIC ⅋○

Italian · Rustic

 ♿ 🏠

Those Godfather Oscars certainly could have funded a posh restaurant for Francis Ford Coppola, but the director has kept it relatively simple at his enormous Geyserville eatery, offering Italian classics from his childhood. Savory pettole in a paper bag kick off the meal, followed by crispy chicken al mattone sautéed in olive oil with strips of red bell pepper. Coppola's personality is a big part of Rustic's appeal, and these walls are covered with his film memorabilia as well as his own wines. Crowds also cherish the Italian-American music, games and nostalgia that define Coppola's past as well as those of his customers.

Come on Tuesdays to find a special prix-fixe menu, as well as the sociable staff donning vintage garb.

▨ 300 Via Archimedes (off Independence Ln.), Geyserville
℘ (707) 857-1485 — **WEB:** www.francisfoodcoppolawinery.com
▨ Lunch & dinner daily　　　　　　　　　　**PRICE: $$**

THE SHUCKERY ⅋○

Seafood · Simple

 ♿

It is a wonder that this easygoing oyster bar is Petaluma's first. The breezy vibe is amplified through oversized windows that let in plenty of natural light.

Everything here seems to be focused on raw delicacies, from minerally Hog Island oysters to meatier Hammersley ones from the Puget Sound. All of these are shucked right at the bar before arriving at your table, so the action and entertainment are constant. Raw items may be the focus, but a handful of fried or baked classics are not to be missed, like oysters Rockefeller laden with parmesan, Pernod, spinach and cured ham. Round out your feast with something more substantial, like puffy golden hushpuppies filled with shrimp morsels in a light corn batter. Fish tacos are yet another big hit.

▨ 100 Washington St. (at Kentucky St.), Petaluma
℘ (707) 981-7891 — **WEB:** www.theshuckeryca.com
▨ Dinner nightly　　　　　　　　　　**PRICE: $$**

SINGLETHREAD ❀❀❀

Contemporary • Luxury

❀ 🍸 ♿

"Exquisite" barely begins to describe a meal at this Healdsburg jewel, where every detail has been considered, from the moss and flowers cradling the amuse-bouche presentation to the packets of heirloom seeds that are sent home as parting gifts. Trained in Japan, Chef Kyle Connaughton adheres to the philosophy of omotenashi, or anticipating a guest's every need.

The menu is acutely tuned to each micro-season in Sonoma County, thanks to the bounty provided by farmer and co-owner, Katina Connaughton. For instance, spring might bring delicately smoked Ora king salmon topped with arctic char roe and myoga; while winter showcases pumpkin tartare with Dungeness crab and a miso-makrut lime foam. An expert in donabe (Japanese clay pot) cooking, the chef proclaims his skills with brilliant fish dishes like "fukkura-san"—black cod that is served over a broth of ember-grilled fish bones. Desserts include a Japanese cheesecake or a delicate snowfall of buttermilk-thyme sherbet.

The service and wine selection are every bit the equal of their thoughtful food and décor, to the point where guests may never want to leave. For them, there's an on-site inn, where lovely breakfasts await the next day.

◾ 131 North St. (at Center St.), Healdsburg

✆ (707) 723-4646 — **WEB:** www.singlethreadfarms.com

◾ Lunch Sat Dinner Wed – Mon   **PRICE: $$$$**

SPOONBAR

Contemporary • Chic

Seeking a modern departure from wine country's faux-rustic aesthetic? This restaurant in the eco-chic h2hotel will fit the bill with reclaimed wood tables and 3-D artwork. Its bar is a local haunt, with wine-weary tasters arriving to palate-cleanse via an extensive list of cocktails. In the kitchen, a husband-and-wife chef team successfully guides the menu in a sophisticated, vegetable-driven direction. Find such inventive dishes as Meyer lemon-ricotta gnudi in a parmesan-mushroom broth; or seared scallops with roasted and pickled brassica and black garlic purée.

Should you order dessert, like the honey-crème fraîche panna cotta, don't be surprised if a second arrives gratis—the chef likes to test out her latest experiments on an all-too-willing public.

■ 219 Healdsburg Ave. (bet. Matheson & Mill Sts.), Healdsburg
✆ (707) 433-7222 — **WEB:** www.spoonbar.com
■ Dinner nightly   **PRICE: $$**

STOCKHOME 😊

Scandinavian • Simple

Halfway across the globe, the husband-and-wife team of Roberth and Andrea Sundell have brought the flavors of their native Stockholm to their adopted hometown, Petaluma. This cheery, minimal spot plays all the hits: pickled herring, hearty meatballs and house-made sodas (try the subtly sweet sea buckthorn). Heavy Mid-Eastern and light California touches still manage to creep in, as seen in the skagen—a classic dill-shrimp salad that adds avocado to the mix, or farm-fresh berries atop giant pancakes. For the hardcore herring haters, the menu also flaunts tasty nods to Sweden's Middle Eastern community by way of falafel, tabbouleh and a terrific beef-lamb pita wrap.

Jars of black licorice and bulks of other Swedish candies are available for daily binging.

■ 220 Western Ave. (at Liberty St.), Petaluma
✆ (707) 981-8511 — **WEB:** www.stockhomerestaurant.com
■ Lunch & dinner Wed – Sun   **PRICE: $$**

TERRAPIN CREEK ⫣○
Californian • Cozy

Whether it's the ochre walls, the bold artwork or the fireplace, Terrapin Creek emits palpable warmth. Liya Lin and Andrew Truong, partners and co-chefs, have created an alluring sanctum where everyone feels like a regular, whether you're a resident or simply here to spot the migrating whales.

The menu is concise, so expect a spectrum of bites that may include grilled Monterey sardines set over shaved radishes and cabbage dressed in a refreshing lime-curry vinaigrette. Pasta is made in house, so dig your fork into those torch-shaped curls with crumbled merguez, chopped spinach, feta cheese, mint and sweet English peas in a spicy tomato-based broth. For dessert, a chocolate cake with cream cheese frosting is bested with a heavenly caramel sauce.

▓ 1580 Eastshore Rd. (off Hwy. 1), Bodega Bay
℘ (707) 875-2700 — **WEB:** www.terrapincreekcafe.com
▓ Dinner Thu – Mon   **PRICE: $$$**

THE FIG CAFÉ ⫣○
Californian • Neighborhood

⅙ ⌲

Sondra Bernstein's Cal-Med café takes on a more modern look with communal tables, orange bar stools and geometric lighting. But pilgrims to this sleepy address shouldn't fret: Rhone-style wines (a house specialty) remain on the shelves and inviting horseshoe-shaped booths are still the best seats in the house. The nightly prix fixe—displayed on butcher paper—is as great a deal as ever, and approachable faves like fried olives and a burger are out in force. Start with a salad like grill-charred romaine Caesar with anchovy-spiked dressing; then segue to a seasonal entrée like trout with wild rice, caramelized onions and green beans.

For like-minded cuisine, visit the girl & the fig in Sonoma's main square.

▓ 13690 Arnold Dr. (at O'Donnell Ln.), Glen Ellen
℘ (707) 938-2130 — **WEB:** www.thefigcafe.com
▓ Lunch Sun Dinner nightly   **PRICE: $$**

VALETTE ⚟

Californian • Neighborhood

Housed in the former Zin space, this contemporary darling is actually a full-circle comeback for Chef Dustin Valette and his brother/General Manager Aaron Garzini, whose grandfather owned the building in the 1940s. Its current look, however, is as cutting-edge as ever thanks to dandelion-like light fixtures, concrete walls and horseshoe-shaped banquettes. The bill of fare is modern American with a few French twists. Scallops arrive beneath squid ink puff pastry, into which a server pours caviar-flecked champagne-beurre blanc. Then, Peking-spiced duck breast set atop hearty forbidden rice is taken to the next level with a touch of tamarind sauce.

For an appetizing end, dig into the smooth block of chocolate mousse with a luscious salted caramel center.

▨ 344 Center St. (at North St.), Healdsburg
☎ (707) 473-0946 — **WEB:** www.valettehealdsburg.com
▨ Dinner nightly   PRICE: $$$

YETI ⚟

Nepali • Elegant

Its sleepy location may be unusual, but with a creekside view and friendly service, Yeti makes for a pleasant getaway from the wine country grind. Inside the sunken dining room, soft folk music, Tibetan artwork and a blisteringly hot tandoor set an authentic scene.

Though this food may hail from the Himalayan frontier, most dishes are from both India's North (think grilled meats and biryanis) as well as her Southern coastal regions (fish curries and coconut sauces). Try the lamb chops coated with garam masala and served over a bed of charred onion and bell pepper. Vegetable momos (steamed dumplings stuffed with cabbage, carrots, beans and green onion) served with spicy sambal, cilantro and sweet tamarind dipping sauces are a party in your mouth.

▨ 14301 Arnold Dr., Ste. 19 (in Jack London Village), Glen Ellen
☎ (707) 996-9930 — **WEB:** www.yetirestaurant.com
▨ Lunch & dinner daily   PRICE: $$

61

ZAZU KITCHEN + FARM 🍴○

American • Rustic

 ♿ 🍴 🛋

A fun change from the rustic décor seen in much of wine country, this big and bright industrial space is practically translucent, thanks in large part to its garage-like doors and glossy cement floors. Natural wood tables and huge wildflower arrangements keep it from feeling chilly, as do surprisingly great acoustics—you won't struggle to be heard, even if the massive 20-seat family table is full.

Pork is the priority here, as evidenced by the sharp, spicy and addictive Cuban sandwich with house-made mortadella. Vegetarians will delight in the tart tomato soup with an oozing Carmody grilled cheese, or the black beans with baked eggs.

But the real key for carnivores is to bring home the bacon; it's a little bit pricey, but worth every penny.

▨ 6770 McKinley St., Ste. 150 (bet. Brown & Morris Sts.), Sebastopol

✆ (707) 523-4814 — **WEB:** www.zazukitchen.com

▨ Lunch Fri – Sun Dinner Wed – Mon   **PRICE: $$**

SACRAMENTO

SACRAMENTO

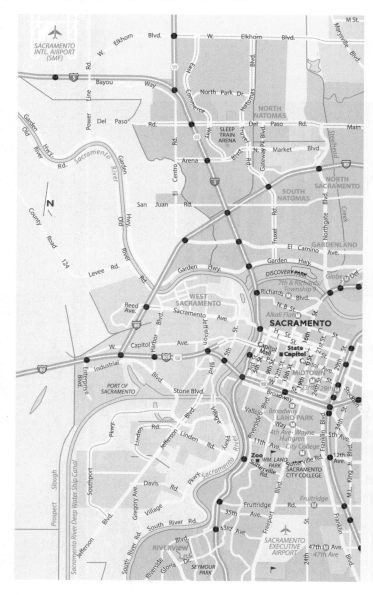

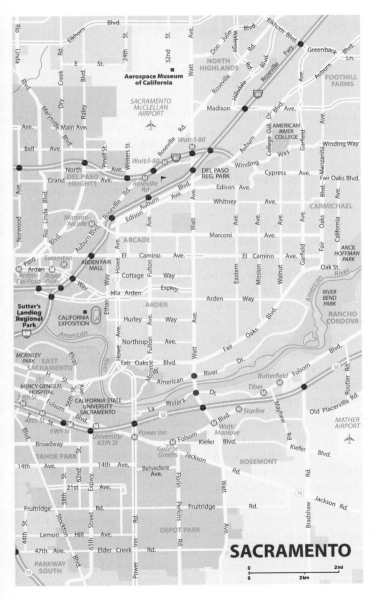

SACRAMENTO

EATING IN...
SACRAMENTO

This capital city of California is a pretty place, punctuated by government buildings, picture-perfect lawns and fruit orchards. Having said that, look further to uncover Sacramento's history, predating its life as the seat of government. Like much of the Golden State itself, it is known for its warm weather, with this part of the central valley being the largest agricultural producer in the nation. This in turn makes it one of the more interesting culinary regions around. Come in September to partake in their **Farm-to-Fork Festival** to sample it all.

Everyone heads downtown for a surfeit of cuisines. Start your morning with meticulously roasted coffee at **Temple Coffee Roasters**. Its largest location (on 22nd and K) flaunts a floor covered with a half-million pennies, as well as a Kyoto slow-drip. Then sojourn at **Freeport Bakery** which has been serving its colossal cinnamon buns for over 30 years now. **Ettore's Bakery & Cafe** is the area's answer to European pastries along with American-style bites. Make your way into this cute café to discover everything from pies and petit fours, to pizzas and sammies.

Moving south of the border, Sacramento also boasts a noticeably strong Mexican heritage. This extends through the central valley, and visitors are always surprised to discover such a diverse culinary scene—one that taps into pan-Latino and other cuisines. **Lalo's**, for instance, is known for its tacos de lengua, chilaquiles and unbeatable prices; while over on Franklin Blvd., **El Novillero** forms the very picture of a comfortable dining room for family-style meals. Young'uns on the run may catch a game of futbol or simply get their groove on at **Chando's Cantina**,

a late-night darling for Mexican cooking and cocktails; but sweet fiends convene at **Pushkin's Restaurant**, a downtown gem with a modern sensibility—think vegan specials. Charming chocolate boutique **Ginger Elizabeth** is another dessert sensation whose goodies star on myriad restaurant menus in town. Finally, both home cooks and top chefs seek out the **Sacramento Natural Foods Co-op**, which may have opened in 1973 but a recent remodel left it thoroughly fresh and farm-y.

"Sactown," as locals like to call it, takes its happy hour seriously, so start your night right...and early. Beer drinkers head to **Ruhstaller**—the city's first craft beer made from local barley and hops—while cocktailers have more of a choice at **The Red Rabbit**—a cool spot as adept with a classic Pimm's Cup as it is with its cooking. **Shady Lady Saloon** is a speakeasy-style stalwart for sips with unique ingredients. Of course, live music five nights a week along with such solid cooking simply makes a visit to here quite the nostalgic memento.

ALLORA ⅋○

Italian • Contemporary décor

Clean, modern and convivial, Allora is filled with the neighborhood feels, largely thanks to the owners' passion and dedication. Tastefully decorated in shades of white, wood and deep green, this Cal-Ital kitchen is focused on fresh and sustainable ingredients. Seafood is supremely enticing and consistently woven through their menu of fresh pasta, local fish and Italian wines. The cavatelli, for instance, is made from scratch before being napped in a garlic-and-tomato sauce bobbing with chunks of sausage and summer squash.

Come dessert, stick with a straightforward gelato, or just indulge in another glass from Sommelier/co-owner Elizabeth-Rose Mandalou's large and reasonably priced selection that's displayed through the glass-enclosed cellar.

■ 5215 Folsom St. (bet. 52nd St. & Rodeo Way)
℘ (916) 538-6434 — **WEB:** www.allorasacramento.com
■ Dinner Tue – Sat   **PRICE: $$**

BACON & BUTTER ⅋○

American • Simple

If the name doesn't have you salivating yet, the dishes being ferried to and fro by the bustling staff certainly will. Bacon & Butter lures diners and lots of them—you'll see lasting queues late into the morning—thanks to its promise of good old-fashioned American breakfast and brunch.

From flapjacks and crisped potatoes to super-sized cinnamon rolls, this kitchen's goods taste like Sunday morning at your Mom's, including all the noise and nagging. The absolute don't miss however is the biscuit sandwich, featuring egg, cheese, bacon and caramelized onion layered atop fluffy, flaky biscuits and then smothered with bacon gravy for a "wet," messy and all-out delicious dish. Everything here is big enough for two, but who wants to share when it's this good?

■ 5913 Broadway (bet. 59th & 60th Sts.)
℘ (916) 346-4445 — **WEB:** www.baconandbuttersac.com
■ Lunch Tue – Sun   **PRICE:** ⊜

BINCHOYAKI 🍴

Japanese • Simple

♿

This mini izakaya greets guests with a mouthwatering whiff of smoky meat at the door, while also honoring its cool surrounds. Imagine a farm-to-table menu and flats of microgreens growing on the bar.

Head straight to that counter for a front-row seat with views of the charcoal grill. There, Chef/owner Craig Takehara is prepping and grilling juicy hot bites that arrive straight from the binchotan. These skewered meats include highlights like negima, chicken thighs and green onion, as well as a beautifully charred Kurobuta pork jowl perfect with just a squeeze of lemon and salt. The menu goes on to list small plates, rice dishes and noodles, such as chewy sukiyaki udon in gingery-soy sauce with thinly sliced ribeye and an abundance of those microgreens.

 2226 10th St. (bet. W & V Sts.)
✆ (916) 469-9448 — **WEB:** www.binchoyaki.com
▨ Lunch & dinner Tue – Sat   PRICE: $$

CANON 😋

Contemporary • Chic

🍹 ♿ 🏠 ⛱ 🛋 🖐

Find the convivial Canon sequestered away from the downtown bustle. This cool space that contrasts deep tones against bright whites is enveloped by the aromatic smell of smoke, so it's no surprise that the house is packed most nights.

Chef Brad Cecchi is the culinary mastermind and his menu is pivoted around playful small plates. Keeping that in mind, arrive armed with a group as involvement is the bottom line. Whether you're sipping a cocktail while snacking on Urfa chili drumsticks at the bar, or savoring lamb pavé matched with roasted pineapple and blue corn tortillas, dining here is a global tour de force. Picky palates will find much to enjoy among the many vegan or gluten-free items; and dessert tapas will have your sweet tooth working overtime.

▨ 1719 34th St. (bet. Folsom & Stockton Blvds.)
✆ (916) 469-2433 — **WEB:** www.canoneastsac.com
▨ Lunch Sat – Sun Dinner Tue – Sun   PRICE: $$

ELLA

American • Elegant

This upscale spot in the heart of downtown Sacramento is equal parts rustic and refined, with floor-to-ceiling curtains, white linens and a colorful overhang comprised of antique wood. You're likely to be seated among regulars, who chat with attentive servers and sample their wine pairing suggestions (there are plenty of half-glass options for the lunchtime Capitol crowd).

The menu offers creative takes on a global array of favorites, from a sweet-savory gazpacho made with aromatic ambrosia melons and a dollop of olive oil ice cream to perfectly crispy and well-executed Southern fried chicken. Desserts are a must—the ambitious "fruity pebble" semifreddo accompanied by a vanilla-coriander meringue and finished with raspberry milk is a sight to behold.

- 1131 K St. (at 12th St.)
- ℰ (916) 443-3772 — **WEB:** www.elladiningroomandbar.com
- Lunch Mon – Fri Dinner Mon – Sat   **PRICE: $$$**

FRANK FAT'S 😊

Chinese • Family

Celebrated as the "third house" because of its popularity among politicians making deals in the back booths, this venerable Chinese-American jewel has been family-owned since 1939. Step inside and you'll be transported into another era by way of a retro bar serving up happy-hour martinis and an elegant dining room attended to by tie-wearing servers and festooned with valuable relics.

The menu is as much of a throwback as the décor, with yu kwok (crispy beef, pork and water chestnut dumplings) sharing equal billing with their not-so-Chinese items, including banana cream pie. But don't be dissuaded by the seeming inauthenticity as everything is beautifully executed, from the fried chicken marinated with brandy and ginger to addictive garlic-chili green beans.

- 806 L St. (at 8th St.)
- ℰ (916) 442-7092 — **WEB:** www.frankfats.com
- Lunch Mon – Fri Dinner nightly   **PRICE: $$**

GRANGE

American • Contemporary décor

The Citizen Hotel is primo for those with business on their minds, but that doesn't mean it's all just corporate here downtown. In fact, Grange, tucked inside the hotel, is proof positive that business and pleasure mix with fine results. High ceilings and an arched shelf stacked with liquor instantly draw the eye, while wood tables lined with orange leather banquettes balance style and comfort. If visiting midday, opt for the Power Lunch and enjoy three courses for a palatable price.

The menu shares a farm-focused sensibility with rustic creations. Mojo pork loin spread with calabrese bomba on toasted bread is simple and tasty, not unlike the dependably creamy broccoli-arugula soup. Hazelnut cake with strawberry and chocolate ends things on a sweet note.

- 926 J St. (at 10th St.)
- (916) 492-4450 — **WEB:** www.grangerestaurantandbar.com
- Lunch & dinner daily   **PRICE: $$**

LOCALIS

Californian • Fashionable

Taste the passion and pride with which Chef/owner Christopher Barnum-Dann scrupulously sources everything on his carte. A charming host who loves to chat with customers, he is happy to explain his "conscious eater" ethos to anyone at the counter. That dedication extends to his diners as well, as this kitchen bends over backwards to adapt the hyper-seasonal five-course tasting menus for those with dietary restrictions (though 24-hours' notice is appreciated).

The setting is a covered patio with hanging lights, spacious windows and an assuredly casual crowd. Beautifully crafted dishes include polenta cakes with bacon, sous-vide eggs, a peach purée and sweet corn. Also try "market" offerings like crisp-skinned salmon with pops of colorful vegetables.

- 2031 S St. (at 21st St.)
- (916) 737-7699 — **WEB:** www.localissacramento.com
- Dinner Tue – Sat   **PRICE: $$$**

THE KITCHEN ⌘

Contemporary • Friendly

The name may sound generic, but dining here is an experience unlike any other. Since opening in 1991, The Kitchen has felt like a party from start to finish, hosted by the talented Chef Kelly McCown. Diners (celebrants are inevitably included) are encouraged to get up and walk around, maybe even peek into the kitchen to chat up the cooks. Really like that truffle dish? The chef invites you to ask for seconds. Having fun is central to everything here.

The menu changes monthly and features far-reaching inspiration that incites guests to honor a world of culinary traditions in a single night. Start off with a Japanese bonenkai party of shrimp with a bit of ginger-infused sake sauce. Then move on to the Périgord truffles grated heavily over butternut squash cannelloni with creamy sauce forestiere. Other highlights include a pan-fried cake of house-made kimchi and Dungeness crab, topped with tamarind-glazed pork belly and an edible orchid. In the holiday season, this may be tailed by an old-timey Christmas supper, starring butter-poached beef tenderloin dressed with red wine sauce and potato fondant.

Nibble on a divine chocolate chip cookie while waiting for desserts like caramel pudding.

🔲 2225 Hurley Way, Ste. 101 (at Howe Ave.)
℘ (916) 568-7171 — **WEB:** www.thekitchenrestaurant.com
🔲 Dinner Wed – Sun   **PRICE: $$$$**

MAYAHUEL ﾟ○

Mexican • Colorful

Ernesto Delgado's sprawling downtown tribute to Mexico isn't just a restaurant—it's a notable tequila bar (Tequila Museo), a luxe private dining space (Coa), as well as a casual taco spot (Maya). But head to Mayahuel proper for serious south-of-the-border cooking, whether you're seeking a lunchtime bowl of chile poblano with the perfect jolt of heat, or a hearty evening meal of chicken enchiladas doused in a deeply flavored mole composed with over 32 ingredients.

Dimly lit but bursting with color from its vibrant yellow-muraled walls, this dining room draws a smart and business-oriented crowd. They flock to the "Museo" at happy hour for a wide selection of tequilas and mezcals, as well as hand-crafted mango margaritas swirled with smoky ancho chile.

■ 1200 K St. (at 12th St.)
🕾 (916) 441-7200 — **WEB:** www.experiencemayahuel.com
■ Lunch & dinner daily   **PRICE: $$**

MING DYNASTY ﾟ○

Chinese • Family

This all-day dim sum destination earns top marks for its seafood items, from slippery rice noodle rolls topped with shrimp, dried scallops and snap peas to classic siu mai. Carnivores will dig the pork and scallion steamed buns with a hint of sesame, while the pleasantly bite-sized Shanghai soup dumplings accompanied by a wallop of gingery vinegar will sate all and sundry.

Though simple in décor, the arena is vast, with plenty of parking and room for banquet parties—don't be surprised to see tables of ten or more fighting over the last egg custard bun. Service is a major highlight here. In fact, the gracious staff will happily help diners navigate the large menu, suggesting unusually delightful items like handmade green-tea dumplings stuffed with lobster.

■ 1211 Broadway (bet. 13th St. & Riverside Blvd.)
🕾 (916) 491-2233 — **WEB:** www.mingdynastysacramento.com
■ Lunch & dinner daily   **PRICE: ⊜**

MOTHER

Vegetarian • Trendy

Down-home and hipster may seem like strange bedfellows, but here they are the perfect marriage. This creative kitchen is equal parts friendly and forward-thinking, with dishes ranging from veggie standbys (turmeric hummus and that magical elixir, kombucha) to Southern staples with a twist. Just try snagging a table, as a loyal crowd convenes for the chitchat as much as the crave-worthy comfort food that eschews meat.

Be sure to tuck into a chicken-fried mushroom po' boy. Stacked precipitously with house-made pickles and smoky aïoli, these delicately fried oyster mushrooms burst with meaty umami. Dessert is in the bag, quite literally, as it's served in a brown paper bag stamped with the chef's face and filled with golden-edged oatmeal cookies.

 1023 K St. (bet. 10th & 11th Sts.)

📞 (916) 594-9812 — **WEB:** www.mothersacramento.com

▧ Lunch Mon – Fri Dinner Tue – Sat   **PRICE:** 🕮

MULVANEY'S B&L 🍴

American • Historic

&

A firehouse in its previous life, this Sacramento gem features food that will have you returning time and again, but sentimentalists beware, as the menu changes daily. While you can't be sure what's on offer here, fresh, seasonal and satisfying cooking is a guarantee. Imagine the likes of tortellini stuffed with winter squash, followed by a "beggar's purse" filled with pumpkin pie, and you'll be in no doubt as to the time of year.

The waitstaff is well versed in the carte and ingredients—watch them name drop local farms like a celebrity stylist on the rise. If the heirloom tomato and mozzarella is available, don't hesitate. It's the most popular dish for a reason, starring ripe Ray Yeung Farms heirloom tomatoes and hand-pulled, still-warm cheese.

▧ 1215 19th St. (bet. Capitol Ave. & L St.)

📞 (916) 441-6022 — **WEB:** www.mulvaneysbl.com

▧ Lunch Tue – Fri Dinner Tue – Sat   **PRICE:** $$$

ZÓCALO 🍴

Mexican • Elegant

Set right in the Capitol Mall, this upscale stunner (which also has outposts in University Village and Roseville) dons an elegant demeanor by way of heavy wooden doors, dark metal chandeliers and plenty of lush greenery. The sprawling outdoor patio boasts terrific people-watching. And though it's named for Mexico City's central plaza, this kitchen's menu offers regional highlights from around the country.

Puebla-style chicken enchiladas, for instance, smothered in handmade mole poblano burst with flavor, while crispy tostadas contrast rich Michoacan-style carnitas against a zesty and bright salsa. Tequila nerds will thrill to the extensive selection, but there's no shame in just ordering a margarita—the "Mango Fresco" with a tajín salt rim is a winner.

▨ 1801 Capitol Ave. (at 18th St.)
℘ (916) 441-0303 — **WEB:** www.zocalosacramento.com
▨ Lunch & dinner daily   **PRICE: $$**

Look for our symbol 🍺
spotlighting restaurants
with a notable beer list.

MARIN

MARIN

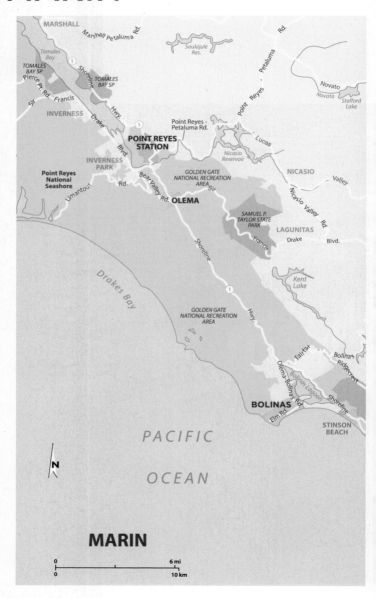

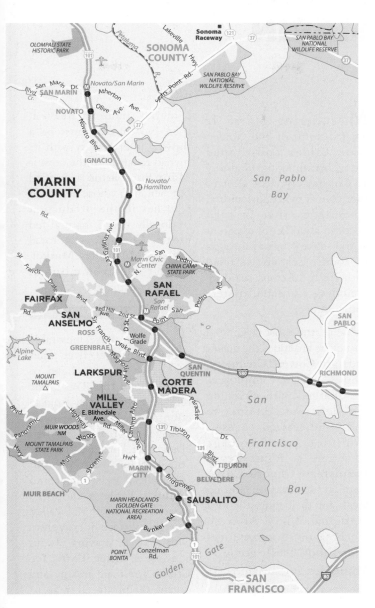

EATING IN...
MARIN

Meandering Marin is located north of the Golden Gate Bridge and draped along breathtaking Highway 1. Coastal climates shower this county with agricultural advantages that in turn become abundantly apparent as you snake your way through its food oases, always filled with fresh, luscious seafood, including slurpable oysters and cold beer.

One of the most celebrated purveyors around is the quaint and rustic **Cowgirl Creamery**, whose "cowgirl" employees are charged with churning out delicious, distinctive and hand-crafted cheeses. Continue your fromage adventure at **Point Reyes Farmstead Cheese Co.**, a popular destination among locals for their famously lush "Original Blue." After so much savory goodness, get your candy crush going at **Munchies** in Sausalito. If cheese and meat are indeed a match made in heaven, then North Bay must be a thriving intermediary with its myriad ranches. At the crest is **Marin Sun Farms**, a glorified butcher shop whose heart and soul lies in the production of locally raised, natural-fed meats. Championing local eating is **Mill Valley Market**, a can't-miss commitment among gourmands.

STOP, SIP & SAVOR

To gratify those inevitable pangs of hunger after miles of scenic driving, head to **The Pelican Inn**. This idyllic retreat, serving hearty English country cooking along with a range of brews from their classic "bar," promises to leave you yearning for more. But forge ahead by strolling into **Spanish Table**, a shopper's paradise settled in Mill Valley. Finally, peckish travelers with a sweet craving always convene at **Three Twins Ice Cream** for their creamy and organically produced treats.

Waters off the coast here provide divers with exceptional hunting ground for supremely fresh oysters, briny clams and meaty mussels. The difficulty in (legally) sourcing these large mollusks make the likes of red abalone a treasured species in area (particularly Asian) restaurants, though seafood does seem to be the accepted norm among most in town. And if fish doesn't float your boat, **Fred's Coffee Shop** in Sausalito is a no-frills find for breakfast signatures like deep-fried French toast with a side of calorie-heavy, crazy-good caramelized "Millionaire's bacon." Not far behind is **M.H. Bread & Butter** where carb addicts routinely pay their respects. While fertile San Rafael county's natural ingredients may be sold in countless farmers' markets, many other celebrations of food and wine continue to pop up throughout—especially during spring and summer months.

BAR BOCCE ⑪○

Pizza • Trendy

This little bungalow on the Bay draws big crowds for the harbor views from its covered patio, complete with a namesake bocce court. Equipped with beachside benches for watching youngsters at play and toasty fire pits for warding off the late-afternoon fog, it's often packed to the gills on weekend afternoons with locals lingering over a second (or fourth) glass of wine.

Should the buzz get too strong, there's hearty Italian cooking to set you right, including wood-fired pizzas topped with pesto, ricotta and kale; tender meatballs in a rich San Marzano tomato sauce; and rib-sticking eggplant parmesan dolloped with burrata. Perk yourself up for the ride home with a vanilla gelato affogato, drowned in espresso and sprinkled with Heath bar crumble.

■ 1250 Bridgeway (bet. Pine & Turney Sts.), Sausalito
✆ (415) 331-0555 — **WEB:** www.barbocce.com
■ Lunch & dinner daily   PRICE: $$

BARREL HOUSE TAVERN ⑪○

Californian • Contemporary décor

The former San Francisco-Sausalito ferry terminal has found new life as this lovely Californian restaurant, which gets its name from its barrel-like arched wood ceiling. A front lounge with a crackling fireplace and well-stocked bar is popular with locals, while tourists can't resist the expansive dining room and back deck, which boasts spectacular views of the Bay.

The cocktail and wine offerings are strong, as is the house-made soda program, which produces intriguing, never-too-sweet combinations like yellow peach, basil and ginger. These pair beautifully with meaty Dungeness crab sliders coupled with watermelon-jicama slaw; though they might be too tasty to keep around by the time grilled swordfish and pork belly with white beans hit the table.

■ 660 Bridgeway (at Princess St.), Sausalito
✆ (415) 729-9593 — **WEB:** www.barrelhousetavern.com
■ Lunch & dinner daily   PRICE: $$$

BUCKEYE ROADHOUSE ⅏

American • Elegant

This hideout has welcomed generations of locals through its doors since 1937, even as its location on Highway 1 gave way to the more bustling 101. Enter the whitewashed Craftsman building, and you'll be given your choice of dining—either at the clubby bar or the grand main room with wood-paneled walls and red leather banquettes.

The food here is classic but never dull, with a simple menu of salads, sandwiches and grilled meats. Oysters bingo set over spinach and topped with garlic aïoli oozes with California panache, while succulent and crisp-skinned chili-lime brick chicken is just as delicious as its accompanying sides—think polenta sticks and cheese-stuffed pasilla peppers. Finish with a slice of pie—the s'mores version or key lime are both winners.

▨ 15 Shoreline Hwy. (off Hwy. 101), Mill Valley
℘ (415) 331-2600 — **WEB:** www.buckeyeroadhouse.com
▨ Lunch & dinner daily   **PRICE: $$**

BURMATOWN ⅏

Burmese • Cozy

Bypass the tired Asian-fusion offerings and head straight for the authentic Burmese dishes at this out-of-the-way cutie. A nutty, crunchy and flavorful tea leaf salad is the perfect answer to a hot summer day, while hearty spiced potato-stuffed samosas and fresh, springy egg noodles tossed with barbecue pork and fried garlic chips will warm your soul in the cooler months.

Given the high quality of its food, it's no surprise that Burmatown is Corte Madera's most popular neighbor: it's big with local families from the surrounding residences who pack every single table, attended to by warm servers. If you're willing to make a special trip to this charming bright-orange bungalow, the laid-back vibe will have you feeling right at home.

▨ 60 Corte Madera Ave. (bet. Bahr Ln. & Redwood Ave.), Corte Madera
℘ (415) 945-9096 — **WEB:** www.burmatown.com
▨ Dinner Tue – Sun   **PRICE: $$**

CAFE REYES

Pizza • Rustic

This unassuming charmer in quaint Point Reyes Station is a perfect stop for day-trippers who are sure to enjoy the many delicious dishes that emerge from its duo of wood-fired ovens. Pizza is the focus, with ten varieties ranging from a classic Margherita to meaty staples like fennel sausage and mushroom. The deliciously crusty pies are named after local destinations, like the Limantour and Bodega, as well as the Farallon, with its slivers of roasted garlic, mini pepperoni with crisped edges and a pile of mozzarella.

Given its cooking method, it's no surprise that Cafe Reyes is stacked high with wood, both against the walls and under the counter. The big, spacious, barn-like dining room is rustic, unfussy and perfect for groups.

■ 11101 Shoreline Hwy. (at Mesa Rd.), Point Reyes Station
✆ (415) 663-9493 — **WEB:** www.cafe-reyes.com
■ Lunch & dinner Wed – Sun   **PRICE: $$**

COPITA

Mexican • Family

Set sail aboard the Sausalito ferry for dinner at this Mexican smash-hit just steps from the harbor's bobbing yachts. Colorful and casual, Copita's most coveted seats are on the patio (complete with partial views of the water and quaint downtown), but a spot at the well-stocked tequila bar or in the brightly tiled dining room is no disappointment.

A light meal of tacos may include the al pastor, spit-roasted on the fire for a bit of smoke and paired with pineapple for sweet essence. Dungeness crab empanada is then drizzled with chipotle aïoli for a surprising yet delightful pairing. Options also abound for heartier appetites, like the 24-hour carnitas or chicken mole enchiladas. Of course, its lively surrounds are a hit with kids, who love sipping on the house-made horchata.

■ 739 Bridgeway (at Anchor St.), Sausalito
✆ (415) 331-7400 — **WEB:** www.copitarestaurant.com
■ Lunch & dinner daily   **PRICE: $$**

ELEVEN ⅋⃝

Italian • Cozy

& ⛱

Life in laid-back Bolinas is all about simple pleasures, like this hippie-chic pizzeria that's a favorite on the après-surf scene. At magic hour, its outdoor tables fill with salt-kissed patrons refueling on oven-charred carbs and crisp green salads as they soak up the last rays of sunshine. You might even nestle into the window alcove to sip on some grüner veltliner and watch the day surfers pack up at sunset.

This menu spins to the seasons but is as streamlined as a surfboard: oysters, greens and a handful of crisp pies, like a Margherita with fresh tomatoes and mozzarella. Of the entrées, flaky branzino stuffed with herbs and Meyer lemon peel is a standout. Linger over a swirl of soft-serve made from local buffalo milk, or a second glass of vino.

▪ 11 Wharf Rd. (at Brighton Ave.), Bolinas
℘ (415) 868-1133 — **WEB:** www.11wharfroad.com
▪ Dinner Thu – Mon   **PRICE: $$**

INSALATA'S ☺

Mediterranean • Contemporary décor

& ⛶ ⬙

San Anselmo restaurateur, Chef Heidi Krahling honors her late father, Italo Insalata, at this crowd-pleasing Marin hangout. The zucca-orange stucco exterior alludes to the Mediterranean air within. Insalata's upscale setting is framed by lemon-yellow walls hung with grand depictions of nature's bounty, setting the scene for an array of fresh and flavorful cuisine to come.

Sparked by Middle Eastern flavors, the kitchen's specialties include velvety smooth potato-leek soup made brilliantly green from watercress purée. Also sample grilled lamb skewers drizzled with cumin-yogurt atop crunchy salad and flatbread. The takeout area in the back is stocked with salads, sides and sandwiches made with house-baked bread. Boxed lunches are a fun, tasty convenience.

▪ 120 Sir Francis Drake Blvd. (at Barber Ave.), San Anselmo
℘ (415) 457-7700 — **WEB:** www.insalatas.com
▪ Lunch & dinner daily   **PRICE: $$**

MADCAP ✿

Contemporary • Chic

♿

Upscale yet friendly and approachable, Madcap is fast becoming one of the Bay Area's beloved destinations for contemporary dining. The superb culinary skills on display should be no surprise considering that Chef/owner Ron Siegel worked at some of the West Coast's more renowned kitchens, including The French Laundry. This is his first solo project and it reflects much of his background as a chef with Californian sensibilities and subtle Japanese influences—note the paper lamps and minimalist décor. At its soul, this is a humble hangout, striving to highlight the best local and seasonal ingredients with little fuss.

Both à la carte and fixed menus are offered and are sure to feature some of the kitchen's more surprising concoctions. While each composition is likely to change with the seasons, every bite remains well crafted, balanced and teeming with unique flavor combinations. Highlights unveil house-made, toothsome tortelloni filled with delicately braised rabbit, resting on a miso-mushroom purée and capped with parmesan espuma.

Desserts are also artful and fun, as seen in a cube of Japanese cheesecake set on a lid over shiso-panna cotta with hot pink huckleberry foam.

◾ 198 Sir Francis Drake Blvd. (bet. Bank St. & Barber Ave.), San Anselmo
✆ (415) 453-9898 — **WEB:** www.madcapmarin.com
◾ Dinner Thu – Mon   **PRICE: $$$$**

MASA'S SUSHI ¶○
Japanese • Simple

Respected veteran Chef Takatoshi Toshi has returned to his roots and taken over the reins to bring Novato locals hearty and affordable sushi. Don't be surprised to see him behind the counter here, breaking down a whole salmon while making small talk with his neighbors. The space is simple, understated and quiet, which seems to match its quaint downtown location, set amid boutiques and restaurants.

Lunch combinations are an excellent deal, offering chirashi bowls as well as sushi and nigiri with miso soup. Come dinner, the affordable omakase selection unveils nigiri, salmon and tuna tastings. Bigger platters might arrive as lovely amalgamations of avocado and albacore rolls alongside ebi, yellowtail and cherry wood-smoked goldeneye snapper (kinmedai).

▩ 813 Grant Ave. (bet. Reichert & Sherman Aves.), Novato
✆ (415) 892-0081 — **WEB:** www.masasnovato.com
▩ Lunch Mon – Fri Dinner Mon – Sat   **PRICE: $$**

OSTERIA STELLINA ¶○
Italian • Family

♿

Its name is Italian for "little star," and this gem does indeed shine in the heart of tiny Point Reyes Station, a one-horse clapboard town with little more than a filling station and a post office to its name. But the Wild West it's not: this frontier village is Marin-chic, and its saloon is a soothing retreat with wide windows and local produce on the menu.

You'll taste the difference in the pillowy house-made focaccia, the soothing chicken brodo and the crisp salad of little gem lettuce with blue cheese, toasted walnuts and honeycrisp apples. Organic, grass-fed beef stew is packed with spices and served over herbed polenta. Finish with the warm, moist Guinness gingerbread cake with a scoop of lemon ice cream and butterscotch drizzle. Yum!

▩ 11285 Hwy. 1 (at 3rd St.), Point Reyes Station
✆ (415) 663-9988 — **WEB:** www.osteriastellina.com
▩ Lunch & dinner daily   **PRICE: $$**

PICCO 🍴○

Italian • Contemporary décor

Picco is Italian for "summit," and this charming Larkspur hilltop home has long been a beacon among Marin County diners. Chef/owner Bruce Hill is a true local-food devotee: his Italian-influenced fare heaps on Marin ingredients like the fresh turnips that dot his silky-smooth duck tortelli, or the Meyer lemon yogurt and beets that sit atop a nourishing kale salad. The "Marin Mondays" menu is a particular steal.

The precise staff moves ably through the busy dining room, carrying bowls of creamy risotto made on the half-hour. With a high ceiling and exposed brick walls, the vibe is graceful but never fussy, making this the perfect setting for couples and groups of friends who congregate here.

Also check out Pizzeria Picco next door.

▦ 320 Magnolia Ave. (at King St.), Larkspur
📞 (415) 924-0300 — **WEB:** www.restaurantpicco.com
▦ Dinner nightly   **PRICE: $$$**

PIG IN A PICKLE ☺

Barbecue • Simple

Don't be fooled by this smoke spot's suburban location—this is transcendent, next-level barbecue. Chef/owner Damon Stainbrook takes his sourcing seriously, as evidenced by the chalkboard outlining where each humanely raised, hormone-free cut of meat arrives from. The counter service is warm, casual and friendly; while rustic wood tables filled with regional, homemade hot sauces dot the rest of the room.

There's really no wrong way to go on their mouthwatering menu. Imagine the likes of melt-in-your-mouth pulled pork; 18-hour smoked brisket; perfectly moist, dry-rubbed ribs; or juicy hotlinks bursting with flavor. Even the mac-and-cheese, a gloopy afterthought at so many other such places, is tended to with care, offering rich flavor and toothsome texture.

▦ 341 Corte Madera Town Centre (at Tamalpais Dr.), Corte Madera
📞 (415) 891-3265 — **WEB:** www.piginapickle.com
▦ Lunch & dinner daily   **PRICE: $$**

PLAYA

Mexican • *Family*

The foggy beaches of Marin County may be a far cry from the sand and surf of Baja, but this lively spot keeps the vacation vibe alive with margaritas, mezcal and madly delicious Mexican cooking. And while Playa feels upmarket with its colorful tiles, blown-glass lights and walls of windows, its food is wonderfully authentic.

The menu makes for tough choices: opt for the outstanding al pastor tacos layered with sweet-spicy caramelized pineapple salsa, or the crispy empanadas stuffed with chorizo, currants and green olives, drizzled with chimichurri. Whether you choose a cocktail and a mushroom-squash blossom quesadilla at the bar or bowls of chips and queso fundido with a big group on the sunny back patio, good times are guaranteed.

🔲 41 Throckmorton Ave. (bet. Blithedale & Miller Aves.), Mill Valley
📞 (415) 384-8871 — **WEB:** www.playamv.com
🔲 Lunch Tue – Sun Dinner nightly   PRICE: $$

POGGIO

Italian • *Trattoria*

A restaurant of Poggio's vintage could easily rest on its tourist-trap laurels—after all, its alfresco terrace has views of the Sausalito harbor that any starry-eyed visitor would long to savor. But this enduring favorite also provides plenty to enjoy on the plate, as well as a comfortable atmosphere, friendly service and a solid Italian wine selection.

The menu takes some northern California detours, like the Dungeness crab salad with blood oranges and radishes. But even the most die-hard Italian would give a seal of approval to the homemade agnolotti, served in a succulent pork ragù with a dusting of parmesan. Want something a little more special? In season, they're happy to give your pasta a hefty shaving of black or white truffles.

🔲 777 Bridgeway (at Bay St.), Sausalito
📞 (415) 332-7771 — **WEB:** www.poggiotrattoria.com
🔲 Lunch & dinner daily   PRICE: $$

SALTWATER ⅼ○

Seafood • Contemporary décor

&. 🏠

If you love oysters, this coastal-chic spot will have you as happy as a clam. Nearly half its menu features these ultra-fresh bivalves plucked straight from nearby Tomales Bay—whether raw, broiled with chili-garlic butter or simmered in a creamy leek stew. If oysters aren't your thing, there's also plenty of other local seafood to choose from, including crisp-skinned steelhead trout or risotto with clams and uni. Carnivores can opt for a roasted pork chop with collard greens.

Set in a country-style house, Saltwater is a small town hot spot that attracts casual couples of all ages for local beer and wine on tap. The menu changes often to reflect the best of its markets, so be sure to pounce on such dishes as spicy gingerbread cake before they vanish.

▓ 12781 Sir Francis Drake Blvd. (at Inverness Way), Inverness
✆ (415) 669-1244 — **WEB:** www.saltwateroysterdepot.com
▓ Lunch Sat – Sun Dinner Thu – Mon   **PRICE: $$$**

SIR AND STAR ⅼ○

Californian • Cozy

&. 🏠 ⌲

This quirky roadhouse in the historic Olema Inn is one-of-a-kind, from the displays of branches in the light-flooded dining room to the poetic menu descriptions ("small feast of fishes," otherwise known as mussels). But in the hands of Chef/owners and longtime Marin fixtures Daniel DeLong and Margaret Gradé, you can always expect a fine meal made with painstakingly sourced ingredients.

Sip a glass of Marin-made mead by the fire; then head to the dining room, where you'll sample dishes like Point Reyes Toma cheese "fondue," golden beet soup and fluffy cardamom sugar beignets with local honey and strawberries—all accompanied by excellent crusty bread.

Come Saturday, there is also a prix-fixe menu, available by reservation only.

▓ 10000 Sir Francis Drake Blvd. (at Hwy. 1), Olema
✆ (415) 663-1034 — **WEB:** www.sirandstar.com
▓ Dinner Wed – Sun   **PRICE: $$**

SOL FOOD
Puerto Rican • Family

You won't be able to miss this Puerto Rican favorite, recognizable by its grasshopper-green exterior and overflowing crowds of festive diners. In fact, their comida criolla is so popular that it's taken over the block: a sister bodega does a booming takeout business, while gift store Conchita sells wares from San Juan and beyond.

Sol Food's soul food is hearty and abundant, from tamale-like pasteles of mashed plantain and taro stuffed with garlicky pork to fragrant sautéed shrimp loaded with tomato, onion and spices. Outstanding daily specials, like arroz con pollo and pernil, are also big draws. Wash it all down with a delicious mango iced tea, and don't skip the decadent pineapple bread pudding, soaked in warm, buttery mango sauce, for dessert.

▪ 903 Lincoln Ave. (at 3rd St.), San Rafael
✆ (415) 451-4765 — **WEB:** www.solfoodrestaurant.com
▪ Lunch & dinner daily   **PRICE: $$**

SUSHI RAN 😀
Japanese • Contemporary décor

Chefs have come and gone at this Sausalito staple, but its zen-like atmosphere and exquisite selection of raw fish remain unchanged—and that's just how the regulars like it. With its charming beachside-bungalow ambience, attentive service staff and thoughtfully curated sake selection, Sushi Ran is as dependable as a restaurant can get.

Start off with a small bite like shrimp tempura over crisp veggies, tobiko and asparagus, or a steamed red crab salad mingled with seaweed, cucumber and a sweet soy dressing. Then move on to the main event: meticulously sourced, extraordinarily pure hamachi, big-eye tuna, steamed blue prawns and Santa Barbara uni. Whether you choose sashimi or nigiri, rest assured that these talented chefs will steer you right.

▪ 107 Caledonia St. (bet. Pine & Turney Sts.), Sausalito
✆ (415) 332-3620 — **WEB:** www.sushiran.com
▪ Lunch Mon – Fri Dinner nightly   **PRICE: $$**

VILLAGE SAKE 👀

Japanese • *Rustic*

○⃝ ⛑ 🍴

Set along a bustling stretch, Village Sake is a mighty hot and mod izakaya delivering authentic goods in the heart of quaint Fairfax. All the classic small plates are in full force here: crisp and creamy takoyaki (octopus croquettes), okonomiyaki, tataki (made with silky smoked hamachi) and coconut mochi cake complete with cardamom gelato. If you must have sushi, there's a small selection of excellent nigiri, too—make sure to sample the shima aji and kinmedai.

The look of the room suggests Tokyo, with closely spaced tables, an array of wood accents (including a live-edge wood counter) as well as a friendly staff, many of them Japanese natives. This is a popular spot that doesn't take reservations, so expect long lines, especially on weekends.

◼ 19 Bolinas Rd. (bet. Broadway Blvd. & Mono Ave.), Fairfax
✆ (415) 521-5790 — **WEB:** www.villagesake.com
◼ Dinner Wed – Sun   PRICE: $$

SAN FRANCISCO

SAN FRANCISCO

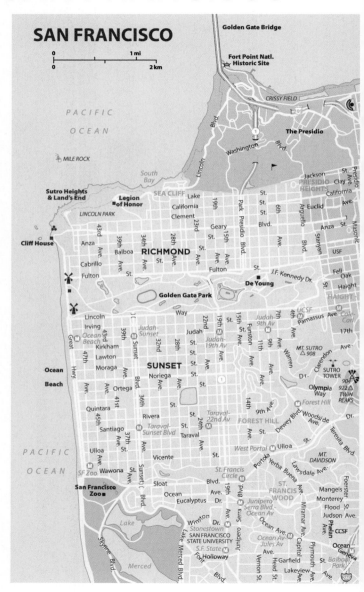

SAN FRANCISCO

Golden Gate Bridge

Fort Point Natl. Historic Site

CRISSY FIELD

PACIFIC OCEAN

MILE ROCK

South Bay

The Presidio

Washington Blvd.

Jackson St.

PRESIDIO HEIGHTS Clay Ave.

California

Sutro Heights & Land's End

Legion of Honor

SEA CLIFF

LINCOLN PARK

Lake

California

Clement

St.

St.

6th

Euclid Ave.

Anza St.

Cliff House

43rd Ave.

39th Ave.

34th St.

28th Ave.

23rd St.

Geary St.

15th Ave.

Park Presidio Blvd.

Blvd.

Arguello Blvd.

Masonic

Anza

Balboa St.

RICHMOND

St.

Ave.

Ave.

USF

Cabrillo St.

Fulton

St.

Fulton

St.

J.F. Kennedy Dr.

De Young

Fell

Oak

Haight

HAIGHT

Golden Gate Park

Way

22nd Ave.

19th Ave.

15th St.

7th Ave.

Judah 9th Av

UCSF

Parnassus Ave.

Cole-Cor.

Lincoln

Irving

Ocean Beach

43rd

39th

Judah-Sunset

Judah

32nd St.

28th St.

Judah 19th Av

Funston Ave.

9th

11th

Warren

MT. SUTRO △ 908

Clarendon Ave.

17th

Kirkham

Lawton

Moraga

SUNSET

Noriega St.

Sunset Blvd.

Ave.

St.

Ave.

14th

SUTRO TOWER

Olympia Way

922 △ TWIN PEAKS

904

Ocean Beach

47th

41st Ave.

36th Ave.

Ortega St.

Quintara

Rivera

Taraval-22nd Av

24th St.

9th Ave.

Forest Hill

FOREST HILL

Dewey Blvd

Woodside Ave.

Teresita Blvd.

45th Ave.

37th Ave.

Santiago

Taraval-Sunset Blvd.

Taraval

Ave.

St.

West Portal Ulloa

Portola Dr.

Yerba Buena

Lawsdale Ave.

MT. DAVIDSON

PACIFIC OCEAN

Ulloa Ave.

Wawona St.

Sunset Blvd.

Vicente St.

St. Francis Circle

19th Ave.

ST. FRANCIS WOOD

Mangels Ave.

Monterey

SF Zoo

Sloat Blvd.

Ocean Ave.

Eucalyptus Dr.

Junipero Serra Blvd.

Ocean Av

Ocean Ave.

Flood

Judson Ave.

Foerster

San Francisco Zoo

Winton Dr.

Stonestown

SAN FRANCISCO STATE UNIVERSITY

S.F. State

Holloway

Ocean Av-Jules Av

Ave.

Junipero Serra Blvd.

Ocean Ave.

Phelan Ave.

CCSF

Capitol

Plymouth Ave.

Ocean Ave.

Geneva Ave.

Lake

Merced Blvd.

Merced

Skyline Blvd.

Garfield

Vernon St.

Head St.

Lakeview Ave.

St.

Balboa Park

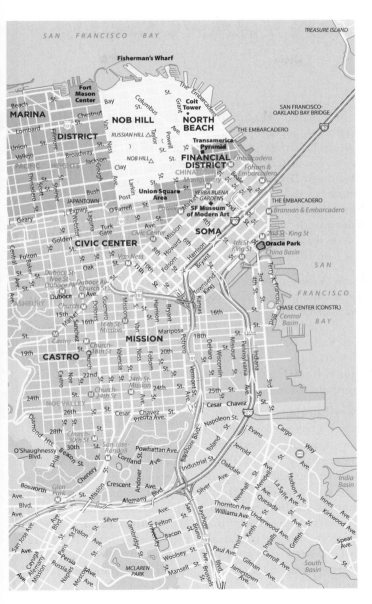

SAN FRANCISCO BAY

TREASURE ISLAND

Fisherman's Wharf

Fort Mason Center

MARINA DISTRICT

PACIFIC HEIGHTS

JAPANTOWN

HAIGHT ASHBURY

CIVIC CENTER

CASTRO

NOE VALLEY

NOB HILL

RUSSIAN HILL

NOB HILL

North Beach

Coit Tower

NORTH BEACH

Transamerica Pyramid

FINANCIAL DISTRICT

CHINATOWN

Union Square Area

YERBA BUENA GARDENS

SF Museum of Modern Art

SOMA

MISSION

SAN FRANCISCO-OAKLAND BAY BRIDGE

THE EMBARCADERO

Embarcadero

Folsom & Embarcadero

THE EMBARCADERO

Brannan & Embarcadero

2nd St - King St

Oracle Park

China Basin

SAN FRANCISCO BAY

CHASE CENTER (CONSTR.)

Central Basin

India Basin

South Basin

MCLAREN PARK

EATING IN...
SAN FRANCISCO

The Castro district is a perpetual party brimming with cool cafeterias. Start your day here at **Kitchen Story** or **Thorough Bread & Pastry**. Linger on the patio at **Café Flore** or stop in at the original **Rosamunde Sausage Grill**. Kitschy kiosk **Hot Cookie** is just right for a bit of sweet.

Cole Valley may be small, but flaunts a big personality. Lines snake out the door for pernil asado at **Parada 22**. **Noe Valley Bakery** bakes the best bread around, after which a pour from **Castro Coffee Company** is simply a must.

Neighboring Tenderloin's Larkin Street is crowded with shops like **Saigon Sandwich** just as nearby **Turtle Tower SF** is frequented for fragrant pho ga. Hayes Valley's **Chantal Guillon** spotlights exquisite macarons but carnivores delight in **Fatted Calf Charcuterie**'s meats. On the other hand, those vegan-leaning hipsters seem to love the Lower Haight, especially **Noc Noc,** for its sake-infused libations.

Over in the Financial District the **Ferry Building** hosts a myriad of eateries, including **Boulettes Larder + Boulibar, Cowgirl Creamery** and **Acme Bread Company**. Marina denizens may gather at **Jane** or **The Tipsy Pig,** but carnivores flock to **Roam Artisan Burgers**. Presidio's **Off the Grid-Fort Mason** is most coveted for its food trucks—from **Curry Up Now** to the **Lobsta Truck.** Not far behind is Japantown—swing by **Super Mira** market for lunch or even grab a bento box at **Nijiya Market**.

Speaking of which, the Mission boasts some of the best bazaars in town, including **La Palma Mexicatessen, Lucca Ravioli** and **Bi-Rite Creamery**. Locals might also mob **Pizzeria Delfina, Tartine Bakery,** or **St. Francis Fountain** for its age-old sundaes.

Then venture on to mighty posh Nob Hill to impress out-of-towners at **Swan Oyster Depot** or **Top of the Mark**. Russian Hill's **Nick's Crispy Tacos** is a perennial foodie haven, while the chocolate earthquake from **Swensen's Ice Cream**'s (in business since 1948) is a treasured dessert.

Richmond has earned the nickname "New Chinatown" for good reason. Tuck into the juicy siu mai at **Good Luck Dim Sum** or enjoy a spread of sweet and savory dim sum at **Wing Lee Bakery**.

If in the Sunset area however, pick up fresh-baked pastries at **Arizmendi Bakery** or simply stroll around the corner to the **Beanery**. Over on Noriega Street, the line snakes out the door and down the block at **Cheung Hing**.

Baseball fans may then indulge in a casual bite at SoMa's **21st Amendment Brewery** or **Little Skillet**, which may just serve the best fried chicken and waffles in town. Seal the deal over green tea at **Samovar Tea Lounge** in Yerba Buena Gardens.

CASTRO
& CIVIC CENTER

A MANO ⚫🍴

Italian • Contemporary décor

&

"A mano" is Italian for "by hand," and that's exactly how your pasta will be made at this delicious Italian, where diners can witness dough being rolled, cut and folded just minutes before arriving at the table. Options include vivid green pea and pesto tagliatelle and delicately shaped agnolotti dal plin. For those who'd rather eschew carbs, there are hearty mains like braised short ribs.

The crowd is diverse, with young professionals and families alike sharing Margherita pizzas and spicy chicken meatballs. Loud, funky music and floor-to-ceiling windows that open onto the bustle of Hayes Valley's main drag add to the lively vibe. Order up another cocktail or an affordable glass of Italian red to make the fun last a little longer.

🔲 450 Hayes St. (bet. Octavia & Gough Sts.)
𝒞 (415) 506-7401 — **WEB:** www.amanosf.com
🔲 Lunch & dinner daily   PRICE: $$

ANCHOR OYSTER BAR 😊

Seafood • Simple

Landlubbers seeking a taste of the sea can be found pulling up a stool at this Castro institution, where waves of waiting diners spill out the doors. This tiny, minimally adorned space filled with old-fashioned charm is better for twosomes than groups.

While the menu may be petite, it's full of fresh fare like a light and flavorful Dungeness crab "burger" on a sesame bun; Caesar salad combining sweet prawns and tangy anchovy dressing; or a cup of creamy Boston clam chowder loaded with clams and potatoes. As the name portends, raw oysters are a specialty—so briny that the accompanying mignonette may not be necessary. And of course, the cioppino is unmissable, as this signature item turns sublime when paired with delicious and buttery garlic bread.

🔲 579 Castro St. (bet. 18th & 19th Sts.)
𝒞 (415) 431-3990 — **WEB:** www.anchoroysterbar.com
🔲 Lunch Mon – Sat Dinner nightly   PRICE: $$

AVERY 🍴◯

Contemporary • Minimalist

Like many a restaurant success story these days, Avery began as a pop-up before taking up brick-and-mortar residence. Its ambitious menu pays homage to the chef's prior experiences at some of the city's more elite kitchens: elements of smoke, for instance, are a signature move as is the influence of Eastern Asian cuisines. Grilled oysters, served with seaweed, ramps, spring peas and Meyer lemon, are beloved by all, as is the A5 Wagyu fat topped with a sweet-smoky barbecue sauce, crème fraîche and golden osetra caviar.

The narrow ground floor offers the more impressive menu, while the mezzanine offers a concise tasting. Walls smeared with blue-and-white paint, oversized wooden tables and modern music give the space a youthful yet refined vibe.

■ 1552 Fillmore St. (bet. Ellis St. & Geary Blvd.)
𝒸 (415) 817-1187 — **WEB:** www.averysf.com
■ Dinner Wed – Sun   **PRICE: $$$$**

BAR CRUDO 🍴◯

Seafood • Contemporary décor

Visitors without reservations should be prepared to wait for a table at this Divisadero gem. In fact, they may even find people lined up on the sidewalk for a seat at the counter. As the name suggests, this seafood haven offers supreme crudos. Whether it's Arctic char with horseradish crème fraîche, wasabi tobiko and dill; or scallop with sweet corn purée, tarragon oil and popped sorghum, the combos are delicious. Shellfish platters are available, and there are a few hot dishes including a chowder chock-full of fish, shrimp, squid and bacon.

Inside, the space is often standing room-only, with just a few tables; most guests gather around the bar. Grab a glass of wine or beer, peek into the kitchen and be sure to check out the futuristic art on the walls.

■ 655 Divisadero St. (bet. Grove & Hayes Sts.)
𝒸 (415) 409-0679 — **WEB:** www.barcrudo.com
■ Dinner Tue – Sun   **PRICE: $$**

BARVALE

Spanish • Trendy

Move over, Mission District. Divisadero is quickly becoming this city's new dinner 'hood darling, and Barvale is the perfect place to start your tour. If you're worried about not having a reservation, don't. Once you see the lively scene flowing inside, you'll realize that this tapas house saves half their tables for walk-ins.

The menu toys with fun riffs on traditional Spanish tapas and bite-sized pintxos—all of them matched to terrific sangria and cocktails. Try the smoky chorizo and manchego before indulging in the petite but hugely delicious paella, laced with a creamy aïoli, charred lemon, prawns, mussels and clams. Service moves quickly but attentively, and weekend brunch offers a handful of egg dishes as well as—you guessed it—tapas.

 661 Divisadero St. (at Grove St.)
℘ (415) 654-5211 — **WEB:** www.barvalesf.com
Lunch Sat – Sun Dinner nightly   **PRICE: $$**

CALA 🍴

Mexican • Contemporary décor

A Mexico City superstar with the seafood-centric Contramar, Gabriela Cámara has brought her magic touch to this Civic Center hottie, where she serves similar food. Nothing is lost in translation: filleted black cod with red chile adobo is silky and smoky after a wood grilling in collard leaves, while Cámara's famed tuna tostadas get a Bay Area sustainability update with ocean trout. And you won't want to miss the griddled black bean sopes, which seem simple but sing with flavor.

Cala's minimalist aesthetic matches that of Contramar, with vaulted, skylight-dotted ceilings, a planter box full of climbing vines and lots of light wood for a rustic-urban feel. Service can be spotty, but for a flavorful, unfussy meal, it's quickly become a hot ticket.

149 Fell St. (bet. Franklin St. & Van Ness Ave.)
℘ (415) 660-7701 — **WEB:** www.calarestaurant.com
Dinner nightly   **PRICE: $$$**

CHE FICO

Italian • Trendy

Che fico ("what a fig") is Italian slang for "How cool!" And the sharply dressed crowd at this good-looking spot is indeed very cool—but they give quite a fig about landing a highly coveted reservation. If you're not a celebrity or tech mogul with an inside line, expect to wait in one. The balanced and beautiful array of cocktails, like a gently spicy banana milk punch, will help bide the time nicely.

The vibe is chic, but this food is approachable with rotating pastas like the saffron spaghetti with 'nduja, quirky, compelling pizzas (try the pineapple, red onion and fermented chili number) and Roman-Jewish appetizers like the artistically plated grilled duck liver with matzo.

Desserts are an absolute must: the coffee-blueberry pavlova may sound odd, but it's divine.

▪ 838 Divisadero St. (bet. Fulton & McAllister Sts.)
☏ (415) 416-6959 — **WEB:** www.chefico.com
▪ Dinner Tue – Sat   PRICE: $$$

FRANCES

Californian • Cozy

This tiny, intensely personal restaurant from Chef/owner Melissa Perello has been a local hit from the get-go. Chic and always packed, it's as perfect for a low-key date night as it is for dinner with the kids. And while reservations are nigh-impossible to score here, its astonishingly cozy setting attended to by a gracious staff justifies planning ahead.

Perello eschews trendy powders and foams for hearty and seasonal fare like charred baby octopus with homemade yogurt and olive tapenade. Honey-brined pork chop rests over creamed escarole and fennel slaw; while McGinnis Ranch carrots are roasted with sunchokes for an interesting blend of sweet and savory. Desserts like a black sesame pavolva with chicory root ice cream offer a light, fresh conclusion.

▪ 3870 17th St. (at Pond St.)
☏ (415) 621-3870 — **WEB:** www.frances-sf.com
▪ Dinner Tue – Sun   PRICE: $$

JARDINIÈRE ¶○

Californian • Elegant

For a memorable night on the town, don your best dress, find a hand to hold and head to this longtime favorite tinged with a sense of bygone romance. Stop off at the circular bar and join the well-heeled couples sipping cocktails pre- or post-opera. Prime seats on the upstairs balcony overlook the bustling lower level, and stunning arched windows show off views of the street. Approachable, seasonal dishes abound on Jardinière's menu, from tender tajarin pasta with morel mushrooms and butter to a Mediterranean-inspired duo of lamb belly and shoulder with fresh fava beans and smoked yogurt sauce.

Indecisive sweet tooths will thrill to the bonne bouche, an array of candies, cookies, small cakes and profiteroles that makes a striking conclusion.

■ 300 Grove St. (at Franklin St.)
φ (415) 861-5555 — **WEB:** www.jardiniere.com
■ Dinner nightly   PRICE: $$$

MONSIEUR BENJAMIN ¶○

French • Bistro

Chef Corey Lee's take on timeless bistro cuisine is as sleek and striking as the space it's served in. Fit for the cover of a magazine, this black-and-white dining room's minimalist, yet intimate décor is trumped only by its pièce de résistance: an exhibition kitchen where you'll find the meticulous brigade of cooks hard at work, producing impressively authentic French food.

Begin with the pâté de campagne, enhanced with liver and shallots and presented with strong mustard, cornichons and country bread. The Arctic char amandine is excellent, dressed with fragrant beurre noisette and served over a bed of crispy haricot verts and sunchokes. For a sweet finish, purists will delight in the dessert menu's île flottante.

■ 451 Gough St. (at Ivy St.)
φ (415) 403-2233 — **WEB:** www.monsieurbenjamin.com
■ Lunch Sat – Sun Dinner nightly   PRICE: $$$

JŪ-NI 🏵

Japanese • Contemporary décor

◔ &

"Jū-ni" is Japanese for "twelve," which also happens to be the number of seats available in this petite, omakase-only spot, housed just off the busy Divisadero corridor. Its segmented, L-shaped sushi bar ensures personalized attention from the trio of chefs, often led by Chef/owner Geoffrey Lee. They're a young, lively crew and they've designed this space with a crowd of similarly young, moneyed professionals in mind. Note the spotlights above the counter, placed for perfect Instagram snapshots of dishes, and the thoroughly curated sake selection.

A meal may begin with a tasting of seasonal vegetables—think tomatoes over edamame hummus—before proceeding to an array of nigiri, painstakingly sourced straight from Japan and delicately draped over well-seasoned rice. Standouts include sakura masu with a salt-cured cherry blossom leaf, buttery Hokkaido scallop and the signature ikura—cured in soy sauce, sake and honey, then finished with a grating of velvety frozen monkfish liver.

Decadent supplements, like torched A5 Wagyu beef and luscious uni, can be added along the way. But the meal finishes with a surprisingly gentle send-off: sweet, tender mochi dabbed with adzuki bean paste.

■ 1335 Fulton St. (bet. Broderick & Divisadero Sts.)
𝄢 (415) 655-9924 — **WEB:** www.junisf.com
■ Dinner Mon – Sat   **PRICE: $$$$**

NIGHTBIRD

Californian • Elegant

Located just behind a beautiful wooden door with a carved owl and in a prime Hayes Valley location, Nightbird invites you into its nest with a small and sleek dining room. If you arrive early, don't miss a delicious craft cocktail at their sibling spot next door, Linden Bar, as it's the perfect lead-up to Chef/owner Kim Alter's five-course tasting.

Though the menu changes often, Alter's presentations are consistently gorgeous. Witness a tender scallop "cooked" in yuzu juice, topped with uni, spring peas, radish, pea shoots and a truffle vinaigrette. Or go for a beautiful tableside presentation of white asparagus from the Loire Valley with paddlefish and salmon roe, a single leaf of nasturtium, as well as a drizzle of beurre blanc studded with escargot.

330 Gough St. (at Linden St.)
(415) 829-7565 — **WEB:** www.nightbirdrestaurant.com
Dinner Tue - Sat **PRICE: $$$$**

NOPA

Californian • Contemporary décor

Before you're able to enjoy a single forkful at this Bay Area sensation, you'll have to secure a table—and that takes some serious effort. Reservations are snapped up at lightning speed, and hopeful walk-ins must line up prior to the start of service to add their name to the list.

The good news? Your efforts will be well rewarded. Inside, an open kitchen, soaring ceilings and hordes of ravenous sophisticates produce a cacophonous setting in which to relish Nopa's wonderful, organic, wood-fired cuisine. Dig into a bruschetta of grilled levain spread with smashed avocado, pickled jalapeños, lemon-dressed arugula and shaved mezzo secco, or go for the roasted king salmon fillet over creamed corn, smoky maitakes, crisp green beans and sweet tomato confit.

560 Divisadero St. (at Hayes St.)
(415) 864-8643 — **WEB:** www.nopasf.com
Lunch Sat - Sun Dinner nightly **PRICE: $$**

NOPALITO 😊

Mexican • Trendy

 ♿ 🏓

Whether they're digging into a refreshing ensalada de nopales or sharing a platter of blue-corn tacos stuffed with spicy-smoky marinated fish, local couples and families adore this sustainable Mexican spot. Sister to Cal-cuisine icon Nopa, Nopalito is so beloved that an equally good and popular Inner Sunset location is also thriving.

The small, cheerful space with reclaimed wood and bright green accents doesn't take reservations; call ahead to get on the list, or try takeout. Once seated, friendly servers will guide the way with house-made horchata for the kids and an extensive tequila selection for grown-ups. Both groups will certainly agree on a sweet finish: the excellent vanilla bean flan topped with orange caramel and orange supremes is unbeatable.

◼ 306 Broderick St. (bet. Fell & Oak Sts.)
✆ (415) 437-0303 — **WEB:** www.nopalitosf.com
◼ Lunch & dinner daily   **PRICE: $$**

PETIT CRENN 🍴○

French • Bistro

 ♿ 🛋

In a homey corner of booming Hayes Valley, Chef Dominique Crenn serves a menu more approachable (in both technique and price) than her acclaimed Atelier Crenn. With its open kitchen, chalkboard menus and nautical feel inspired by Brittany, Petit Crenn is a hit among locals.

While the eats are lip-smacking—think kampachi crudo with matsutake mushrooms, or rustic "Cassoulet de la Mer" showcasing creamy beans, lightly crisped black cod and plump mussels—the execution of this kitchen is precise. Find further evidence of this in such exquisite desserts as pain de Gênes presented with creamy cardamom ice cream and Meyer lemon curd. Whether you opt for the early evening à la carte seating or multi-course prix-fixe, expect to leave wholly sated and smitten.

◼ 609 Hayes St. (bet. Buchanan & Laguna Sts.)
✆ (415) 864-1744 — **WEB:** www.petitcrenn.com
◼ Lunch Sat – Sun Dinner Tue – Sun   **PRICE: $$$$**

THE PROGRESS

Californian • Contemporary décor

This is the rare restaurant that guarantees its diners will never be bored, thanks to the sophisticated energy that flows directly from a notably ambitious kitchen.

The gorgeous space has that Nordic look that California so loves, with plenty of bare wood, skylights and an affluent crowd appearing informal in their Patagonias. The hipster staff echoes the casual mood but performs attentive service.

The focus is on family-style dining, but go ahead and order a few smaller dishes to accompany their platter-sized plates. Perfectly crisp artichokes, for instance, are at the center of an exceptionally good combination of preserved lemon and coriander chermoula, garnished with fragrant herbs and tender artichoke leaves. Barbecued Liberty Farms duck is cooked to absolute delight and presented with garlic- and ginger-infused crisped rice as well as meat so tender that it is practically falling off the bone. When they hit their mark, creations like this transcend their ingredients and technique to result in something genius, including the properly executed île flottante. Be sure to match this with one of their refreshing cocktails, like the house martini, finished with a droplet of rosemary oil.

■ 1525 Fillmore St. (bet. Geary Blvd. & O'Farrell St.)
𝒫 (415) 673-1294 — **WEB:** www.theprogress-sf.com
■ Dinner nightly   **PRICE: $$$**

REVELRY BISTRO ¶◯

French • Bistro

    ♿ 🚋 ⬜ 🍽

Though this colorful corner bistro boasts some fusion-forward items, diners in the know stick with the French classics. No quarter is given to tired menu standards like onion soup and boeuf bourguignon; instead, you'll find truly seasonal fare, like endive in a creamy, umami-rich gratin that nicely softens its bitterness. The rotating specials might include decadent tournedos Rossini—perfectly tender filet mignon.

Low-key vibes, excellent food and soft tunes make this a date-night bijou; and couples typically occupy the tightly packed tables. However, even if you're rolling solo, you might find yourself falling for the pristine profiteroles, stuffed with vanilla ice cream and drenched in a thick, rich chocolate sauce.

■ 297 Page St. (at Laguna St.)
✆ (415) 241-6833 — **WEB:** www.revelrybistro.com
■ Lunch Sat – Sun Dinner Tue – Sun   **PRICE: $$$**

ROBIN ¶◯

Japanese • Trendy

    ♿

Trust is the name of the game at Robin, a hip sushi-focused destination, where no menu is ever presented. Instead, guests happily submit themselves to the very capable skills of Chef Adam Tortosa and eagerly await his modern take on omakase. This kitchen's decadent vision includes lots of elite ingredients like A5 Wagyu beef and caviar, though the staff will kindly ask what your budget is (or if you have allergies). The upscale space is a mix of posh and street cool—think graffiti-esque bathrooms and hip-hop beats. Young sushi chefs are the focal point of the room, working fastidiously with tweezers, torches and gel in front of a bright backdrop.

A small, carefully curated list of beer, sake and wine pairs nicely with the food.

■ 620 Gough St. (at Ash St.)
✆ (415) 548-2429 — **WEB:** www.robinsanfrancisco.com
■ Dinner nightly   **PRICE: $$$$**

RICH TABLE
Contemporary • Trendy

A rustic-chic décor highlighting reclaimed and raw wood gives Rich Table a farmhouse feel, and the crowds that pack it are equally stylish. The young professionals and pre-theater diners know that reserving in advance is a must. If you're not lucky enough to secure a table, get in line 30 minutes before opening to snag one of the dozen coveted bar seats.

Why all the fuss? Because Chefs/owners Evan and Sarah Rich execute casual Californian fare with fine-dining precision, interweaving a bevy of global influences along the way. The seared pierogies, stuffed with ricotta, morels and peas, are pristine enough to win a Polish grandmother's approval, and a char siu-style pork chop is beautifully smoky and charred.

The super-hip staff is thoroughly polished and happy to recommend a cocktail or wine. They'll push the duo of famous "snacks"—crispy sardine-threaded chips and umami-packed porcini doughnuts with raclette dipping sauce. But skip them in favor of a seasonal dessert, like the tart cherry ice with almond ice cream and shiso.

■ 199 Gough St. (at Oak St.)
℘ (415) 355-9085 — **WEB:** www.richtablesf.com
■ Dinner nightly   **PRICE: $$$**

RT ROTISSERIE ¶○

Californian • Simple

Can't manage to snag a seat at Rich Table? You'll dine equally well at the restaurant's fast-casual sibling, just a block away. Though it resembles the mothership with its simple, wood-heavy décor and earthenware plates, RT's compact menu and counter service make it far more affordable—a bonus with the Hayes Valley crowds seeking a quick-but-quality lunch or pre-theater dinner.

The menu is centered on a few rotisserie items, including tender, juicy half-chicken with crisp, burnished skin. When accompanied by perfectly roasted cauliflower that shines in a pita sandwich, with beet hummus, cucumber salad, lemon and herbs, it's an utter delight. Add on a dipping sauce like chipotle yogurt or a side of charred corn with ricotta, and you're in business.

- ▦ 101 Oak St. (at Franklin St.)
- ℰ (415) 829-7086 — **WEB:** www.rtrotisserie.com
- ▦ Lunch & dinner daily **PRICE:** ☜

SARU ¶○

Japanese • Simple

Hilly Noe Valley is the perfect setting for this jewel of a sushi restaurant, so make your way inside to discover a bustling (read: energetic) vibe. The menu is thoroughly Japanese with a few Californian touches—think grilled shishito peppers tossed with crunchy daikon in a ponzu dressing.

Be sure to start with the signature tempura-fried seaweed cracker topped with spicy tuna and avocado. Then, perfectly sized tasting spoons of seared ankimo with scallions, as well as halibut tartare with yuzu make for delightful quick bites. Though rolls are available, regulars opt for the nigiri, which might include kampachi, baby snapper and snow crab. If you'd like the chefs to choose, several omakase (including an all-salmon variation) are also on offer.

- ▦ 3856 24th St. (bet. Sanchez & Vicksburg Sts.)
- ℰ (415) 400-4510 — **WEB:** www.akaisarusf.com
- ▦ Lunch & dinner Wed – Sun **PRICE:** $$

STARBELLY 😊

Californian • Rustic

The simplest things are often the best, as a meal at Starbelly deliciously proves. Whether you're twirling a forkful of spaghetti with garlicky tomato sauce, jalapeños and house-made bacon, or tucking into a juicy burger on a grilled sesame seed-challah bun, you're sure to savor something beautifully made, seasonal and unfussy. Desserts are just as satisfying, like a salted caramel pot de crème served with rosemary shortbread cookies.

A nexus of the Castro social scene, this cheerful, wood-paneled space is always full of locals hopping from table to table to greet their friends, and the back patio (heated and sheltered when it's foggy) is an appealing refuge.

Be sure to make reservations: this is an area favorite, and for good reason.

■ 3583 16th St. (at Market St.)
℘ (415) 252-7500 — **WEB:** www.starbellysf.com
■ Lunch & dinner daily   PRICE: $$

TSUBASA 😊

Japanese • Simple

Amidst the pricey boutiques and top-dollar restaurants of Hayes Valley, a good deal can be hard to come by. However, Tsubasa is a delightful exception, offering well-made nigiri, sashimi and maki at a price point that belies the high quality of its fish.

The sleek dining room offers table seating, but the best seats in the house are at the sushi bar, where you'll be presented with generously portioned nigiri that range from cleanly flavored turbot to intense, vinegar-kissed saba (mackerel). There are also more elaborate maki, like a salmon and avocado roll topped with raw scallops and miso sauce. But the deepest pleasures are simple ones: excellent miso soup, a tuna roll with beautifully seasoned rice and rich, custardy tamago.

■ 429 Gough St. (bet. Hayes & Ivy Sts.)
℘ (415) 551-9688 — **WEB:** www.tsubasasf.com
■ Dinner Tue – Sun   PRICE: $$

STATE BIRD PROVISIONS ⣎

American • Trendy

Welcome to the evolution of fine dining, where streams of plates are passed between guests in dim sum-style, and the supremely seasonal Californian cooking is always very good; even vibrant and surprising. You may not understand all of what you ordered at first, but prices are reasonable so pile on a few extras and try everything that comes your way. No one leaves hungry here.

Servers circulate through the room carrying platters or pushing carts brimming with creative and utterly unique dishes. Highlights that will leave you begging for more include pan-seared dumplings—filled with tender, pulled guinea hen and earthy shiitake mushrooms—accompanied by a tableside pour of aromatic and umami-rich broth. Heartier but wow-inducing plates of fried black cod tail glazed in a delicious tamari-butter and garnished with toasted sesame seeds, followed by hot-pink rhubarb-and-passion fruit granita draped over an oat mousse make for a fine study in wonderfully unexpected flavors and textures.

Be forewarned: getting a reservation here is the ultimate challenge and walk-in spots require lining up around 4:30 P.M. Best to avoid nights when large parties are booked, as this may negatively impact your experience.

◼ 1529 Fillmore St. (bet. Geary Blvd. & O'Farrell St.)
✆ (415) 795-1272 — **WEB:** www.statebirdsf.com
◼ Dinner nightly   PRICE: $$

UMA CASA

Portuguese • Contemporary décor

&

High ceilings and azulejo-adorned walls set the scene at this Noe Valley jewel, which succeeds longtime local spot Incanto. It's also one of the few high-end San Francisco restaurants spotlighting the cuisine of Portugal, and Chef Telmo Faria delivers a traditional seafood-centric menu. Read: grilled sardines, salt cod fritters, as well as garlic- and chili-inflected camarão moçambique.

Most diners opt to share a flurry of small plates, commencing with potato chips and piri-piri sauce. The entrées are satisfying, too. Try the alcatra, red wine-braised short ribs; or pan-roasted sea bass with molho cru, the Portuguese take on chimichurri. Finally, sip on one of the bar's signature low alcohol cocktails, made with port, sherry and other fortified wines.

■ 1550 Church St. (at Duncan St.)
℘ (415) 829-2264 — **WEB:** www.umacasarestaurant.com
■ Dinner Tue – Sun   **PRICE: $$**

SAN FRANCISCO ▶ CASTRO & CIVIC CENTER

VILLON

Contemporary • Chic

This up-and-comer in the sleek Proper Hotel has style to spare—from its polished checkerboard floors all the way up to the floor-to-ceiling library shelves behind the stunning bar. No detail is too small here, especially those heavy etched glasses that hold complimentary sparkling water, and the smart shirts donned by the waitstaff. Even the gold flatware will catch your eye.

The good looks extend to the plate as well, where the chef and team offer clever riffs on everything from Hawaiian sweet rolls topped with "everything" seasoning and served with a trio of spreads, to Japanese okonomiyaki, which gets a Spanish twist with prawns and chorizo.

Seek out the outstanding cocktail list as it boasts 49 options, one for each square mile of San Francisco.

■ 1100 Market St. (at Charles J. Brenham Pl.)
℘ (628) 895-2040 — **WEB:** www.properhotel.com
■ Lunch & dinner daily   **PRICE: $$**

ZUNI CAFÉ ¶O

Mediterranean • Bistro

Forty years young and still thriving as if it were newborn, locals and visitors remain drawn to this SF institution. Famous for its laid-back California vibe and great, locally sourced eats, this iconic space embraces its unique shape, and is styled with bold artwork-covered walls, a copper bar and wood-burning oven sending out delightful pizzas that fill the room with mouthwatering aromas.

Given its ace location, Zuni makes for a divine lunch destination—and proof is in the many business folk, trendy ladies-who-lunch and tourists who fill its tables midday. Menu treasures include sliced persimmon scattered with shaved Jerusalem artichokes and baby arugula leaves, tailed by artisanal rigatoni clutching a fragrant lamb sugo.

■ 1658 Market St. (bet. Franklin & Gough Sts.)

℘ (415) 552-2522 — **WEB:** www.zunicafe.com

■ Lunch & dinner Tue – Sun   PRICE: $$

FINANCIAL
DISTRICT

AKIKO'S 🍴○

Japanese • Cozy

〇◡

Though Akiko's may look like an average neighborhood sushi joint from the outside (especially since it's often confused with a nearby spot of the same name), a meal here is a reminder that appearances can be deceiving. Those planning on dining in will want to make a reservation, as the small, industrial space is mighty popular—especially those coveted counter seats.

Second-generation Chef/owner Ray Lee does wonders with nigiri from around the globe, from silky New Zealand king salmon to full-flavored Cyprian sea bream. Cooked dishes like gently battered agedashi tofu, in a flavorful broth accented with "pearls" of ikura, are just as appealing. And be sure to sample the excellent applewood-aged soy sauce, which brings out the flavors of each dish.

◾ 431 Bush St. (bet. Grant & Kearny Sts.)
℘ (415) 397-3218 — **WEB:** www.akikosrestaurant.com
◾ Lunch Mon – Fri Dinner Mon – Sat   PRICE: $$$

COQUETA ☺

Spanish • Contemporary décor

♿

A tasty little morsel of a space serving up mouthwatering tapas, Michael Chiarello's Pier 5 destination offers shimmering views of the Bay from its rustic dining room, equipped with rough-hewn wooden tables, cowhide rugs and a big, theatrical open kitchen and bar. There's a bit more space on the tented outdoor patio, but if your heart is set on a table, book early.

Its name is Spanish for "flirt," and Coqueta's alluring menu has caused more than one enraptured diner to over-order. Some fine options: crunchy-creamy chicken and pea croquetas, mini sandwiches of smoked salmon with queso fresco and truffle honey and wood-grilled octopus with tender fingerling potatoes. Complete the experience with the Asturian apple pie with Cabrales blue cheese ice cream.

◾ Pier 5 (at The Embarcadero)
℘ (415) 704-8866 — **WEB:** www.coquetasf.com
◾ Lunch Tue – Sun Dinner nightly   PRICE: $$

CAMPTON PLACE ⭐⭐

Indian • Elegant

The breadth and complexity of Indian cuisine gets its due at this tasteful retreat, tucked into a posh hotel just steps from the luxury boutiques of Union Square. Attired in a soft palette of cream and white, with a striking central glass light fixture, it's a smooth showcase for the freewheeling, colorful food from Chef Srijith Gopinathan.

Diners have a choice of vegetarian or omnivorous dishes from the six-course tasting—with an extravagant add-on of white truffle naan for the high rollers in the room. Either way, you'll be sent on a riotous journey through different textures, flavors and temperatures, along with some truly whimsical plating. Whether it's a pea-shoot "flowerpot" with quinoa soil or a frozen stone bearing persimmon-kulfi popsicles, the chef's panache is sure to garner wide smiles.

That's not to discount this kitchen's exceptional use of flavors as relished in the butter-poached lobster dressed with a coastal curry derived from the chef's grandmother's recipe, or the crisp dosa matched perfectly with a filling of sweet day boat scallops. Cauliflower roasted on charcoal with tomato tokku, kohlrabi and yogurt paired with fluffy kallappam makes for yet another high point.

■ 340 Stockton St. (bet. Post & Sutter Sts.)
☏ (415) 955-5555 — **WEB:** www.camptonplacesf.com
■ Dinner nightly   **PRICE: $$$$**

DEL POPOLO 🏵️

Pizza • Minimalist

&

If you've got eyes for pies, you'll want to make a beeline to this chic and simple Italian hot spot. The open space is centered around a big, blazing oven and crowds arrive early to score every last no-reservations seat.

Del Popolo may have gotten its start as a food truck, but one bite of their wood-fired pizzas and it's clear how it earned its address. Chewy, blistered and deliciously caramelized, the crusts arrive laden with toppings both traditional (mozzarella, crushed tomato and basil) and California cool (roasted winter squash, mascarpone, spring onions). Don't sleep on the antipasti either, since the starters are first-rate. The lightly charred carrots set atop house-made yogurt and garnished with crispy red quinoa are dizzyingly delicious.

■ 855 Bush St. (bet. Mason & Taylor Sts.)
✆ (415) 589-7940 — **WEB:** www.delpopolosf.com
■ Dinner Tue – Sun   PRICE: $$

GIBSON 🍴

Contemporary • Chic

🍸 & 🍽️

This swanky spot in the Hotel Bijou is truly a tale of two cities—while the Tenderloin-bordering exterior is unassuming, the shimmering interior is a Gatsby-worthy altar of Deco glamour. But look beyond the ornate ceilings and aquamarine banquettes, and you'll find a menu that revolves around two ancient techniques—live-fire cooking on an open hearth, and a robust fermentation program with jars lining the kitchen walls.

The results are impressive. Imagine fire-baked sourdough rolls with a delicate duck liver mousse, tailed by charred roast carrots served over an impressively rich sunflower seed "risotto." Portions are petite, so all the better to share them over cocktails or house-made sodas.

For a deeper dive, opt for the prix-fixe menu.

■ 111 Mason St. (at Eddy St.)
✆ (415) 771-7709 — **WEB:** www.gibsonsf.com
■ Dinner Mon – Sat   PRICE: $$$

HARBORVIEW

Chinese · Chic

With a behemoth $14-million space in the Embarcadero Center to call its own, this restaurant and bar is no mom-and-pop Cantonese joint. In fact, its dining room showcases impressive views of the Ferry building and Bay Bridge from its sunny upper deck patio; add to that a beautiful and polished interior space offering sun-drenched rooms as well as more intimately lit nooks.

For lunch, you can order from the extensive dim sum selection, a separate kitchen menu or simply pick whatever strikes your fancy from the passing carts. From sesame balls to fried daikon and shrimp rolls, one really can't go wrong. For dinner though, go for the crispy, golden-brown Peking duck, served with crunchy cucumber and scallions, steamed buns and a decadent house-made sauce.

■ 4 Embarcadero Center (at The Embarcadero)

✆ (628) 867-7350 — **WEB:** www.harborviewsf.com

■ Lunch & dinner daily　　　　　　　　　　**PRICE: $$**

HOG ISLAND OYSTER CO. ⑪

Seafood · Trendy

Can't make the trip to Marin to shuck oysters on Hog Island's docks? They'll bring Tomales Bay's finest to you at this buzzing cityside outpost in the Ferry Building, which draws long lines of both tourists and locals for platters of some of the sweetest, freshest bivalves on the West Coast. You'll receive all the accompaniments—lemon, Tabasco, mignonette—but they're good enough to slurp solo.

Once you've had your fill, be sure to sample the other aquatic offerings: Peruvian-style crudo with silky sea bass; a hefty bowl of cioppino loaded with prawns, clams, mussels and squid; and the exceptional Manila clam chowder, a bestseller for good reason. Throw in the expansive Bay views from the patio and dining room, and those lines come as no surprise.

■ 1 Ferry Building (at The Embarcadero)

✆ (415) 391-7117 — **WEB:** www.hogislandoysters.com

■ Lunch & dinner daily　　　　　　　　　　**PRICE: $$$**

KIN KHAO ❀

Thai • Trendy

Tucked into an alcove of the unprepossessing Parc 55 hotel, this restaurant won't win any awards in the décor department—it's spare and casual, with tables set with chopstick canisters and bowls of chili oil. But when it comes to delivering authentically layered, fiery Thai flavor with a produce-driven northern California flair, it has no equal.

Kin Khao's menu conjures up dishes from across Thailand and is a virtual homage to local purveyors. Imagine a meaty and rich five-spice noodle soup infused with duck bones and stocked with bok choy as well as delightfully tender duck leg confit; or a deliciously fresh take on som tum, with julienned green papaya tossed with golden tomatoes, long beans, dried shrimp and crushed red chili. More traditional options may include classic pad kee mao showcasing wide, flat noodles stir-fried with a potent mixture of ground pork bits, bell pepper, onion and holy basil.

Needless to say, those avoiding spicy food or craving plain old pad Thai should look elsewhere. But, if you're in the mood for a vibrant and zesty meal, then strap in for a wild and enticing ride. Come dessert, try the black rice pudding served warm and with myriad toppings.

■ 55 Cyril Magnin St. (entrance at Ellis & Mason Sts.)
✆ (415) 362-7456 — **WEB:** www.kinkhao.com
■ Lunch & dinner daily   PRICE: $$

KUSAKABE 🍴◯

Japanese • Minimalist

🍶 ♿

Serene with warm lighting and clean lines, distinctive creativity is the motto of this sushi-focused operation. Inside, a stunning counter crafted from a piece of live-edge elm, oyster-hued leather chairs and a ceiling of wood slats complete the Japanese-chic look.

While the preparation of their nightly omakase might seem like a production line by employing myriad cooking techniques, the kitchen ensures that every bite is memorable. Begin with warm kelp tea, before embarking on a sashimi parade of bluefin slices served with a yuzu-onion-sesame sauce. A soup course may feature a soy foam-miso broth with rice dumplings and duck meatballs. And finally, a top rendition of sushi yields shima aji with daikon and ayu that is torched just enough to blister the skin.

▨ 584 Washington St. (bet. Montgomery & Sansome Sts.)
✆ (415) 757-0155 — **WEB:** www.kusakabe-sf.com
▨ Dinner Mon – Sat   **PRICE: $$$$**

PERBACCO 🍴◯

Italian • Contemporary décor

🍸 ♿ 🍽

Slick financial types flex their expense accounts at this longtime Northern Italian retreat. Its polished décor belies a comforting menu of house-made pastas and items like roast chicken and meatballs at lunch, with slightly more refined takes at dinner. Dishes are executed with care—from slow-roasted vitello tonnato and semolina-dusted petrale sole to handmade pastas.

The space is larger inside than it looks, with plenty of booths and seats at the gleaming marble bar up front to the buzzy tables in the back with a view of the open-plan kitchen. Well-versed servers will encourage saving room for the end of the meal—as the cheese display, an impressive selection of grappas and the inventive, delicious desserts are all highlights.

▨ 230 California St. (bet. Battery & Front Sts.)
✆ (415) 955-0663 — **WEB:** www.perbaccosf.com
▨ Lunch Mon – Fri Dinner Mon – Sat   **PRICE: $$**

MICHAEL MINA ƒ

Contemporary • Elegant

ƒ ♿ ⊕ ↴

Power players can't seem to get enough of mega-popular Chef Michael Mina's San Francisco flagship, even though it sports a completely revamped menu. If the crisp, contemporary dining room was a favorite, don't fret, as the overall demeanor remains the same. It's still ground zero for fine dining and you're likely to see the same expense-account types, along with a handful of occasion-celebrating duos.

The kitchen's approach showcases Middle Eastern flavors and incorporates classic ingredients, like labneh, which appears in both sweet and savory dishes. Wild king salmon is accompanied by a coriander-green tomato sauce; the dry-aged strip loin with matbucha sauce is a prime example of the kitchen's novel direction. While you won't find the famed trios on this carte any longer, you'll relish the signature tuna tartare, mixed with quail egg, diced pear and ancho chili powder. A multi-course tasting allows you to select your own options, including the hand-cut tajarin and a properly rendered dark chocolate cremeux with fresh strawberries.

Be sure to spend time with the wine list as well: though expensive, it offers an impressive roster of familiar labels and unusual varietals.

■ 252 California St. (bet. Battery & Front Sts.)
☎ (415) 397-9222 — **WEB:** www.michaelmina.net
■ Lunch Mon – Fri Dinner nightly   **PRICE: $$$$**

NICO

Contemporary • Bistro

&

After moving to the Financial District, Chef Nicolas Delaroque has succeeded in ensuring that this contemporary French bistro does not miss a beat. The petite dining room is polished and sophisticated but never stuffy, combining brown leather banquettes and exposed brick with a backlit white marble bar. Find the best seats towards the immaculate, white-tiled open kitchen located in the back.

The menus change frequently, promising that each dish showcases peak-season ingredients. The lunch carte is well priced and bound to attract a flock of business diners. At dinner, the six-course chef's tasting is a worthwhile recommendation, in addition to the à la carte offerings. Regardless of the time of day however, this all translates into tremendous value for such expertly prepared cuisine.

Everything turned out of the kitchen is perfectly cooked and seasoned, beginning with lightly poached white asparagus accompanied by trout roe and lemon. Freshly shelled peas with spring onion, meaty clams and smoked cod custard combine acidity, creaminess and incredible flavors. Delectable desserts have included apricot confit on almond crumble with refreshing bay leaf-ice cream.

■ 710 Montgomery St. (bet. Jackson & Washington Sts.)
℘ (415) 359-1000 — **WEB:** www.nicosf.com
■ Lunch Tue – Fri Dinner Tue – Sat   **PRICE: $$$**

THE SLANTED DOOR 🍴

Vietnamese • Contemporary décor

Reservations are a challenge at this modern stunner, located on the Embarcadero and with a killer view of the Bay Bridge. The Slanted Door has managed to stay atop tourists' hit lists thanks to its Northern Californian spin on classic Vietnamese cuisine. It's an efficient and professional place; and while the décor is quite stark, the servers are all warmth.

Instead of the cellophane noodles with crab or overpriced shaking beef, diners should stick to more solid offerings like gau choy gow, featuring pan-fried dumplings with Gulf shrimp and garlic chives accompanied by a zippy soy and fish-sauce dip. Take advantage of this kitchen's varied repertoire by sampling more than one of their vegetable sides, like the crisp and spicy broccoli with pressed tofu.

- 1 Ferry Building (at The Embarcadero)
- ℰ (415) 861-8032 — **WEB:** www.slanteddoor.com
- Lunch & dinner daily   **PRICE: $$**

TRESTLE 😊

American • Cozy

In SF's dizzyingly expensive dining landscape, this hot spot, which offers a three-course menu for under $40, is an incredible steal—provided you're willing to sacrifice freedom of choice. The two options for each course change daily based on what's freshest: your repast may feature fork-tender short ribs draped atop a luscious parmesan polenta and spigarello, followed by frozen chocolate parfait garnished with crushed cashews and huckleberries.

As with any killer deal, there are caveats: reservations are necessary (and hard to score) and the noise level is through the roof. However, this historic brick space is lots of fun, with cool, contemporary art and a namesake central trestle table. The fact that the price is right only adds to the overall allure.

- 531 Jackson St. (at Columbus Ave.)
- ℰ (415) 772-0922 — **WEB:** www.trestlesf.com
- Dinner nightly   **PRICE: $$**

WAYFARE TAVERN ⅈ◯

Gastropub • Elegant

  ♿   🍴   🛋

Though it feels like it's been around for decades, celebrity chef Tyler Florence's FiDi favorite is actually a toddler—at least in tavern years. In fact, it's become a standby for business types doing deals or enjoying post-work cocktails. Complete with dark wood and leather furnishings, a private billiards room and bustling bar, Wayfare Tavern has the air of a gastropub-turned-private club.

Hearty Americana with seasonal accents defines the menu. Meals here usually begin with piping-hot popovers, and then proceed to buttermilk-brined fried chicken—both of which are the chef's signature dishes. Even fish specials, like pan-roasted salmon with wilted leeks, are pure comfort, as is the strawberry cheesecake finished with a graham cracker tuile.

◼ 558 Sacramento St. (bet. Montgomery & Sansome Sts.)

✆ (415) 772-9060 — **WEB:** www.wayfaretavern.com

◼ Lunch & dinner daily   **PRICE: $$$**

MARINA

AN JAPANESE 🍴

Japanese • Intimate

This tucked-away space in Japantown promises a great evening complete with specialized Japanese cuisine. At the helm of the kitchen is the talented chef, Kiyoshi Hayakawa, who along with his wife, the head server, plus a second sushi chef, provides a concise menu with a $30 à la carte minimum. Serious sushi lovers, however, can always go for the two nigiri-only menus or an all-out omakase with some hot appetizers.

The nigiri are excellent—their gently seasoned rice draped with exceptionally pristine fish. And for the finale—a buttery slice of seared Wagyu beef. Cooked dishes might include a vivid matsutake mushroom soup featuring an intense kelp broth.

Though the dress code is casual, the room is still small and very hushed, making for an intimate meal.

◼ 22 Peace Plaza, Ste. 510 (bet. Buchanan & Laguna Sts.)
✆ (415) 292-4886 — **WEB:** www.sushiansf.com
◼ Dinner Tue – Sat   PRICE: $$$

A16 😋

Italian • Trendy

🕸 ♿

An undying favorite of yuppies, families and tourists alike, A16 is known for rustic Italian cooking and a vast selection of delicious, unusual wines from all over the boot. Dinner reservations are indispensable, especially if you want one of the prime counter seats facing the open kitchen and wood-burning pizza oven.

The menu's pies, pastas and antipasti change with the season, so you could sample anything from a highly enjoyable zuppa di ceci verde flecked with green garbanzo beans and parsley, to perfectly al dente cavatelli tossed in a slow-cooked lamb sugo made extra hearty with the addition of plump borlotti beans. For dessert, look no further than the fig crostata with vanilla gelato, which tastes like the work of a particularly talented nonna.

◼ 2355 Chestnut St. (bet. Divisadero & Scott Sts.)
✆ (415) 771-2216 — **WEB:** www.a16pizza.com
◼ Lunch Fri – Sun Dinner nightly   PRICE: $$

ATELIER CRENN ✿✿✿

Contemporary • Elegant

At the hands of accomplished Chef Dominique Crenn, guests have rightly come to expect a thrilling meal at her singular atelier, replete with lustrous combinations, a keen understanding of flavors and an impeccable sense of grace. Another exclusive hallmark of dining here is the deeply hospitable and exemplary staff. They appear to virtually float in and out of the kitchen, which in turn prides itself on a sense of poetry expressed figuratively through dishes and quite literally via the actual poem composed by Chef Crenn to her father—it's even etched into marble and on full display.

Original is the name of this culinary game—one that is as thoughtful in serving brioche with cultured butter as it is with caviar crowned by turbot gelée and gold leaf. Poached sea bass with black truffles then happily wins over the most discerning of palates. It is indeed possible to dine here and not see any meat, but it's also never missed, thanks to the team's masterful hand with seafood.

The cheese course is stellar, but Pastry Chef/partner Juan Contreras' desserts make for a novel finale. A faux-coconut shell coated in dark chocolate and filled with pineapple as well as coconut foam takes home the gold.

■ 3127 Fillmore St. (bet. Filbert & Pixley Sts.)
☏ (415) 440-0460 — **WEB:** www.ateliercrenn.com
■ Dinner Tue – Sat   **PRICE: $$$$**

BAR CRENN ⍟
French • Chic

🏵

It may be located next to Chef Dominique Crenn's notable Atelier Crenn, but Bar Crenn is a destination in its own right. Designed with an eye on Paris during Les Années Folles with a splash of speakeasy, this room is a flea market-chic amalgam of cozy lounge furniture, glinting chandeliers and vintage accents. Fine silver, crystal, champagne and caviar complete the decadence. The wine list is presented as a gold-embossed book of wooden pages.

The classic French cooking strives to recreate many of the century's great dishes through recipes on loan from culinary masters, such as Alain Ducasse and Paul Bocuse. The concise menu evolves with the seasons as it offers traditional cooking alongside some of Bar Crenn's own creations. Start with the rendition of Chef Guy Savoy's huîtres en nage glacée, with two Washington State oysters on the half shell topped with oyster cream and a gelée made from its liquor. Chef Pierre Troisgros is honored with perfectly poached king salmon in a pool of beurre blanc with a few wilted leaves of lemony sorrel for tang. Finish with this kitchen's own take on an exquisite apple tart, stacking thin slices of apples that almost melt into one another beneath a rich caramel sauce.

▇ 3131 Fillmore St. (at Pixley St.)
℘ (415) 440-0460 — **WEB:** www.barcrenn.com
▇ Dinner Tue – Sat   **PRICE: $$$**

BELGA

Belgian • Brasserie

Belgian brews and bites are the cornerstones of this buzzing brasserie. All the classics are accounted for: well-salted frites with garlic aïoli; bowls of mussels; and of course, house-made sausages—try the combo board, which comes with andouille, boudin noir, boudin blanc and currywurst, not to mention a generous bowl of spaetzle. From schnitzel to salads, there's something to satisfy all appetites (including a quinoa salad; that culinary siren song of the Lululemon-clad). Flatbreads and salads round things out.

The Euro-café vibe is fun with red banquettes, classic bistro chairs and marble floors to complement the big beer selection (both European and domestic) and cocktails. Happy hour, either at the bar or on the dog-friendly patio, is a madhouse.

▪ 2000 Union St. (at Buchanan St.)
℘ (415) 872-7350 — **WEB:** www.belgasf.com
▪ Lunch & dinner daily   **PRICE: $$**

BISTRO AIX

Mediterranean • Bistro

In the competitive Marina market, lovely Bistro Aix remains a charming and relatively affordable neighborhood option for thoughtfully made Southern French fare with a California touch. The dining room offers two distinct culinary experiences, beginning with seats in front at the convivial marble bar and small bistro tables. Beyond this, find the sunny bubble of the intimate back atrium, verdant with olive trees and flooded with natural light. A well-heeled crowd enlivens the space.

Dishes are simple and well executed, like roasted eggplant with toasted sesame seeds, gypsy peppers and a topping of creamy burrata; or the excellently grilled sea scallops with earthy chanterelles and silky beurre blanc. Thoughtfully chosen French wines complement each dish.

▪ 3340 Steiner St. (bet. Chestnut & Lombard Sts.)
℘ (415) 202-0100 — **WEB:** www.bistroaix.com
▪ Dinner Mon – Sat   **PRICE: $$**

DOSA

Indian • Elegant

Glamour infuses every inch of this stylish restaurant, whose soaring ceilings, colorful walls and swanky demeanor augment the bold and fragrantly spiced food. As the name suggests, dosas are indeed a highlight here. Warm servers will explain Cali-inspired takes on other South Indian dishes like almond ambur curry, which replaces traditional cashews with local almonds; or shake things up with idli fries, tailed by a Bengali gimlet with gin, curried nectar and lime. Desserts are every bit as exotic as the rest of the menu, and may reveal rasmalai—patties of fresh cheese in sweet cream flavored with cardamom and rosewater.

A second, smaller location on Valencia Street draws fans, while those in a hurry opt for fast casual at the East Bay sib, dosa by DOSA.

■ 1700 Fillmore St. (at Post St.)
✆ (415) 441-3672 — **WEB:** www.dosasf.com
■ Lunch Fri – Sun Dinner nightly   **PRICE: $$**

ELITE CAFÉ 🍴○

Southern • Contemporary décor

This Southern charmer might have you California dreaming with its array of seasonal salads and other lighter bites, but wise diners know to skip straight to the old-school goods: crunchy fried chicken (try the spicy "Nashville hot" version), buttery grits and tender, porky collard greens. Of course, you'll need to save room for pie. Thick and custardy chocolate pecan, to be exact.

Such an indulgent menu might not be expected from this cool, modern space set on a posh stretch of Fillmore Street, but Chef Chris Borges, a New Orleans native, ensures the authenticity of such faves as crawfish mac and cheese, blackened catfish and duck gumbo. Be sure to keep an eye out for daily specials, including half-priced fried chicken dinners on Tuesdays and wine bottles on Wednesdays.

■ 2049 Fillmore St. (bet. California & Pine Sts.)
✆ (415) 346-8400 — **WEB:** www.theelitecafe.com
■ Lunch Sat – Sun Dinner nightly   **PRICE: $$**

FLORES 🍴○

Mexican • Colorful

It's always a fiesta at this lively spot on Cow Hollow's main drag, where you're as likely to find young families sharing a bowl of guac as you are Marina girls getting tipsy on mezcal margaritas. Patterned tiles, bright murals and chill beats create a modern vibe, and though you may have to wait (only limited reservations are available), the friendly staff will make it worth your while.

Flores is among the city's best upscale Mexican spots—with the bonuses of heftier portions and a lower price tag. You'll be able to taste the difference in the handmade corn tortillas that encase an oozy huitlacoche quesadilla, and the tender, citrusy carnitas. Save room for churros: the spicy "Mexican hot chocolate" dipping sauce is well worth the calories.

- 2030 Union St. (bet. Buchanan & Webster Sts.)
- (415) 796-2926 — **WEB:** www.floressf.com
- Lunch Sat – Sun Dinner nightly   **PRICE: $$**

GARDENIAS 🍴○

Californian • Contemporary décor

Though it's moved across town from the Mission to the Fillmore, the former Woodward's Garden has maintained its tasteful, unpretentious vibe with a bolder, more current aspect. It now even has an actual garden, with a few outdoor tables for dining in the warmer months. Thoughtful service makes Gardenias an equally beloved destination among groups of millennials and leisurely couples on a dressy date night.

Owners Dana Tommasino and Margie Conard are local restaurant veterans. Their Californian cooking may not be cutting-edge, but it has a timeless appeal. Whether you're savoring fork-tender red wine-braised short ribs with celery root purée or a rustic plum and raspberry tart, it's the kind of seasonal, soul-warming food that never goes out of style.

- 1963 Sutter St. (bet. Fillmore & Webster Sts.)
- (415) 621-7122 — **WEB:** www.gardenias-sf.com
- Dinner nightly   **PRICE: $$$**

GREENS ⑪◯
Vegetarian • Rustic

♿ 🛋

Annie Somerville's legacy of California cooking continues at this wholesome restaurant that's been around since 1979. Still, vibrant cuisine abounds, with a light touch and slight global inspiration. Brunch draws a crowd, so be prepared to wait for perfectly fried eggs over griddled potato cakes. Vegetarians and carnivores will rejoice after sampling the honest, colorful and seasonal entrées at dinner, followed by such lovely desserts as huckleberry upside down cake with a subtle kick from Meyer lemon.

Housed in historic Fort Mason, this warehouse-style space is rustic but refined, offering sweeping views of the Golden Gate Bridge and sailboats on the Bay. It's pricey, but the cheery aura makes it worthwhile.

For a quick bite, opt for the to-go counter.

▪ 2 Marina Blvd. (at the Fort Mason Center, Bldg. A)
✆ (415) 771-6222 — **WEB:** www.greensrestaurant.com
▪ Lunch Tue – Sun Dinner nightly   PRICE: $$$

OMA SAN FRANCISCO STATION ⑪◯
Japanese • Simple

♿

This simple wood counter serves some of the area's better nigiri, right from the corner of a mall in Japantown. Blink and you'll miss it—Oma is about the size of a kiosk near the Webster Street exit.

Behind the counter, find Chef Wilson Chan deftly slicing each morsel before your eyes, artfully placing it before every guest, piece by piece. Choose from five- eight- or twelve-piece prix-fixe menus to match your appetite and budget, though prices are reasonable for such quality. Clean flavors and rich, silky fish are the hallmarks of dining here. Highlights include a lightly torched wild star butterfish that melts in the mouth, and a delicious handroll combining chopped bluefin tuna balanced with pickled yellow daikon wrapped in crisp nori.

▪ 1737 Post St. #337 (in Japan Center West)
✆ N/A — **WEB:** www.omasfstation.com
▪ Lunch & dinner daily   PRICE: $$$

OCTAVIA
Californian • Chic

Chef/owner Melissa Perello may already be a local culinary personality at Frances, but her sequel, Octavia, shines even brighter from its home in the tony lower Pacific Heights. Packed with a dynamic and diverse group of diners, the airy, open space feels minimalist and bistro-chic, from the white-tiled kitchen to those raw-wood benches lined with woolen pillows. Service is polite and efficient.

Chef Perello has a gift for elevating straightforward dishes through the use of superb ingredients and beautifully executed technique, beginning with a smoked trout fillet on a bed of cream cheese with green mustard seeds and steamed potatoes. Kale salad is deliciously crunchy and nicely matched with diced fennel, creamy avocado, salty aged parmesan and breadcrumbs in a light vinaigrette. A petite filet of beef arrives tender and perfectly cooked to order, atop potatoes mashed with olive oil, grilled broccolini and cabbage dressed in rapini pesto. Desserts are imaginative and masterful, so save room for their completely new take on profiteroles, soft and fresh, filled with poppy seed-ice cream that is accented with tart rhubarb and kumquat.

Tables fill early, so be sure to reserve well in advance.

◼ 1701 Octavia St. (at Bush St.)
✆ (415) 408-7507 — **WEB:** www.octavia-sf.com
◼ Dinner nightly   PRICE: $$$

OZAOZA ⚪

Japanese • Intimate

This hidden gem in Japantown offers authentic kaiseki cuisine in a second-floor room seating just nine. Kyoto native, Tetsuro Ozawa, oversees the kitchen, while his wife (Gana) infuses this austere space with genuine hospitality. Expect a set menu of around eight courses, each with superb cyclical ingredients and thoughtful garnishes—imagine freshly shaved wasabi and house-made kombu pickles to fresh flowers.

Depending on the month, you might sup on deep-fried, seaweed-wrapped smelt and sea urchin with kabocha squash; or even red snapper rice in a gingery dashi broth. While an array of pristine sashimi is a perpetual highlight, regardless of the season, expect to begin with creamy, delicate tofu and conclude over sweet, chewy mochi with plum wine gelée.

◾ 1700 Post St. Ste. K (bet. Buchanan & Webster Sts.)

✆ (415) 674-4400 — **WEB:** www.ozaoza.net

◾ Dinner Wed – Sat   **PRICE: $$$$**

THE SNUG ⚪

Gastropub • Contemporary décor

In keeping with its location on boutique-y Fillmore Street, The Snug reimagines the neighborhood bar in a very au courant context. Dark wood is subbed for sun-drenched white walls, big windows are lined with an array of house-made tinctures and visitors might even spot that rarest of SF species—children—alongside the laptop-bound techies wrapping up the day with a 4:00 PM craft beer.

Upscale but unpretentious, The Snug's menu is serious for a bar, spanning both snacks (think green garlic fritters rolled in an umami-rich wasabi pea powder) and more substantial plates like charred octopus with smoked avocado purée, ramps and melon. They meld nicely with the refreshing draft cocktails, like the nitrogenated, mezcal-spiked take on a Last Word.

◾ 2301 Fillmore St. (at Clay St.)

✆ (415) 562-5092 — **WEB:** www.thesnugsf.com

◾ Lunch Sat – Sun Dinner Tue – Sun   **PRICE: $$**

SOCIALE
Italian • Romantic

Italian in name but Californian in spirit, Sociale is a go-to for comfort fare that blends the best of both worlds. Chef/owner Tia Harrison crafts wonders; creamy burrata over pumpkin purée and melt-in-your-mouth braised pork belly are just two winners. Dessert is a must; you'll be hard-pressed to find a table that can resist ordering the signature chocolate oblivion cake, a sinfully rich ganache enhanced with olive oil, sea salt and amaretti cookie crumble.

Located at the end of an alley with a heated patio, the vibe here is bistro-chic, with a hint of European flair accented by the warm, accommodating staff and the Italian and French chanteuses on the playlist. It's the kind of neighborhood gem that everyone wishes they had on their block.

3665 Sacramento St. (bet. Locust & Spruce Sts.)
𝒞 (415) 921-3200 — **WEB:** www.sfsociale.com

Dinner Mon – Sat   PRICE: $$

Look for our symbol 🍇
spotlighting restaurants
with a notable wine list.

SORREL ⌘

Californian • Contemporary décor

 ♿ ⛶

Perched on the edge of Pacific Heights, this sleek Cal-Ital eatery draws a casual-chic neighborhood crowd. Dimly lit and inviting, its dining room boasts two particularly eye-catching appurtenances: a white marble bar with glamorous green swirls as well as a bright and vibrant open kitchen, abuzz with a youthful, lively and passionate staff.

Trained at Quince, Chef Alexander Hong has a true gift for pasta, like smoky potato zlikrofi drizzled with sharp plum mostarda and shaved horseradish, or thick strascinati bathed in a 'nduja-infused sauce with tender butter beans and lovage. His ricotta gnudi are exemplars of the form: cloud-soft, accented by crisp fried sage and bright pops of sour cherry.

In keeping with Sorrel's approachable mien, everything is offered à la carte, but the five-course tasting menu boasts of exceptional value. In addition to a pair of pastas, discover some deliciously contemporary small bites, including madai crudo with yuzu and cured egg yolk, or dry-aged beef tartare with a hint of pink peppercorn. The duck breast course is truly a sight to behold—complete with its brilliant trinity of golden-crisped skin, juicy meat and earthy red kuri squash purée.

▥ 3228 Sacramento St. (bet. Lyon St. & Presidio Ave.)

✆ (415) 525-3765 — **WEB:** www.sorrelrestaurant.com

▥ Dinner Tue – Sat   **PRICE: $$$**

SPQR ✿

Italian • Contemporary décor

Pleasant and homey with excellent modern Italian cooking, there is little wonder why this destination is always bustling. Book in advance and assume that the dining counter reserved for walk-ins is already overflowing for the night. The space itself is narrow with tightly packed wood tables and furnishings; it would seem cramped were it not for the soaring ceiling, skylights and open kitchen to brighten the mood. No matter where you look, the passion and enthusiasm for Italian specialties are palpable here—even contagious.

From antipasti to dolci, celebrated Chef Matthew Accarrino's extensive menu evolves with the seasons, yet remains as satisfying as it is impressive. Memorable and very creative pastas include the supremely rich linguine Alfredo with abalone liver, grated bottarga and the faintest hint of Meyer lemon. A degustazione of suckling pig arrives as six unique preparations, including medallions of succulent loin, slices of crisp-edged porchetta and a cool terrine with pops of mustard seed.

Desserts feature the wonderfully sweet and tart flavors of thick and creamy maple panna cotta topped with wine-poached apple, a cloud of whipped cream and cookie crumble.

■ 1911 Fillmore St. (bet. Bush & Pine Sts.)
☏ (415) 771-7779 — **WEB:** www.spqrsf.com
■ Lunch Sat – Sun Dinner nightly   PRICE: $$$

SPRUCE ❁

Californian • Chic

Set in one of San Francisco's snazziest neighborhoods, Spruce draws a regular following of wealthy retirees and corporate types by day. Evenings bring couples out for date night. The dining room, with its cathedral-style ceilings and skylight, is masculine yet modern—think studded leather chairs and splashes of charcoal and chocolate. A small front café serves coffee and pastries, while the marble bar lures happy-hour crowds for a cocktail or glass of wine from the extensive list.

Micro-seasonal and thoroughly Californian, Spruce spotlights cooking that's both simple and undeniably elegant. Rustic and homey starters may include hand-shaped ravioli filled with fresh ricotta and bathed in a broth of tart whey with fava leaf purée. A roulade of guinea hen stuffed with pork and duck sausage is exquisitely moist, juicy and accompanied by thick fingers of nutty-sweet brown ale toast that is perfect for sopping up every last drop.

For dessert, a dense and decadent crème fraîche cheesecake is thick and creamy, with sweet vanilla flavor and a classic graham-cracker crust. Juicy citrus segments and a quenelle of brilliantly tart makrut lime ice cream add a delicious bit of zing.

▇ 3640 Sacramento St. (bet. Locust & Spruce Sts.)

✆ (415) 931-5100 — **WEB:** www.sprucesf.com

▇ Lunch & dinner daily   **PRICE: $$$**

MISSION

CASEY'S PIZZA 🍴○
Pizza • Contemporary décor

&

After making its name as a food truck, Casey Crynes' pizza party has come indoors in fast-developing Mission Bay, where it's caught on hard with the condo-dwelling millennials who've swept into the neighborhood. This industrial space has all the of-the-moment markers, including cement walls, subway tiles, pendant lights and a roaring clientele.

The menu is simple and appealing, starring a handful of pizzas, seasonal salads and plenty of craft beers. Spice things up with the "Hot Pie," a combo of sizzling pepperoni, hot cherry peppers and feta; or go full Californian with a kale pie composed with bacon and red onion. At the end, opt for a hot fudge sundae, made adult-friendly with the addition of dark fudge sauce, sea salt and Luxardo cherries.

▪ 1170 4th St. (bet. Channel & Long Bridge Sts.)
℘ (415) 814-2482 — **WEB:** www.caseyspizzas.com
▪ Dinner Tue – Sun   **PRICE: $$**

CENTRAL KITCHEN 🍴○
Californian • Contemporary décor

& ⊡

A chic and sleek crowd of area foodies gathers at this trendy restaurant, nestled in a complex and right beside sister shop/deli Salumeria (by night it transforms for private parties), cocktail bar Trick Dog and coffee shop Sightglass. Wend your way to the central courtyard, with a trickling fountain and glass doors leading into the main space, where a vast open kitchen with a wood-burning hearth faces the simple wood tables.

Along the way, you might taste a mound of burrata surrounded by melon cubes, cucumber slices and purslane tossed in a chili-herb vinaigrette. Gamey pork trotter agnolotti is balanced by lemon verbena; while smoked short ribs dotted with harissa and served with charred eggplant purée and mint sauce are fork-tender and flavor-packed.

▪ 3000 20th St. (at Florida St.)
℘ (415) 826-7004 — **WEB:** www.centralkitchensf.com
▪ Dinner nightly   **PRICE: $$$**

AL'S PLACE ✿

Californian • Contemporary décor

 ♿ ⛱

Vegetables are the star of the menu at this bright blue oasis on busy Valencia Street, even though it adheres to a mostly pescatarian philosophy, with meat options also available on the side. Chef/owner Aaron London (a.k.a. AL) is wildly adept with the seasons' bounty, making a dish of blistered squash with pickled kohlrabi, hummus and creamy burrata feel as complex and luxurious as the offerings at a steakhouse.

London's menu is chockablock with creativity, from the brine-pickled French fries and flavorful ras el hanout olives that kick off each meal, to the silky grits topped with tangy goat's milk curds, Brussels sprouts, chanterelles and yuzu. At times, the combinations can read like a five-car pile-up—cured trout, mashed turnips and bagna cauda? But the crew always manages to smoothly navigate the layers of flavor, blazing new trails in diners' imaginations.

Like the menu, Al's space is bright, open and cheerful, with plenty of natural light, bold colors and a casual but engaging staff. Embrace this energy, perhaps with a glass of French wine or a craft beer, and let the boisterous, creative spirit of the restaurant win you over.

◾ 1499 Valencia St. (at 26th St.)
℘ (415) 416-6136 — **WEB:** www.alsplacesf.com
◾ Dinner Wed – Sun   **PRICE: $$**

ASTER ✿

Californian • Contemporary décor

&

The idea of a fine-dining space that features mainstream music, spare décor and young clientele in jeans may seem overdone, but Aster makes everything appear new and inventive, never forced. Set in a quiet residential neighborhood, its tawny banquettes, wood tables and strands of lights fashion a studied yet casual vibe that doesn't feel like it is trying too hard. The staff is attentive yet friendly, and eager to please.

The kitchen heightens every element of healthy, light Californian cuisine made from only the best organic ingredients around.

Like the space, the food has no sense of excessive complication; everything is cooked, seasoned and paired perfectly. Here, a simple garden salad is a graceful blend of tangerines, turnips and flowers tossed with pumpkin seeds over a bed of mashed avocado. This might be followed by a generous trout fillet, seared to crisp-skin perfection and set atop snap pea purée. Lighter main courses leave room for enjoying their excellent desserts, such as a sweet poached pear stuffed with vanilla ice cream and set beneath a crunchy pistachio scone and pear coulis. The fixed-price menu is reasonable for the trendsetting combination of cuisine and space.

▨ 1001 Guerrero St. (at 22nd St.)
℘ (415) 875-9810 — **WEB:** www.astersf.com
▨ Dinner Tue – Sat   PRICE: $$$

CALIFORNIOS ❀❀
Mexican • Chic

Set in a bohemian area known for its street tacos and bare bones eateries, Californios aims to elevate the Mission district's south-of-the-border fare to contemporary Mexican cuisine and it more than succeeds. A complex, layered mole here isn't just likely to please—it's bound to turn your entire understanding of this nation's cuisine on its head.

The luxurious space only ups the appeal. Caramel-hued banquettes pop against dark-lacquered walls, while chandeliers and shelves of cookbooks further punctuate the upscale mien of the intimate room. You'll feel as though you're dining in Chef Val M. Cantu's very own atelier, made extra personal by the deeply knowledgeable staff, who seem to pride themselves on knowing every detail about the dishes coming out of the open kitchen.

One lengthy tasting menu is served nightly. It changes often, but expect inventive items like squid-ink tostadas heaped with guacamole, Monterey squid and truffles. A wonderfully spicy flauta is filled with duck barbacoa; while butter-poached lobster is tucked into blue corn tortillas and topped with fennel and aji amarillo. Sorbet made from local guavas, nestled in a spread of pistachio butter is an astounding send-off.

■ 3115 22nd St. (bet. Capp St. & Van Ness Ave.)
℘ (415) 757-0994 — **WEB:** www.californiossf.com
■ Dinner Tue – Sat   **PRICE: $$$$**

COMMONWEALTH ✿

Contemporary · Simple

&

The cool kids of the Mission flock to this upscale spot, all sleek vibe and warm welcome. Set on one of the neighborhood's grittiest stretches, the one-story brick building wears its history in the form of an old painted doughnut ad. And though frosted windows keep the environs at bay, Commonwealth cares for its own by donating a portion of profits from each night's seven-course tasting menu to charity.

Everything here is offered à la carte, but most opt for the aforementioned option, for which the cheerful servers are happy to mix and match dishes. The results are as creative and ambitious as the techie-hipster clientele, with breathtakingly beautiful, Asian-influenced bites: think sea urchin under a canopy of seaweed brioche topped with tomato and watermelon pearls, or seared diver scallop in a corn-and-white miso emulsion with tarragon and fennel.

Along the way, expect surprises utilizing the best seasonal produce, like tangy sudachi sorbet in a pool of sake soda, or pressed cantaloupe infused with honey and togarashi. All of this pairs nicely with an intriguing, terroir-driven wine list—or if you're feeling adventurous, a nightly frozen cocktail chilled with liquid nitrogen.

■ 2224 Mission St. (bet. 18th & 19th Sts.)
℘ (415) 355-1500 — **WEB:** www.commonwealthsf.com
■ Dinner nightly   **PRICE: $$**

DELFINA 😋

Italian • Trattoria

&

One of the city of San Francisco's greats for rustic Italian meals, Delfina is nestled on a block of gems for food lovers, including Bi-Rite (and its creamery), Tartine Bakery and sister spot, Pizzeria Delfina. But even with this rarefied competition, Delfina continues to book well in advance and draws long lines for its few walk-in seats.

The simple, yet lively dining room is attended to by a warm cadre of servers, and the bill of fare shifts with the seasons. Soul-satisfying dishes might include house-made francobolli with prosciutto and mascarpone, as well as perfectly roasted chicken with silky olive oil-mashed potatoes. Seasonal desserts, like a warm pear Charlotte with salted caramel and brandy-crème anglaise, are notably delightful.

■ 3621 18th St. (bet. Dolores & Guerrero Sts.)
✆ (415) 552-4055 — **WEB:** www.delfinasf.com
■ Dinner nightly   **PRICE: $$**

EL BUEN COMER 🍴

Mexican • Simple

&

"Good eats" are promised right in the name of this homey restaurant on the outskirts of the Mission, and La Cocina alum Isabel Caudillo delivers. Her menu centers on guisados, the luscious slow-cooked stews of her native Mexico City. Whether you opt for piquant meatballs in chipotle sauce or tender pork with green mole, you'll receive plenty of warm, handmade corn tortillas to mop up every last drop of her delectable blends.

The tightly edited menu is rounded out with other Mexican classics: tacos, tortas, chilaquiles and fresh-fried tortilla chips accompanied by a hefty scoop of tangy guacamole. Chase it all down with an ice-cold Mexican Coke, but remember to save room for Caudillo's creamy, caramelized flan—it's one of the best renditions in the city.

■ 3435 Mission St. (at Kingston St.)
✆ (415) 817-1542 — **WEB:** www.elbuencomersf.com
■ Lunch & dinner Tue – Sun   **PRICE: $$**

FARMHOUSE KITCHEN THAI

Thai • Colorful

&

For authentic Thai flavors, this lively gem is hard to beat—boasting a dedicated following among the young techies and families who reside in this area's industrial lofts. The space is eclectic with art installations and flower arrangements that spin to the seasons. It's the kind of affordable spot designed for repeat business.

The menu is vast but mostly unchanging, with dishes that display careful attention to detail, bold flavors and top ingredients—think marinated flank steak rolled around cucumber or coconut- and turmeric-marinated barbecue chicken with sticky rice. The herbal rice salad tossing green mango and dried shrimp is a signature and deservedly so.

An equally dazzling meal is assured at the newly minted sib in Jack London Square.

▨ 710 Florida St. (bet. 19th & 20th Sts.)
✆ (415) 814-2920 — **WEB:** www.farmhousethai.com
▨ Lunch & dinner daily   **PRICE: $$**

FLOUR + WATER ¶⃘

Italian • Trendy

& ⊡

As the name implies, two ingredients create a world of possibilities at this always-packed Mission hot spot. Neapolitan pizzas and handmade pastas (like al dente garganelli with whole-grain mustard and braised pork) will have you sighing after each bite, and a selection of more traditional mains (such as seared duck breast with chanterelles and pecorino-dusted charred Brussels sprouts) score every bit as big as the noodles and pies.

Laid-back service, up-to-the-moment music and a buzzy, effervescent vibe make flour + water the epitome of California cool.

Throw in a glass of their refined Italian wine, along with an alluring dessert like the salted caramel apple tart, and you can see why getting a table here is well worth the challenge.

▨ 2401 Harrison St. (at 20th St.)
✆ (415) 826-7000 — **WEB:** www.flourandwater.com
▨ Dinner nightly   **PRICE: $$**

GRACIAS MADRE

Vegan • Rustic

&

Less mamacita and more Mother Earth, Gracias Madre is definitely not just another laid-back Mexican cantina. This is largely thanks to its strict sourcing standards (tortillas are made from scratch with heirloom corn) and wholesome plant-based food. Large portions showcase plenty of local produce, but that nacho cheese drizzled all over your butternut squash- and caramelized onion-filled tortilla is crafted from—nuts, of course. These colorful, vegan items explode with flavor, as seen in the enchiladas con mole packed with potato, zucchini and peas, then topped with tomatillo salsa, crema and avocado. The surprises keep coming throughout the meal.

Take note of the flan, which created sans eggs still manages to have that trademark wobble.

■ 2211 Mission St. (bet. 18th & 19th Sts.)
✆ (415) 683-1346 — **WEB:** www.gracias-madre.com
■ Lunch & dinner daily   **PRICE: $$**

IZAKAYA RINTARO 😊

Japanese • Minimalist

& 💠

Delicate izakaya cuisine with a produce-centric NorCal sensibility awaits at this Japanese sanctum, which transforms even the most humble dishes into works of art. Freshly made soft tofu is infused with fragrant bergamot peel, while meaty king trumpet mushrooms join classic chicken thighs and tender tsukune on the menu of smoky, caramelized charcoal-grilled skewers. The blancmange, infused with white sesame and topped with sweet black soybeans, is particularly unmissable.

Housed in the former Chez Spencer, which was destroyed in a fire, Rintaro has kept its predecessor's gorgeous (and charred) arched ceiling beams, but added a delicate, wood-framed bar and booths. The result is a serene environment perfect for sharing and sampling the exquisite food.

■ 82 14th St. (bet. Folsom & Trainor Sts.)
✆ (415) 589-7022 — **WEB:** www.izakayarintaro.com
■ Lunch Fri – Sun Dinner nightly   **PRICE: $$**

KHAMSA 🍴○

Moroccan • Contemporary décor

♿ ⛱ 🛋

Set in a luxury condo building amidst a row of auto body shops, this relaxed urban oasis brings the charm of Morocco to an otherwise divey stretch of the Mission. Inside, you'll find a cheerful turquoise dining room bedecked with colorful tiles, a small courtyard for outdoor dining and a diverse clientele—ranging from young techies to women dressed in traditional garb.

The pricey food boasts a few Californian accents, like Moroccan-inspired salads featuring seasonal produce, but most dishes are designed to please purists. The basteeya pie with shredded chicken and almonds in a phyllo crust is nothing less than flaky precision; while chicken tagine with preserved lemon followed by pistachio baklava and a pot of mint tea is all sweetness and appeal.

▪ 1503 15th St. (bet. Capp St. & Van Ness Ave.)
📞 (628) 233-1503 — **WEB:** www.khamsasf.com
▪ Dinner nightly   **PRICE: $$**

LA CICCIA 🍴○

Italian • Mediterranean décor

Sardinian cuisine takes the spotlight at this family-run charmer, which draws a loyal crowd of Noe Valley regulars—particularly parents on a well-earned date night. The intimate, dark green dining room is always full, and nestled right up against the kitchen, from which the chef regularly pops out to greet guests with welcoming banter.

Start with the house-made bread and the home-cured salumi of the day (think citron-studded mortadella). The pasta lunga with cured tuna heart slivers twirls fresh, delicious linguini with sea urchin and tomato, while an entrée of stewed goat is gamey but tender, served alongside braised cabbage, black olives and fried capers. For a pleasant conclusion, cap it all off with the fluffy and airy ricotta-saffron cake.

▪ 291 30th St. (at Church St.)
📞 (415) 550-8114 — **WEB:** www.laciccia.com
▪ Dinner Tue – Sat   **PRICE: $$$**

LA TAQUERIA 🍴

Mexican • Taqueria

This local favorite always has a queue because everyone loves it—from tech bros in hoodies to families out for Sunday lunch. The jovial Miguel Jara runs this show—you may find him working the register or handing out roses to customers. Counter service makes it feel no-frills, but this is the kind of place that relishes in its simplicity.

Everything here is supremely fresh, as exhibited in the open kitchen with its mountains of char-grilled steak alongside vibrant tomato, cilantro and onion. The carne asada super burrito is everything you dream it should be. It may not be on the menu, but order your taco "Dorado-style," which begins as a corn tortilla crisped on the plancha, layered with cheese and another tortilla before getting loaded with toppings.

- 2889 Mission St. (bet. 24th & 25th Sts.)
- ℰ (415) 285-7117 — **WEB:** N/A
- Lunch Wed – Sun Dinner Wed – Sun   PRICE: 🍴

LOCANDA 🍴

Italian • Osteria

This chic Roman-style osteria packs in the hipsters with a lively scene, killer cocktails and inspired pastas, like radiatore tossed in tomato-lamb ragù with pecorino and hints of fresh mint. Hearty main courses might include smoky and tender pancetta-wrapped chicken served over nutty farro verde. None of this is surprising, considering Locanda is from the team behind Mission favorite, Delfina.

Reservations here are a tough ticket, but the attire and vibe are casual and welcoming (if noisy). Can't get a table? Seats at the bar, where the full menu is served, are a solid backup.

Locanda's ultra-central address makes parking a challenge, so plan on using the valet or allotting extra time.

- 557 Valencia St. (bet. 16th & 17th Sts.)
- ℰ (415) 863-6800 — **WEB:** www.locandasf.com
- Lunch Sat – Sun Dinner Wed – Sun   PRICE: $$

LAZY BEAR ⚜⚜

Contemporary • Chic

Communal eating is at the heart of this fine-dining dinner party. Lazy Bear may have its origins as an underground phenom, but today anyone can try to score a seat. That is, after jumping through a few virtual hoops: buy a ticket in advance and wait for an e-mail listing house rules to be followed in earnest. Rest assured this is all worth the effort.

The nightly tasting menu is dished out in a cool, bi-level warehouse and starts upstairs in the loft with aperitifs and snacks, like tempura beer-battered maitake mushrooms with a sour cream and onion dip or pig's head cheese with black truffle shavings. Then move downstairs to a dining room boasting two giant tree slabs as communal tables, each lined with 20 chairs. Diners are given a pencil and pamphlet informing them of the menu (with space for note-taking underneath) and are invited to enter the kitchen to chat with the talented cooks themselves. This leaves the young crowd dreamy-eyed with chef worship.

Highlights include smoked trout on a blanket of trout roe, sorrel and brown rice, or dry-aged Sonoma County duck with a wonderful sweet and bitter yin and yang, courtesy of fermented kumquat and partially scorched broccolini.

■ 3416 19th St. (bet. Mission & San Carlos Sts.)
✆ (415) 874-9921 — **WEB:** www.lazybearsf.com
■ Dinner Tue – Sat   **PRICE: $$$$**

THE MORRIS ¶○

Contemporary • Neighborhood

⅏ ♿

After working at a number of SF's top restaurants, veteran sommelier Paul Einbund has settled down at this neighborhood charmer in the Mission, named for his father. Unsurprisingly, The Morris boasts a selection of wine (displayed in a handsome glass cellar), along with top-notch cocktails and a sophisticated yet highly craveable comfort-food menu.

Quell your hunger with slices of Tartine country loaf—baked just down the street—as you peruse the menu, which offers appealing bites both small (pork cracklins with honey and Aleppo pepper) and large (charred broccolini with succulent grilled squid in chili-lime dressing). Be sure to also sample their signature smoked duck. Brined for two days and aged for four, it is a smoky, tender and meaty marvel.

▪ 2501 Mariposa St. (at Hampshire St.)
✆ (415) 612-8480 — **WEB:** www.themorris-sf.com
▪ Lunch Mon – Fri Dinner Mon – Sat   **PRICE: $$$**

PAPITO ¶○

Mexican • Cozy

🍴 ⊿

It might be French-owned (neighboring bistro Chez Maman is a sibling), but Papito is appealingly Mexican, as your first bite of the outstanding shrimp tacos, piled with spicy adobo and sweet mango salsa, will attest. An ear of caramelized, grilled corn slathered in spicy mayo, lime juice and Cotija cheese will transport you to the streets of CDMX, while the smoky coloradito sauce that bathes tender chicken enchiladas will have you scraping your plate for more. Papito's flavors are big, but its space is no more than a shoebox, so be prepared to wait or take your order to-go. If you dine in, the vibrant look matches the energetic food, with bright walls and a bustling side bar.

Note: Hayes Valley's Papito, once a satellite, now has different owners.

▪ 317 Connecticut St. (at 18th St.)
✆ (415) 695-0147 — **WEB:** www.papitosf.com
▪ Lunch & dinner daily   **PRICE:** ⊜

PICCINO ♟○

Italian • Family

 ♿ 🪑 🛋

A progenitor of the increasingly hot Dogpatch restaurant scene, Piccino embodies this neighborhood's many flavors, drawing families with kids in tow, young tech types, gregarious retirees and more. Its memorable yellow exterior houses a relaxed, artsy-urban interior with lots of wood and natural light—a perfect venue for unwinding with friends.

Everyone comes here for deliciously blistered pizzas like the funghi, with roasted mushroom duxelles, sautéed wild mushrooms, stracchino and slivers of garlic. Though pizza is a focus, Piccino excels in appetizers like tender, skillfully prepared polpette in tomato sauce, and must-order desserts such as a delectable hazelnut-cocoa nib cake. Their adjacent coffee bar is an area favorite.

◼ 1001 Minnesota St. (at 22nd St.)
℘ (415) 824-4224 — **WEB:** www.piccino.com
◼ Lunch & dinner daily   **PRICE: $$**

RAMENWELL ♟○

Japanese • Simple

 ♿

This unobtrusive yet buzzy ramen house arrives courtesy of Chef Harold Jurado. His modest space displays a clean, streamlined décor, complete with rows of counter seats and a smattering of tables. This menu is simple—and while tatakis are creative, these bowls are next-level delicious. For instance, the pork tonkatsu selection is wholly addictive, featuring perfectly chewy noodles in a 20-hour pork broth, bobbing with smoky, melt-in-your-mouth chashu, soft cooked egg and a flutter of bamboo shoots, corn, green onion and black garlic. Pair this with a daikon, hijiki and nori salad tossed in ponzu for a touch of refreshing crunch.

Don't leave without your Instagram-worthy swirl of matcha and taro soft serve, offered in a cone—to stay or to go.

◼ 3378 18th St. (bet. Mission & Capp Sts.)
℘ (773) 620-0605 — **WEB:** www.ramenwell.com
◼ Dinner Mon – Sat   **PRICE: $$**

RITU INDIAN SOUL FOOD 🍴

Indian • Colorful

&

Formerly known as Dum, this hip Indian eatery has rebranded with a fresh menu of seasonal Californian produce ("Ritu" is Hindi for "seasons"). CIA-trained Chef/owner Rupam Bhagat remains at the helm, and longtime fans will recognize some of the kitchen's faves, including a light and frothy mango lassi that pairs delightfully with a reimagined version of the fried tandoori chicken featuring mustard-and curry-leaves.

Veterans of this cuisine shouldn't sleep on such seasonal gems either, like asparagus chaat with pickled carrots and spiced yogurt; or crisp artichoke pakoras. Even bog-standard butter chicken takes on new life here, with a tomato-rich gravy. Arrive on the later side to enjoy flaky naan and fluffy biryani along with the cool Mission crowds.

◼ 3111 24th St. (bet. Folsom & Shotwell Sts.)
✆ (415) 874-9045 — **WEB:** www.ritusf.com
◼ Lunch Fri – Sun Dinner Wed – Sun   **PRICE: $$**

SASAKI 🍴

Japanese • Minimalist

&

Masaki Sasaki is well known among Bay Area sushi enthusiasts, having worked at a number of the area's top spots. Now, he's finally launched his own restaurant, housed on the ground floor of a quaint Mission Victorian. With only 12 seats at the counter, reservations are a must, but each guest is rewarded with personal attention from Masa-san.

As with many high-end temples of sushi, only one omakase-style menu is offered. But Sasaki throws out the rulebook on proceeding from light to heavy fish. Commence with silky maguro, rich mackerel and creamy monkfish liver, before veering back to a lighter crab and pickled cucumber dish. A parade of nigiri is equally deft, with specially seasoned rice that is individually chosen for each type of fish.

◼ 2400 Harrison St. (at 20th St.)
✆ (415) 828-1912 — **WEB:** www.sasakisf.com
◼ Dinner Tue – Sat   **PRICE: $$$$**

SERPENTINE

American • Contemporary décor

This warehouse-chic spot was one of the first to plant its flag in the once-sleepy Dogpatch, where it quickly made a name for its «honest» American food and top-notch cocktails. After hitting the decade mark, it's now in the hands of Chef/owner Tommy Halvorson, who's recharged the space with stainless steel tables, black banquettes and dim Edison lights that accentuate the high ceilings.

The menu also received an update, though it hasn't strayed too far from its comfort food roots. There's something for everyone here, including burgers, salads and entrées like slow-cooked short ribs in a rich demi-glace. Lighter bites like steamed mussels in a smoky and spicy white wine-broth tease those taste buds, not unlike the cocktails, which must not be missed.

◼ 2495 3rd St. (at 22nd St.)
✆ (415) 252-2000 — **WEB:** www.serpentinesf.com
◼ Lunch Thu – Sun Dinner Mon – Sat   PRICE: $$

SHIZEN

Vegan • Minimalist

At first glance, this stylish izakaya and sushi bar could be another in a line of similar places that dot the San Francisco landscape were it not for a major twist: everything on the menu is vegan. Purists and die-hard carnivores may scoff, but the food is exceptional, skillfully manipulating vegetables and starches to recreate seafood-centric Japanese favorites.

Spicy tuna gets a run for its money from the impressive tofuna rolls, with chili-inflected minced tofu and cucumber, crowned with creamy avocado and dusted in chili "tobiko." A yuba salad with miso dressing and tempura-battered shiitake mushrooms stuffed with faux-crab is equally compelling. Throw in a sleek, contemporary setting, and Shizen is a winner for eaters of all stripes.

◼ 370 14th St. (at Stevenson St.)
✆ (415) 678-5767 — **WEB:** www.shizensf.com
◼ Dinner nightly   PRICE: $$

TARTINE MANUFACTORY 🍴

Californian • Contemporary décor

&

Like its much-loved loaves, Tartine Bakery's spinoff turns rusticity into an art form. Sharing a massive industrial space with the Heath Ceramics factory, it boasts large windows, floods of natural light and a crowd of millennial worker bees seeking morning ham-and-cheese danishes, as well as afternoon pick-me-ups of house-roasted coffee with cherry-almond bostocks. Also on the menu: beer, wine, soft-serve ice cream and perfectly tangy house-made shrub sodas.

In the evening, those piping-hot bread ovens shut down to create a more intimate space for dinner, with entrées like roast chicken and little gem salad. Still, the best time to visit is while the sun is up and the scent of bread is wafting through the air.

 595 Alabama St. (at 18th St.)
📞 (415) 757-0007 — **WEB:** www.tartinebakery.com
◼ Lunch & dinner daily   PRICE: $$

TRUE LAUREL 🍴

Contemporary • Design

🍸 &

Hipster-friendly and Mission-approved, this is an instant hit for everyone from early happy hour drinkers through late-night snackers. Sidle up to the custom bay laurel bar for delicious (if pricey) cocktails made with unique liquors like gooseberry brandy. The menu focuses on small plates of refined comfort food, as well as creative presentations like tender sweetbreads tucked into grilled cabbage with broccoli spigarello and Caesar dressing. You may even taste an amuse-bouche from sibling restaurant Lazy Bear, such as crisp hen of the woods mushrooms with allium dip.

Desserts seem straightforward but are beautifully crafted, especially the sweet, savory and even bitter combination of bay leaf-ice cream drizzled with new olive oil and citrus confit.

◼ 753 Alabama St. (bet. 19th & 20th Sts.)
📞 (415) 341-0020 — **WEB:** www.truelaurelsf.com
◼ Dinner nightly   PRICE: $$$

NOB HILL & NORTH BEACH

ACQUERELLO ✿✿

Italian • Elegant

With its air of old-world sophistication, Acquerello is the kind of establishment where one dresses for dinner, which is always an occasion. The room feels embellished yet comfortable, with vaulted wood-beamed ceilings, warm orange walls and contemporary paintings. It seems to draw celebrants of a certain age who are happy to splurge on a white truffle-tasting menu.

Chef Suzette Gresham's menus promise expertise and finesse, with a carefully curated wine list to match. Count yourself lucky if your meal begins with their famed parmesan budino surrounded by black truffle "caviar." Pasta must not be missed, such as the very fine and vibrant tajarin with a tableside shaving of impossibly earthy truffles. Venison medallions wrapped in crisped pancetta are served with beautiful simplicity alongside pear slices, onion jam, chanterelles and butternut squash purée. Refreshing desserts include delicate almond milk-panna cotta covered with vin santo jelly and crowned by buttery crushed almonds, quince and tufts of dehydrated balsamic vinegar.

Save room for one of the best mignardises carts you will ever encounter, stocked with superlative house-made chocolates, macarons, pâtes de fruits and caramels.

■ 1722 Sacramento St. (bet. Polk St. & Van Ness Ave.)
☎ (415) 567-5432 — **WEB:** www.acquerello.com
■ Dinner Tue – Sat   PRICE: $$$$

ALTO VINO 🍴⊙

Italian • Bistro

♿ ⛲

This restaurant is divided into two equally lively spaces: a bar packed with millennials drinking Italian vino while nibbling crostini; and a dressier dining room where a sophisticated crowd settles in to a multi-course meal. Others may choose to venture into the heated outdoor patio to sip rosé and watch the cable cars go by.

Much of the menu seems ideal for sharing, particularly snacks like fried olives stuffed with oxtail, giardiniera and grissini. Don't miss the chicken liver pâté crostini with apple, mint and flower petals. You may want to keep the house-made pasta all to yourself, with offerings like two large ravioli doppio—one packed with ricotta and spinach, the other with wine-braised veal—in a lovely jus with Meyer lemon, English peas and fava.

◼ 1358 Mason St. (at Pacific Ave.)
℘ (415) 834-5766 — **WEB:** www.altovinosf.com
◼ Dinner Tue – Sun   PRICE: $$

BARRIO 🍴⊙

Mexican • Pub

🍺 ♿

The simple pleasures of tacos and beer get taken to the next level at this laid-back spot, where hand-ground, hand-griddled blue corn tortillas star on every corner of the menu, and craft brews leave Corona in the dust. With just one chef and one bartender, the service is friendly and personal, with a healthy dose of genuine passion for the food (and a fun classic rock soundtrack).

Snag an IPA before taking a full lap of the short menu: freshly fried chips with outstanding guacamole, warm tortillas piled with achiote-marinated pork and pickled onions, as well as a gooey Oaxacan cheese quesadilla stuffed with tender chicken. A trio of house-made hot sauces (including a habanero "death sauce") make for the perfect grace note.

◼ 1609 Powell St. (bet. Green & Union Sts.)
℘ (415) 923-8997 — **WEB:** www.barriosf.com
◼ Lunch Fri – Sun Dinner nightly   PRICE: $$

CAFÉ JACQUELINE ¶○

French · Romantic

You'll float away on a cloud at the first taste of Jacqueline Margulis' signature soufflés, light and fluffy masterworks that have kept her tables full for over 35 years. Since the chef makes each of her creations by hand, expect to spend three or so hours at the table—it's the perfect romantic escape for couples lingering over a bottle of wine.

To sate your appetite while you wait, a bowl of light carrot soup or a delicate cucumber salad in champagne vinaigrette will do the trick. But the soufflés are the real draw, and keen diners plan on both a savory and a sweet course. For the former, a combination of flaky salmon, tender asparagus and caramelized Gruyère is a delight. And the utterly perfect lemon soufflé will haunt any dessert lover's dreams.

- 1454 Grant Ave. (bet. Green & Union Sts.)
- (415) 981-5565 — **WEB:** www.cafejacqueline.com
- Dinner Wed – Sun   **PRICE: $$$$**

COTOGNA 😊

Italian · Rustic

Though rustic compared to high-end sibling Quince just next door, Michael and Lindsay Tusk's casual offshoot would be elegant by any other standard. Exposed brick, a shiny copper chef's counter and bar, wooden tables...it's Italian to a T, and a hot-ticket reservation.

The space centers around an exhibition kitchen, from which crisp pizzas and hearty roasted meats emerge. The absolutely delicious menu highlights Chef Tusk's pristine pastas, like agnolotti del plin, stuffed with tender rabbit, veal and pork. Seasonal starters are equally pleasing, like kale and radicchio salad in a tangy vinaigrette with hard-boiled farm egg and pecorino. The rustic plum and ginger torta is moist and delicious, but those ever-so-sweet, ripe plums steal the show.

- 490 Pacific Ave. (at Montgomery St.)
- (415) 775-8508 — **WEB:** www.cotognasf.com
- Lunch Mon – Sat Dinner nightly   **PRICE: $$**

COI

Contemporary • Elegant

Warm, neutral tones and a soft, diffused glow from rice-paper panels welcome diners to this jewel. Over in the kitchen, Chef Erik Anderson is kicking things up with his very own culinary style. He has steered away from seafood, and as a result one is more likely to find a panoply of game birds on the menu now. Changes aside, meals remain a well-executed show.

Settle in to this admired retreat for an intimate parade of elegantly prepared and thoughtfully composed dishes. Topped with oxalis and matchsticks of radish, the citrus-infused "marshmallow" accompanied by curd is delicate and impressive. Thin slices of geoduck with tremulous clam-juice jelly is luscious, while Dungeness crab kissed by crab mayo and lemongrass-panna cotta is on point. Then relish a tourte of duck and sweetbreads, enriched by Armagnac prunes and black truffles. It's hit after haute hit, where even the humble blood orange sorbet dances on the tongue and seals the deal.

The experience doesn't end there. Flip to the last page of the leather-bound wine list to discover a unique tea pairing, as well as a sweet-and-savory souvenir to enjoy tomorrow—if indeed you can wait that long.

■ 373 Broadway (bet. Montgomery & Sansome Sts.)
📞 (415) 393-9000 — **WEB:** www.coirestaurant.com
■ Dinner Tue – Sat   **PRICE: $$$$**

EIGHT TABLES BY GEORGE CHEN ⅩO

Chinese • Elegant

The jewel of Chinatown's stylish China Live complex actually has nine tables, but it's still one of the most intimate spots in town (and priced accordingly). Patterned after the "private chateau" restaurants that are all the rage in the Far East, this one has good looks to spare—from its midcentury-meets-Chinese décor to the marvelous cocktails that are turned out by the hugely talented bartenders.

The nine-course tasting menu repurposes luxe Western ingredients in classic dishes, from crisp, lacy dumplings to char siu made with Ibérico pork. The notable "nine tastes of China" starter offers the greatest of pleasures, including poached chicken stuffed with cured egg yolk and beef tendon with those tingling Sichuan peppercorns.

- 8 Kenneth Roxroth Pl. (at Vallejo St.)
- ℰ (415) 788-8788 — **WEB:** www.eighttables.com
- Dinner Tue – Sat   **PRICE: $$$$**

GARY DANKO ❀

Contemporary • Elegant

The elite meet to eat at this throwback favorite, which has been hosting the crème de la crème of the city (and its visitors) since the 90s. Set near Ghirardelli Square in Fisherman's Wharf, it features two lovely wood-paneled dining rooms and a small, bustling bar, all of them regularly full of hobnobbing business types and couples celebrating big occasions. With bursting flower arrangements, attentive servers and well-dressed diners everywhere you look, it's hard not to be captivated.

The menu focuses on classic cuisine with some global twists; diners can create their own three- four- or five-course prix-fixe, or hand over the reins to the chef's tasting menu. Luxurious dishes include a luscious rock shrimp and Dungeness crab risotto, accented with butternut squash; branzino with fennel purée, olives and a saffron-orange emulsion; as well as a perfectly cooked herb-crusted lamb loin, draped over date-studded farro and rainbow carrots.

While Gary Danko may not be on the cutting-edge of fine dining, its top-notch wine list and outstanding service epitomize old-school luxury. Like the chocolate soufflé with vanilla bean crème anglaise that caps the meal, this is a classic for a reason.

■ 800 North Point St. (at Hyde St.)
☎ (415) 749-2060 — **WEB:** www.garydanko.com
■ Dinner nightly   **PRICE: $$$$**

KEIKO À NOB HILL ❀

Fusion • Elegant

Elegant, discreet and romantic, Keiko à Nob Hill blends unique culinary style with traditional appeal. Cushioned banquettes wrap the square dining room, outfitted with subdued lighting, fabric-covered walls and heavy brown trim, resulting in a space that is lovely (if of a certain age).

It is always best to be prompt: the formal service team is gracious but handles each night's single seating with precision, serving all guests at once. Such punctuality is crucial as this kitchen takes its work and its mission rather earnestly.

Chef Keiko Takahashi's nightly tasting menu is a progression of French culinary technique with subtle hints of Japanese flavors. Her success is undeniable from the first taste of spiny lobster presented in a martini glass with lobster-tomato water foam and a chilled layer of fruity bell pepper mousse. Moist, fragrant and remarkably delicious Cornish hen then arrives tucked with razor-thin shavings of black truffle beneath its skin, complemented with parmesan foam, Ibérico ham-cream sauce and asparagus. A simple parfait is an extraordinary finale that includes coffee pâte de fruit, marron glacé and bits of crunchy meringue atop whipped cream with grilled pears.

■ 1250 Jones St. (at Clay St.)
☎ (415) 829-7141 — **WEB:** www.keikoanobhill.com
■ Dinner Tue – Sun   **PRICE: $$$$**

KINJO ❀

Japanese • Minimalist

&

With Chef/co-owner Billy Kong and consultant Chef Fujii Tahahiro holding the reins of this kitchen, it's no wonder that this Edomae sushi spot is white-hot.

Decked out in neutral tones, pale wood and fine ceramics, the expansive dining room exudes a sense of zen. The equally large kitchen though is animated and action-packed—in fact, that eight-seat counter remains the place to be. Plunk down your plastic where $155 will grant you a kaiseki-inspired omakase extravaganza that includes a striking hassun course. Each small dish will transport you to Kyoto by way of Kinjo — imagine water shield spiked with vinegar; red miso soup with delicate tofu skin (yuba) and Sansho pepper; or a tender tiger prawn poached in delicious dashi. Continue to wend your way through cooked items like truffled chawanmushi with earthy shiitake mushrooms, sweet bits of shrimp and Thai snapper; before sinking into a procession that may reveal the likes of kanpachi from Kyushu or anago from Nagasaki.

Each menu also includes a dessert, so even though you may be tempted to order more nigiri, save room for such sweet treats as the warabimochi, which is cut into two rustic rectangles and topped with an addictive brown sugar syrup.

■ 2206 Polk St. (at Vallejo St.)
✆ (415) 921-2222 — **WEB:** www.kinjosf.com
■ Dinner Wed – Sun   **PRICE: $$$$**

KOKKARI ESTIATORIO 😋

Greek • Chic

 ♿ ⛶

Zeus himself would be satisfied after a soul-warming meal at this Greek favorite, which serves up San Francisco-chic with a side of old-world taverna hospitality. Translation? Once you're seated at the bar or settled near one of the roaring fireplaces, the thoughtful staff will cater to your every need. Kokkari's sophisticated menu leans heavily on the wood grill and rotisserie, which produce smoky souvlaki with warm pita and tangy chickpea salad, as well as roasted head-on prawns in garlic butter. Braised lamb shank with orzo is a feast, but resist the urge to conquer their Olympus-sized portions: you'll want to sample the galaktoboureko, crispy phyllo rolls filled with creamy custard and topped with honey, figs and crème fraîche ice cream.

■ 200 Jackson St. (at Front St.)
☎ (415) 981-0983 — **WEB:** www.kokkari.com
■ Lunch Mon – Fri Dinner nightly   **PRICE: $$**

LA FOLIE 🍴

French • Elegant

 🐾 ♿ ⛶ 🧼

Few grandes dames of high-end French cuisine remain in the city, but this long-running elder from Chef/owner Roland Passot has held strong. With two formal dining rooms featuring starched tablecloths, polished servers and a tall art deco wine case, it's a favorite among occasion-celebrating couples and the luxury-loving tourist crowd.

Diners can build their own three- to five-course prix-fixe, with classic dishes like a double bone-in lamb chop or a tower of crispy goat cheese, eggplant and portobello mushroom. Thicker wallets can splurge on the chef's-choice tasting menu or the array of sumptuous supplements, like butter-poached lobster. For dessert, chocolate lovers should be sure not to miss out on the velvety Valrhona mousse.

■ 2316 Polk St. (bet. Green & Union Sts.)
☎ (415) 776-5577 — **WEB:** www.lafolie.com
■ Dinner Tue – Sat   **PRICE: $$$$**

LAI HONG LOUNGE

Chinese • Family

This windowless dim sum lounge looks small from the outside, but there's room for over 100 diners inside its cherry-red dining room—with dozens more hopefuls lined up on the street outside. The largely Chinese crowd attests to the authenticity of the food, which ranges from steamed pork buns and taro dumplings to chicken feet with peanuts and Peking duck—if you're hoping to skip out on the wait, go at dinner instead of lunch, or call for takeout.

Favorites include rice noodle rolls stuffed with ground beef and aromatic herbs and crispy, golden pan-fried tofu with a silky interior. Shanghai pork soup dumplings arrive in a steam basket in individual metal cups. Served with black vinegar for dipping, they're achingly fragile but terrifically tasty.

■ 1416 Powell St. (bet. Broadway & Vallejo St.)
 (415) 397-2290 — **WEB:** www.lhklounge.com
■ Lunch & dinner daily   **PRICE: $$**

LIHOLIHO YACHT CLUB

Hawaiian • Trendy

There are no yachts to be found on the urban Tenderloin/Nob Hill border, but hordes of enthusiasts remain quite eager to book passage on Liholiho's love boat. Fusing Californian technique with the flavors of Chef/owner Ravi Kapur's native Hawaii, this sleek and sunny Instagrammer's paradise is known for strong cocktails, shareable plates and near-impossible reservations. Two bars are available for walk-ins, but those tend to fill up quickly.

Watched over by a big 70s-era snapshot of Kapur's mom, the dining room hums with groups savoring beef tongue bao, luscious coconut-clam curry and nori crackers heaped with tuna poke. If you turn your nose up at Spam, a Hawaiian staple, try the house-made (and off-menu) version. It just might convert you.

■ 871 Sutter St. (bet. Jones & Leavenworth Sts.)
 (415) 440-5446 — **WEB:** www.liholihoyachtclub.com
■ Dinner Mon – Sat   **PRICE: $$$**

LORD STANLEY ✿

Californian • Contemporary décor

&

Like the husband-and-wife team who own it, Lord Stanley is half European and half Californian. Superlative ingredients and a sun-filled space lend it an undeniable West Coast vibe, while house-made breads, confections and an intriguing wine list of European vintages make it clear that these chefs were trained across the pond.

Yet this is a charming little establishment right at home in its central Polk Street location, filled with a casual crowd of locals streaming in—imagine windows which offer a stellar, sweeping view of the neighborhood. Inside, the dining room is furnished with small bistro tables, while a larger communal table on the balcony welcomes groups. Bare wood tabletops set with hand-crafted cutlery and warmed by candlelight set a simple and cozy atmosphere for enjoying meals that highlight artisanal and organic ingredients. Not unlike the space, the cooking here is approachable yet refined. A Berkshire pork chop is meltingly tender, balanced with just the right blend of sweet and sour flavors. Come dessert, a deconstructed dark chocolate pudding with sesame crisp is unmissable.

Be sure to quiz the attentive staff on the dishes—they'll happily explain each intricate layer.

■ 2065 Polk St. (at Broadway)
☏ (415) 872-5512 — **WEB:** www.lordstanleysf.com
■ Dinner Tue – Sat   **PRICE: $$$**

MENSHO 🍴

Japanese • Trendy

This little ramen shop is the first in the U.S. from the chef behind the highly popular Tokyo outposts, and its wait times are nothing short of epic—even in queue-crazed San Francisco. No matter how early you arrive, snagging one of the 28 communal seats is at least a 30-minute affair that can easily run up to two hours. And the dicey Tendernob address means the line is often beset by aggressive panhandlers.

Only true aficionados can say if the ramen is worth it, but the tori paitan is one undeniably spectacular bowl, packed with springy, chewy noodles and outstanding duck chashu in a luxuriously creamy and umami-rich broth. Just know you'll be asked to slurp it down quickly: the hungry, huddled masses outside are anxious to take your seat.

■ 672 Geary St. (bet. Jones & Leavenworth Sts.)
☏ (415) 800-8345 — **WEB:** www.mensho.tokyo
■ Dinner Tue – Sun   PRICE: 🍜

TOSCA CAFÉ 🍴

Italian • Historic

This historic bar has been expertly revived under NYC chef, April Bloomfield, who spent millions to add a kitchen and make its old-school charm seem untouched. White-coated bartenders shake and stir behind the glorious carved wood bar, while diners feast in the cushy red leather booths. Tables are few, so expect a wait if you don't have a reservation.

The food is Italian-American with Bloomfield's signature meaty influences, like flavorful, gamey grilled lamb ribs that nearly fall off the bone. Pastas are strong, from creamy gemelli cacio e pepe to rich, spicy bucatini all'Amatriciana. But don't neglect their vegetables: a dish of tender cauliflower and potatoes in a rich Taleggio sauce with crunchy breadcrumbs is a showstopper.

■ 242 Columbus Ave. (bet. Broadway & Pacific Ave.)
☏ (415) 986-9651 — **WEB:** www.toscacafesf.com
■ Dinner nightly   PRICE: $$$

MISTER JIU'S ✿

Chinese • Contemporary décor

Chef/owner Brandon Jew has brought some of the sparkle back to Chinatown with this contemporary treasure, which puts a modern Californian spin on the Cantonese classics that once made this neighborhood a national dining destination. Impressively, the chef also makes all his Chinese pantry staples in-house, like the oyster sauce that coats a stir-fry of smoked tofu with long beans, tripe and tendon; or lap cheong (Chinese sausage), which comes stuffed into roasted quail with sticky rice and jujube. The menu is full of these clever touches, from the tomalley that adds depth to a rich Dungeness crab egg custard to the "tentacles" of fried fennel that echo the texture of salt-and-pepper squid.

Desserts are excellent, equally skillful and may incorporate black sesame, red bean and osmanthus cream into preparations that will satisfy any sweet tooth.

Set in a longtime banquet hall, Mister Jiu's is bright and airy, with dramatic brass lotus chandeliers overhead. Food is served family style, making it ideal for groups. But solo diners will also enjoy the sophisticated front bar that serves up thoughtful and complex cocktails with Asian inflections—like lemongrass milk and green tea.

■ 28 Waverly Pl. (bet. Clay & Sacramento Sts.)
☏ (415) 857-9688 — **WEB:** www.misterjius.com
■ Dinner Tue – Sat   PRICE: $$$

QUINCE ✿✿✿

Contemporary • Elegant

An air of refinement touches this dining room—note the massive Murano chandelier, the stylish guests and everything in between. No wonder this is where affluent tourists and locals alike come to celebrate their special occasions. From the moment the champagne cart arrives at your table to the last bite of the guéridon's mignardises, the service is perfectly timed and attentive. Following suit, the room is as lovely as ever, allowing more space for private parties.

There was a time when Quince was home to traditional cooking, but Chef Michael Tusk's menu is increasingly contemporary. Thin strands of zucchini "noodles" are intertwined with strips of cool and tender squid in a refreshing composition, while a "lasagna" arrives as a square of squab liver layered with greens, accompanied by a piece of medium-rare breast meat and a morel mushroom stuffed with perfect squab mousse. Milk-fed lamb, prepared as a seared chop, braised shoulder and crisped belly, makes for a particularly delightful trio.

That mignardise cart is a sight to behold with its dazzling array of diminutive treats, such as the kouign amann, filled with huckleberry jam, as well as macarons, chocolates and nougats.

▪ 470 Pacific Ave. (bet. Montgomery & Sansome Sts.)
☎ (415) 775-8500 — **WEB:** www.quincerestaurant.com
▪ Dinner Mon – Sat   **PRICE: $$$$**

SONS & DAUGHTERS ✿

Contemporary · Cozy

Everyone at this inviting space is warmly professional, including the eager, well-paced staff. Add in the mature, stylish crowd, architecturally detailed dining room—a hybrid between your grandmother's home and an art gallery with its black-and-cream palette, leather seating and vintage chandeliers—and you'll be counting down the days until your next visit.

Small but mighty, this kitchen under the guidance of Chef Teague Moriarty turns out a seasonal prix-fixe menu that consistently pleases. A meal here might begin with an unctuous butternut squash soup garnished with fried salsify; or crunchy asparagus accompanied by gently pickled mushrooms and topped with shaved cured egg yolk. Then crisp bits of lamb are incorporated with minted peas to form a clever counterpoint of sweet and savory flavors.

Deep red and juicy cherry-ice cream is a sublime dessert. But it is the combination with intensely moist pistachio cake, tart verjus granité, juniper foam and fresh cherries that showcase the technical prowess of this gifted kitchen.

▦ 708 Bush St. (bet. Mason & Powell Sts.)
☏ (415) 391-8311 — **WEB:** www.sonsanddaughterssf.com
▦ Dinner Wed – Sun   **PRICE: $$$$**

Z & Y BISTRO 😊

Fusion • Contemporary décor

Z & Y Restaurant might be the most popular destination in Chinatown, drawing crowds for its killer takes on Sichuan staples, like dan dan noodles or chicken with explosive chili peppers. Now, savvy diners can skip the wait there and enjoy the same items at this upscale spin-off set right across the street, which boasts a chic and modern wine bar-feel with brick walls and pendant lighting.

The Sichuan food served here is the equal of the mothership's—sample tender strips of beef in a tingling peppercorn-infused broth that's crowned with flaming chili oil. But the pristine Japanese yakitori skewers, like smoky-tender duck breast with spring onions, will come as a pleasant surprise. Accompany these with sips at the bar, or bring a group for a family-style fusion feast.

■ 606 Jackson St. (bet. Grant Ave. & Kearny St.)
✆ (415) 986-1899 — **WEB:** www.zybistro.com
■ Lunch & dinner Wed – Mon   PRICE: $$

Z & Y 😊

Chinese • Family

Some like it hot, and here they are in heaven. Be forewarned: timid palates should steer clear of the super-spicy Sichuan dishes that have made Z & Y a Chinatown smash hit. Nearly every dish is crowned with chilies, from the huge mound of dried peppers that rests atop tender, garlicky bites of fried chicken to the flaming chili oil anointing tender, flaky fish fillets in a star anise-tinged broth with Sichuan peppercorns aplenty.

The well-worn dining room may seem unremarkable and the service perfunctory, but the crowds are undeterred. Plan to wait among eager fans for a seat; then settle in for delicate pork-and-ginger wontons swimming in spicy peanut sauce and more chili oil. Allot time to navigate the challenging parking situation.

■ 655 Jackson St. (bet. Grant Ave. & Kearny St.)
✆ (415) 981-8988 — **WEB:** www.zandyrestaurant.com
■ Lunch & dinner daily   PRICE: $$

RICHMOND
& SUNSET

BURMA SUPERSTAR 🍴○

Burmese • Trendy

&

Like any celebrity, it's easy to recognize this unusual dark wood superstar from the eager crowds swarming like paparazzi. Everyone endures their no-reservations policy to Instagram their favorite Burmese dishes. See the iPhones poised over the famed rainbow and tea leaf salads or samusa soup (also available as a lunchtime combo). Regulars stick to traditional items, marked by asterisks on the menu. Palate-tingling options include rice noodles with pickled daikon and tofu in a spicy tomato-garlic sauce, or pork and kabocha squash stewed in a gingery broth with coconut sticky rice. A creamy Thai iced tea is the perfect counterbalance to the spicy, boldly flavored fare.

Hipper digs, a cooler crowd and updated favorites can be found at sib, Burma Love.

▨ 309 Clement St. (bet. 4th & 5th Aves.)
⊘ (415) 387-2147 — **WEB:** www.burmasuperstar.com
▨ Lunch & dinner daily   **PRICE: $$**

CHAPEAU! 🍴○

French • Bistro

&

For an oh-so-French experience on Asian food-centric Clement, denizens head to Philippe Gardelle's authentic bistro, where tightly spaced tables and paintings of the titular hats create a convivial atmosphere. Packed with regulars receiving bisous from the chef, Chapeau! is warm and generous, a vibe that's aided by its strong Gallic wine list.

Dishes are traditional with a bit of Californian flair, like fingerling potato chips in a friseé and duck confit salad or salted-caramel ice cream that tops the pain perdu. The cassoulet, wholesome with braised lamb, rich with smoky sausage and earthy with white beans, is perfect for a foggy night in the Avenues. Come before 6:00 P.M. on certain nights for an early bird prix-fixe, or create your own from their many set menus.

▨ 126 Clement St. (bet. 2nd & 3rd Aves.)
⊘ (415) 750-9787 — **WEB:** www.chapeausf.com
▨ Dinner Wed – Sun   **PRICE: $$$**

FIORELLA ‖○

Italian • Osteria

 ♿ 🛋

In the foggy Outer Richmond, this casual neighborhood pizzeria has quickly become as hot as its wood-fired oven. Local families come in droves to share a pie or a plate of pasta in the vintage-chic dining room, where laid-back servers chat with patrons beneath funky wallpaper depicting a bevy of Bay Area landmarks and legendary locals.

The chewy, blistered crusts churned out of the kitchen are loaded with flavor, whether in a classic Margherita or salami pie with provolone and red chili. Throw in a seasonal salad, a pile of chicken wings tossed in a Calabrian chili-honey glaze and a glass of Italian wine from the compact list. Be sure to save room though for the warm almond- and Meyer lemon-ricotta cake, which gets toasted alongside the pies in the oven.

▦ 2339 Clement St. (bet. 24th & 25th Aves.)

✆ (415) 340-3049 — **WEB:** www.fiorella-sf.com

▦ Lunch Sat – Sun Dinner nightly   **PRICE: $$**

FIVE HAPPINESS ‖○

Chinese • Elegant

 ♿

Its façade might not seem like much—look for the bright orange tile and prominent sign advertising Mandarin cuisine—but rest easy as this quiet, longstanding Chinese staple is a favorite of cooking icon, Cecilia Chiang. Inside, you'll find a warm and inviting décor, starring white linens and a crimson carpet—it's the sort of space that lends itself to group celebrations.

The dizzying menu features numerous items, but the genial staff is wonderfully helpful at directing guests to house favorites. Standouts include a beautifully bronzed Peking duck (plan to order it 24 hours in advance); slippery hand-cut noodles studded with savory moo shu pork and crunchy vegetables; or the meltingly tender Shanghai braised rib topped with a flutter of green onions.

▦ 4142 Geary Blvd. (bet. Fifth & Sixth Aves.)

✆ (415) 387-1234 — **WEB:** N/A

▦ Lunch & dinner Tue – Sun   **PRICE: $$**

LOKMA

Mediterranean · Neighborhood

This cozy neighborhood recruit has a quaint, laid-back vibe that seems a perfect match to its quiet corner location. The owner is a constant presence, welcoming young families (with tots in tow) and hustling to set up tables. Don't be dismayed by the regular crowds—those weekend lines move quickly and the food is absolutely worth it.

Traditional brunch dishes are served as lunch here, with such hearty favorites as a Turkish breakfast of fried eggs, crumbled feta, sliced sausages, pastyrma (cured beef) and much, much more. Come dinner, try a lemony grilled branzino or skewers of chicken with basmati rice. Every item flaunts a Mediterranean twist—think savory carrot hummus or sweet bal-kaymak (clotted cream with honey) and homemade pitas for scooping.

■ 1801 Clement St. (at 19th St.)
𝒞 (415) 702-6219 — **WEB:** www.lokmasf.com
■ Lunch Tue – Sun Dinner Tue – Sun   **PRICE: $$**

OUTERLANDS

American · Trendy

For the residents of this Outer Sunset beachside community, this sweet spot is an ideal hangout. The salvaged wood-dominated décor is perfectly cozy, and all-day hours ensure that crowds flock here for breakfast and Bloody Marys to start their day. A friendly staff, good, locally roasted coffee and a nicely stocked bar with a fine listing of beers on tap encourages further lingering.

While snackers stop in for fresh-baked pastries, coffee cake or doughnuts, heartier appetites come at lunch for such warming items as a cast iron-grilled cheese with two-bean and parsnip soup. Dinner however brings more ambitious dishes, including a Berkshire pork chop, which when accompanied by a dandelion-salsa verde, forms the very essence of fresh and vibrant flavors.

■ 4001 Judah St. (at 45th Ave.)
𝒞 (415) 661-6140 — **WEB:** www.outerlandssf.com
■ Lunch & dinner daily   **PRICE: $$**

PEARL 6101

American • Contemporary décor

This recruit in a retro drugstore is already the toast of town, with crowds young and old packing in—not unlike neighboring sister, Pizzetta 211. The big and airy space is designed for all-day dining —whether that may be coffee and wood-fired bagels during the day, or a substantial dinner (and cocktail) later.

Co-chefs Mel Lopez and Joyce Conway turn out a Cal-Mediterranean menu heavy on seafood and pastas, like rustic handkerchiefs in a velvety white Bolognese sauce. Carnivores can get down on a grilled bone-in pork chop, accompanied by gently charred broccolini and nectarines. And that San Francisco must—brunch—is brilliantly executed here, with enticing eggs in purgatory or Dutch baby pancakes with fresh fruit and whipped crème fraîche.

■ 6101 California St. (at 23rd Ave.)
✆ (415) 592-9777 — **WEB:** www.pearl6101.com
■ Lunch Sat – Sun Dinner Tue – Sun   PRICE: $$

PIZZETTA 211 ‖○

Pizza • Cozy

This shoebox-sized pizzeria may reside in the far reaches of the Richmond, but it's easily identifiable by the crowds hovering on the sidewalk to score a table. Once inside, you'll be greeted by pizzaiolos throwing pies in the tiny exhibition kitchen—ask for a counter seat to get a better view.

The thin, chewy, blistered pizzettas each serve one, making it easy to share several varieties. Weekly specials utilize ingredients like seasonal produce, house-made sausage and fresh farm eggs, while standbys include a pie topped with wild arugula, creamy mascarpone and San Marzano tomato sauce. Whatever you do, arrive early: once the kitchen's out of dough they close for the day, and the omnipresent lines mean the goods never last too long.

■ 211 23rd Ave. (at California St.)
✆ (415) 379-9880 — **WEB:** www.pizzetta211.com
■ Lunch & dinner Wed – Mon   PRICE: $$

SICHUAN HOME 🏠

Chinese • Simple

One of the brightest offerings on Geary Boulevard, Sichuan Home lures diners far and wide. Its spotless dining room is a vision of varnished wood panels and mirrors, with plexiglass-topped tables for easy chili oil clean-up and menus that feature tempting photos of each item.

A sampling of the wide-ranging Sichuan cuisine should include tender, bone-in rabbit with scallions, peanuts and a perfect dab of scorching hot peppercorns. Fish with pickled cabbage gets a delightfully restorative hit of bold flavors from mustard greens and fresh green chilies, while red chilies star in aromatic dry-fried string beans with minced pork. For dessert, rich and velvety mango pudding, topped with grapefruit sorbet and fresh pineapple, is a tropical treat.

- 🍽 5037 Geary Blvd. (bet. 14th & 15th Aves.)
- ☎ (415) 221-3288 — **WEB:** www.sichuanhomesf.com
- 🍽 Lunch & dinner daily   **PRICE: $$**

VIOLET'S TAVERN 🍴

American • Tavern

Edgy restaurants are finally arriving to meet the needs of the Richmond's increasingly young and moneyed population, and Violet's is the first among equals, serving an enticing menu of cocktails, raw-bar favorites and hearty entrées. Done up in hues of blue and green and outfitted with a wraparound walnut bar, it has the same intimate and lively vibe as nearby sib—Fiorella—ideal for date night.

Don't miss the fresh, tender and chilled lobster, accompanied by Meyer lemon-mayonnaise, or the highly Instagrammable sipper Violet Skies, infused with strawberry brandy, mezcal and crème de violette. A grilled half-chicken with bread salad tailed by a tangy key lime tart is pure comfort, while the late-night $20 burger and cocktail combo is worth staying up for.

- 🍽 2301 Clement St. (at 24th Ave.)
- ☎ (415) 682-4861 — **WEB:** www.violets-sf.com
- 🍽 Lunch Sat – Sun Dinner nightly   **PRICE: $$**

WAKO 🌼

Japanese • *Contemporary décor*

Wako blends right in with the sea of Asian restaurants on Clement Street, but don't let its nondescript exterior fool you. Once inside, you will find a serene and spare dining room that is composed with beautiful, multi-hued wood surfaces and attended to by an exceedingly polite service staff. Fresh flowers add a bit of flourish and fun.

It's the kind of pristine culinary experience that connoisseurs and foodies crave. And since this kitchen boasts some of the best sushi in town, be sure to make reservations. The omakase (with a choice of two menus of varying length) may be the only option on offer, but rest assured as it's available throughout the restaurant. Nevertheless, a seat at the ubiquitous counter is likely to deliver a happier outcome.

From the non-sushi items, diners may be presented with poached monkfish liver, a creamy potato croquette dolloped with salmon roe or a salad of shaved apple and mizuna. The real knockouts though arrive on rice: squid with a touch of shiso and Meyer lemon zest; silky salmon with house-made yuzu kosho; custardy uni imported from Japan, wrapped in roasted seaweed; and to finish, a melt-in-your-mouth slice of gently seared A5 Wagyu beef.

▦ 211 Clement St. (bet. 3rd & 4th Aves.)
℘ (415) 682-4875 — **WEB:** www.sushiwakosf.com
▦ Dinner Tue – Sat   **PRICE: $$$$**

© J.-P. Lescourret/hemis.fr

SOMA

ANGLER ❀

Contemporary • Design

❀ 🍸 ♿ 🍽 🧼

Pitched as a more casual counterpart to the stellar Saison, this Embarcadero dining gem demands your attention. Its pair of plush rooms feels like a hunter's cabin gone Danish chic, complete with taxidermy galore and fiberglass fish commingling surprisingly well with sparkling stemware and modern, throw-draped furniture. But all eyes eventually drift to the gorgeous display kitchen, where cooks tend to a live fire that gently perfumes the room with wood smoke.

The touch of those embers can be felt everywhere—from the infused cream in an elevated White Russian to an intensely concentrated and roasted tomato relish piled atop a fresh-peeled beefsteak tomato. Impeccable sourcing is another one of Chef Joshua Skenes' signatures: fluke crudo in a sour plum vinaigrette is likely to have been caught that morning and picked from the tank just moments before serving.

Despite such meticulousness, Angler retains some humor by transforming rabbit into the world's most lavish riff on Nashville hot chicken, or slipping a bracing tot of beer into the creamy ganache of a chocolate mille-feuille. Like a perfectly tailored suit in an arrestingly bright shade, it's polished yet very playful.

◼ 132 The Embarcadero (bet. Howard & Mission Sts.)
📞 (415) 872-9442 — **WEB:** www.anglerrestaurants.com
◼ Lunch Thu – Sat Dinner nightly   **PRICE: $$$$**

BELLOTA 🍴

Spanish • Chic

Iberian flavors and Cali-cool join forces at this Spanish stunner, where legs of the namesake jamón ibérico de Bellota hang in a central glass case. They're flanked by a sumptuous exhibition kitchen framed in bronze and hand-painted tiles, as well as a glamorous U-shaped bar. Chic professionals (some of them from the neighboring offices of Airbnb) have already staked their claim for date night.

The menu adds seasonal touches to traditional Spanish tapas: picture yogurt-braised chicken albóndigas drizzled with pomegranate agridulce; or a fluffy tortilla Española with rainbow chard and chorizo crumbles. Paellas sized for 2-4 people are another popular option—try the Pluma, with Ibérico pork shoulder, summer squash and slivered squash blossoms.

- 888 Brannan St. (bet. 7th & 8th Sts.)
- (415) 430-6580 — **WEB:** www.bellotasf.com
- Lunch Mon – Fri Dinner Mon – Sat   PRICE: $$$

BOULEVARD 🍴

Californian • Historic

Housed in one of the city's most historic buildings, this Belle Époque stunner is still breathtaking after more than 20 years, with glamorous mosaic floors, colorful glass and polished bronze at every turn. The Embarcadero-adjacent location offers lovely views of the Bay Bridge and the water, and business lunchers as well as evening romance-seekers adore its transporting vibe—there's not a bad seat in this restaurant.

Chef/owner Nancy Oakes is known as a pioneer of Californian cooking, with comforting takes on standards like silky-smooth lobster bisque and a tweaked Cobb salad that eschews chicken for roasted white prawns and comes tossed with crispy bacon bits, feta cubes, cucumbers and tomato slices in different, visually appealing shapes.

- 1 Mission St. (at Steuart St.)
- (415) 543-6084 — **WEB:** www.boulevardrestaurant.com
- Lunch Mon – Fri Dinner nightly   PRICE: $$$

Lavish. Luxurious. Polaris lounge. Pick three.

Relax and recharge in our reimagined lounge experience. Available at LAX and SFO.

fly California's global airline

BENU ✿✿✿

Asian • Design

✿ ♿ ⬚ 📱

Benu is an oasis in the heart of the city. The mandatory stroll through the serene courtyard not only sets the mood, but also offers insight into the meal to come. Peruse the earthenware pots with fermenting ingredients you'll later find on your plate and glimpse the kitchen hard at work. The interior is awash in earthy colors and sleek banquettes, and the slate-gray dining room is serene, with clean lines drawing the eye across the meticulous design. Given the restaurant's high caliber, the staff is impressively warm and relaxed.

A series of highly technical small bites kicks off the meal. These delicacies alone rival some of the country's most ambitious tasting menus, but wait, there's more. Faux shark's fin and soup dumplings remain a constant, while Chef Corey Lee continues to reimagine and redefine his nightly tasting menu. Dishes like Beluga caviar and sweet sea urchin or Cantonese-style pork belly served alongside blood sausage crepinette reflect a unique marriage of contemporary Asian influences.

Patience seems to define this kitchen in its relentless pursuit of excellence, whether perfecting technique or waiting for just the right moment to serve an ingredient at its peak.

◼ 22 Hawthorne St. (bet. Folsom & Howard Sts.)
☎ (415) 685-4860 — **WEB:** www.benusf.com
◼ Dinner Tue – Sat   **PRICE: $$$$**

BIRDSONG ✤

American • Contemporary décor

✤ ♿ ⛶

The front windows are stacked with logs, dried fish hangs from the rafters and the dining room is gently scented with wood smoke, but lofty ceilings and a contemporary aura make Birdsong feel lumberjack-chic. While Chef Christopher Bleidorn prides himself on live-fire cooking and using every part of the animal, he's still attuned to creature comforts, including a restful color scheme, gorgeous earthenware, elegant stemware and a staff that's as sharp as a well-made axe. The funky 80s rock music in the background certainly helps preserve a laid-back vibe.

His tasting menu underlines the cuisine of the Pacific Northwest, with a deeper emphasis on the intense flavors of wood fire. Perfectly grilled lamb-stuffed mushrooms are standouts, accompanied by the likes of custardy blue-corn bread matched with charcoal butter. The chef also flaunts immense skill with dehydrated and cured ingredients, transforming humble carrots into a tender, "meaty" marvel, or wrapping a cylinder of crisp pork belly around luscious caviar and chives for an enticing blast of flavor.

Even desserts get their turn in the embers: brioche soaked in jasmine custard is rich and moist, with deliciously caramelized edges.

■ 1085 Mission St. (bet. 6th & 7th Sts.)
✆ (415) 369-9161 — **WEB:** www.birdsongsf.com
■ Dinner Tue – Sat　　　　　　　　　　　　**PRICE: $$$$**

THE CAVALIER

Gastropub • Brasserie

One of the city's high-profile hangouts, this is the third effort from the team behind Marlowe and Park Tavern. Everything here has a British bent, echoed in the hunting-lodge-gone-sophisticated décor with red-and-blue walls accented by taxidermied trophies and tufted banquettes. Across-the-pond classics have Californian twists like a deep-fried Scotch duck egg wrapped in heritage pork sausage. The restaurant has quickly become a see-and-be-seen haunt of the tech oligarchy (complete with a private club). However, the food is spot-on and homey, as seen in the corned beef-and-potato hash topped with a gently poached egg.

Though reservations are recommended, its location in the Hotel Zetta means service runs from morning to night, giving diners plenty of options.

◼ 360 Jessie St. (at 5th St.)
✆ (415) 321-6000 — **WEB:** www.thecavaliersf.com
◼ Lunch & dinner daily   PRICE: $$

COCKSCOMB

American • Rustic

Carnivores will thrill to the offerings at this favored spot from offal-loving Top Chef Masters champ, Chris Cosentino. It doesn't shy away from aggressively rich fare like wood-grilled bruschetta topped with uni butter, sweet Dungeness crab and buttery lardo or smoky butterflied roast quail in a rich, salty tetrazzini gravy. Even the vegetable-centric celery Victor gets a meaty spin, thanks to such delectable toppings as crispy chicken skin.

Thanks to the hearty menu and location in a tech-centric corridor, Cockscomb draws a mostly male crowd that packs in for shellfish platters and intense, boozy cocktails named for SF landmarks. Laid-back, yet attentive service and a soaring, industrial space make it the very picture of a hot spot.

◼ 564 4th St. (at Freelon St.)
✆ (415) 974-0700 — **WEB:** www.cockscombsf.com
◼ Lunch Mon – Fri Dinner Mon – Sat   PRICE: $$$

HASHIRI ✿

Japanese • Design

This omakase-only sparkler in Mint Plaza may be one of the city's most expensive restaurants, but those who can afford the bill will be rewarded with a truly luxurious culinary experience. Every detail of Hashiri has been finely crafted, from the hand-painted dishes and crystal sake glasses, to the parting seasonal treat presented to diners at the end of their meal. This dining room is home to a host of Asian diners and suits, but don't be surprised if you see a hoodie-clad millionaire or two seated next to you.

Chef Shinichi Aoki and team offer their own creative hybrid of two classic cuisines—the artistry of sushi fused with the ceremony of a kaiseki meal. Exceptional dishes showcase the best of the season and have included tender pen shell clam with citrus-splashed fava beans and bamboo shoots, as well as lightly grilled A5 Wagyu beef over a celeriac purée and charred ramps. Then move on to some outstanding nigiri like buttery Spanish mackerel enhanced by citrus; aji with minced chives; chutoro; otoro; and Hokkaido uni.

Sake connoisseurs will enjoy the bar's exclusive selection, while novices can rest assured as the helpful staff is happy to steer the way to the right choice.

■ 4 Mint Plaza (at 5th St.)
℘ (415) 908-1919 — **WEB:** www.hashirisf.com
■ Dinner Tue – Sat   PRICE: $$$$

IN SITU ✾

International • Design

 ♿ 🍽️

Like the SF Museum of Modern Art in which it's housed, Corey Lee's "culinary museum" bends notions of time and place to offer a unique array of iconic dishes from top chefs around the world, honoring more than two decades of innovative cooking. Guided by each respective creator, Lee has trained his cooks to faithfully replicate more than 100 menu items from a starry lineup that includes Chefs Thomas Keller, Albert Adrià and David Chang.

The concise menu rotates seasonally, ensuring that diners will always have new "exhibits" to sample. These might include David Thompson's intensely spicy Chiang Mai-style guinea fowl larb salad, Mehmet Gürs' luscious lamb shank manti with yogurt mousse and tomato or Hiroshi Sasaki's succulent glazed chicken thigh with a creamy onsen egg. If Adrià's decadent and masterfully prepared Jasper Hill Farm cheesecake with a hazelnut crust and white chocolate cookies is in the lineup, don't hesitate.

In addition to the culinary concept, In Situ's design is in keeping with its museum home, featuring a spare dining room and a few gems from SFMOMA's collection adding pops of color. Be forewarned that a sophisticated but casual crowd fills up this room quickly.

◼ 151 Third St. (bet. Howard & Minna Sts.)
✆ (415) 941-6050 — **WEB:** insitu.sfmoma.org
◼ Lunch Thu – Mon Dinner Thu – Sun   **PRICE: $$$$**

INTERNATIONAL SMOKE ⅋○

International · *Trendy*

 ♿ ⚚

International Smoke is definitely en fuego. This downtown eatery nails that industrial-chic look with its black brick, copper accents and graffiti-emblazoned pillars. But, it's the buzzing clientele that makes this a smoking-hot spot. Attentive servers make everyone feel like a VIP, though there's a good chance you'll be dining next to a bonafide baller—after all, this is a collaboration between Michael Mina and lifestyle maven/basketball wife, Ayesha Curry.

Expect a meat-centric menu with creative takes on barbecue. Don't pass up the ribs, with three distinct flavors—all equally juicy, and yes, smoky. There's a nice balance here between messy finger food and elevated dishes employing smoke-filled cloches for tableside prep— and a bit of drama.

■ 301 Mission St. (at Fremont St.)
☏ (415) 543-7474 — **WEB:** www.internationalsmoke.com
■ Lunch Mon – Fri Dinner nightly   PRICE: $$$

KHAI ⅋○

Vietnamese · *Intimate*

♿

A celebrity in his native Vietnam, Chef/owner Khai Duong has chosen to settle down in a strip mall near the Design District, where he offers a ten-course tasting menu with two nightly seatings. The petite dining room is a bit eccentric, with its daytime takeaway counter mostly obscured by curtains. Still, you'll get a lot of face time with the chef, who's an active presence and a great character.

Trained in France, Duong offers beautifully crafted updates on classic Vietnamese dishes, from vermicelli with shredded omelet and pork belly to Hanoi's famous cha ca thang long—turmeric-marinated fish with dill and scallions. Other highlights include rich matsutake mushroom pâté, and for dessert, slippery coconut noodles with durian paste and coconut cream.

■ 655 Townsend St. (bet. 7th & 8th Sts.)
☏ (415) 724-2325 — **WEB:** www.chefkhai.com
■ Dinner Tue – Sat   PRICE: $$$$

LUCE ✿

Contemporary • Elegant

Know that the ambience is pleasant, the space is elegant, the service team is quick and polite and the food is consistently excellent. Also know that you probably won't have a hard time getting a reservation at this InterContinental Hotel restaurant—Luce is often inexplicably empty. Let its lack of popularity be your reminder to come here when looking for a little privacy—think date night.

Soaring ceilings, dark and dramatic spherical lights, a transparent wall of wine bordering the kitchen and shiny cushioned banquettes give the dining room a sumptuous, airy feel that promises the high level of luxury echoed in the cuisine. This may be one of the city's more venerable mainstays, but a contemporary sensibility is clear throughout the décor and menu.

Luce serves breakfast, lunch and brunch, but dinner is when the serious diner arrives for an altogether stellar experience. Highlights include a generous portion of perfectly white halibut poached in California olive oil and placed on a colorful bed of fresh shelling beans with artichokes and clams. Desserts may combine the wonderfully light flavors of sweet corn panna cotta with kernels of honey-caramel popped corn and huckleberry compote.

▉ 888 Howard St. (at 5th St.)
✆ (415) 616-6566 — **WEB:** www.lucewinerestaurant.com
▉ Lunch & dinner daily   **PRICE: $$$**

MOURAD ✵

Moroccan • Chic

This glamorous outpost at the base of the PacBell building introduces the unique soul of Chef/owner Mourad Lahlou's eponymous restaurant. The neighborhood's food-obsessed techies along with tourists flock to this boldly designed space, replete with soaring ceilings, glowing central columns and a superb (suspended) wine cellar. The crowd is contented and lively, and while the servers fit the bill, the sommelier is especially impressive.

Chef Lahlou's expression of Moroccan cuisine is peppered with local and contemporary influences like maple and brown butter, as well as more traditional inflections such as charmoula and preserved lemon. Diners may commence with the basteeya, a traditional Moroccan pastry made modern with finely shredded duck and composed with verjus crème fraîche, compressed pear, edible flowers as well as cocoa paste. Couscous is jazzed up with savory brown butter and a host of vegetables, then hit with spicy harissa for a slight kick.

Even dessert comes packed with flavor. For instance, the slender slice of pistachio cake set with candied pink grapefruit, fresh grapefruit segments, a quenelle of tangerine sorbet and orange-infused cream, is lush and delicious.

■ 140 New Montgomery St. (bet. Minna & Natoma Sts.)
✆ (415) 660-2500 — **WEB:** www.mouradsf.com
■ Lunch Mon – Fri Dinner nightly   **PRICE: $$$**

M.Y. CHINA ⬤

Chinese • Contemporary décor

&. ✗

Need proof that Yan Can Cook? Just snag a table at the famed PBS chef's elegant restaurant. Housed under the dome of the Westfield San Francisco Centre shopping mall, M.Y. China is a dark, sultry space full of posh Chinese furniture, antiques and dramatic lighting. Shopping-weary patrons fill the dining room, whereas chowhounds hit the exhibition counter to watch the staff masterfully hand-pull noodles and toss woks.

The menu reads like an ode to regional Chinese cuisine, spanning chewy scissor-cut noodles with wild boar, fluffy bao stuffed with sweet and smoky barbecue pork and, when it's in season, delectable pepper-dusted whole crab. Be sure to order strategically, as you'll want room for the flaky, buttery, creamy and outright superb Macanese egg tarts.

■ 845 Market St. (bet. 4th & 5th Sts.)
𝒫 (415) 580-3001 — **WEB:** www.tastemychina.com
■ Lunch & dinner daily   **PRICE: $$**

OKANE ⬤

Japanese • Simple

&.

Can't afford to indulge in the exquisite sushi at Omakase? Consider heading to its next-door little sib, where the fish is still top-notch (it's all sourced from Japan) but the atmosphere is more laid-back. Okane draws lots of nearby Adobe and Zynga employees at lunch and big groups at dinner, all sharing bottles of sake and making the most of the small-plates menu.

Sushi is, of course, a must: the nigiri is pristine and delicious, as are more Americanized rolls like the Harajuku (filled with shrimp tempura, avocado and salmon and topped with tuna, eel sauce and lotus root chips). But don't sleep on the non-sushi dishes—cod marinated in sake lees is grilled to perfection, and broiled salmon aburi with avocado and ikura is delicious too.

■ 669 Townsend St. (bet. 7th & 8th Sts.)
𝒫 (415) 865-9788 — **WEB:** www.okanesf.com
■ Lunch & dinner daily   **PRICE: $$**

OMAKASE ⌘

Japanese • Simple

&

True, the vibe is friendly and the location is convenient for tech entrepreneurs, but superb Edomae sushi is the real reason why Omakase is always full. Ergo, reservations are required and punctuality is a must. The kimono-clad servers strain to place dishes in front of diners, who usually sit elbow-to-elbow at the tight L-shaped counter, but the chummy young professionals and gourmands don't seem to notice anything but the chefs.

Choose from two omakase menus; the more extensive (and expensive) one offers additional sashimi and nigiri. Begin with buttery ocean trout steamed in sake and presented with a wedge of heirloom black tomato as well as an herb salad in rice wine vinaigrette. Beautifully arranged sashimi features bluefin tuna with red-fleshed sea perch, garnished with cured kombu, shiso leaf, wasabi and a bit of chrysanthemum petal salad. Still, no dish can compare with the exquisite level of nigiri, which may showcase marinated chutoro, cedar-torched sea bream, Hokkaido uni with house-brined ikura and a fluffy piece of lobster-infused tamago.

Extreme attention to detail is the hallmark of dining here, with customized portions of rice and wasabi adjustments for each guest's palate.

■ 665 Townsend St. (bet. 7th & 8th Sts.)
✆ (415) 865-0633 — **WEB:** www.omakasesf.com
■ Dinner nightly   **PRICE: $$$$**

PROSPECT ⅋○

American • Elegant

🎱 🍸 ♿ 🎏

For a polished and contemporary experience that doesn't sacrifice approachability, SoMa denizens turn to Prospect, a crowd-pleaser for the full-pocketbook crowd. Set on the ground floor of a soaring high-rise, its airy space offers attractive, roomy tables, adept service and a popular, well-stocked cocktail bar.

Simple, well-constructed American fare abounds, with menu mainstays like an heirloom tomato salad with creamy dollops of burrata and crisp, garlicky breadcrumbs; or a perfectly flaky coho salmon fillet set over earthy black rice, sweet yellow corn and caramelized summer squash. Dessert should not be missed: the butter brickle icebox cake with honey-glazed plums and toasted pecan butter crunch is a truly memorable treat.

🔳 300 Spear St. (at Folsom St.)
☎ (415) 247-7770 — **WEB:** www.prospectsf.com
🔳 Lunch Mon – Fri Dinner Mon – Sat   **PRICE: $$$**

ROOH ⅋○

Indian • Contemporary décor

♿ 🍷

Amidst a slew of upscale Indian restaurants descending upon San Francisco, Rooh rises to the top, thanks to an innovative menu that fuses the subcontinent's myriad flavors with modern restaurant staples (oysters, pork belly, burrata). The bold India-goes-industrial décor is a bit paint-by-numbers, with vivid jewel tones and an oversized mural depicting a traditionally dressed woman. But the vibe is engaging and the cocktails quite unique.

Rooh's approach is casual, but tabs can grow stratospheric in this pricey tech corridor. For the best value, opt for a meal of delicious small plates like the piquant paneer chili, coated in crispy shreds of kataifi noodles. Wrap up with the exquisite carrot halwa cake, accented by cardamom kulfi and yogurt mousse.

🔳 333 Brannan St. (at Stanford St.)
☎ (415) 525-4174 — **WEB:** www.roohsf.com
🔳 Lunch & dinner Mon – Sat   **PRICE: $$$**

SAISON ✿✿
Californian • Chic

Set within an imposing warehouse, this iconic kitchen's footprint overlaps the dining room, where the cooks themselves can often be seen serving diners. While savoring each course, you may have a full view of the impressive team tending the fiery hearth that is the very soul of Saison's culinary philosophy. This enticing chamber combines the original brick ceilings with cushy seats and giant taxidermy that allude to founder Joshua Skenes' hunting prowess. Over at the bar, a salon fills with couples dining at cocktail tables.

The menu demonstrates a range of skill and tastes. Begin with a ceviche of fairly firm and meaty jackfish enhanced by yuzu and glistening with finger lime, or use your hands to pick up a delicate mound of plump sea urchin on crunchy toast—a house signature. Then, translucent, moist and bite-sized king salmon matched with smooth celeriac purée will leave you yearning for more—quite like the enticingly sauced filet of meltingly tender venison, and in true California style, charred avocado.

Desserts too flaunt an intense devotion to local ingredients and seasonal flavors as seen in the refreshing pear sorbet set afloat in house-made apple kombucha.

■ 178 Townsend St. (bet. 2nd & 3rd Sts.)
℘ (415) 828-7990 — **WEB:** www.saisonsf.com
■ Dinner Tue – Sat   **PRICE: $$$$**

1601 BAR & KITCHEN 😊
Sri Lankan • Contemporary décor

&

Sri Lankan flavors infuse the dishes at this quiet winner, which also employs Western ingredients to arrive at its very own delicious concoctions. For a more extensive exploration of this island nation's cuisine, go for the degustation menu. Or stick to such decidedly untraditional items as lamprais, which might stuff a classically French bacon-wrapped rabbit loin and eggplant curry into a banana leaf. Halibut "ceviche" is more like flavored sashimi, with hints of coconut milk and serrano chilies.

This contemporary space with its wraparound windows and slate walls is a perfect showcase for the cooking. Dine solo at the bar with a bittersweet Dubonnet sangria, or come with friends to share food and wine—the polished staff makes either experience enjoyable.

 1601 Howard St. (at 12th St.)
℘ (415) 552-1601 — **WEB:** www.1601sf.com
■ Dinner Tue – Sat   **PRICE: $$**

TRAILBLAZER TAVERN ⫯○
Hawaiian • Contemporary décor

🍹 & 🛖 🖵

Deep in the concrete jungle, this newbie from super chef Michael Mina aims to offer a taste of the islands. In collaboration with Hawaiian culinary power couple, Michelle Karr-Ueoka and Wade Ueoka, this tavern's lofty ceilings, leafy plants and tropical turquoise accents offer a punchy contrast against its expansive views of the surrounding skyscrapers.

Native Hawaiian ingredients from lilikoi to poi make appearances, often alongside Asian influences—the huli huli chicken, for example, comes with rice cakes and Chinese broccoli. But for a luxe workday lunch, the prix-fixe is a steal. Start with the ahi tuna poke with fried wonton "nachos," and wrap up over the tart strawberry-hibiscus shaved ice, piled atop haupia tapioca and mochi ice cream.

■ 350 Mission St. (at Fremont St.)
℘ (415) 625-5445 — **WEB:** www.michaelmina.net
■ Lunch Mon – Fri Dinner nightly   **PRICE: $$**

YANK SING 😊

Chinese • Family

 ♿ 🚪 🥢

With a higher price tag than the average Chinatown joint, Yank Sing is arguably the place in town for dim sum. The upscale setting boasts reasonable prices, but the zigzagging carts can get hectic. While peak hours entail a wait, one can be assured of quality and abundant variety from these carts rolling out of the kitchen.

The signature Peking duck with its crispy lacquered skin and fluffy buns makes for a memorable treat, not unlike the deliciously sweet and salty char siu bao. Of course, dumplings here are the true highlight, and range from fragrant pork xiao long bao to paper-thin har gao concealing chunks of shrimp. Don't see favorites like the flaky egg custard tarts? Just ask the cheerful staff, who'll radio the kitchen for help via headsets.

■ 101 Spear St. (bet. Howard & Mission Sts.)
✆ (415) 781-1111 — **WEB:** www.yanksing.com
■ Lunch daily   **PRICE: $$**

ZERO ZERO 😊

Pizza • Rustic

 ♿ 🛋

Zero Zero may be named for the superlative flour used in its blistered pies, but it is so much more than a pizzeria. While the Castro topped with oozing mozzarella and spicy soppressata is delicious, this casual spot offers far more than just a good slice. Absolute knockouts include a beautifully composed panzanella accompanied by basil pesto, as well as gnocchi tossed in a hearty pork belly ragù, decked with dollops of ricotta making it light and bright, despite the indulgent ingredients.

A mix of families, hipsters and business folk from the Moscone Center fills the warm, bi-level space. Group dining is ideal for sampling more of the menu, and the sizable bar will ensure that everyone's furnished with a terrific cocktail or pint of local draft root beer.

■ 826 Folsom St. (bet. 4th & 5th Sts.)
✆ (415) 348-8800 — **WEB:** www.zerozerosf.com
■ Lunch & dinner daily   **PRICE: $$**

EAST BAY

EAST BAY

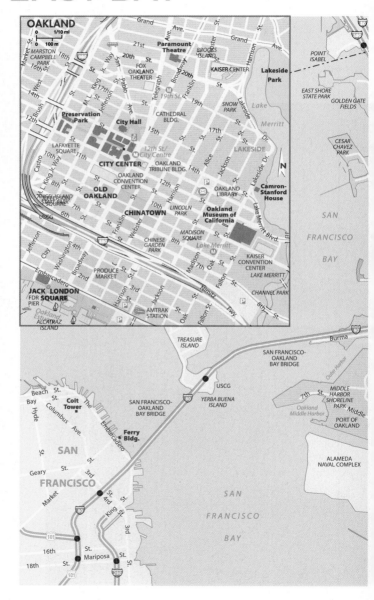

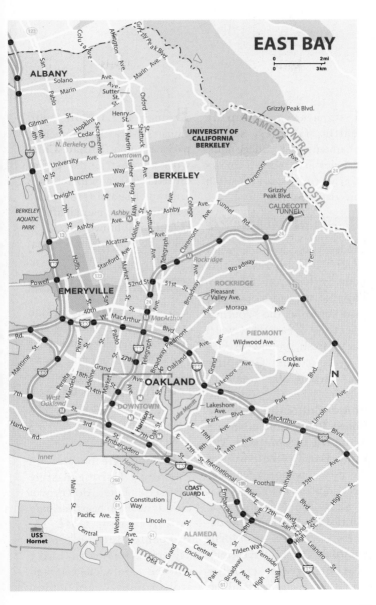

EAST BAY

0   2mi
0   3km

EATING IN...
EAST BAY

A signature mash-up of wealthy families, senior bohemians and college kids, Berkeley is extolled for its liberal politics and lush university campus.

GOURMET GHETTO

Budget-conscious Berkeleyites needn't look to restaurants alone for local, organic food. Their North Shattuck corridor (also known as the "gourmet ghetto") gratifies with garden-fresh produce as well as takeout from **Grégoire**. This area is also home to co-ops like the **Cheese Board Collective**, **Cheese Board Pizza Collective** and **Acme Bread Company**. The **Juice Bar Collective** lures the diet-conscious, whereas meat addicts can't get enough of Chef Paul Bertolli's **Fra' Mani Handcrafted Foods**. Every Thursday, the **North Shattuck Organic Farmer's Market** attracts cooking enthusiasts from near and far.

Brunch at **La Note**, with cinnamon-brioche pain perdu, packs a punch. **Tomate Cafe,** with a pup-friendly patio, churns out a wholesome Cuban breakfast; while **Udupi Palace**, named after a region in Southwest India, is wildly popular for its regional cuisine.

OAKLAND

Located across the bridge from the city, Oakland has seen a resurgence in recent years. With panoramic views of the Bay, terrific restaurants and shops, Jack London Square is revered for sun-soaked docks and a Sunday farmers' market.

Mornings are busy at **La Farine**, a European-style patisserie. Later, downtown crowds nosh on heartwarming po'boys from **Café 15**. **Bakesale Betty** caters to big appetites with bulky chicken sandwiches served atop ironing-board tables.

Post-work revelry reaches epic status at **The Trappist**, pouring over 100 Belgian and other specialty beers. End the day at **Fentons Creamery**, which has been churning handmade ice creams for over 120 years. **Lush Gelato** spotlights homegrown producers like **Strauss Creamery**, while **Tara's Organic Ice Cream** scoops unique flavors (beet-balsamic anyone?) in compostable cups. Down-home Mexican food fans can get their fiesta on at taco trucks parked along International Boulevard, or at local joints like **Taqueria Sinaloa**. Bonus bites await at **Rockridge Market Hall**, featuring **Hapuku Fish Shop** and **Highwire Coffee Roasters**. Set between Oakland and Berkeley, Rockridge boasts a plethora of quaint boutiques and quirky eateries—including **Oaktown Spice Shop** on Grand Avenue, which showcases herbs and exotic spices, available in both small amounts and bulk bags.

BARCOTE ¶⃝

Ethiopian • Simple

♿ ⛲

The competition may be stiff on Oakland's Ethiopian restaurant row, but thanks to a warm and welcoming team of chef/owners as well as a menu that excels in weaving together the spices and seasonings, the cuisine at Barcote stands out and sparkles like no other. Whether you opt for a meaty plate of kitfo (spiced minced beef cooked in clarified butter); a sampler of vegetarian stews like spicy misir wot (lentils simmered in berbere sauce); or hearty atakilt wot (cabbage, potato, and carrot stew with turmeric); you'll be captivated by the layers of flavor.

The space is clean and simple, but friendly service and a tree-shaded front patio ensure that it's homey, not ho-hum. Don't come in a rush—this is a place to kick back and enjoy a leisurely meal.

▪ 6430 Telegraph Ave. (bet. Alcatraz Ave. & 65th St.), Oakland

✆ (510) 923-6181 — **WEB:** www.barcoteoakland.com

▪ Lunch & dinner daily   **PRICE:**

BELOTTI RISTORANTE E BOTTEGA ¶⃝

Italian • Contemporary décor

🖐

Pasta aficionados will find paradiso in this petite and casual restaurant-turned-enoteca, set on a busy but bucolic stretch of Rockridge's main artery. Boasting an impressive passel of regulars who frequently park at the bar to chat with the owner in Italian between bites, Belotti dabbles in the traditional cuisine of Piemonte.

Envision such hearty dishes as brasato—braised beef with mushrooms served over polenta and finished with a nebbiolo reduction. House-made pastas are also a major attraction here, including the heirloom grain spaghettini in a tomato sauce with creamy burrata. But more unexpected dishes excel as well: try the delicious butter lettuce salad with lemon and pine nuts, or the decadent tortino, a spinach flan with egg yolk and truffle.

▪ 5403 College Ave. (bet. Kales & Manila Aves.), Oakland

✆ (510) 788-7890 — **WEB:** www.belottirb.com

▪ Lunch & dinner Mon – Sat   **PRICE:** $$

BENCHMARK OAKLAND ⅑◯

Italian • Contemporary décor

🍸 ♿

This stylish pizzeria is a spinoff sister restaurant to Benchmark in Kensington, but feels right at home in food-centric Old Oakland and sits across from Swan's Market. The space showcases beautiful tiled floors, vibrant red wall accents and jumbo windows that overlook a charming, bustling and typically Oakland neighborhood scene.

The kitchen is known for perfectly blistered, wood-fired pies, but house-made pastas are no second fiddle. Perfectly chewy, strozzapreti is glossed with a featherlight coating of Bolognese sauce and halo of finely grated parmesan cheese. Then a crisp and local romaine salad (Star Route Farms), laced with creamy Caesar, shaved Grana Padano and freshly cracked black pepper, steps up as the perfect accompaniment.

▪ 499 9th St. (at Washington St.), Oakland
✆ (510) 488-6677 — **WEB:** www.benchmarkoakland.com
▪ Lunch Mon – Fri Dinner nightly   **PRICE: $$**

CAFÉ ROMANAT ⅑◯

Ethiopian • Regional décor

In a stretch of Oakland that teems with Ethiopian restaurants, Café Romanat is a standout, thanks to its deliciously spiced dishes served in generous portions. Locals (including some Ethiopian families) fill the small room that is set with traditional low stools, woven tables and features colorful fabric curtains and artwork.

Order up a homegrown beer, honey wine or a nutty ground flax or sesame seed juice to pair with the sambussas, triangular pastries stuffed with piquant jalapeño-spiked lentils. All the combination platters, served on spongy, slightly sour injera, are perfect for sharing. And the veggie combo, with dishes like sautéed collard greens, lentils in smoky berbere and split peas with turmeric and ginger, will delight any crowd.

▪ 462 Santa Clara Ave. (near Grand Ave.), Oakland
✆ (510) 444-1800 — **WEB:** www.caferomanat.com
▪ Lunch Sat – Sun Dinner Tue – Sun   **PRICE:** ⊜

CDP ◯

Contemporary · Chic

In addition to its façade, CDP shares a great deal with its sibling, Commis. The name itself is a continuation of classic French kitchen hierarchy nomenclature—the initials stand for Chef de Partie—and it displays the same professional service and elegant cuisine as its counterpart.

While Chef Syhabout serves both restaurants, this menu features affordable, snack-sized portions unlike next door. Those seeking a more hearty meal can opt for the côte du boeuf prix-fixe. Begin with canapés like brown butter blinis topped with smoked trout roe or popcorn dressed with dashi seasoning. The signature egg with a slow-poached yolk is poised delicately atop smoked cream, while a Japanese-style cheesecake is more sweet than tangy, with a scoop of strawberry sorbet.

■ 3861 Piedmont Ave. (at Rio Vista Ave.), Oakland
✆ (510) 653-3902 — **WEB:** www.commisrestaurant.com
■ Dinner Wed – Sun   **PRICE: $$$**

CHEZ PANISSE ◯

Californian · Historic

A legendary address among the foodie set, Alice Waters' Arts and Crafts bungalow continues to flourish as the Bay Area's temple of Californian cuisine. The talented team of chefs here work their magic in a gleaming open kitchen that is set at the very back of the dining room and served by an aromatic wood-burning oven.

Diners are privy to one nightly fixed menu of four rotating courses (three on Mondays). What they will get is a matter of chance, but rest assured it will feature only peak-season produce—from the fresh peas, asparagus and black truffle in a spring risotto, to the sweet corn and squash blossoms served with a summer preparation of pork loin.

Seeking more freedom of choice? Head to the upstairs café, which offers meals á la carte.

■ 1517 Shattuck Ave. (bet. Cedar & Vine Sts.), Berkeley
✆ (510) 548-5525 — **WEB:** www.chezpanisse.com
■ Dinner Mon – Sat   **PRICE: $$$$**

CHINA VILLAGE 😊
Chinese · Family

 ♿

It takes a village to feed a big group, and this laid-back spot is a favorite with families. A stylish makeover featured a sleek front bar, contemporary chandeliers and dramatic Chinese art, but one look at the scorching-hot menu options—think spicy Sichuan frog and flaky sautéed fish with pickled chili peppers—confirms the authenticity factor.

Skip the Hunan, Mandarin and Cantonese offerings in favor of the Sichuan specialties like dry-fried, bone-in chicken laced with ground chilies and numbing peppercorns. And be sure to order the five-spice hot and spicy pork shoulder. A house specialty, this mouthwatering dish is fork- (or chopstick) tender and rests atop a deliciously piquant chili-oil jus with baby bok choy, scallions and garlic.

▦ 1335 Solano Ave. (at Ramona Ave.), Albany
☏ (510) 525-2285 — **WEB:** www.chinavillagealbany.com
▦ Lunch & dinner daily   **PRICE:** 🍤

COMAL 😊
Mexican · Contemporary décor

🍸 ♿ 🛖

For bold and zesty Mexican food crafted with pristine ingredients, Berkeleyites pack this industrial-chic hot spot, where an excellent cocktail program and an extensive tequila and mezcal selection keep things buzzing. The large flat tortilla griddles for which Comal is named are on full display in the open kitchen, while a covered and heated back patio draws locals for year-round outdoor dining

Fryer-fresh warm tortilla chips paired with perfect guacamole are irresistible; summon an order as you peruse other options like the refreshing white shrimp ceviche and earthy hen-of-the-woods mushroom quesadilla. Just make sure that those smoky wood-grilled rock cod tacos, with creamy avocado aïoli and spicy cabbage slaw, are on your must-order list.

▦ 2020 Shattuck Ave. (bet. Addison St. & University Ave.), Berkeley
☏ (510) 926-6300 — **WEB:** www.comalberkeley.com
▦ Dinner nightly   **PRICE:** $$

COMMIS ❀ ❀
Contemporary · Intimate

&

Oakland continues to evolve and maintain its destination status thanks in large part to Commis and its hard-working troupe. This serene elder from Chef/owner James Syhabout is packed every night for its menu of measured, elegant and well-conceived dishes.

Tucked into colorful Piedmont Avenue, the dining space is long and neat, with a smattering of tables up front; cozy banquette seating in the back; and a lively counter overlooking the humming kitchen. Soft music and a vibrant staff set the mood—cool and contemporary; relaxed but never casual.

In the kitchen, Chef Syhabout pairs local, well-sourced ingredients with precise technique to create a sophisticated nightly tasting menu. Dinner might unveil silky scallops with tangy crème fraîche, poached asparagus and charred lemon granité. That signature slow-poached egg yolk sitting in a bed of onion- and malt-infused cream is a consistent and thrilling revelation; while white sturgeon caviar with creamed potato and beer-marinated onion resembles an exquisitely elevated sour cream-and-onion dip. Perfectly cooked mussels set over porridge-like grains is yet another beautiful plate that reflects this kitchen's keen attention to detail.

■ 3859 Piedmont Ave. (at Rio Vista Ave.), Oakland
📞 (510) 653-3902 — **WEB:** www.commisrestaurant.com
■ Dinner Wed – Sun   **PRICE: $$$$**

CORSO 🐷
Italian • Trattoria

&

A Tuscan follow-up from the couple behind nearby Rivoli, Corso is every bit the equal of its big sister, thanks to generous, Florentine-inspired dishes like roasted squid panzanella with torn flatbread, buttery white beans and bright dashes of lemon juice and chili oil. Pasta fiends will swoon for house-made tagliatelle in a meaty beef and pork sugo, while butter-roasted chicken boasts juicy meat, golden-brown skin as well as fresh peas and asparagus alongside.

Soul-warming in its hospitality, Corso is the kind of place where servers will bring complimentary pistachio biscotti simply because they're "so good when they're warm." It's no surprise that the tiny trattoria is a favorite among couples, so be sure to reserve in advance and come hungry.

■ 1788 Shattuck Ave. (bet. Delaware & Francisco Sts.), Berkeley
✆ (510) 704-8004 — **WEB:** www.corsoberkeley.com
■ Dinner nightly   **PRICE: $$**

DELAGE ¶◯
Japanese • Rustic

&

The word is out about this tiny, omakase-only Japanese gem, located adjacent to Swan's Market in Old Oakland. It's a simple, casual space with a small counter and handful of tables, but it also provides a fine spotlight for a mixture of high-quality nigiri and kaiseki dishes.

Meals typically run about eight courses, with seasonal starters like a grilled apricot and mizuna salad; salmon sashimi adorned with a slice of Saturn peach; or garlic shoots enhancing seared Miyazaki beef.

Excellent nigiri, from tuna to mackerel to fluke, arrive at intervals alongside other captivating items, like seared duck breast with moro miso or scallops with shiso and umeboshi. The only downside is that reservations can be a challenge—so be sure to plan well ahead.

■ 536 9th St. (bet. Clay & Washington Sts.), Oakland
✆ (510) 823-2050 — **WEB:** www.delageoakland.com
■ Dinner Wed – Sun   **PRICE: $$$**

DYAFA

Middle Eastern • Contemporary décor

🍸 ♿ 🚻 🛋️

After making a splash with casual Middle Eastern café Reem's, Chef Reem Assil has gone upscale with this big outpost in Jack London Square, a partnership with Daniel Patterson's Alta Group.

"Dyafa" is Arabic for "hospitality," and you'll find plenty of it here, with outstanding service, stunning views of the marina and an array of tempting family-style platters, including braised lamb shanks with garlic yogurt and almonds. Light and fluffy flatbreads are Assil's specialty, and you'll want plenty of her pita to scoop up the delectable dip sampler of creamy hummus, vibrant muhammara and rich labneh. Equally unmissable: the freshly made mana'eesh, which cradles charred and juicy chicken kebabs topped with garlic aïoli and pickled turnips.

■ 44 Webster St. (at Embarcadero W.), Oakland
℘ (510) 250-9491 — **WEB:** www.dyafaoakland.com
■ Lunch & dinner daily   **PRICE:** 👄

FOB KITCHEN 🍴

Filipino • Trendy

🍸 🚻 🛋️

This highly desirable Filipino restaurant brought to you by dynamic duo, Brandi and Janice Dulce, got its start as a popular pop-up. Its current brick-and-mortar space, tucked into the Temescal neighborhood, might still be small but is ingeniously designed—with whimsical black-and-white palm frond paper lining the walls and saturated pops of teal accents transmitting a relaxed, island vibe throughout the room.

Be prepared to cozy up to the pretty bar while you wait for a table—a situation made infinitely more bearable with a Fresh Off the Boat cocktail, humming with rum, red bean, pandan and coconut milk. For dinner, don't miss Janice's Ribs—glossy and slow-roasted with notes of coffee, coconut beer and banana ketchup; or the delightfully crisp lumpia.

■ 5179 Telegraph Ave. (bet. 51st & 52nd Sts.), Oakland
℘ (510) 817-4169 — **WEB:** www.fobkitchen.com
■ Lunch Sat – Sun Dinner Wed – Fri   **PRICE:** $$

FUNKY ELEPHANT 🍴

Thai · *Simple*

& 🛖

Look completely past the strip mall location and head into this storefront for some of the more nuanced Thai cooking around. Pop music and colorful plastic tablecloths create a leisurely, relaxed mood, so place your order and head to a table on the patio. This kitchen is helmed by an ex-Hawker Fare chef, so expect spice blends and house-made curry pastes at the base of each dish.

The menu is small but mighty, with items that exude a playful spirit. Nowhere is this clearer than in the "party wings," which sound like a good time but in fact have great depth of flavor. The som tom is an idyllic toss-up of shredded green papaya as well as dried shrimp and long beans pounded together with fish sauce, sugar and lime for a dreamy bite of cool, sweet and heat.

▨ 1313 Ninth St. (bet. Camelia & Gilman Sts.), Berkeley

📞 (510) 356-4855 — **WEB:** www.funkyelephantthai.com

▨ Lunch & dinner Tue – Sun   **PRICE:** 🍴

GATHER 🍴

Californian · *Family*

& 🛖 🛏

With its heavily Californian bill of fare, repurposed décor and Berkeley clientele, Gather is a must for hordes of wholesome foodies of all ages. The aptly named hit serves busy professors during the bustling lunch hour before welcoming a more relaxed evening crowd, who come to sip at the bar and sup en plein air on the patio.

Pescatarians will delight in thick-cut toast spread with albacore tuna rillettes and topped with pan-fried broccoli di cicco, pickled radishes and potatoes, while vegetarians will find it hard to resist a hefty portion of arugula salad tossed with goat cheese, almonds, pomegranate and balsamic dressing. Be sure to try some dessert—specifically the luscious lime curd tart and its thick dollop of meringue. You won't be sorry.

▨ 2200 Oxford St. (at Allston Way), Berkeley

📞 (510) 809-0400 — **WEB:** www.gatherrestaurant.com

▨ Lunch & dinner daily   **PRICE:** $$

GREAT CHINA 😊
Chinese • Family

Chic enough for the style-savvy, cheap enough for students and authentic enough for local Chinese families, Great China is one of the few Berkeley restaurants everyone can (and does) agree on. Spicehounds should look elsewhere, as the food is somewhat mild, but the ingredients are higher quality than the average Chinese spot.

Kick things off with an aromatic bowl of hot and sour soup or an order of vegetarian egg rolls. Then sample generously portioned favorites like the sweet-and-spicy kung pao chicken; beautifully lacquered tea-smoked duck; or the beloved "double skin"—a platter of mung bean noodles tossed with pork, mushrooms, squid and a soy-mustard dressing. Only larger parties can reserve, so be aware there may be lines at peak hours.

■ 2190 Bancroft Way (at Fulton St.), Berkeley
✆ (510) 843-7996 — **WEB:** www.greatchinaberkeley.com
■ Lunch & dinner Wed – Mon   **PRICE: $$**

HOMESTEAD ⅃○
American • Rustic

&

If it wasn't housed in a beautiful Julia Morgan-designed building, this farm-to-table jewel would be defined by the enticing smells that engulf you upon entrance. It's a rustic space, full of large windows peering onto Piedmont Avenue and the jars of dry ingredients, pickling vegetables and cookbooks on the counter create an upscale country-kitchen demeanor.

The menu focuses on the best and freshest of local produce, such as yellowtail ceviche nestled in a tangy aguachile that is interspersed with bits of sweet corn and potato. Roasted duck breast boasts an intensely caramelized skin and is served in its own jus along with maitake mushrooms for a wonderfully woodsy touch. Craving a bright breakfast? Look no further than the homemade pastries or quiche.

■ 4029 Piedmont Ave. (bet. 40th & 41st Sts.), Oakland
✆ (510) 420-6962 — **WEB:** www.homesteadoakland.com
■ Dinner Tue – Sun   **PRICE: $$$**

IPPUKU 😋

Japanese • *Rustic*

◌ ⟵ ⟶

Can't swing a ticket to Tokyo? Dinner at Ippuku is the next best thing. With its low Japanese-style tables, extensive woodwork and enormous selection of sake and shochu, it feels like an authentic izakaya transplanted into a corner of downtown Berkeley. The low-profile entrance adds to the feeling that you've lucked upon a special dining secret—assuming you don't stroll right past it, that is.

Yakitori is the big draw here, with smoky, salty chicken thighs, necks, hearts and gizzards arriving fresh off the binchotan. Other excellent small plates include korokke, or golden-brown Dungeness crab croquettes, crisp on the outside and with a creamy interior, or yaki imo, caramelized white sweet potato with a sweet-and-salty glaze.

◼ 2130 Center St. (bet. Oxford St. & Shattuck Ave.), Berkeley
✆ (510) 665-1969 — **WEB:** www.ippukuberkeley.com
◼ Dinner Tue – Sun   **PRICE: $$**

IYASARE ⵏⵁ

Japanese • *Contemporary décor*

⟵ ⟶

Japanese techniques and Californian ingredients blend harmoniously at this charming Berkeley getaway, which flaunts a buzzing dining room and a delightful (heated) patio. Start the evening off right with an excellent (and reasonably priced) local wine on tap or a selection from the well-edited sake list. Then, order a variety of their exquisite small plates for sharing.

Every dish is a carefully crafted delight for the senses. Baby kale and mustard greens might not sound very Japanese, but they blend beautifully in a salad with Fuji apple and a sesame-miso dressing. The superb hamachi crudo is dusted with a sprinkle of wasabi snow and lemon-tamari oil, while fresh Manila clams arrive in an aromatic broth of sake, bacon, potatoes and earthy shiitakes.

◼ 1830 4th St. (bet. Hearst Ave. & Virginia St.), Berkeley
✆ (510) 845-8100 — **WEB:** www.iyasare-berkeley.com
◼ Lunch & dinner daily   **PRICE: $$$**

JUANITA & MAUDE

Contemporary • Rustic

Downtown Albany is abuzz about this chic arrival named for the mother and grandmother of Chef/co-owner Scott Eastman. It has all the accoutrements of a fancy local joint—think unique sculptures from an area artist, rustic plates and fun craft cocktails like the rum- and coconut-based White Picket Fence. And yet, this rookie eschews the tragically hip crowds for an easier, more communal feel.

The roving menu is heavy on odes to seasonal produce, like a succotash of summer squash, corn and cherry tomatoes topped with flaky halibut. You'll also be able to taste the chef's nine years of cooking at Berkeley favorite—Corso—in his perfect veal Bolognese sauce. Creative, well-balanced desserts like a creamy banana custard with coconut granita are menu musts.

■ 825 San Pablo Ave. (bet. Solano & Washington Aves.), Albany
✆ (510) 526-2233 — **WEB:** www.juanitaandmaude.com
■ Dinner Tue – Sat **PRICE: $$$**

LA MARCHA

Spanish • Cozy

This Spanish delight from the team behind acclaimed caterer Ñora Cocina Española does double duty as a mecca for both tapas and paella, offered in varieties from the traditional mixta (prawns, chicken, chorizo, garlic, peppers) to the inventive "tres cerditos" (three little pigs) featuring pork chorizo, shoulder and belly. The classic tapas are also out in full force—from grilled head-on garlic shrimp and salt cod croquettes with nutty romesco, to tortilla Española.

Located on busy San Pablo Avenue, the lively space offers enticements for groups of all sizes: foursomes can make the most of the sizable paellas, while a duo of happy hours offer discounts on wine at the L-shaped bar and a selection of free tapas, perfect for solo diners or couples.

■ 2026 San Pablo Ave. (bet. Addison St. & University Ave.), Berkeley
✆ (510) 269-7374 — **WEB:** www.lamarchaberkeley.com
■ Lunch Sat – Sun Dinner nightly **PRICE: $$**

MILLENNIUM 😳

Vegan • Rustic

 ♿ 🛆

After more than 20 years in San Francisco, this vegan paradise relocated to Oakland, where it's continuing to put out some of the most unique, delicious plant-based cuisine in the country. This rustic-chic space is laid-back and unfussy, with lots of dark wood, a patio for alfresco dining and a crowd of young families and professionals attended by welcoming servers.

While dedicated vegans are sure to swoon, even hardcore carnivores might reconsider the lifestyle after a dose of Chef/owner Eric Tucker's culinary creativity, showcased best on a five-course "Taste of Millennium" menu. Roasted pumpkin tamales with pumpkin seed pastor and cashew nut crema are knockouts, as are the crunchy king trumpet fritters with chili-persimmon jam.

▨ 5912 College Ave. (bet. Chabot Rd. & Harwood Ave.), Oakland
✆ (510) 735-9459 — **WEB:** www.millenniumrestaurant.com
▨ Lunch Sun Dinner nightly   **PRICE: $$**

MISS OLLIE'S 🍴

Caribbean • Rustic

♿

Even on the coldest (a.k.a. 50-degree) Oakland day, the soul-warming Caribbean cuisine at this little cutie will transport you to the islands. Barbados-born Chef/owner Sarah Kirnon named her restaurant after her grandmother, and it now serves up many of her childhood favorites, including plump, sweet grilled shrimp in a jerk marinade and some of the best fried chicken in town—with a flaky golden-brown crust.

Housed in the historic Swan's Market building in Old Oakland, Miss Ollie's has a particularly loyal crowd of lunchtime regulars, who sip tart ginger limeade as they liberally dose their food with the excellent Scotch bonnet hot sauce. With all the colorful art on the walls as well as a welcoming staff, it's a rustic slice of Caribbean soul.

▨ 901 Washington St. (bet. 9th & 10th Sts.), Oakland
✆ (510) 285-6188 — **WEB:** www.realmissolliesoakland.com
▨ Lunch & dinner Tue – Sat   **PRICE: $$**

NIDO ♚○
Mexican • Rustic

♿ 🛋

The industrial area west of the I-880 freeway doesn't boast many good restaurants, but this hidden Mexican is an exception. Complete with a hip reclaimed-wood décor and local clientele of suits as well as trendy foodies, it's definitely a cut above a taqueria in terms of quality and price, with fresher, lighter food in smaller—but by no means stingy—portions.

Lunchtime tacos feature handmade corn tortillas perhaps piled high with carnitas and salsa verde, chamoy-glazed grilled chicken or braised beef with chile arbol salsa. Dinner might bring carne asada with black beans and salsa de chile cascabel, or pork pibil panuchos with pickled onion and sikil pak. With a truly relaxed vibe and home-cooked feel to the food, it's worth the extra effort to drop by.

■ 444 Oak St. (at 5th St.), Oakland
☎ (510) 444-6436 — **WEB:** www.nidooakland.com
■ Lunch Tue – Sun Dinner Tue – Sat   PRICE: $$

NYUM BAI 😊
Cambodian • Simple

♿ 🏖

Thanks to the support of crowd-funding, Nyum Bai started as a pop-up but grew into this cozy, sun-filled local jewel. Inside, pastel colors and wood accents fashion a retro vibe. Outside, find a beer garden of sorts that is filled with picnic tables for soaking in the sunshine while filling up on Cambodian food.

Chef/owner Nite Yun puts her signature spin on traditional Khmer dishes that layer tangy, sweet, tart and spicy flavors. Some items are so popular that they might run out early, especially the amok—a fish soufflé made with coconut milk. Others like kuy teav cha, a stir-fry of chewy noodles with tamarind, soy, egg and palm sugar, are sure to satisfy. Finish on a sweet note with nom krouch rolled in palm sugar and presented piping-hot from the fryer.

■ 3340 E. 12th St. Ste. 11 (bet. 33rd & 34th Aves.), Oakland
☎ (510) 500-3338 — **WEB:** www.nyumbai.com
■ Lunch & dinner Tue – Sun   PRICE: ᢒ

RANGE LIFE

Californian • Trendy

Livermore may not seem like a go-to spot for inventive California cuisine, but this charming newbie from husband-and-wife chefs Bill and Sarah Niles would be the envy of any city slicker. The rustic space with big arched windows and plenty of succulents screams «hipster hotspot,» but few big-city restaurants can offer such an enthusiastic, passionate staff and friendly local crowd.

Order up a refreshing tequila-lime "Range Water" and dive into the appealing menu of beautifully plated bites like duck liver toast with roasted cherries on chewy house-made bread; flavorful artichoke and chickpea curry; as well as rich and creamy chocolate budino with cinnamon whipped cream. A jar of house-made fermented chili sauce from the on-site market makes a delicious souvenir.

▦ 2160 Railroad Ave. (bet. K St. & Livermore Ave.), Livermore
✆ (925) 583-5370 — **WEB:** www.rangelifelivermore.com
▦ Dinner Wed – Mon   **PRICE: $$**

RIVOLI

Californian • Neighborhood

Northern Californian cooking with a hint of regional Americana is the main draw at this charmer on the Albany-Berkeley border. It's popular with smartly dressed couples, who come here to savor items like an artfully presented arugula salad with winter citrus, Marcona almonds and avocado, or a highbrow riff on gumbo with chicken confit and andouille sausage perched atop Carolina rice. The excellent gâteau Basque, a caramelized wedge of creamy custard, is a must-order.

Set in an adorable cottage, Rivoli's dining room boasts enormous picture windows overlooking a lush "secret" garden blooming with tender fronds, camellias and magnolia trees. Smartly serviced by an engaging waitstaff, the greenery is a nice contrast to the crisp, white-linen tables.

▦ 1539 Solano Ave. (bet. Neilson St. & Peralta Ave.), Berkeley
✆ (510) 526-2542 — **WEB:** www.rivolirestaurant.com
▦ Dinner nightly   **PRICE: $$**

SHAKEWELL 🍴

Mediterranean • Contemporary décor

♿ 🛋️

This trendy eatery, the brainchild of Top Chef alums Jen Biesty and Tim Nugent, was made for sipping and supping. Outfitted with a bar up front and several dining nooks on either side of a central walkway, Shakewell keeps things Medi-chic with Moorish accents, reclaimed wood and organic elements.

Service is particularly warm, and an even warmer teal-green wood-fired oven in the back turns out deliciously smoked items like crisp falafel served with romesco. A summer squash salad with heirloom tomatoes, fried bread and feta offers an inspired blend of Greek and Tuscan flavors, and bomba rice with braised fennel, piperade, chicken and prawns is a fluffy take on paella. Finish with the caramel syrup-spiked crema Catalana for a flavorful finale.

▦ 3407 Lakeshore Ave. (bet. Longridge & Trestle Glen Rds.), Oakland

☏ (510) 251-0329 — **WEB:** www.shakewelloakland.com

▦ Lunch Wed – Sun Dinner Tue – Sun   **PRICE: $$**

SOBA ICHI 😊

Japanese • Minimalist

♿ ⛩️

It takes effort to visit this remarkable little noodle bar, as it's located in deep industrial West Oakland, open only at lunchtime and waits can run upwards of 45 minutes—if the designated 100 daily orders of soba don't sell out first. But rest easy as this delay is happily passed with a drink in the sunny garden, and the warm hospitality rewards the hassle.

Handmade Japanese noodles come in two varieties: 100% or 80% buckwheat, served hot or cold in dishes like tenseiro, chewy cold soba with feather-light tempura shrimp and vegetables alongside a flavorful dipping sauce. For something warmer, kamo nanban, a rich broth with tender slices of duck breast, hits the spot. Be sure to sample the sake, served here in the traditional "overflowing" style.

▦ 2311A Magnolia St. (bet. 24th St. & Grand Ave.), Oakland

☏ (510) 465-1969 — **WEB:** www.sobaichioakland.com

▦ Lunch Sat – Sun Dinner Wed – Sun   **PRICE: $$**

TACOS SINALOA ¶○
Mexican • Taqueria

East Oakland's taco truck titans have put it in park with this Berkeley taqueria, which is making its name as a Mexican fave in the Bay Area. Sinaloa's logo is a smiling shrimp holding a taco, so your first choice may be the top-notch shrimp tacos (full of plump, succulent, spice-rubbed shrimp). However, rest assured that there's more in store: smoky carnitas with fiery red chili salsa, tender roast chicken and beautifully caramelized al pastor. For the adventurous eater, there's tripe, suadero and pork stomach, too.

Like the truck, this operation is no frills: pay at the counter, grab some plastic utensils and seat yourself. But with food this good—and prices so low that even a penniless Cal student can afford to dine—who needs frills?

▨ 2384 Telegraph Ave. (bet. Channing Way & Durant Ave.), Berkeley
☏ (510) 665-7895 — **WEB:** N/A
▨ Lunch & dinner daily   **PRICE:** ⊜

TACUBAYA ¶○
Mexican • Taqueria

& ⛩

Tacubaya is so beloved by locals that they moved a few doors down to an expanded space in an attempt to accommodate its enlarged fan base. This taqueria in the Berkeley shopping complex is where families flock to grab a bite during errands. In fact, there is a perpetual line of patrons ordering limeade at the counter and claiming seats in the festive dining room (look out for the hanging pink papel picados) or sunny front patio.

They are here for chilaquiles and churros at breakfast; then transition into chorizo-and-potato sopes with black bean purée at lunch. Other standbys unveil beef enchiladas doused in a smoky guajillo-tomatillo sauce and covered with melted cheese; followed by tamales de verdure bested with spicy salsa verde and cool crema.

▨ 1782 4th St. (bet. Hearst Ave. & Virginia St.), Berkeley
☏ (510) 525-5160 — **WEB:** www.tacubaya.net
▨ Lunch & dinner daily   **PRICE:** ⊜

TENI EAST KITCHEN 😊

Burmese • Contemporary décor

&

Burmese food with a California spin is on the menu at Chef/owner Tiyo Shibabaw's cheery spot in Temescal, where the tea leaf salads come with kale and there's plenty of flaky, golden roti bread to go around. Everything is affordable here, but the lunchtime specials are an especially good deal: a hot and flavorful entrée (like spicy coconut curry chicken with rice noodles) and a fresh salad—go for the pea shoots topped with radishes and fried garlic in a turmeric dressing.

Bright and airy, with exposed wooden beams on the ceiling, Teni draws a crowd of hipsters of all ages. Its dining room can certainly fill up fast at prime hours, but it's worth the wait for food that's fresh, flavorful, unfussy and generously portioned.

 4015 Broadway (bet. 40 & 41 Sts.), Oakland
℘ (510) 597-1860 — **WEB:** www.tenieastkitchen.com
Lunch & dinner daily   **PRICE:** 😊

THAI HOUSE 😊

Thai • Elegant

🏕 🍽

Many a warm evening has been spent on the garden patio of this fantastic Thai restaurant, where potted plants create a leafy retreat. Whether you're dining alfresco or tucked inside the tiny, colorful bungalow, you can be assured of a warm welcome and boldly flavorful food—a secret that's out with the locals, making this house a packed one from noon to night.

The consistently outstanding menu makes it hard for one to go wrong, but you can't miss with the creamy red pumpkin curry, full of tender scallops, prawns and perfectly balanced notes of sweet, spicy, salty and sour. Other showstoppers may reveal pad prik khing, chicken in a spicy peanut-tamarind sauce or the aromatic basil tofu, jam-packed with fresh vegetables, chili and garlic.

254 Rose Ave. (bet. Diablo Rd. & Linda Mesa Ave.), Danville
℘ (925) 820-0635 — **WEB:** www.thaihouseca.com
Lunch Mon – Fri Dinner nightly   **PRICE:** $$

VIK'S CHAAT 🍴

Indian • Family

&

This bright orange and yellow building looks big enough to be a warehouse, which makes sense as the inside is not only a counter-service restaurant but also a market. Its namesake chaat may be the star here, but lunch specials are a fantastic bargain. For $15, you can get perfectly tender tandoori chicken with a mouthwatering smoky char, served alongside basmati rice, dal, raita and papadum. Family-friendly and casual, this Indo canteen seems to attract everyone with its excellent chaat, authentic flavors and breads—especially the fried and puffy bhature ideal for sopping up spicy chole. A glass case filled with colorful sweets reminds everyone to save room for dessert.

The kitchen closes early at dinner, so unless you're an early bird, go for lunch.

■ 2390 Fourth St. (at Channing Way), Berkeley
✆ (510) 644-4412 — **WEB:** www.vikschaat.com
■ Lunch Sun – Sat Dinner Fri – Sun   **PRICE:** ∞

WOOD TAVERN 😊

American • Contemporary décor

&

There's always a crowd at this lively neighborhood standby, where groups of friends, parents on date night and trendy couples congregate for drinks at the copper-topped bar. Flanked by organic groceries, indie bookstores and antique shops, its surroundings speak of peace, weaving a pleasantly bohemian spell that captivates both regulars and newcomers alike.

Rustic American cooking with a hint of Italian flair dominates this tavern's menu, and the local Belfiore burrata—served atop diced pears, honey-cashew cream and peppery arugula—is a surefire hit. A bit of Calabrian chili adds a welcoming bit of heat to the otherwise earthy pan-roasted Maple Leaf duck breast, while the warm mini Bundt cake bursts with chocolate goodness.

■ 6317 College Ave. (bet. Alcatraz Ave. & 63rd St.), Oakland
✆ (510) 654-6607 — **WEB:** www.woodtavern.net
■ Lunch Mon – Sat Dinner nightly   **PRICE:** $$

PENINSULA

PENINSULA

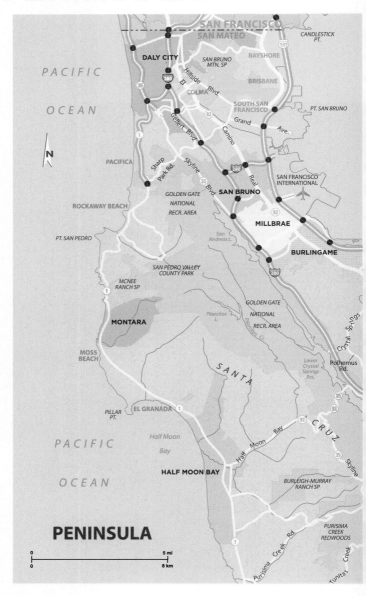

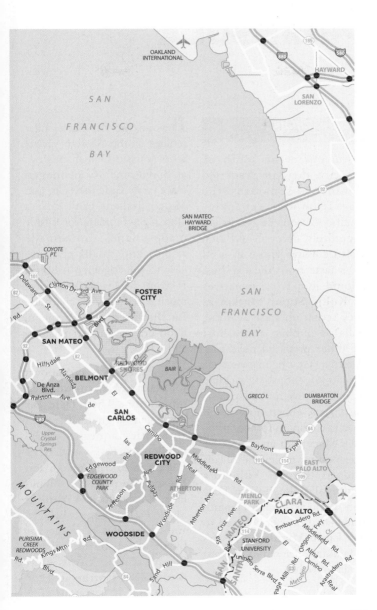

EATING IN...
PENINSULA

Situated to the south of the city, the San Francisco Peninsula separates the Bay from the expansive Pacific Ocean. It boasts an incredibly diverse and rich Asian culture. Those in need of a taste from the Far East should join Korean natives at **Kukje Super Market** as they scoop up fresh seafood, rolls of gimbap and a host of other prepared delicacies. Alternatively, one may practice the art of chopstick wielding at one of the many Japanese sushi bars, ramen houses and izakayas. Filipino foodies tickle their fancy with an impressive selection of traditional breads and pastries at **Valerio's Tropical Bakeshop** in Daly City. Fittingly set in a Filipino-dominated quarter referred to as "**Little Manila**," Valerio's is famously revered as the best bakery around.

Beyond the Far East, sugar junkies of the Western variety savor classic Danish pastries at Burlingame's **Copenhagen Bakery & Cafe**. Over in San Mateo, Italians can't miss a stop at **pasta pasta** for freshly made shapes, homemade sauces and salads that are easy to put together at home. If your domestic skills leave much to be desired, charming **La Biscotteria** has premium, hand-crafted Italian pastries and cookies.

The Peninsula is also known for its large Mexican-American population. Their taste for home can be gratified at such authentic taquerias as **El Grullense** in Redwood City; **El Palenque** in San Mateo; and **Mexcal Taqueria** in Menlo Park. Divey **Back A Yard** in Menlo Park is eternally beloved among foodies yearning for flavorful Caribbean cuisine. Pescetarians know that **Barbara's Fishtrap** in Half Moon Bay is a sought-after

"catch" for fish 'n chips by the harbor, whereas pig trumps fish at **Gorilla Barbeque**. Here, fat-frilled pork ribs are all the rage, especially when served out of an orange railroad car parked on Cabrillo Highway in Pacifica.

SUMMER'S BOUNTY

Motivated home chefs stop by **Draeger's Market** in San Mateo to pick up some wine and cheese for dinner, while **Wursthall Restaurant & Bierhaus** brings a festive spirit and a bevy of German beer and bites to this tech center. Others revel in the riot of Japanese treats at **Suruki Supermarket**.

Half Moon Bay is a coastal city big on sustainable produce. Here, residents load up on local fruits and vegetables from one of the many roadside stands on Route 92. Find them also scanning the bounty at **Coastside Farmer's Market**, which has been known to unveil such Pescadero treasures as **Harley Farms** goat cheese, as well as fresh, organic eggs from **Early Bird Ranch**.

ALL SPICE 🍴○
International · Cozy

Like a bracelet glittering with different jewels, All Spice is home to a bevy of vibrant dining rooms, made extra colorful with artwork and sparkling chandeliers. It's a delightful blend of old-school charm and contemporary verve that appeals to a sophisticated crowd. They're usually here to catch up with friends or celebrate a birthday.

This kitchen offers a variety of creative selections on both the à la carte and tasting menus, which spin to highlight the seasons. Chilled butternut squash soup in a shot glass makes a soigné amuse-bouche and is a delicious way to start a meal; while carrot-date fritters with charred eggplant and mango with carrot curls is accompanied by toasted almonds as well as smoked date chutney for added enrichment.

▓ 1602 El Camino Real (bet. Barneson & Borel Aves.), San Mateo
℘ (650) 627-4303 — WEB: www.allspicerestaurant.com
▓ Lunch Tue – Fri Dinner Tue – Sat   PRICE: $$$

BROADWAY MASALA 🍴○
Indian · Contemporary décor

&

Set in the heart of downtown Redwood City, this contemporary Indian boasts great views onto the main thoroughfare it's named for. In all likelihood though, you might be distracted by what's on your plate, as these traditional dishes are executed to precision. Begin with crispy potato-and-pea samosas that exude a nice kick of spice, before moving on to smoky butter chicken served atop basmati rice. Even the warm and flaky naan is an outstanding delight.

While service is distracted, it's hard to argue with a place that has such hefty portions for such reasonable prices. Lunch specials are a steal, and the kitchen does a booming takeout business. Adventurous diners may also enjoy such fusion items as chapati lamb tacos or Cajun-spiced chicken tikka masala.

▓ 2397 Broadway (at Winslow St.), Redwood City
℘ (650) 369-9000 — WEB: www.broadwaymasala.net
▓ Lunch & dinner daily   PRICE: $$

CAFÉ CAPISTRANO 🍴
Mexican • Family

Chef/owner Arturo Mul grew up on the Yucatán peninsula, and the traditional Mayan dishes of his youth are now the backbone of this cute café in the heart of Half Moon Bay. Housed in an older home surrounded by gardens and a small side deck, this retreat is warm, inviting and, to the delight of local families, off most tourists' radars.

Start with a plate of fried panuchos (stuffed with earthy black bean purée and topped with achiote-marinated tender pulled chicken). Then dig into the Mayan pork adobo served with fresh salsa, guacamole, a lightly pickled coleslaw and crema. But, save room for the true star of the show—grilled red snapper coupled with warm tortillas for wrapping, as well as queso for rich and creamy goodness.

▪ 523 Church St. (at Miramontes St.), Half Moon Bay
☏ (650) 726-7699 — **WEB:** N/A
▪ Lunch & dinner daily   **PRICE:** 🍽

CAMPER 🍴
Californian • Contemporary décor

This sweet little Menlo Park charmer arrives courtesy of Chef/partner Greg Kuzia-Carmel. The vibe inside is as welcoming as it gets—the light-flooded space is strewn with homey throw pillows, and the crowd is a sophisticated mix of professionals and families (the kids' menu looks delicious enough to tempt an adult).

The Californian fare is refined, creative and seasonal, so anticipate the likes of charcuterie and oysters, followed by handmade pastas (like a sweet corn agnolotti with bacon). Their hearty mains are also quite the rage, and may include warming Camper Chicken served with basmati rice and fresh greens. Be sure to save room for the house cornbread—an otherworldly cake-like concoction, served with perfectly tempered honey butter.

▪ 898 Santa Cruz Ave. (at University Dr.), Menlo Park
☏ (650) 321-8980 — **WEB:** www.campermp.com
▪ Lunch Tue – Fri Dinner Mon – Sat   **PRICE:** $$

FLEA ST. CAFE ⅊○

Contemporary • Cozy

This classic "café" retains the feeling of being in a house, with dining areas distributed throughout. Interesting artwork adorns each of these rooms, simply adding to the sense of intimacy, not unlike the warm and inviting front bar area, filled with friendly banter and soft tunes.

The team ensures that each item from this kitchen is well conceived and adheres to California's farm-to-table ethos. Everything on this seasonally driven menu strives to emphasize freshness, starting with the warm and buttery biscuits that welcome you to your table. Don't miss the shell bean soup featuring a braised tomato broth complete with summery flavors. On Thursday through Saturday evenings, explore The Oysterette—a changing carte of oysters served at the bar.

■ 3607 Alameda de las Pulgas (at Avy Ave.), Menlo Park
℘ (650) 854-1226 — **WEB:** www.cooleatz.com
■ Dinner Tue – Sat   **PRICE: $$**

GINTEI ⅊○

Japanese • Minimalist

San Bruno's reputation as a dining wasteland is due for a re-evaluation thanks to this sleek and stylish sushi spot, whose offerings can hang with the best in San Francisco. Bright and contemporary, with dramatic pressed-tin ceilings and a coveted eight-seat counter, it's known as a reservations-required must for omakase enthusiasts, with deeply hospitable service.

Fans of nigiri should make a beeline for the chef's selection, but the more discerning palate will revel in market specials like the silky Hokkaido scallops, sweet and succulent live spot prawns (with the traditional deep-fried heads alongside) as well as firm yet tender octopus. Everything is minimally dressed here—all the better to accentuate the fish's outstanding quality.

■ 235 El Camino Real
(bet. Crystal Springs Rd. & San Felipe Ave.), San Bruno
℘ (650) 636-4135 — **WEB:** www.gintei.co
■ Lunch Tue – Fri Dinner Tue – Sun   **PRICE: $$**

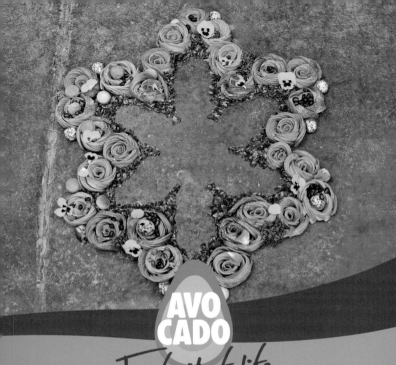

HONG KONG FLOWER LOUNGE ⊘

Chinese • Family

♿ ⛵ 🍴 🈂️

Generations of dim sum diehards have patronized this palace of pork buns, where a small army of servers will surround you with carts from the moment you take your seat. They bear innumerable delights: rich barbecue pork belly with crispy skin, pan-fried pork-and-chive wontons steamed to order and doused in oyster sauce, delicate vegetable dumplings and a best-in-class baked egg custard bun. Evenings are a bit more sedate, emphasizing Cantonese seafood straight from the on-site tanks.

As with all dim sum spots, the early bird gets the best selection (and avoids the non-negotiable weekend waits). Thankfully, the super-central Millbrae location, towering over El Camino Real, boasts plenty of parking—and a machine-like staff that knows how to pack them in.

▨ 51 Millbrae Ave. (at El Camino Real), Millbrae
☎ (650) 692-6666 — **WEB:** www.mayflower-seafood.com
▨ Lunch & dinner daily   PRICE: $$

KABUL ⊘

Afghan • Family

♿

Fans of Afghan cuisine flock from miles around to this homestyle spot in San Carlos, tucked away in a deceptively large space within a modest shopping plaza. Kabul's walls are festooned with deep red tapestries and other Afghan embroidery, and even on weekday nights it fills up with local families. There's even a semi-private side dining room for big groups.

The friendly staff is happy to suggest favorite dishes, from smoky chicken and lamb kebabs over spiced basmati rice to sweet, fork-tender sautéed pumpkin served with garlicky yogurt sauce and fluffy flatbread. And though everything comes in generous portions, you'll want to save room for the firnee, a sweet milk pudding flavored with cardamom and rosewater and topped with pistachios.

▨ 135 El Camino Real (bet. F & Holly Sts.), San Carlos
☎ (650) 594-2840 — **WEB:** www.kabulcuisine.co
▨ Lunch Mon – Fri Dinner nightly   PRICE: $$

KOI PALACE ⫶◯

Chinese • Elegant

Long regarded as one of the Bay Area's best spots for dim sum, Koi Palace continues to earn its serious waits (guaranteed on weekends, and common at weekday lunch). The dining room is a step up from its competition, with shallow koi ponds weaving between tables, high ceilings and huge tables to accommodate the Chinese-American families celebrating big occasions.

They come to share plates of perfectly lacquered, smoky-salty roasted suckling pig or sticky rice noodle rolls encasing plump shrimp, minced ginger and sesame oil. Not far behind, find lotus leaves stuffed with glutinous rice, dried scallop and roast pork, as well as big pots of jasmine tea. Save room for desserts like the fluffy almond cream-steamed buns and flaky, caramelized custard tarts.

■ 365 Gellert Blvd. (bet. Hickey & Serramonte Blvds.), Daly City
✆ (650) 992-9000 — **WEB:** www.koipalace.com
■ Lunch & dinner daily   PRICE: $$

LA COSTANERA ⫶◯

Peruvian • Contemporary décor

Set atop one of the most beautiful perches in the entire Bay Area, this bungalow boasts a gorgeous patio and a dining room that's walled with windows.

While the panoramas are amazing—endless ocean, spectacular sunsets and even frolicking dolphins if you're lucky—so are the boldly flavored plates produced by Chef Carlos Altamirano and his team. Cebiche pescado bathed in leche de tigre is perhaps the best way to experience Peru's national dish, while succulent langostino crocantes served over silky potatoes, or herb-marinated pollo salvaje accompanied by fried yuca are other treasures worth devouring.

Be sure to sample the creative cocktails. Alternatively, try a delicious and refreshing chicha morada, which is safer for the drive home.

■ 8150 Cabrillo Hwy. (bet. 1st & 2nd Sts.), Montara
✆ (650) 728-1600 — **WEB:** www.lacostanerarestaurant.com
■ Dinner Tue – Sun   PRICE: $$$

LA VIGA 🍴

Mexican · Cozy

&

Named after Mexico City's massive seafood market, La Viga is a Redwood City favorite for oceanic fare with a Latin twist. Wedged between an industrial area and downtown, the basic but cheerful dining room draws both blue- and white-collar workers for heaping tacos— soft white corn tortillas stuffed with fried snapper fillet, cabbage and chipotle crema; or crisp prawns with tomatillo-garlic sauce and pico de gallo.

At the dinner hour, residents stream in for the famed tallarines con mariscos, a sizable mound of al dente fideos studded with pristine seafood cooked in a spicy tomato sauce. With such fresh ingredients and bold flavors, the low prices and generous portions are particularly pleasing. Don't forget to leave room for a delicate flan to finish.

■ 1772 Broadway (bet. Beech & Maple Sts.), Redwood City
✆ (650) 679-8141 — **WEB:** www.lavigaseafood.com
■ Lunch & dinner daily   **PRICE: $$**

NAVIO 🍴

Californian · Contemporary décor

Nestled inside the luxe Ritz-Carlton, Half Moon Bay, Navio is blessed with a classic northern California setting. Whether you're fresh off the course or arriving just for dinner, settle in with a ruby-red Sassamanash punch before admiring the emerald-green links and crashing surf. Golden sunsets are ripe for romantics, but you're almost as likely to find families with young children as lovebirds here.

Just like the coastal décor that is both polished and casual, this kitchen takes classic Americana and ramps it up. Seafood is underlined—diver scallops with a red wine sauce and boudin basque atop seared pear circles are particularly good. But that spaghetti alla chitarra, punctuated by the delicate sweetness of Dungeness crab, is an absolute show-stealer.

■ 1 Miramontes Point Rd. (at Hwy. 1), Half Moon Bay
✆ (650) 712-7000 — **WEB:** www.ritzcarlton.com
■ Lunch Sat – Sun Dinner Wed – Sun   **PRICE: $$$$**

MADERA ✿

Contemporary • Trendy

As evidenced by all those Teslas parked out front, this is a swanky spot for fine dining in the Rosewood Sand Hill hotel. The grand open kitchen, roaring fireplace and large outdoor patio complete with gorgeous views of the Santa Cruz mountains draw a moneyed crowd of local techies.

While its location may mean it is open for three meals a day, come for dinner to taste this kitchen's ambition and pure talent. The cuisine is contemporary, thoughtfully composed with seasonal ingredients and even surprising at times. An excellent risotto sings with the flavors of roasted butternut squash, Périgord black truffles, airy Lacinato kale chips and the unexpected, wondrous touch of finger lime. The kitchen also flaunts its dexterity in three preparations of guinea hen, including its tender breast meat with crackling-crisp skin, sliced thigh and excellent springy sausages accompanied by charred peaches bursting with sweetness, pickled chanterelles, toasted pecans and green onion soubise.

Desserts are fun, delicious and do not hold back, especially the insanely rich peanut butter and black sesame parfait, layered as fudgy brownie, rich ganache, mousse and brittle in a glass goblet.

🔲 2825 Sand Hill Rd. (at I-280), Menlo Park
📞 (650) 561-1540 — **WEB:** www.maderasandhill.com
🔲 Lunch & dinner daily   PRICE: $$$

NEW ENGLAND LOBSTER EATERY 🍴○

Seafood • Simple

♿ ☂

You'll know your meal is fresh at this Peninsula palace of seafood, where flat-screen TVs showcase the bevy of crustaceans in their huge seawater-holding tanks. Set in an industrial warehouse, this eatery is both a fish market and a counter-service restaurant—complete with a nautical theme, picnic tables indoors and out and a happy crowd of young and old diners donning lobster bibs.

Kick things off with the justifiably beloved lobster-corn chowder, thick with sweet, succulent meat in a rich and creamy—but not overly heavy—stock. (For dedicated fans, frozen to-go quarts are offered.) Then go for broke with the outstanding lobster roll, lightly dressed with mayo on a fluffy, buttery roll and accompanied by excellent house-made potato chips.

▦ 824 Cowan Rd. (off Old Bayshore Hwy.), Burlingame
☏ (650) 443-1559 — **WEB:** www.newenglandlobster.net
▦ Lunch & dinner daily   **PRICE: $$**

PASTA MOON 🍴○

Italian • Trattoria

♿ ☐

One of Half Moon Bay's most popular restaurants, Pasta Moon is always packed to the gills with locals and tourists filling up on massive portions of hearty Italian-American fare. With its vaulted ceilings and multiple intimate dining rooms, it's a hit among diners of all ages, especially those seated at tables with a view of the lovely side garden.

House-made pastas steal the show, with tempting options like the delicate 30-layer lasagna filled with ricotta, parmesan and house Sicilian sausage (even the half portion is huge). A grilled pork chop stuffed with peaches, pancetta and caramelized onions then arrives with mascarpone mashed potatoes. The butterscotch pudding (with shards of Ghirardelli chocolate, natch) is bound to send you over the moon.

▦ 315 Main St. (bet. Mill St. & Stone Pine Rd.), Half Moon Bay
☏ (650) 726-5125 — **WEB:** www.pastamoon.com
▦ Lunch & dinner daily   **PRICE: $$**

PAUSA ⊛

Italian • Contemporary décor

Come to this San Mateo sweetie for authentic Italian eats, where Chef/co-owner Andrea Giuliani dishes up the cuisine of his native Veneto. Thanks to the modern space and late hours (by San Mateo standards, at least), it's a big draw for the growing crowds of young tech types in town.

The dining room has a view of the charcuterie-aging room and those enticing cured meats like delicate, fennel-flecked finocchiona or exceptional pork ciccioli terrine. The wood-fired Neapolitan pizzas are equally strong—try the porchetta variation, topped with gorgonzola and radicchio. And of course, the pasta doesn't disappoint either: seafood is a specialty of Veneto, and their perciatelli with a tomato-flecked shrimp and octopus ragù is downright perfect.

◼ 223 E. 4th Ave. (bet. B St. & Ellsworth Ave.), San Mateo
☏ (650) 375-0818 — **WEB:** www.pausasanmateo.com
◼ Lunch Mon – Fri Dinner nightly   **PRICE: $$**

PAZZO ⅋○

Pizza • Family

New Haven transplants longing for the region's signature chewy, charred apizza will find a taste of home at this San Carlos jewel, which churns out authentically blistered pies. Keep it traditional with red sauce topped with house-made fennel sausage and cremini mushrooms. Or go slightly Californian with the garlicky asparagus pie, draped with creamy crescenza cheese.

Pazzo (Italian for "crazy") is anything but, thanks to a relaxed, family-friendly vibe. Kids of all ages will delight in the back counter, with a great view of the chef slipping pizzas into the cherry-red, wood-fired oven. And don't sleep through the house-made pastas: pillowy ricotta gnocchi, tucked into a lemony mascarpone and artichoke sauce, is good enough to steal the show.

◼ 1179 Laurel St. (bet. Brittan & Greenwood Aves.), San Carlos
☏ (650) 591-1075 — **WEB:** www.pazzosancarlos.com
◼ Dinner Tue – Sat   **PRICE: $$**

RAMEN DOJO 🍴

Japanese • Simple

The two-hour lines may have died down, but a 40-minute wait on the sidewalk is still standard at this noodle hot spot. The interior, when you finally reach it, is utterly spare—the better to showcase steaming bowls of tasty and satisfying soup. Customize your broth (soy sauce, garlic pork, soybean), spiciness and toppings (like spicy cod roe and kikurage mushrooms), then dive in.

The ramen arrives in minutes, loaded with the standard fried garlic cloves, hard-boiled quail egg, scallion, chili and two slices of roast pork. Your job is to slurp the chewy, delicious noodles (and maybe some seaweed salad or edamame), then hit the road—the hyper-efficient staff needs to keep the line moving, after all. But for one of the best bowls in town, it's worth it.

▧ 805 S. B St. (bet. 8th & 9th Aves.), San Mateo
☏ (650) 401-6568 — **WEB:** N/A
▧ Lunch & dinner Wed – Mon   **PRICE:** ⬡

ROYAL FEAST 😀

Chinese • Family

♿

You'll dine like royalty at this Millbrae retreat, which offers an array of Chinese delicacies rarely seen outside banquet menus. Helmed by Chef Zongyi Liu, a onetime Bocuse d'Or China competitor, the décor here is light on regal glamour, opting for a simple, spare interior with well-spaced tables. But the menu teems with sought-after items, from abalone to sea cucumber.

Dishes here run the gamut of China's eight great cuisines, with a special emphasis on spicy Sichuan food like white fish in a rich chili-laced broth, or steamed chicken dusted with peppercorns and served in a pool of chili oil. For those seeking milder flavors, the shredded pork in a sweet garlic sauce, as well as fluffy pan-fried sesame cakes, make for ideal choices.

▧ 148 El Camino Real (bet. Linden & Serra Aves.), Millbrae
☏ (650) 692-3388 — **WEB:** www.royalfeastus.com
▧ Lunch & dinner daily   **PRICE:** $$

RASA ✿

Indian • Contemporary décor

&

In a bustling tech corridor that's also home to Indian expats with high culinary standards, Rasa has managed to find the perfect middle ground. No-joke dishes that aren't toned down for Western palates cater to both software execs and date-night couples, and though the bi-level space boasts a sleek, minimalist-mod décor with bright splashes of orange, stylish pendant lights and dark wood fittings, the focus here is on food.

The elevated South Indian cuisine draws added elegance from superb ingredients and inventive presentations, like fluffy "Bombay slider" buns stuffed with well-seasoned crushed potatoes and drizzled with spicy, smoky "gunpowder" butter. The dosas are appropriately paper-thin and shatteringly crisp, while uttapams topped with peppers and ground masala lamb are earthy and delicate—but watch out for the punch from the accompanying ghost pepper chutney.

A serious spread could be made just out of Rasa's excellent small plates, but for bigger appetites, the flaky white fish moilee, stewed in a creamy coconut curry, is rich and satisfying. No one should skip the cardamom brûlée for dessert: equal parts bread pudding and crème brûlée, it's dizzyingly delicious.

▪ 209 Park Rd. (bet. Burlingame & Howard Aves.), Burlingame
☏ (650) 340-7272 — **WEB:** www.rasaindian.com
▪ Lunch & dinner daily   PRICE: $$

SHALIZAAR ⅡО
Persian • Elegant

A perennial favorite for Persian flavors, Shalizaar is friendly, charming and authentic. Lunchtime draws a large business crowd, while dinners cater to couples on dates. The upscale space features chandeliers, linen-topped tables, Persian carpets and walls of framed windows that flood everything with light.

Meals here are always a pleasure, thanks to the high quality of every ingredient. Try the signature koobideh, smoky ground beef and chicken kebabs served with char-broiled whole tomatoes and rice. Or, tuck into baghali polo, fork-tender lamb shank over bright green rice studded with dill and young fava beans. For dessert, take the friendly servers' advice and order the zoolbia bamieh, sticky-crisp squiggles of fried cake soaked in rosewater syrup.

▩ 300 El Camino Real (bet. Anita & Belmont Aves.), Belmont
✆ (650) 596-9000 — **WEB:** www.shalizaar.com
▩ Lunch & dinner daily   **PRICE: $$**

SICHUAN CHONG QING ⅡО
Chinese • Family

The medical staff at the Mills Health Center take plenty of heat in an average day, but that doesn't stop them from piling into this compact neighboring Sichuan restaurant for their fix of spicy chili oil and numbing peppercorns. Both ingredients are featured in the crispy Chong Qing chicken and shrimp, each laden with chili peppers (be sure to watch out for shards of bone in the cleaver-chopped chicken).

Skip the mild Mandarin dishes and stick to the house's fiery specialties, like the nutty, smoky cumin lamb with sliced onion, still more chilies and chili oil. Aside from a few contemporary touches, the décor isn't newsworthy and the staff is more efficient than engaging—but you'll likely be too busy enjoying the flavor-packed food to mind.

▩ 211 S. San Mateo Dr. (bet. 2nd & 3rd Aves.), San Mateo
✆ (650) 343-1144 — **WEB:** N/A
▩ Lunch & dinner Tue – Sun   **PRICE: $$**

SPICY HEAVEN ¡O
Chinese • Simple

The surroundings are bare enough to qualify as purgatory, but for lovers of spicy fare, this humble eatery in downtown San Mateo is worthy of ascension into the astral plane. In an area with plenty of Sichuan dining options, the mostly Chinese-speaking crowd demands that the flavors are authentic and on point.

As is typical, most dishes here revolve around the interplay of tingling peppercorns, mouth-scorching dried chilies and luscious chili oil, from the delicate pork wontons topped with crushed peanuts and scallions to the silky fish fillets and firm tofu swimming in a delectable bright-red and fiery oil bath. Calm your palate with bites of garlicky sautéed water spinach. Then dive in for another chopstick-full of the spicy, tangy chili pork.

■ 35 E. 3rd Ave. (bet. El Camino Real & San Mateo Dr.), San Mateo
℘ (650) 781-3977 — **WEB:** www.spicyheavensanmateo.com
■ Lunch & dinner Thu – Tue   **PRICE: $$**

SWEET BASIL ¡O
Thai • Simple

&

Set near a charming bayside walking and biking trail on Foster City's perimeter, Sweet Basil makes for a great meal after a leisurely stroll or strenuous ride. The space is snazzy and contemporary-looking with bamboo floors and colorful hanging lights, but the vibe is casual with the staff hustling to serve the daytime rush of office workers as well as families (at night).

Though you may have to wait for a table, their signature kabocha pumpkin and beef in a flavorful red curry will merit patience. Other delights include moist and well-marinated chicken satay; tofu stir-fried with bell peppers and basil; or sticky rice topped with mango. You can choose your own spice level here, but watch out—when this kitchen says hot, they're not kidding around.

■ 1473 Beach Park Blvd. (at Marlin Ave.), Foster City
℘ (650) 212-5788 — **WEB:** www.sweetbasilfostercity.com
■ Lunch & dinner daily   **PRICE: $$**

SUSHI YOSHIZUMI ✿

Japanese • Minimalist

&

Reservations may be, at times, hard to secure, but rest assured that it is completely worth the effort to dine here. This is a dining room cherished by expats yearning for a taste of home and sushi purists snapping iPhone shots faster than you can say "omakase." The setting is discreet in every way, with a tidy interior that consists of little more than eight seats, a cypress bar, as well as a chef's work station.

The menu is built around Edomae sushi, a style that Chef Akira Yoshizumi spent years perfecting in both Japan and New York. His training clearly pays off with food that is refined, delicate and beautifully balanced. Employing wild seafood, mostly from Japan, to create an intimate omakase experience, Chef Yoshizumi offers detailed explanations and welcomes questions with his warm and open demeanor.

Clean flavors shine in each course; garnishes and sauces are kept to a minimum. Wonderfully firm and surprisingly mild geoduck sashimi arrives with nothing more than fresh wasabi and a sprinkle of black sea salt. Still, the height of any meal is their nigiri, starring flavorful rice seasoned with akazu (red vinegar) and fish so pristine that its taste seems to name its species.

■ 325 E. 4th Ave. (bet. B St. & Railroad Ave.), San Mateo
☎ (650) 437-2282 — **WEB:** www.sushiyoshizumi.com
■ Dinner Wed – Sun   **PRICE: $$$$**

TASTY PLACE 🍴

Chinese • Simple

If you like dumplings and noodles—and plenty of them—Tasty Place is your kind of place. Hot or cold, steamed or pan-fried, solo or in soup, this cornucopia of carbs is made entirely by hand, a process diners can watch unfold in a glassed-in room adjacent to the kitchen. It's likely you'll find yourself with some time to do so, as waits can get long at peak hours.

As with many Chinese eateries, the menu is overly vast, spanning from Sichuan to Cantonese. The happiest diners stick to dough-based items, like tender chicken dumplings with sweet corn, or chewy handmade cold noodles topped with ground pork, mung bean sprouts, green onion and chilies. Pork dumplings with fermented cabbage are ferociously good—equal parts juicy, tangy and toothsome.

■ 1625 El Camino Real (bet. Park Blvd. & Park Pl.), Millbrae
📞 (650) 872-2338 — **WEB:** www.tastyplacemillbrae.com
■ Lunch & dinner daily   **PRICE:** 🍜

VESTA 😊

Pizza • Contemporary décor

Whether they're rolling in from their offices at lunch or their condos at dinner, Redwood City locals are always up for a wood-fired pie at this stylish downtown pizzeria. With an airy, mosaic-filled dining room extending into a large front patio, this is a relaxed, roomy space perfect for groups and families.

The menu is divided into red and white pies, and they're equally delicious: zesty tomato sauce enlivens a combo of peppery soppressata, smoked mozzarella and spinach, while a white version with crumbled French feta, fresh slices of garlic, cherry tomatoes and chopped applewood-smoked bacon is irresistible. Get your greens in with the arugula salad, tossed with shaved Parmigiano Reggiano, toasted hazelnuts and a delicious apricot vinaigrette.

■ 2022 Broadway St. (bet. Jefferson Ave. & Main St.), Redwood City
📞 (650) 362-5052 — **WEB:** www.vestarwc.com
■ Lunch & dinner Tue – Sat   **PRICE:** $$

THE VILLAGE PUB ❀

Contemporary • Elegant

Though it has the feel of a chichi private club, this attractive restaurant is open to all—provided they can live up to the style standards set by its fan base of tech tycoons and ladies-who-lunch. Draw your eyes away from those sleek wheels in the parking lot, and head inside for fine dining that exceeds this sophisticated restaurant's humble name.

Despite the glitz, the cuisine here is surprisingly approachable, from platters of house charcuterie served with fire-warmed artisan bread to the superb lobster bisque with braised new potatoes and fennel available in both the cozy front lounge and more formal dining area. It's there that the kitchen shines its brightest though, with such elaborate entrées as ricotta gnudi neatly arranged with chanterelles à la Greque, tender squash and golden raisins. The popular key lime tart is an equally impressive display—its crisp and perfect shell topped with toasted marshmallows, viola petals and meringue batons.

Given the clientele, the wine list is designed to court the deepest of pockets, with an outstanding selection of French vintages, particularly Bordeaux. On a budget? Aim for lunch, which is lighter not only in approach, but also on the wallet.

■ 2967 Woodside Rd. (off Whiskey Hill Rd.), Woodside
✆ (650) 851-9888 — **WEB:** www.thevillagepub.net
■ Lunch Sun – Fri Dinner nightly　　　　**PRICE: $$$**

WAKURIYA ✿

Japanese • Contemporary décor

🍶 ♿

Innovative, serious and very well-established, Wakuriya successfully combines a deep respect for the kaiseki tradition with a contemporary touch. This is largely thanks to the lone chef behind the counter, Katsuhiro Yamasaki; his wife is the one so deftly managing and serving the dining room. The location is charmless, but there is a sober elegance here that is enhanced by the kitchen's quiet confidence. The room books a month in advance—set your alarm for midnight, phone them exactly 30 days ahead and pray for a call back.

Each month brings a new, refined menu that combines the chef's personal style with superlative Japanese and Californian ingredients. Course after course arrives uniquely presented, perhaps on handcrafted ceramics or even a silver spoon, cradling chunks of poached lobster with intensely smoky dashi gelée, soft-boiled Jidori egg, crisp asparagus and fried kombu.

This may not be a sushiya, but the sashimi course is nonetheless excellent. Find that same level of talent in the yamaimo gratin with silky morsels of black cod and tender Brussels sprouts that are crisp, yet light as air and so delicious. The shirako tofu topped with kabocha squash tempura is beyond delightful.

🔲 115 De Anza Blvd. (at Parrot Dr.), San Mateo

☎ (650) 286-0410 — **WEB:** www.wakuriya.com

🔲 Dinner Wed – Sun   **PRICE: $$$$**

WONDERFUL 😊

Chinese • Simple

&

Hunanese cuisine often takes a back seat to the Bay Area's bumper crop of Cantonese and Sichuanese restaurants, so it's no wonder that this hot spot has caught on with the area's Chinese transplants seeking Hunan dishes. Expect a wait at peak meal hours—especially for large parties, as the dining room is compact.

The boldly flavored dishes incorporate oodles of smoked, cured and fermented ingredients—from the bacon-like pork wok-tossed with leeks, garlic and soy, to the pungent pork, black bean and pickled chili mixture that tops those spicy, chewy, hand-cut Godfather's noodles. The whole chili-braised fish, fresh and flaky in its bath of bright red chili sauce flecked with scallions and garlic, is an absolute must.

◼ 270 Broadway (bet. La Cruz & Victoria Aves.), Millbrae
☏ (650) 651-8888 — **WEB:** www.wonderful.restaurant
◼ Lunch & dinner Wed – Mon   **PRICE: $$**

YUMMY SZECHUAN 🍴

Chinese • Simple

&

Long waits for a great Chinese meal are common in the Peninsula, which makes this as yet line-free favorite doubly special. The space is no-frills, but the kitchen is all-thrills, knocking out classic dish after classic dish: crisp Chongqing-style fried chicken buried under a mound of dried chilies and numbing peppercorns, tender pork wontons swimming in gloriously mouth-searing chili oil and chewy dan dan noodles tossed with ground pork, peanuts and plenty of chili oil.

As with all Sichuan restaurants, those who can't stand the heat will have a hard go of it, but non-fiery options include a flaky rolled beef pancake and garlicky pea shoots. The moral of this story: while Yummy may not be anyone's idea of high style, the food assuredly lives up to its name.

◼ 1661 El Camino Real (bet. Park Blvd. & Park Pl.), Millbrae
☏ (650) 615-9648 — **WEB:** www.yummy1661.com
◼ Lunch Thu – Tue Dinner daily   **PRICE: $$**

SOUTH BAY

SOUTH BAY

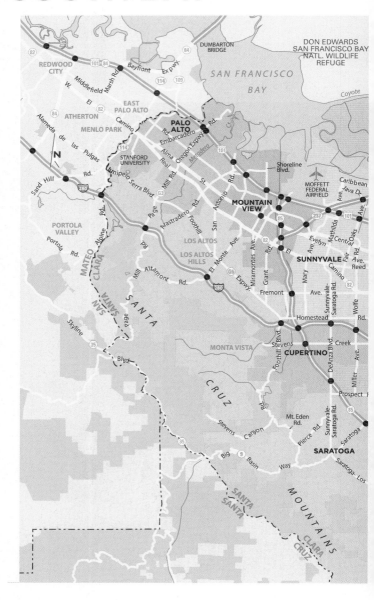

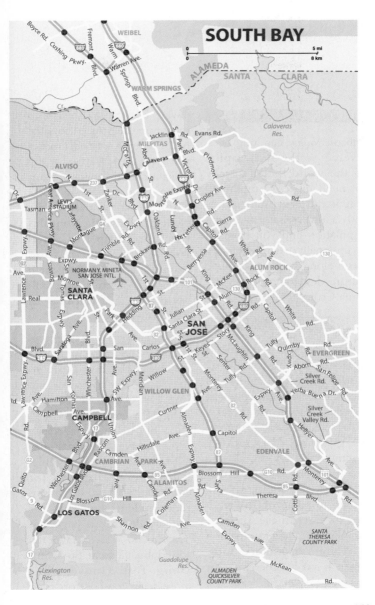

SOUTH BAY

EATING IN...
SOUTH BAY

SILICON VALLEY

Silicon Valley has long been revered as the tech capital of the world, but it's really so much more. Combine all that venture capital money with a diverse, international population and you have an exceptionally dynamic culinary scene along with a rich wine culture descending from the Santa Cruz Mountains.

CULTURAL DYNASTY

Catering to its global residents, this area south of the bay boasts of friendly pho shops and bánh mì hangouts, including **Bui Phong Bakery**, all of which serve to gratify its growing Vietnamese community. They can also be found gracing the intersection of King and Tully streets (home to some of the city's finest Vietnamese flavors) sampling decadent cream puffs at **Hong-Van Bakery**. **Lion Plaza** is yet another hub for bakeries, markets and canteens

paying homage to this ninth most populated Asian country. Neighboring Cambodia makes an appearance by way of delicious noodle soups at **Nam Vang Restaurant** or **F&D Yummy**. Encompassing the globe and traveling from this Far Eastern tip to Central America, Mexican food enthusiasts in San Jose seem eternally smitten by the still-warm tortillas at **Carnitas El Rincon**.

A STUDENT'S DREAM

And yet there is more to the South Bay than just San Jose. Los Gatos, for instance, is home to prized patisseries like **Fleur de Cocoa** and such historic, specialized wineries as **Testarossa**. Meanwhile, Palo Alto is the base for celebrated Stanford University. Find students lining up for homemade frozen yogurt at **Fraîche**. Food lovers favor the soondubu jjigae at **So Gong Dong Tofu House**, while those seeking a comfort food

fix have a field day over the caramelized sweet potatoes at **Sweet Potato Stall**—just outside the Galleria. Then treat your senses to a feast at Mountain View's European-style **Milk Pail Market**, which has transformed from a drive-through dairy to an open-air market showcasing over 300 varieties of local and imported cheese, plus baked goods and produce. Residents of Los Altos have their German food cravings covered between **Esther's German Bakery** and **Dittmer's Gourmet Meats & Wurst-Haus**. Los

Gatos Meats & Smokehouse is another beloved staple serving meat-loving mortals an embarrassment of riches (14 varieties of beef jerky!). Pair these salty licks with a sip from Mountain View's **Savvy Cellar Wine Bar & Wine Shop**. With blind tasting challenges and classes, this spot certainly knows how to pour on the fun. Others however may opt to unwind in luxury at the members-only **Los Gatos Cigar Club**, where the choices are exceptional and conversation intriguing.

ADEGA

Portuguese · Neighborhood

Adega may be located on a commercial strip, but its busy surrounds melt away once you step inside. Exposed wood beams, farmhouse sliding doors and wood tables dominate the scene and thereby fashion a modern-rustic appeal. There is a three-course menu, but the seven-course tasting is the best way to take stock of this husband-and-wife team's Portuguese cooking.

Seafood is plentiful here—from the house favorite arroz de mariscos with shrimp, clams and mussels to the peixe do dia com espargos, a daily changing selection of fresh fish. Codfish croquettes topped with confit tomato have terrific textures with creamy centers, while caldo verde flaunts a tempting presentation. Desserts, too, are on theme and toe the line between traditional and retro.

■ 1614 Alum Rock Ave. (bet. 33rd & 34th Sts.), San Jose
℘ (408) 926-9075 — **WEB:** www.adegarest.com
■ Dinner nightly   PRICE: $$$

ALEXANDER'S STEAKHOUSE

Steakhouse · Contemporary décor

This behemoth and swanky flagship steakhouse is housed in the suburban Main Street Cupertino center. But make your way inside to unearth this sharp and stylish dining room done up with sleek grey hues, beautiful floral arrangements and thick white linen-topped tables.

Pricey steaks emerge from the glass-enclosed dry-aging room to sate the executives doing deals over their meals. They may range from Japanese Wagyu variations to dry-aged domestic Porterhouse, but let the warm and well-dressed servers take the lead when it comes to these impeccable cuts of meat. Other luscious offerings like icy oysters and fiery shishito peppers simply prepare you for a delightful finale by way of the white chocolate and strawberry mousse served atop devil's food cake.

■ 19379 Stevens Creek Blvd. (bet. Tantau Ave. & Wolfe Rd.), Cupertino
℘ (408) 446-2222 — **WEB:** www.alexanderssteakhouse.com
■ Lunch Tue – Sat Dinner nightly   PRICE: $$$$

BACK A YARD ♍○

Caribbean • Colorful

&

Though this Caribbean spot is located in the heart of downtown San Jose, dining here feels like a vacation thanks to cheerful murals, a lively soundtrack and hospitable servers. Unlike its Menlo Park predecessor, which mainly does to-go orders, this location boasts a capacious brick dining room.

Back A Yard is a Jamaican term meaning "the way things are done back home," and the food doesn't disappoint on that count. Specialties include smoky, spicy and tender jerk chicken, flavorful curry goat and vinegar-marinated escovitch fish fillets, all accompanied by coconut rice and red beans, a side salad and caramelized fried plantains. Cool off your palate with a glass of coconut water, then order a slice of dense, flan-like sweet potato pudding.

 80 N. Market St. (bet. Santa Clara & St. John Sts.), San Jose
☏ (408) 294-8626 — **WEB:** www.backayard.net
 Lunch & dinner Mon – Sat   PRICE: ✎

BIRD DOG ♍○

Contemporary • Chic

🍸 & 📷

Anyone on the hunt for a happening scene in Palo Alto should follow the scent to Chef Robbie Wilson's Bird Dog, where the décor is sleek and the cocktails flow freely.

The food is ambitious, and while it may misstep here and there, it gets points for a modern approach. Delicious options abound; start with a wood-grilled avocado filled with ponzu and a dab of fresh wasabi before tucking in to the KFC, three bone-in Jidori chicken thighs coated in a thick, crunchy batter and served with a kicky chickpea gochujang. House-made sodas, with flavors like blueberry lemon, banana lime and ginger cinnamon-chai, are especially refreshing. Finish with the doughnuts and coffee, a trio of warm and dainty coffee-glazed, sugar-dipped and chocolatey delights.

80 420 Ramona St. (bet. Lytton & University Aves.), Palo Alto
☏ (650) 656-8180 — **WEB:** www.birddogpa.com
Lunch Tue – Fri Dinner nightly   PRICE: $$

BAUMÉ ✿ ✿

Contemporary · Elegant

&

A bold and bright glass door in an otherwise nondescript building along Palo Alto's main thoroughfare marks the entrance to the mystical Baumé. Inside, find a dining room with a modernist sensibility that carries through with orange-hued walls and fabric room dividers. Chef Bruno Chemel offers a select number of seatings. Tables are spaced widely for privacy and never rushed. Mrs. Chemel oversees this luxurious enclave, adding warmth, detailed knowledge and clear enthusiasm for her husband's progressive (albeit pricey) cuisine. It's a family affair indeed, as the couple's young son, decked out in whites, assists in the kitchen as well.

Each contemporary dish is refined, balanced and demonstrates an enormous attention to detail. The kitchen focuses on seasonal ingredients and coaxing flavor to profound levels. Roasted California squab with its caramelized, ever-so-perfect crispy skin and light dusting of fennel is an absolute showstopper in all of its velvety, well-seasoned glory.

Desserts include a pear bavarois artfully crested with delicious cassis jam and a frozen flower composed with grape sorbet. A plate of perfectly ripe stone fruit is a wonderfully seasonal send-off.

▨ 201 S. California Ave. (at Park Blvd.), Palo Alto
℘ (650) 328-8899 — **WEB:** www.maisonbaume.com
▨ Lunch Thu – Sat Dinner Wed – Sat   **PRICE: $$$$**

THE BYWATER 😋

Southern • Family

 ♿ 🍽 🚲

If dining at Manresa is like a weeklong stay at a luxury resort, this New Orleans-inspired little sib from Chef/owner David Kinch is more like a weekend of partying in the Big Easy. With its zinc bar, pressed ceilings and open kitchen stacked with bottles of Crystal hot sauce, it might just fool you into thinking you're in Louisiana—right down to the zydeco and jazz playing on the stereo.

Reservations aren't accepted, so locals (some with kids in tow) line up early to get a taste of spicy, andouille-flecked gumbo z'herbes, golden-brown hushpuppies, oyster po'boys and other Cajun and Creole classics. For the finale, a luscious butterscotch pot de crème may sound less traditional, but rest assured that it tastes like heaven.

◼ 532 N. Santa Cruz Ave. (bet. Andrews St. & Roberts Rd.), Los Gatos
℘ (408) 560-9639 — **WEB:** www.thebywaterca.com
◼ Lunch & dinner Tue – Sun   **PRICE: $$**

DIN TAI FUNG 🍴

Chinese • Contemporary décor

You'll need to wait (and wait, and wait) to get a taste of the much-coveted dumplings at the first Bay Area outpost of this acclaimed international chain, which has drawn crazy crowds to the Westfield Valley Fair mall since day one.

With only a handful of reservations taken a month in advance, expect to cool your heels for anywhere from 45 minutes to two hours. Is the wait worth it? Depends on how much you love xiao long bao, the Shanghai-style soup dumplings that are offered here in outstanding pork-crab and utterly decadent black truffle variations. Bring a crew so you can sample the non-dumpling offerings as well: delectably spicy wontons, top-flight barbecue pork buns, springy house-made noodles and lightly sweetened black sesame buns for dessert.

◼ 2855 Stevens Creek Blvd.
(bet. Monroe St. & Winchester Blvd.), Santa Clara
℘ (408) 248-1688 — **WEB:** www.dintaifungusa.com
◼ Lunch & dinner daily   **PRICE: $$**

CHEZ TJ

Contemporary · Elegant

Nestled into a charming 19th-century Victorian in the heart of downtown Mountain View, Chez TJ likes to kick it old school. This elder statesman in the fine-dining scene flaunts an elegant and welcoming streak thanks to antique pictures and Venetian blown-glass table lamps that infuse the space with a romantic feel. And the waitstaff is formally suited—naturally.

Having launched the career of many a culinary legend, including its current leader—Jarad Gallagher—this kitchen showcases contemporary French cuisine by way of one tasting. Featuring a number of courses, the menu aims at highlighting ingredients sourced from within 100 miles of the restaurant as well as exploring global territory.

Dinner might begin with a fried yuba skin beggar's purse stuffed with Kumamoto oysters bobbing in spicy kimchi juice and served atop a porcelain soup spoon. Later, a delicate French onion soup, crowned with a Gruyère crostini and paired with homemade sourdough levain, makes its way to your table. Sashimi courses typically precede richer items, including a duo of veal, served beneath paper-thin shingles of turnip and slipped into a small crispy croquette set over sautéed Bloomsdale spinach.

938 Villa St. (bet. Bryant & Franklin Sts.), Mountain View
𝒞 (650) 964-7466 — **WEB:** www.cheztj.com
Dinner Tue – Sat   PRICE: $$$$

DIO DEKA ▯○

Greek · Elegant

Dio Deka may specialize in Greek food, but this is no typical taverna, as the stylish dining room (complete with a roaring fireplace) ably demonstrates. A wealthy, well-dressed Los Gatos crowd flocks to the front patio on warm evenings, dining and people-watching within the vine-covered walls of the Hotel Los Gatos. The bar also draws a brace of cheery regulars.

Skip the dull mesquite-grilled steaks and keep your order Greek: think stuffed grape leaves with tender braised beef cheek, or a bright pan-seared local salmon with roasted yellow peppers, potatoes and artichokes. The adventurous shouldn't miss out on the fun offering of Greek wines, and sweet buffs should allow space for the crema me meli, a fantastic burnt-honey mousse with almond and lemon.

▮ 210 E. Main St. (bet. Jackson St. & Villa Ave.), Los Gatos
✆ (408) 354-7700 — **WEB:** www.diodeka.com
▮ Dinner nightly   PRICE: $$$

DISHDASH ▯○

Middle Eastern · Regional décor

Dining on the run is certainly possible at this Mid-East gem on historic Murphy Avenue—just ask the techies who rush in to take food back to their desks. Families and groups congregate in the colorful dining room; and even though the space has expanded to include five outposts, you might want to linger on the front sidewalk patio—all the better to people-watch while savoring a bright, tangy tabbouleh, tender-crisp falafel or baba ghanoush topped with black olives and roasted garlic cloves.

Served on griddled bread and enriched with a garlicky yogurt-parsley sauce, wraps like the incredibly smoky and juicy chicken shawarma are full-flavored and downright memorable. For dessert, go for the m'halabieh, a creamy and fragrant rosewater-and-pistachio pudding.

▮ 190 S. Murphy Ave. (bet. Evelyn & Washington Aves.),
Sunnyvale
✆ (408) 774-1889 — **WEB:** www.dishdash.com
▮ Lunch & dinner Mon – Sat   PRICE: $$

DOPPIO ZERO PIZZA NAPOLETANA ⅋○

Italian • Neighborhood

 ♿ ⛺

It's easy to overlook pizza as a way to quell hunger pangs, but sink your teeth into the selections here and you're quickly reminded that it's an art form unto itself. The pies are, well, epic (and certified by the Associazione Verace Pizza Napoletana, one of just a few in the state), and well-seasoned—topped with a zesty tomato sauce and bold ingredients. Then there is that crust—chewy and blistered with just the right amount of char. You could come just for pizza, but that would mean missing out on such delicious dishes as polpo—smoky octopus dressed with anchovy vinaigrette and set atop tomatoes. It's so much more than just a "salad."

The bustling interior doesn't distract from the goods. On a nice day, grab a seat on the sidewalk to imbibe the bliss.

■ 160 Castro St. (bet. Evelyn Ave. & Vista St.), Mountain View
☎ (401) 863-0308 — **WEB:** www.dzpizzeria.com
■ Lunch & dinner daily   **PRICE: $$**

EVVIA ⅋○

Greek • Mediterranean décor

 ♿ 🛀

Inviting with its rustic wood beams, hanging copper pots and roaring wood-burning fireplace, this central Palo Alto spot is a draw for Maserati-driving tech billionaires by day and couples in the evening. Dress to impress here, where the scene dictates high prices (though lunch features lighter dishes and more palatable pricing).

Much of the menu emerges from the wood-fired grill, including smoky, tender artichoke and eggplant skewers drizzled in olive oil and paired with garlicky Greek yogurt. The rustic, impossibly moist lamb souvlaki is nicely contrasted by a refreshing tomato, cucumber and red onion salad. For dessert, pumpkin cheesecake is subtle, sweet and accented with syrup-poached chunks of pumpkin.

■ 420 Emerson St. (bet. Lytton & University Aves.), Palo Alto
☎ (650) 326-0983 — **WEB:** www.evvia.net
■ Lunch Mon – Fri Dinner nightly   **PRICE: $$$**

JANG SU JANG ⅱ○
Korean • Family

 ♿ ⛲

Smoky Korean barbecue, luscious soft tofu stews and enormous seafood pancakes are among the standards at this Santa Clara classic and Koreatown jewel. Its strip-mall façade may not seem enticing, but the interior is classier than expected, thanks to granite tables equipped with grill tops and ventilation hoods, and a glass-enclosed exhibition kitchen located in the back.

This is fiery-flavored cuisine for gourmands who can stand the heat. A heavy-handed dose of kimchi flavors soft beef and pork dumplings, while the fierce red chili paste that slicks garlicky slices of marinated pork may actually cook the meat in daeji bulgogi. Cool down with mul naengmyun, a cold beef broth with tender, nutty buckwheat noodles and a pot of boricha.

■ 3561 El Camino Real, Ste. 10 (bet. Flora Vista Ave. & Lawrence Expwy.), Santa Clara
✆ (408) 246-1212 — **WEB:** www.jangsujang.com
■ Lunch & dinner daily   **PRICE: $$**

LAU HAI SAN ⅱ○
Vietnamese • Simple

Most Westerners don't think of hot pot when they're craving Vietnamese food, but it's actually a traditional favorite well worth sampling—and the proof is in this sunny spot. The overstuffed menu boasts 20 different variations on the theme, including a spicy seafood version with shrimp, mussels, squid, fish balls stuffed with salmon roe and other aquatic delights. Dip them into the sour, tangy broth; twirl them with noodles; garnish with herbs—the choice is yours.

If hot pot isn't adventurous enough, bring a group to sample delicacies like chewy, flavorful curried coconut snails and crispy fried pork intestine. The diner-like space and strip-mall setting are nothing special, but the hot pot is so outstanding that lines are to be expected.

■ 2597 Senter Rd. (bet. Feldspar Dr. & Umbarger Rd.), San Jose
✆ (408) 938-0650 — **WEB:** N/A
■ Lunch & dinner Thu – Tue   **PRICE: $$**

MANRESA ✿✿✿

Contemporary • Elegant

🍇 🍷 ♿ 🍽

It may have a reputation for being one of the Bay Area's most well-regarded restaurants, but Manresa is welcoming, distinctively stylish and extraordinarily hospitable for a fine-dining operation. Chef David Kinch works with some of the region's most revered growers, turning products from Andy's Orchard, Pistils & Petals Farm and Dirty Girl, among others, into works of art.

The nightly compositions are unknown until they arrive on the table (a souvenir copy of the menu will be handed to you at the end). The food is at once cerebral and luxurious, approachable and thoroughly delicious. Each course is likely to represent a moment within a season, beginning with savory petit fours that are an illusory play on the palate. Sample red-pepper pâtes de fruits or black olive madeleines along with excellent bread baked at the offshoot bakery made with house-milled flour. Tender striped bass in a saffron bouillabaisse is topped with a crisp wafer of brioche. Even something as simple as asparagus is elevated here with a charred beurre blanc and its fantastic smokiness.

Don't miss those excellent vanilla-bean caramels offered on your way out.

◾ 320 Village Ln. (bet. Santa Cruz & University Aves.), Los Gatos

✆ (408) 354-4330 — **WEB:** www.manresarestaurant.com

◾ Dinner Wed – Sun   **PRICE: $$$$**

MAUM ✿

Korean • Contemporary décor

🍴 ♿

Founded as a private dining club for its wealthy owner, this Korean-influenced, tasting-menu shoebox was too good to remain a secret for too long. Suss out its well-hidden location, amidst the shops of downtown Palo Alto, and you'll be ushered into this impossibly chic nightly dinner party, with just 16 seats at the communal table. Get ready to chat up your neighbors—and given Maum's prominence on the VC scene, hear a bit of shop talk as well.

The name is Korean for "from the heart," and naturally, family is at this restaurant's heart. Chefs Michael and Meichih Kim are a married couple, whose hospitality and welcoming demeanor create a social and exuberant contrast against their refined cuisine and wine—starting with such exquisite canapés as soondae (blood sausage) dotted with preserved shrimp, or Kusshi oysters dusted with kimchi snow.

Korean food aficionados will be astounded by the heights to which these chefs can take simple ingredients. Imagine the likes of fresh warm tofu with a savory drizzle of soy sauce, or galbi ssam bap starring tender grilled Wagyu wrapped in lettuce and enhanced with soybean paste. A lovely strawberry sorbet makes for a lingering send-off.

◼ 322 University Ave. (bet. Bryant & Waverly Sts.), Palo Alto
✆ (650) 656-8161 — **WEB:** www.maumpaloalto.com
◼ Dinner Wed – Fri   **PRICE: $$$$**

LUNA MEXICAN KITCHEN 😋

Mexican • Colorful

   ♿ 🛆 🛏

The name means "moon" in Spanish, and this Mexican kitchen also uses it as an acronym to reflect its philosophy of "L(local) U(unrefined) N(natural) A(authentic)" cooking. The food is decidedly highbrow, thanks to special ingredients like Rancho Gordo beans, Mary's free-range chickens and everything else that's made from scratch. Chef/owner Jo Lerma-Lopez's love for cooking is clear in every single bite, especially the fire-roasted chiles rellenos, generously stuffed with a fragrant beef stew and deep-fried to perfection. Ask for extra handmade tortillas to go with your simmered charro beans.

The dining room seems to burst with color. A full-service bar lures with backlit tequila bottles and vibrant tiles. Come summer, the back patio is the place to be.

🔳 1495 The Alameda (at Magnolia Ave.), San Jose

☏ (408) 320-2654 — **WEB:** www.lunamexicankitchen.com

🔳 Lunch & dinner daily   **PRICE: $$**

NASCHMARKT 🍴

Austrian • Simple

   ♿ 🛆

A slice of Vienna in downtown Campbell, Naschmarkt scores high marks for its authentic flavors, inviting space and friendly service. The cozy, brick-walled dining room is a favorite among couples, and solo diners will have a ball at the wraparound counter, which has a great view of the busy open kitchen.

Most of the menu is traditional: think bratwurst, krautrouladen and Wiener schnitzel. The pan-roasted chicken breast, moist and juicy with a golden-brown seared crust, is served over a "napkin dumpling" made with compressed bread, tomato and herbs. But, rest easy as there are a few items that have lighter Californian twists, like spätzle made with quark (a fresh white cheese) and tossed with smoked chicken, yellow corn, English peas and wild mushrooms.

🔳 384 E. Campbell Ave. (bet. Central & Railway Aves.), Campbell

☏ (408) 378-0335 — **WEB:** www.naschmarkt-restaurant.com

🔳 Dinner Tue – Sun   **PRICE: $$**

NICK'S NEXT DOOR ¶O

American • *Contemporary décor*

 ♿ 🌲

There is a loyal crowd of locals flooding Nick's Next Door, but this delightful haunt is as welcoming to rookies as it is to regulars. Inside, the bar and semi-open kitchen beckon; while outside, there's plenty of space to linger just a little bit longer.

The mood, thanks to a chic black-and-gray palette, and the food scream upscale American bistro. Pan-fried abalone served with creamy risotto and crispy Brussels sprouts leans edgy, while Nani's meatloaf, a thick slab of juicy meat in a savory mushroom gravy and resting atop fluffy, buttery mashed potatoes, is straight-up comfort. Finish with the apple bread pudding, a blend of sourdough and brioche, a variety of apples as well as a decadent caramel sauce that smacks of pure pleasure—and joy.

▪ 11 College Ave. (at Main St.), Los Gatos
☏ (408) 402-5053 — **WEB:** www.nicksnextdoor.com
▪ Lunch & dinner Tue – Sat   **PRICE: $$**

ORCHARD CITY KITCHEN 😊

International • *Rustic*

 ♿ 🌲 🛎

Jeffrey Stout is at the helm of this international small-plates spot, where a wall-to-wall crowd of loyal followers flock despite the humble shopping-center environs. Polished yet casual with a big front bar and patio, a meal here is best enjoyed with a group—so come prepared to max out the menu.

The menu spins in a number of directions, but this team won't steer your wrong. Kick it off with a cocktail, then tuck into a hodge-podge of dishes, including a riff on poutine with tater tots, muenster cheese, bacon and fried egg; and a spicy budae jjigae with slurpy ramen noodles and Spam. Served in a cast iron pan, the orange dream pulls together orange soft serve, kiwi, honey cream and poppy seed for an unusual twist on the ice cream truck favorite.

▪ 1875 S. Bascom Ave., Ste. 190 (off Campisi Way), Campbell
☏ (408) 340-5285 — **WEB:** www.orchardcitykitchen.com
▪ Lunch & dinner daily   **PRICE: $$**

PLUMED HORSE ❀

Contemporary • Elegant

This handsome stallion is certainly a feather in the cap of the inviting, if slightly sleepy, Saratoga. There has been a Plumed Horse in this spot since 1952, though this decade-old iteration is by far the best. The décor inside exudes warmth, first in the fireplace-warmed lounge, then in the stunning dining room, with its arched barrel ceiling. From shimmering Venetian plaster to striking chandeliers that emit a colorful glow, these rich details create a sensational backdrop that is at once elegant and comfortable.

The kitchen turns out modern and upscale cooking with an Asian bent. Duck consommé, poured tableside and enhanced with meaty mushrooms as well as a bright English pea flan, is as impressive to the eye as it is to the palate. Locally sourced abalone is finished with XO sauce for a pop of flavor, while the decadent black pepper- and parmesan-soufflé accompanied by a delicate petal of uni is of the dive-right-in variety.

Almond cake with cocoa-nib mousse and orange foam is delightful, but wait until those chocolates arrive. Wheeled over in a glass-domed cart with row-upon-row of beauties from Chocolaterie by Angelica, they are nothing less than exquisite.

▪ 14555 Big Basin Way (bet. 4th & 5th Sts.), Saratoga
✆ (408) 867-4711 — **WEB:** www.plumedhorse.com
▪ Dinner Mon – Sat   **PRICE: $$$$**

PROTÉGÉ ✿

Contemporary • Chic

This Palo Alto hit boasts an envious pedigree—Chef Anthony Secviar, Pastry Chef Eddie Lopez and Master Sommelier Dennis Kelly all trained under Chef Thomas Keller at The French Laundry. However, this notable kitchen offers an experience that is far from weighty. In fact, the staff aims to keep things more lenient in this dining room, which sports cushy leather booths, beautifully laid tables and even the occasional diner donning flip-flops.

Hungry techies from around the enclave can expect cooking with a suave and edgy panache—reviving such tired players as Alaskan king crab (a seasonal delight here, thanks to sweet corn purée and bacon-tinged corn succotash); or beef tenderloin accompanied by buttery potatoes infused with a sharp horseradish mousseline. Such keen attention to detail and surprisingly well-balanced flavors continue through to dessert—as evidenced by the dulce de leche mousse coated with salted hazelnuts, toasted honey and delicious dark chocolate.

In keeping with its accessible slant, the kitchen also offers a lounge menu, which thanks to its popularity, requires reservations.

250 California Ave. (bet. Birch St. & Park Blvd.), Palo Alto
(650) 494-4181 — **WEB:** www.protogepaloalto.com
Dinner Tue - Sat **PRICE: $$$**

ORENCHI 🍴

Japanese • Simple

&

Whether at lunch or dinner, this ramen specialist is known for its lines of waiting diners that curl like noodles outside its door. Even those who arrive before they open may face a long wait, so don't come if you're in a rush. Once inside, you'll be seated at a simple wood table or at the bar, collaged with Polaroid portraits of guests savoring their ramen.

The reason for the wait becomes clear when you're presented with a rich and utterly delicious bowl of tonkotsu ramen full of chewy noodles, roasted pork and scallions. Shoyu ramen is equally delish, but make a point to show up early if you want to try the tsukemen (dipping noodles), as there is a limited number of servings available daily.

Orenchi Beyond is an equally busy younger sib in SF.

■ 3540 Homestead Rd. (near Lawrence Expy.), Santa Clara
📞 (408) 246-2955 — **WEB:** www.orenchi-ramen.com
■ Lunch & dinner daily   **PRICE:** 🍴

SAWA SUSHI 🍴

Japanese • Simple

&

Strict rules and big rewards unite at this zany, unusual and randomly located (in a mall) dive, where Chef Steve Sawa rules the roost. After going through the rigamarole of landing a reservation for his omakase-only affair, throw all caution to the wind and just go with the flow. Yes, the décor is nothing special; however, the food is anything but so-so, and the ad hoc prices are quite high.

So what draws such a host of regulars? Their pristine and very sublime fish, of course—from creamy Hokkaido sea scallops to delicious toro ribbons. Sawa is also an expert on sauces: imagine the likes of yuzukosho topping kanpachi or a sweet-spicy tamarind glaze on ocean trout. Accompany these with a top sake or cold beer and feel the joy seep in.

■ 1042 E. El Camino Real (at Henderson Ave.), Sunnyvale
📞 (408) 241-7292 — **WEB:** www.sawasushi.net
■ Dinner Mon – Sat   **PRICE:** $$$$

TAMARINE

Vietnamese • Simple

Tamarine has long been a Palo Alto standby for its refined take on Vietnamese food that doesn't sacrifice authentic flavor. There's nearly always a corporate lunch happening in the private dining room, and techies, families and couples alike fill the rest of its linen-topped tables.

Family-style sharing of dishes is encouraged, which is good because deciding on just one entrée is nearly impossible. To start, make like the regulars and order one of the "Tamarine Taste" appetizer platters with a round of tropical fruit-infused cocktails. Then move on to the fresh shrimp spring rolls, full of bean sprouts and mint; the springy ginger-chili seitan with steamed coconut rice; and curried long beans, sautéed with fragrant makrut lime leaves and chili.

 546 University Ave. (bet. Cowper & Webster Sts.), Palo Alto
☏ (650) 325-8500 — **WEB:** www.tamarinerestaurant.com
Lunch Mon – Fri Dinner nightly   **PRICE: $$$**

THIÊN LONG ｜○

Vietnamese • Simple

There are plenty of Vietnamese restaurants catering to the local expats in San Jose, but Thiên Long stands out for its pleasant dining room presenting delicious cooking—as the numerous families filling the large space will attest. Tile floors and rosewood-tinted chairs decorate the space, while walls hung with photos of Vietnamese dishes keep the focus on food.

Begin with sweet-salty barbecued prawns paired with smoky grilled pork and served atop rice noodles. But, it is really the pho with a broth of star anise, clove and ginger, topped with perfectly rare beef that is a true gem—even the regular-sized portion is enormous. English is a challenge among the staff, but they are very friendly; plus the authentic flavors make up for any inadequacies.

3005 Silver Creek Rd., Ste. 138 (bet. Aborn Rd. & Lexann Ave.), San Jose
☏ (408) 223-6188 — **WEB:** N/A
Lunch & dinner daily   **PRICE:** ⊜

VINA ENOTECA 🍴⭕

Italian • Contemporary décor

It has been made more than apparent by now that this owner, Rocco Scordella who is a native of Italy, succeeded in bringing a delicious taste of his homeland to Palo Alto. Look around and note that pasta tops everyone's table for good reason. If offered, be sure to try the toothsome spinach tagliatelle in a meaty ragù that's composed with local pork and naturally raised beef. This kitchen clearly prioritizes sourcing—a majority of the greens and vegetables are grown at Stanford Education Farm—and pastas, pizzas and bread are all crafted in-house.

The industrial-chic décor features high ceilings, arches and soft leather chairs. Whether you pop in for snacks and cocktails at the bar or plan on savoring a full meal, service is always friendly and quick.

▪ 700 Welch Rd. Unit 110 (at Arboretum Rd.), Palo Alto
☎ (650) 646-3477 — **WEB:** www.vinaenoteca.com
▪ Lunch & dinner daily   PRICE: $$

WALIA 🍴⭕

Ethiopian • Simple

Authentic Ethiopian flavors are delivered without pretense at this easygoing, affordable restaurant housed in a strip mall just off Bascom Avenue. Though the space is basic, the service is friendly and it's casual enough for kids in tow.

Start things off with an order of sambussas, fried dough triangles filled with lentil, onion and chilies. Then choose from an all-meat, all-veggie or mixed selection of warming stews, like tibs firfir, featuring lamb in a garlicky berbere sauce dolloped on spongy injera. Vegetarians will particularly love dining here, as all of the plant-based options, including alicha wot or split peas in turmeric sauce, shiro (spiced chickpeas) and gomen (wilted collard greens with onion and spices), are big winners.

▪ 2208 Business Cir. (at Bascom Ave.), San Jose
☎ (408) 645-5001 — **WEB:** www.waliaethiopian.com
▪ Lunch & dinner Wed – Mon   PRICE: ⬤

ZAREEN'S ¶○
Indian • *Simple*

&

Taking up residence just steps from the Googleplex, it's no surprise that this wholesome little South Asian restaurant is absolutely packed with tech employees seeking a taste of their homeland. But local families love Zareen's as well, perusing books from the lending library or doodling their heartfelt thanks on the wall. An added bonus: the space is set in a small shopping plaza with a big lot out front, making parking a non-issue.

The chicken Memoni samosas, supposedly made from a recipe known to only a select number of grandmothers worldwide, are a must-order: crispy, well-spiced and flavorful, they're so good they don't need chutney. Follow these with the outstanding chicken shami kebabs, juicy and caramelized on their bed of fluffy basmati rice.

▦ 1477 Plymouth St. (off Shoreline Blvd.), Mountain View
𝒫 (650) 600-8438 — **WEB:** www.zareensrestaurant.com
▦ Lunch & dinner Tue – Sun   **PRICE:** ⊜

ZENI ¶○
Ethiopian • *Simple*

&

From its home at the end of a shopping plaza, Zeni caters to expats, tech types and families alike. The interior has a standard dining area decorated with colorful portraits and tapestries as well as traditional seating on low stools at woven tables. Either way, group dining is encouraged.

Relish the spongy, enticingly sour injera used to scoop up delicious yemisir wot (red lentils with spicy berbere); kik alicha (yellow peas tinged with garlic and ginger); or beef kitfo (available raw or cooked) tossed with that aromatic spice blend, mitmita, and crowned by crumbled ayib cheese. Here, injera is your only utensil, but be assured as there's a sink in the back to tidy up. Balance the fiery food with cool honey wine, or opt for an after-dinner Ethiopian coffee.

▦ 1320 Saratoga Ave. (at Payne Ave.), San Jose
𝒫 (408) 615-8282 — **WEB:** www.zeniethiopianrestaurant.com
▦ Lunch & dinner Tue – Sun   **PRICE:** ⊜

ZOLA ⅋○
French • Bistro

&

A Palo Alto sparkler, Zola charms its way into diners' hearts via a seductive French bistro menu with Californian flair. Whether you're spreading smoky salmon rillettes on toasted artisan levain, twirling pillowy caramelized ricotta gnocchi into the yolk of a soft-cooked egg in brown butter or tucking into tender filet de boeuf with creamy sauce béarnaise and golden-brown fingerling potatoes, you're sure to fall hard for the food.

The stylish space updates a few classics (wood tables, bistro chairs, pressed ceilings) with a dark teal color scheme and enticingly low lighting, and the well-chosen wine list is equal parts Gallic and Golden State. Crème caramel for dessert may be traditional, but it's also perfectly executed and decadently rich.

▨ 565 Bryant St. (bet. Hamilton & University Aves.), Palo Alto
✆ (650) 521-0651 — **WEB:** www.zolapaloalto.com
▨ Dinner Tue – Sat   **PRICE: $$**

MONTEREY

MONTEREY

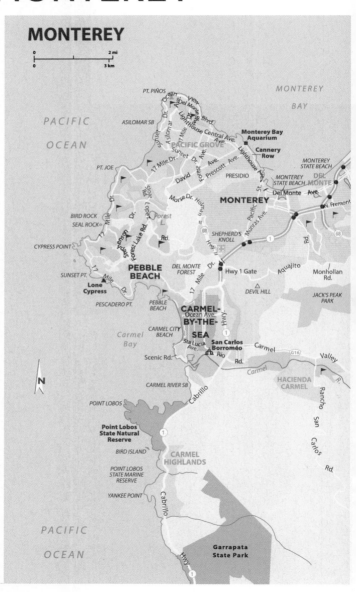

MONTEREY

0   2 mi
0   3 km

PACIFIC

OCEAN

MONTEREY

BAY

PT. PIÑOS

ASILOMAR SB

Del Monte Blvd

View

Ocean

Sunset

17 Mile

Dr.

Sinex

Lighthouse Central Ave.

Ave.

PACIFIC GROVE

Monterey Bay
Aquarium

Cannery
Row

Lighthouse Ave.

PT. JOE

17 Mile Dr.

Sunset Dr.

Forest Ave.

David

Prescott Ave.

PRESIDIO

MONTEREY
STATE BEACH

MONTEREY
STATE BEACH

DEL
MONTE

Morse Dr.

Holsey

Del Monte Ave.

N. Fremont

MONTEREY

Pacific St.

Munras Ave.

BIRD ROCK

SEAL ROCK

CYPRESS POINT

17 Mile

Dr.

Sloat

Spyglass

Forest Lake Rd.

Lopez

Forest

L

Rd.

Dr.

SHEPHERD'S
KNOLL

Hwy 1

68

Rd.

PEBBLE
BEACH

DEL MONTE
FOREST

Hwy 1 Gate

Aquajito

Monhollan
Rd.

JACK'S PEAK
PARK

SUNSET PT.

Lone
Cypress

17
Mile
Dr.

17 Mile Dr.

DEVIL HILL

PESCADERO PT.

PEBBLE
BEACH

CARMEL-
BY-THE-
SEA

Ocean Ave.

Carmel
Bay

CARMEL CITY
BEACH

Sta Lucia
Ave.

San Carlos
Borroméo

Carmel

G16

Valley

Scenic Rd.

Rio

Rd.

Carmel

HACIENDA
CARMEL

CARMEL RIVER SB

Cabrillo

Carmel

R.

POINT LOBOS

N

Point Lobos
State Natural
Reserve

BIRD ISLAND

CARMEL
HIGHLANDS

San

Carlos

Rd.

Rancho

POINT LOBOS
STATE MARINE
RESERVE

YANKEE POINT

Cabrillo

PACIFIC

OCEAN

Garrapata
State Park

Hwy 1

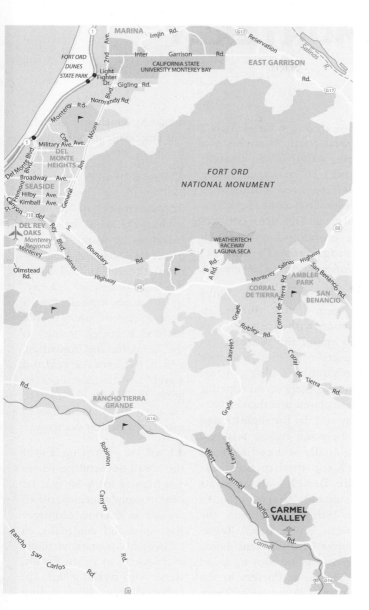

EATING IN...
MONTEREY

Located on California's central coast, Monterey is a well-patronized destination thanks to its breathtaking cliffs, coastal climes and seaside views along Highway 1. This is an area that celebrates the great outdoors through hiking, farmer's markets galore and world-class golfing.

Pebble Beach Golf Links is open to the public, so anyone with deep pockets can spend the morning on the green to enjoy some of the country's best golfing. After working up an appetite, these players and their caddies may stop by for sophisticated homegrown cuisine featuring regionally sourced seafood and top-quality meats at **The Bench**—an open-air restaurant that overlooks the 18th hole. Naturally, the various Pebble Beach Resort courses have different dining scenes, but be sure to spend some time at **Porters in the Forest** at Poppy Hills. From

breakfast, lunch and twilight, this seasonally inspired menu is sure to sate.

Foragers, foodies or anyone looking to get closer to the marina can flock to Monterey to harvest what has been hailed as the world's greatest diversity of seaweed— mind the ten-pound limit, though. Of course, this city-by-the-sea's notoriety as a proponent of sustainable seafood is largely thanks to the Monterey Bay Aquarium, which publishes a seafood watch list that's meant to guide the world on what to eat, what to avoid and how to maintain a healthy ocean.

If all this learning about the area's aquaculture leaves you hungry for local fish, be sure to sample such cherished species as abalone, Monterey Bay squid and sand dabs, all of which decorate virtually every menu in town. Finally, those who notice a line out the door may be standing

near **Phil's Fish Market** in Moss Landing; while others may find themselves parked outside **Passionfish**— another neighborhood gem.

This region also boasts vibrant cafés ideal for an afternoon respite—including **Acme Coffee** and **Café Lumiere**. While **The Lafayette Bakery and Café** is also beloved for its sandwiches and pastries finished with European flair, nowhere is the Old Country more delicious than at **Parker-Lusseau Pastries**. Finally, no evening is complete without

a trip to the **Cannery Row Brewing Company**. It may have given up its former life as the center of the sardine packing industry, but this hot spot now rules the drinks field thanks to its bar, pouring over 70 craft beers and 30 small-batch Bourbons. Close out the night over something totally unique at **Revival Ice Cream** whose award-winning scoops are made from bee pollen, bee's wax, burnt honey and homemade honeycomb candy. What follows? Nothing but the most sweet of dreams.

AKAONI 🍴

Japanese • Simple

With few seats, limited hours and a two-person staff, snagging a table at this no-frills sushiya can be a real challenge. But those willing to make the effort will be rewarded, because Akaoni offers some of the region's most pristine sushi—at surprisingly down-to-earth prices.

A 12-piece chef's choice platter is offered for those who'd like to put their fate in the kitchen's hands, but savvy diners know to go straight for the options on the daily specials board—like buttery local spot prawns served to order from a tank right behind the omnipresent counter. Simply plated and nicely cut, the nigiri far outshines most of the cooked dishes. But if you're looking to supplement your sushi, the light and crispy vegetable tempura is a worthy option.

▨ Mission St. at 6th Ave., Carmel-by-the-Sea
☎ (831) 620-1516 — **WEB:** N/A
▨ Lunch Wed – Sat Dinner Mon – Sat   **PRICE: $$**

CAFÉ RUSTICA 🍴

European • Rustic

♿ ☂

Nestled amid the many wine-tasting rooms of the Carmel Valley, this country charmer is the place to dine in after visiting the local vineyards. As a result of which, tables fill up quickly so get here in time. The big draw is a sunny patio decked with umbrellas, a gem among visitors ranging in age from 1 to 80. It's a delightful place to kick back (and kick back you will, since service can be quite slow).

Indoors, the action revolves around a wood-burning oven, which turns out fire-roasted artichokes with lemon aïoli; and thin-crust pizzas like the Lorraine, topped with caramelized onions, bacon and Gruyère. These may be supplemented by salads at lunchtime and hearty entrées like oven-baked rigatoni at dinner—along with floods of local wine, of course.

▨ 10 Del Fino Pl. (bet. Pilot Rd. & Carmel Valley Rd.), Carmel Valley
☎ (831) 659-4444 — **WEB:** www.caferusticavillage.com
▨ Lunch & dinner Tue – Sun   **PRICE: $$**

AUBERGINE

Contemporary • Romantic

‹ ♿ 🍳

Tucked into the quaint seaside surroundings of Carmel, this high-end restaurant boasts the same appealing mix of luxury and simplicity as its home in the cottage-like L'Auberge Carmel. With only a dozen or so tables, it's an intimate retreat that offers personalized attention—a must for the many couples that flock to this tony town for weekend getaways. Low ceilings, soft lighting, gauzy curtains as well as a soothing palette of seafoam-green and alabaster add to the hushed aura—though a 25,000-bottle wine cellar will perk up any oenophile around.

Helmed by Chef Justin Cogley, the kitchen eschews elaborate technique for a classic approach to fine dining, integrating superlative local seafood and even the sea itself. Imagine the likes of seawater jelly topping a briny Kumamoto oyster heaped with caviar. Then, delicate coastal greens like red vein sorrel pop up in a dish of edamame with buttery chanterelles and black trumpet mushrooms; just as kombu envelops a carefully seared slab of delicious A5 Wagyu beef.

Desserts boast equal refinement, with satisfyingly sweet and savory creations like the goat cheese panna cotta crowned with juicy and paper-thin slivers of bright red apple.

■ Monte Verde at 7th Ave., Carmel-by-the-Sea
📞 (831) 624-8578 — **WEB:** www.auberginecarmel.com
■ Dinner nightly · · · · · · · · · · · · · · **PRICE: $$$$**

CASANOVA ⅋○

European • Romantic

This historic 1920s cottage—once owned by Charlie Chaplin's personal chef—is marked by a bike parked out front with lavender flowing from the basket. Before opening in 1987, the family remodeled the building after their Belgian farmhouse and even dug down to replicate their wine cellar, which today houses a notable collection. Its setting, just a block off quaint Carmel's main drag, makes dining here seem all the more relaxing and charming. A private room invites 2-8 people to enjoy the chef's prix-fixe on Vincent Van Gogh's very own dining table.

The rustic French and Italian cooking features deliciously simple dishes, ranging from the likes of hearty cannelloni to a peak-season grilled peach topped with pickled onion, toasted almonds and torn basil.

■ 95 5th Ave. (bet. San Carlos & Mission Sts.), Carmel-by-the-Sea

✆ (831) 625-0501 — **WEB:** www.casanovacarmel.com

■ Lunch Sat – Sun Dinner nightly   PRICE: $$$

CULTURA ⅋○

Mexican • Tavern

Cultura's cooking is inspired by the cuisine of Mexico, with particular attention paid to the region of Oaxaca. It might not be the right place to take abuela for an authentic taste of home, but the food is very good. Tucked among shops in a courtyard away from the street, this dining room resembles a sort of Mexican taberna, lined with deep red booths, coffered ceilings and wrought-iron accents. On fair nights, dine alfresco around the courtyard's fire pits.

Try the house-made Cultura mole with smoked pork, which arrives as a feast of freshly made tortillas and lightly pickled vegetable slaw for assemble-your-own tacos. Save room for desserts like the dense and dark Oaxacan chocolate brownie with a touch of chili and cinnamon cloaked in ganache.

■ 100 Dolores St. (bet. 5th & 6th Aves.), Carmel-by-the-Sea

✆ (831) 250-7005 — **WEB:** www.culturacarmel.com

■ Lunch Sat Dinner nightly   PRICE: $$

DAMETRA CAFE 🍴◯

Mediterranean • Simple

♿

The name itself tells the story of this restaurant and cuisine: Dametra is a portmanteau of Damascus and Petra. This results in a Middle Eastern and Mediterranean menu of huge portions that won't break the bank. The eponymous veggie delight offers a tasty array of the rustic dishes that they do best. Sample for instance the spinach and feta spanakopita, falafel and mounds of hummus to scoop up with wedges of warmed pita. For dessert, try their rich and buttery baklava, layering flaky phyllo dough with crushed pistachios and walnuts.

The cheery yellow interior, filled with colorful murals and a welcoming staff, makes this a thoroughly enjoyable place for a meal in Carmel. Its charming ambience has made it a hot spot for locals as well as tourists.

■ Corner of Lincoln St. & Ocean Ave., Carmel-by-the-Sea
☎ (831) 622-7766 — **WEB:** www.dametracafe.com
■ Lunch & dinner daily   **PRICE: $$**

LA BICYCLETTE 🍴◯

Mediterranean • Bistro

♿ 🚌 🕳

This is a quintessential bistro and relaxed neighborhood spot in the heart of charming Carmel-by-the-Sea. The quirky corner space offers petite but comfortable wooden chairs and tables, set beneath hanging copper pots and, of course, a bicycle or two.

First and foremost, the kitchen focuses on comforting seasonal cuisine with a California-Mediterranean slant, plus a handful of pizzas and fantastic breads fired in their wood-burning oven. At the same time, they are dedicated to beloved French classics: picture fork-tender duck confit, set on a bed of earthy Puy lentils with halved Brussels sprouts. At the end, a golden, flaky and buttery-sweet tarte Tatin filled with caramelized apples and finished with a tuft of whipped cream is absolutely delicious.

■ 29 Dolores St. (at 7th Ave.), Carmel-by-the-Sea
☎ (831) 622-9899 — **WEB:** www.labicycletterestaurant.com
■ Lunch & dinner daily   **PRICE: $$**

LUCIA 🍴⭕

Californian • Elegant

This dining room in the luxe Bernardus Lodge & Spa boasts its own garden, which provides many of the superb ingredients, and is proof of the kitchen's dedication to local and seasonal food. It might show a talent and focus on vegetables, but highlights from the nightly menu as well as à la carte may include brilliantly tender lamb, served as medallions of deboned ribeye with rosemary jus on a bed of sautéed greens.

There is a casual feel to the upscale lodge-like interior, with its large fireplace and muted colors. It's located just off the lobby but draws diners from well beyond mere hotel guests. The view alone, overlooking the Carmel Valley and Bernardus vineyards, may be worth a visit. Better yet, come on a sunny day and dine alfresco on the patio.

▪ 415 W. Carmel Valley Rd. (at Laureles Grade), Carmel Valley
✆ (831) 658-3400 — **WEB:** www.bernarduslodge.com
▪ Lunch & dinner daily   **PRICE: $$$**

MONTEREY'S FISH HOUSE 🍴⭕

Seafood • Family

Humble and home-style, this seems like a seaside city's answer to a great local diner and an idyllic stop for a cup of hearty clam chowder. The rich and smoky, woodsy smell of their signature oak-grilled oysters and fresh fish may greet you even before you walk in the door. That said, the owner's Sicilian roots are clear from the first bite of homemade linguini tossed with mounds of unctuous seafood. Italian sensibilities emerge again at dessert with a lovely array of cannoli, tiramisu and spumoni.

The white and seafoam-green dining room feels small and quaint, with cloth-covered tables and a fireplace in the back adding a touch of polish.

▪ 2114 Del Monte Ave.
(bet. Casa Verde Way & Dela Vina Ave.), Monterey
✆ (831) 373-4647 — **WEB:** www.montereyfishhouse.com
▪ Lunch Mon – Fri Dinner nightly   **PRICE: $$**

MONTRIO BISTRO 🍴○

Contemporary • Family

♿ 🏠 🍽️

This vast space is actually a 1910 firehouse replete with curving architecture, a beautiful bar and stairs that lead up to private rooms. The environment may seem upscale and contemporary, but don't be afraid to bring the kids—crayons and paper cover the tablecloth and they just might score a balloon on the way out. The kitchen prides itself on being green, sourcing many ingredients from local farmers, using sustainable seafood, prime meats and doing their part for responsible waste management. Expect tasty renditions of familiar favorites, like big, crisp pieces of golden-fried calamari with zesty charmoula.

Happy hour brings deals in the lounge, but come on Sunday night for half-price bottles of California wines, with plenty of pinots to choose from.

▨ 414 Calle Principal (bet. Franklin & Jefferson Sts.), Monterey
✆ (831) 648-8880 — **WEB:** www.montrio.com
▨ Dinner nightly   PRICE: $$$

PACIFIC'S EDGE 🍴○

American • Romantic

❀ ♿ 🍽️

Take a windy drive into the hills off Highway 1, pull in at the Hyatt hotel and brace yourself for a breathtaking experience. Perched on the cliffs over the roaring Pacific and encased by large windows, this aptly named spot boasts panoramic views. A roaring fireplace dissipates any misty chill coming off the ocean.

Dinner may not always live up to the vistas, but there are strong items to be had, especially the Brussels sprouts with kimchi and hazelnuts followed by their signature braised short ribs. Others may go the seafood route—perhaps scallops with romesco and cauliflower—as they are all Monterey Seafood Watch approved for sustainability. And speaking of all things local, behold desserts like a peanut butter mousse cake strewn with Big Sur salt.

▨ 120 Highlands Dr. (off Hwy. 1), Carmel
✆ (831) 622-5445 — **WEB:** N/A
▨ Dinner nightly   PRICE: $$$

PAPRIKA CAFÉ ⅃○

Mediterranean • Rustic

This tiny spot is the perfect sojourn before or after a visit to the Monterey Bay Aquarium, thanks to its delectable and affordable Mediterranean food and friendly service. A diminutive and humble place, it has only six tables, but the chef/owner provides a warm welcome, recommending favorite items before he goes to work in the tiny back kitchen.

Signs in the room advertise the café's famed creamy garlic sauce, best enjoyed in a pita wrapped with chicken, tomato and spinach. The luscious tahini that accompanies crisp, golden falafel is almost as good, and a classic Greek salad is refreshingly satisfying. Don't fill up completely though, as the homemade baklava, which the restaurant also sells at the local Tuesday farmer's market, is sure to sate.

▦ 309 Lighthouse Ave. (bet. Dickman & Drake Aves.), Monterey
℘ (831) 375-7452 — **WEB:** www.paprikacafe-monterey.com
▦ Lunch Wed – Mon Dinner Mon & Wed – Sat   **PRICE:** ⬬

PÈPPOLI ⅃○

Italian • Luxury

⅋ ♿ ☂ ⬭

The ocean and golf course views may be pure California, but a meal here is all about Tuscany. Named for the Pèppoli Vineyard in Italy and owned by the legendary Antinori family of winemakers, this restaurant strives to deliver rustic cooking to their discerning Pebble Beach clientele. Many of their own labels are featured here, as a perfect complement to the cuisine.

The dining room transports guests back to the homeland with rooms styled to resemble an exclusive Italian estate serving a menu of wood-fired Tuscan food. Expect hearty but skillfully prepared dishes like hand-crafted orecchiette tossed in vibrant green pesto, mixing puréed kale and broccoli with house-made sausages. Save room for excellent desserts like tiramisu and other traditional treats.

▦ 2700 17 Mile Dr. (at The Inn at Spanish Bay at Pebble Beach), Pebble Beach
℘ (831) 647-7500 — **WEB:** www.pebblebeach.com
▦ Dinner nightly   **PRICE:** $$$$

THE SARDINE FACTORY 🍴

Seafood • Vintage

The name and exterior of this "factory" can be deceptive as it is pretty damn elegant, if even a bit stodgy on the inside. Imagine silk curtains, monogrammed seatbacks and other ornate touches, including a glassed-in greenhouse "conservatory." If that's not enough, white tablecloths, silver chargers and a menu listing "favorite" and "famous" dishes showcase decades of approval from tourists and elders.

The menu is well executed but far from trendy, featuring a mix of classics like crispy sand dabs alongside '80s-glamour revivals like lobster ravioli in cream sauce. For those more open-minded however, the throwback theatricality can also be a lot of fun—from the ample bread basket with tomato-white bean dip to an engaging staff with fine-dining panache.

▨ 701 Wave St. (at Prescott Ave.), Monterey
℘ (831) 373-3775 — **WEB:** www.sardinefactory.com
▨ Dinner nightly   PRICE: $$$$

SEVENTH & DOLORES 🍴

Steakhouse • Fashionable

This highly anticipated rookie on the downtown scene boasts soaring ceilings, Crayola-bright pop art and crisp white linens. The result is an airy and deliciously polished modern room fit for a stylish crowd. A heated patio with large umbrellas is ideal for alfresco dining, weather permitting; inside, there's a peek-a-boo look into the immaculate kitchen.

If you land for lunch, don't miss their excellent burger, ground from tender filet mignon, brisket and bone marrow. Come dinner however, guests tuck into a chilled asparagus salad with burrata, shaved bottarga and Calabrian chili oil enhanced with supplements like poached prawns. Make sure to get your steak fix by way of the steak frites with bordelaise sauce or the larger Niman Ranch steak and chops.

▨ 7th Ave. & Dolores St. (SE Corner), Carmel-by-the-Sea
℘ (831) 293-7600 — **WEB:** www.7dsteakhouse.com
▨ Lunch & dinner daily   PRICE: $$$

SIERRA MAR 🍴

Californian · Minimalist

This Monterey marvel delivers what is hands-down one of the most spectacular Pacific Ocean views around. The space feels like it was designed for anniversaries, honeymoons and other such celebrations as guests take in the panoramic vistas through floor-to-ceiling windows. Despite being housed in the exclusive resort—the Post Ranch Inn—it retains a comfortable and even relaxed mood, supported by the rustic modern décor.

Be sure to try the attractively presented iron cocotte of melted and caramelized petit Basque cheese with seeded crackers and sweet apple compote. Ambitious desserts may showcase a wonderful range of flavors, as in the single bite-sized sphere of Bartlett pear panna cotta topped with sweet huckleberry gelée and powdered sorrel.

🔲 47900 CA-1 (at the Post Ranch Inn), Big Sur
✆ (831) 667-2800 — **WEB:** www.postranchinn.com
🔲 Lunch & dinner daily   **PRICE: $$$$**

YAFA 😊

Mediterranean · Cozy

This clear hit among locals has even spread to tourists—everyone comes back time and again. The owners bring hospitality to a new level, thanks to a jovial greeting and warm farewells that may involve a hug from the owner.

The smell of roasting meats entices passersby with the promise of their excellent kebabs, like deliciously charred yet tender chicken skewered with tomatoes. The Aleppo kafta, combining ground beef and lamb, is richly seasoned and perfectly paired with a side of zippy tzatziki. Be sure to begin any meal with an enormous plate of their mezze, heaped with minty cucumber and tomato salad, hummus as well as a sundried tomato- and feta-dip for scooping up with warm and fluffy pita.

Weekends bring a host of live music performances.

🔲 Junipero St. (at 5th Ave.), Carmel-by-the-Sea
✆ (831) 624-9232 — **WEB:** www.yafarestaurant.com
🔲 Dinner nightly   **PRICE: $$**

SANTA BARBARA

© Ron_Thomas/iStock

SANTA BARBARA

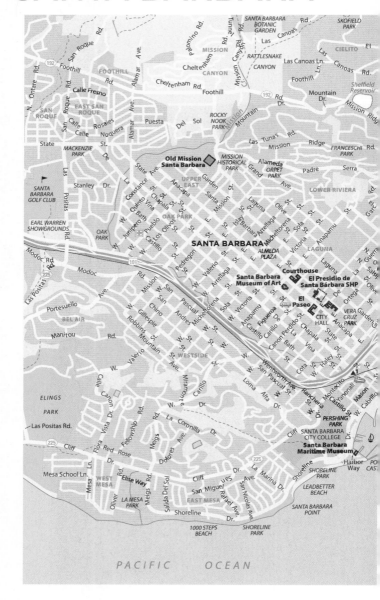

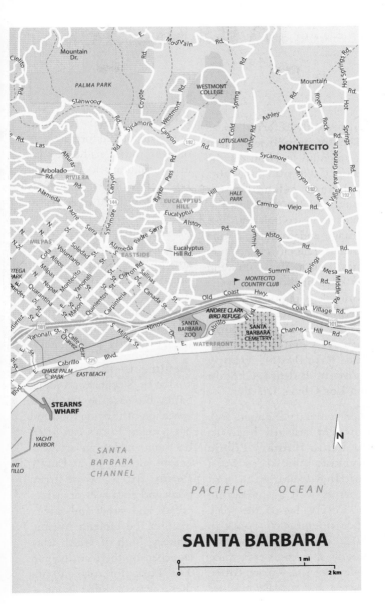

Mountain Dr.

Cielto

Rd.

PALMA PARK

Stanwood

Mountain Rd.

Coyote Rd.

Sycamore Canyon

WESTMONT COLLEGE

Spring

Cold

Ashley

E. Mountain

Rock

Rd.

Hot Springs Rd.

192

LOTUSLAND

MONTECITO

Las

Alturas

Rd.

Arbolado Rd.

Alameda

RIVIERA

Rd.

Padre Serra

Sycamore Canyon

144

Barker Pass Rd.

EUCALYPTUS HILL

Eucalyptus

Alston Rd.

Hill

HALE PARK

Camino Viejo Rd.

Sycamore Canyon

192

Rd.

192

MILPAS

N. St.

Cota

Soledad

Voluntario

Alameda Padre Serra

Alston

Summit Rd.

Rd.

Rd.

Padre Serra

N. Milpas

N. Nopal

Quarantina

ORTEGA PARK

Alisos

Montecito

Yanonali

Clifton St.

Salinas

Eucalyptus Hill Rd.

EASTSIDE

MONTECITO COUNTRY CLUB

Summit

Mesa Rd.

Hot Springs

Middle Rd.

Rd.

Guetierrez

S. Nopal

S. Mason

Quinientos

Carpinteria

Canada St.

Old Coast Hwy.

Coast Village Rd.

101

N. St.

161

Yanonali St.

S. Calle Cesar Chavez

S. Milpas St.

Niños

SANTA BARBARA ZOO

ANDREE CLARK BIRD REFUGE

Cabrillo

E. WATERFRONT

SANTA BARBARA CEMETERY

Channel

Hill Rd.

Dr.

225

Cabrillo Blvd.

CHASE PALM PARK

EAST BEACH

Blvd.

STEARNS WHARF

YACHT HARBOR

INT TILLO

SANTA BARBARA CHANNEL

N

PACIFIC OCEAN

SANTA BARBARA

0   1 mi
0   2 km

EATING IN...
SANTA BARBARA

Commonly referred to as "The American Riviera" given its splendid location on the central California coast, Santa Barbara is celebrated for many things, not the least of which is its colonial Spanish heritage and wonderful wine varietals. This city's viniculture dates back to the 1700's and has since blossomed into the world-class region that it is today. Make sure you explore tastings in the multiple areas with AVA status, including **Sta. Rita Hills**, **Happy Canyon**, **Ballard Canyon** and **Los Olivos District**.

The culinary-inclined folk however should head to the **Santa Barbara Public Market**, which has been pouring local wine and beer, as well as preparing food every day of the week since opening its doors in 2012. This urban emporium proudly showcases everything under the sun—from coffee roasters and cupcake bakeries to artisanal pizzerias and purveyors of Californian olive oils. Of course, its home base in the culturally focused Arts District makes it a perfect stop before or after a theater performance or visit to the Museum of Modern Art. This scenic coastal destination also hosts a farmer's market, originally founded in 1983—don't forget to check its whereabouts online as it moves to a different part of town every day of the week.

Adding to this stunning coastal city's culinary standing, Santa Barbara has its own spectrum of thriving food and bar retreats. Locals can often be found taking an art walk before winding up at **Lucky Penny** for its wood-fired pizza and craft beer or artisan breads and sweet and savory treats at the **Helena Avenue Bakery**, both of which were launched by the team behind **The Lark**. Intertwined with these gems is Funk Zone—

an arts community housed amidst a collection of old homes and industrial lots that draw crowds for its cultural explosion.

Follow the same creative vein by trekking onward to **Bree'osh** to sign up for a lesson in French pronunciation while sampling some of this county's best-loved pastries. Its success as a bakery-turned-cafe should come as no surprise, as a French couple is responsible for turning out these decadent treats which range from croissants and tartines in the morning to midday croque madame and quiche Lorraine. Capping off this culinary fun is **McConnell's**, which started serving its superb made-from-scratch ice cream in 1949. Little has changed, but with flavors like chocolate-covered strawberries, dairy-free Turkish coffee and whiskey and pecan praline, it's a major fave among local gentry—superfans, don't forget to join their pint-of-the-month club. They even ship to 48 states if you're not in town.

BARBAREÑO ¶◯

Californian • Trendy

 ♿ 🚻

This off-the-beaten-path favorite is inspired by California coastal traditions. Set just steps from downtown Santa Barbara, excellent sourcing and quality ingredients may as well be the kitchen's mission.

The outdoor smoker and grill are enough to lure folks over to their covered patio or casually cool dining room. Start with a local craft beer or wine to accompany with any one of their diverse small plates, which are generally centered around the grill. Highlighting their farm-to-table ethos and a love of all things organic is a pulled pork sandwich, with meat that's deliciously tender on the inside yet perfectly crunchy on the out. Standbys like pinquito beans are fulfilling—not unlike a scoop of the pomegranate- tamarind- and blood orange-ice cream.

■ 205 W. Canon Perdido (at De la Vina St.)
✆ (805) 963-9591 — **WEB:** www.barbareno.com
■ Dinner Wed – Mon   **PRICE: $$**

BELLA VISTA ¶◯

Italian • Elegant

 ♿ 🚻 🛋 🍳

Find this remarkable setting as you make your way through the lovely Spanish colonial style interior of the Four Seasons Biltmore resort. However, the ideal place to land is at a table on the terrace overlooking Butterfly Beach, amid fire-pits and Italian marble floors. The expansive menu offers everything one could want from luxury resort dining. Indulge in crudo, homemade pasta and a host of seafood or meat dishes. Refined fish preparations include white bass nostrano with nasturtium pesto and delicate lemon-potato cream. Explore some of the more unusual house-cured salumi, such as lonzino, saucisson sec or even duck prosciutto served with fresh cherry tomatoes, mustard and grilled crostini.

On Sundays, the brunch menu is a laudable attraction.

■ 1260 Channel Dr. (at the Four Seasons Biltmore)
✆ (805) 565-8246 — **WEB:** www.fourseasons.com
■ Lunch & dinner daily   **PRICE: $$$$**

BELMOND EL ENCANTO ¶◯

Contemporary • *Fashionable*

The Santa Barbara Hills may be a more residential neighborhood, but this renowned resort houses an elegant and romantic dining room with vistas that are downright stunning. Outside, sit on the spectacular terrace surrounded by treetops, hills and the ocean off in the distance. Inside, the huge lounge features live piano tunes most nights of the week, adding to the celebratory ambience.

The contemporary cuisine focuses on local and seasonal ingredients, often highlighting herbs from the chef's own gardens as in the colorful presentation of seared tuna with heirloom tomatoes. Classic desserts are also a high point, including the intensely rich and well-puffed dark chocolate soufflé.

The excellent French and domestic wine list merits a bit of exploration.

■ 800 Alvarado Pl. (bet. Lasuen Rd. & Mission Ridge Rd.)
✆ (805) 845-5800 — **WEB:** www.belmond.com
■ Lunch & dinner daily   PRICE: $$$$

BLACKBIRD ¶◯

Contemporary • *Elegant*

Located at the waterfront Hotel Californian, Blackbird is as attractive as its surroundings. Inside, its décor resembles a meeting of art deco and mid-century styles, with an "air kiss" to the private clubs of yesteryear. Striking arched doors seem to let the sea breeze wash over the room, which is as popular for lingering over cocktails as it is for dinner.

The cooking seems to convey an enjoyable play on classics, which may be no surprise given the chef's impressive pedigree. Nowhere is this more deliciously clear than in the green gazpacho comprised of cucumber, papaya and avocado, topped with sweet crabmeat and a bit of curried yogurt. Also sample the wonderfully fresh oysters, almost pearl-like when crowned with a smoky mignonette.

■ 36 State St. (bet. Mason & Cabrillo Blvd.)
✆ (805) 882-0135 — **WEB:** www.thehotelcalifornian.com
■ Dinner nightly   PRICE: $$$$

FIRST & OAK 🍴○
Contemporary • Romantic

In a small, romantic boutique hotel, this is a deliciously old-school restaurant that is coming into its own with ambitious contemporary cuisine. This should be no surprise, as the chef boasts a background in some esteemed and globally acclaimed kitchens.

Guests are invited to create their own prix-fixe menu by selecting four to five dishes from a variety of categories, such as garden, ocean or farm. This might yield a meal that begins with a refreshing gazpacho made from delicately spiced melon with basil blossom and a bit of smoky fried shrimp. Masterful desserts have included a brown-butter sponge cake with dense clotted cream and marinated strawberries.

Be sure to sample the owner's own wine label, Coqueliquot, available in a range of styles.

■ 409 First St. (at Oak St.), Solvang
℘ (805) 688-1703 — **WEB:** www.firstandoak.com
■ Dinner nightly   **PRICE: $$$**

THE LARK 🍴○
Californian • Trendy

This former fish market is located in the Funk Zone arts district, just a stone's throw from the oceanfront. The vibrant dining room has become one of the trendiest places in town, largely thanks to the urban scene it fashions through an edgy décor and vintage lighting. Service remains cool and laid-back as ever, while also taking very good care of each guest.

Meals are served as large, family-style portions that are meant to be shared and spotlight the central coast's finest ingredients. Well-mastered original creations may unveil blistered shishito peppers and roasted eggplant with cilantro yogurt, sweet and sour pickles as well as duck-fat breadcrumbs.

The wine selection is a smart representation of the best of Santa Barbara's producers.

■ 131 Anacapa St. (at Yanonali St.)
℘ (805) 284-0370 — **WEB:** www.thelarksb.com
■ Dinner Tue – Sun   **PRICE: $$$**

LA SUPER-RICA TAQUERIA ℀○

Mexican • *Taqueria*

This beloved institution has been drawing crowds for decades from near and far with its simple, delicious food—and not just because it was Julia Child's favorite spot for tacos. The small corner location has a cheerful exterior shaded by ficus and palm trees, as well as covered patio seats.

Orders are taken at the window, where you can watch the cooks grilling meats and pressing your tortillas at a steady clip. The menu lists an array of tacos filled with grilled steak, chorizo, rajas and much more. The tacos de adobado feature perfectly marinated and grilled pork, ready to be embellished with their pico de gallo and choice of green or spicy red salsa. Offerings go on to include supplements and specials, such as chile rellenos or tamales.

- 622 N. Milpas St. (at Alphonse St.)
- (805) 963-4940 — **WEB:** N/A
- Lunch & dinner Thu – Mon

PRICE: ⬟

LOS AGAVES ℀○

Mexican • *Simple*

Serving generous portions, fresh flavors and some of the most authentic south-of-the-border food around, this place deserves every bit of praise lavished upon it. The room has a cozy and soft sort of Mexican-style décor, with a Latin guitar playing gently in the background. The staff may place chips immediately on your table, but salsa and drinks are both self-service. Remember to order at the counter and collect a number before being seated. Start with the likes of lime-marinated halibut ceviche tostada with cilantro and sliced avocado. Then move on to the Agave burrito, wrapping halibut, shrimp and roasted peppers in a whole-wheat tortilla.

There may be four locations, but this one is the original. The room can get crowded, so takeaway is a popular option.

- 600 N. Milpas St. (at Costa St.)
- (805) 564-2626 — **WEB:** www.los-agaves.com
- Lunch & dinner daily

PRICE: ⬟

MESA VERDE 😳

Vegan • Simple

 ♿ 🛖 🍴

Don't let the less-than-swanky location fool you into thinking that this is anything less than an excellent vegan restaurant. Besides, once inside it feels more like a house with a lovely garden terrace, wood décor and wide-open kitchen. This is the kind of food that even meat-eaters can instantly love.

From the first bite of a mushroom umami burger with crisp lettuce and superb heirloom tomatoes, it is abundantly clear that these ingredients arrive fresh from the farm. Be sure to sample their Latin-style dishes like gluten-free picadillos tacos or empanadas. Polenta fries with jalapeños and caramelized onions are a hands-down favorite; while the sweet cashew cheesecake decked out with strawberries and an almond crust is a signature for good reason.

▪ 1919 Cliff Dr. (at Meigs Rd.)
🕾 (805) 963-4474 — **WEB:** www.mesaverderestaurant.com
▪ Lunch & dinner daily
                    PRICE: $$

SAMA SAMA KITCHEN 😳

Asian • Simple

 ♿ 🛖

This eatery in the heart of downtown is not only good fun but also good for the wallet. Here, the Chefs/partners bring their disparate expertise—one is a barbeque aficionado from Nashville, the other is Indonesian, and together they turn out a menu of thoroughly pleasing Southeast Asian food. Attractions include a well-spiced rendition of green papaya salad, mixing aromatic herbs, chilies and peanuts. Bao can be ordered fried or steamed, which yields a pillowy soft bun to be filled with crunchy fried chicken in a tangy sauce.

The interior is appealingly simple, but the back patio is a hidden gem, filled with string lights and communal tables that can be booked for parties. Weekday happy hour simply means steep discounts on a variety of food and drinks.

▪ 1208 State St. (at Anapamu St.)
🕾 (805) 965-4566 — **WEB:** www.samasamakitchen.com
▪ Dinner Tue – Sun
                    PRICE: $$

SMITHY KITCHEN + BAR 🍴

Californian • Contemporary décor

Named for its long-ago life as a blacksmith shop, but now existing amid the Museum of Art, Granada Theater and other galleries, this spacious restaurant has moved well beyond its humble beginnings. Inside, find sultry lighting and an attractive marble bar serving sophisticated cocktails. However, most prefer the ample patio, with its glowing lights, gnarled olive trees and warm atmosphere that's perfect for any occasion.

The menu changes often, but expect starters like Mexican-style corn, grilled on the cob until supremely sweet, then shaved and tossed with spicy, smoky green harissa, zucchini and chard. Well-balanced pastas are another favorite, especially those tubes of rigatoni tossed with tender pancetta and loads of vegetables in tomato sauce.

▪ 7 E. Anapamu St. (bet. Anacapa & State Sts.)
℘ (805) 845-7112 — **WEB:** www.smithysb.com
▪ Lunch Sun Dinner nightly   PRICE: $$$

THE STONEHOUSE
AT SAN YSIDRO RANCH 🍴

American • Rustic

This setting is totally unique and intensely romantic. Picture lush gardens and a rustic stone cottage lined with rough-hewn beams and a wood-burning fireplace, all overlooking a creek. Many of the herbs, fruits and vegetables are harvested right on the property. Arrive early to ensure there is enough time to walk the grounds before your meal. There is exclusivity in the air, which seems to match the affluent diners and formal service. Start with fresh-baked breads and olives while perusing the menu, which reads like a celebration of old-school American classics—think of a steak Diane, flambéed tableside.

The list of global wines and liquors is far from rote and has everyone smitten.

▪ 900 San Ysidro Ln. (at Mountain Dr.)
℘ (805) 565-1720 — **WEB:** www.sanysidroranch.com
▪ Lunch & dinner daily   PRICE: $$$$

YOICHI'S ₩○

Japanese • Intimate

This quaint little house run by a husband-wife team just happens to be one of the area's favorite spots for traditional Japanese dining. This should be no surprise, as Chef Yoichi Kawabata's background includes cooking at Nobu Tokyo. The dining room is quiet and serene, filled with white walls and dark wood tables—there is no sushi counter. Service is both friendly and informative.

The seven-course menu respects all the rules of kaiseki dining, using top seasonal ingredients and pristine, top-class fish. Meals begin with an array of four appetizers (zenzai) including delectable Wagyu beef that has been grilled and glazed in a sansho pepper sauce. Then grilled duck breast may be prepared with perfect tenderness in sweet soy sauce with green peppers.

◼ 230 E. Victoria St. (at Garden St.)
✆ (805) 962-6627 — **WEB:** www.yoichis.com
◼ Dinner Tue – Sun   **PRICE: $$$$**

LOS ANGELES

LOS ANGELES

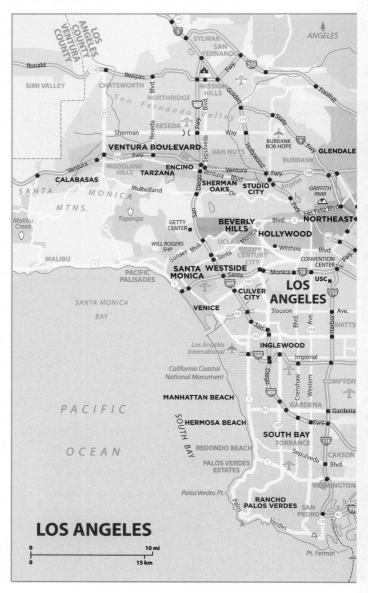

LOS ANGELES

0		10 mi
0		15 km

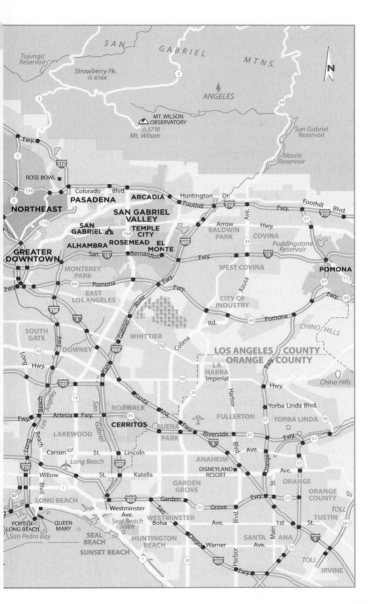

EATING IN...
LOS ANGELES

Beverly Hills is the capital of chic. Shoppers may start their day at the majestic **Fountain Coffee Room** inside the luxe Beverly Hills Hotel. **Tarte Tatin Bakery & Cafe** serves globally infused bites, while classic palates will love the carte at **Founders Ale House**.

Drop in for a Frenchified nibble at downtown's **Bottega Louie** or swing by K-town's **Mapo Galbi**, which boasts many a fan, including celebrity chef David Chang. But other mere mortals may slurp up the noodles at **Hangari Bajirak Kalguksu**; dine on spicy Nashville fried chicken at **Howlin' Rays**—a Chinatown hottie (literally); or chow down on Korean-Chinese fast food at **Zzamong**.

Everyone knows that Hollywood loves its classics; and dating back to 1927, **Pig'N Whistle** offers a taste of yore. While **The Musso & Frank Grill's** menu hasn't changed in eons, **Philippe**

The Original has been turning out sandwiches for an age now. They also allege to have invented the French dip (just don't tell **Cole's**, which stakes its own claim). And then there is **The Ivy**, a celebrity-mobbed hot spot.

Northeast's areas share a common thread of coolness. Artsy Eagle Park locals linger at **The Oinkster**, while **Casa Bianca Pizza Pie** has been a staple since the 1950's. Mexican munchies are also plentiful—hit **Leo's Taco Truck**, **Taco Spot** or **CaCao Mexicatessen**. Just as modern Israeli food lures diners to **Mh Zh**; date night prevails at **Covell**; and carousers convene at **Ye Rustic Inn**—a desirable dive. Less than 10 miles from Downtown, Pasadena sways to a gentler beat. Refuel at **Tortas Mexico** or **ShanDong Dumplings**.

The vibrant San Gabriel Valley teems with restaurants.

Sample deliciously crispy Meizhou roast duck or spicy chicken at **DongPo** as well as Hainanese chicken from **Side Chick**. The Valley is also home to Vietnamese diners and delis, like **Banh Mi Tho** and **Com Tam Thuan Kieu**.

In Santa Monica, drop in at **Huckleberry Bakery and Café**. But, California's café culture may be best seen at **Urth Caffé**. Not far behind, **Rose Café** is quintessential Venice. Meanwhile, South Bay's locals make a beeline to **Baja California Fish Tacos** or **Phanny's** for breakfast burritos. **The Standing Room Restaurant**, is great for burgers and **Abigaile** is a trendy haunt for drinks.

Westside's **Little Osaka** on Sawtelle Blvd. is studded with izakayas. **Tsujita LA** specializes in tsukemen, but it's all about burgers at **Plan Check Kitchen + Bar**. Finally, **The Apple Pan** has been a Century City mainstay and is über-popular among execs and actors from nearby 20th Century Fox Studios.

BEVERLY HILLS

AVRA 🍴○

Greek • Elegant

The laid-back luxury of the Greek islands has arrived, thanks to this vast beauty that has stolen the hearts of all and sundry. Imagine breezy elegance mingled in with clean, fresh and classic flavors from the Aegean and you'll start to get the drift.

Pull up a chair and you'll be met with a welcoming trio of olives, radishes and hummus to snack on while perusing the menu. Greek salad keeps its promise of crunch and punch, while mussels steamed with ouzo and finished with tart feta are spot on. As expected, fish is a focal point, both on the menu and in the dining room, where they are on display over ice. Crudo is great, but should you prefer your food cooked, go for items offered by the pound—be mindful though as these prices can creep up on you.

◼ 233 N. Beverly Dr. (bet. Wilshire Blvd. & Dayton Way)
𝒫 (310) 734-0841 — **WEB:** www.avrabeverlyhills.com
◼ Lunch & dinner daily   **PRICE: $$$$**

THE BAZAAR 🍴○

Spanish • Design

When a place has not merely hype, but also an elite vibe, painstaking service and excellent food, it is no surprise that Chef José Andrés is behind it. This vast "bazaar" never ceases to please the eye, with chandeliers, candy apple-red accents and ebony furnishings, all of which combine to create luxurious drama.

Adding to the sense of pleasure is the fact that this is multiple restaurants in one, each offering a unique experience. The ever-changing menu offers classic tapas with contemporary spins. For instance, the addition of black olives and cucumber makes tomato tartare deeply savory. Similarly, the elaborate presentation of steamed asparagus served with a grilled tomato vinaigrette delivers on taste, while the cheese course is a textural feat.

◼ 465 S. La Cienega Blvd. (at San Vicente Blvd.)
𝒫 (310) 246-5555 — **WEB:** www.thebazaar.com
◼ Dinner nightly   **PRICE: $$$**

THE BELVEDERE 🍴

Contemporary • Elegant

  ♿ 🚪 📷 🛋️ 🍽️

From its home in the posh Peninsula Beverly Hills hotel, this luxuriously designed dining room feels like a cross between the French countryside and the Hamptons. Topiaries guide you outside to the lovely black-and-white dining patio. The clientele looks as casually elegant as the setting and seems to carry an air of privilege, augmented by the occasional security guard hovering around a high profile table.

The menu features classic cooking techniques always done right. The perfectly cheesy and decadent risotto is rich with earthy flavors from mushrooms and asparagus, then topped with pecorino and bits of sea salt. For dessert, a deconstructed baked Alaska tastes like Hawaii, thanks to layers of coconut sorbet and toasted Marcona almonds.

■ 9882 S. Santa Monica Blvd. (at Wilshire Blvd.)
✆ (310) 975-2736 — **WEB:** www.beverlyhills.peninsula.com
■ Lunch & dinner daily   **PRICE: $$$**

CULINA 🍴

Italian • Contemporary décor

  🐾 ♿ 🚪 🪑 📷 🛋️ 🍽️

With a clientele heavy on striking on-screen stars, this upscale operation at the Four Seasons could easily get by on mere glitz and grappa. Instead, dishes that may seem tired are remarkably innovative here, sharpening standards like an artistic plate of prosciutto e melone composed as a mosaic and dressed to the hilt with a drizzle of olive oil, a few sprigs of thyme and grains of coarse sea salt.

The clubby dining room is well appointed, but the best perch is the outdoor patio, surrounded by hedges and a burbling waterfall. It's the ideal retreat to sip on a tart Meyer lemon spritz, twirl forkfuls of perfectly al dente spaghetti with mussels as well as breadcrumbs and sigh over a slice of moist, caramelized brown butter cake with blueberry gelato.

■ 300 S. Doheny Dr. (bet. 3rd & Burton Way)
✆ (310) 860-4000 — **WEB:** www.culinarestaurant.com
■ Lunch & dinner daily   **PRICE: $$$**

CUT 🏵

Steakhouse • Design

🏵 ♿ 🍽 🤲

In contrast to its grand hotel setting, this bright and modern Wolfgang Puck retreat delivers top quality, simply prepared meats and market-driven fare. As is true with so many of his other establishments, the menu here focuses on classics that never seem to go out of style. This is deliciously clear in the Maryland blue crab and Louisiana shrimp dressed in a tangy "Louis" sauce set over horseradish panna cotta.

At the center of the carte find both Japanese and American breeds of Wagyu beef grilled over hardwood. These may arrive on the plate as a trio of sirloin tastings from farms both local and abroad, all served as beautifully charred steaks with blushing pink centers, bursting with savory and buttery textures—pair them with a vibrant chimichurri, béarnaise or traditional steak sauce. Tableside presentations enhance the drama of this classic dining experience. But don't fret if you're not into red meat, as the versatile kitchen pays equal attention to other such delectable items as Maine diver scallops and roasted poussin. Even the sides flaunt some of the best produce around, from spring peas to autumn squash.

Excellent desserts and mignardises promise that no one leaves disenchanted.

◼ 9500 Wilshire Blvd. (at Rodeo Dr.)
☎ (310) 276-8500 — **WEB:** www.wolfgangpuck.com
◼ Dinner Mon – Sat   **PRICE: $$$$**

IL PASTAIO 😊

Italian • Trattoria

♿ 🚻 🍽️ 📋

Boisterous, bustling and always packed, make sure to reserve in advance before attempting to dine at this neighborhood favorite. The sunny outdoor terrace is the kind of place where jubilant crowds of people flock to be seen sipping Montepulciano at a tightly spaced table. Then again, some are surely here because it offers great value for Beverly Hills. The menu is large and aims to have something for everyone—from the wide range of carpaccio with toppings to pleasing bowls of homemade fettucine Bolognese. Decadent white and black truffle specials add flourish and heft to your bill.

Its longevity and status as a flagship of the Drago family empire is thanks to the unwavering quality of genuine and delicious Italian cooking through the years.

■ 400 N. Cañon Dr. (at Brighton Way)
℘ (310) 205-5444 — **WEB:** www.giacominodrago.com
■ Lunch & dinner daily   PRICE: $$

JEAN-GEORGES 🍴

Contemporary • Luxury

🍹 🍸 ♿ 🚻 🍽️ 🛎️ 📋

When a restaurant is housed in the venerable Waldorf Astoria, luxury and glamour are assured. High ceilings and imposing columns strive to fill the space, which is at once airy and modern, crisp and luminous. It also seems rather fitting that the romantic patio is covered with passion fruit vines. Well-heeled types come here to see and be seen, and the menu is calibrated to their pizza and pasta preferences.

Don't hesitate to let this kitchen take you beyond those tasty pizzas and try one of their signatures, like the caviar egg. Seared black cod in a spicy, herbal broth demonstrates that delicious blend of Asian influences that the eponymous chef's kitchen is renowned for. Well-composed desserts include a wonderfully fruity maple-roasted pear.

■ 9850 Wilshire Blvd. (at Santa Monica Blvd.)
℘ (310) 860-6566 —
WEB: www.waldorfastoriabeverlyhills.com
■ Lunch & dinner daily   PRICE: $$$$

MATSUHISA ¶○

Japanese • Vintage

After three decades of success, Matsuhisa remains as fine, lively and creative as it was on its opening day in 1987. It's also still very popular—note the luxury cars filling the parking lot. Inside, the unpretentious décor fosters a casual ambience. Find the best seats in the house right at the sushi bar, where an array of itamae are putting their skills to work while engaging with guests.

The menu highlights a wide range of rolls, ceviche, sashimi and cold dishes with an unexpected but delicious twist. Try the likes of Peruvian-style tiradito, yellowtail with jalapeño and zesty king crab ceviche. Classic sushi may go on to showcase Santa Barbara sea urchin, delicate snapper with shiso leaf and ponzu or fatty toro that melts in the mouth.

■ 129 N. La Cienega Blvd. (bet. Clifton Way & Wilshire Blvd.)
☎ (310) 659-9639 — **WEB:** www.nobumatsuhisa.com
■ Lunch Mon – Fri Dinner nightly　　　　**PRICE: $$$$**

NERANO ¶○

Italian • Fashionable

This seafood-friendly restaurant is appropriately named for an idyllic town on the Amalfi Coast. Nerano is LA's perfect spot for anyone craving honest, well-sourced and always-delicious food that strives to master the bounty of Campania. The upscale dining room maintains a pleasant vibe with friendly, competent service. Offerings are consistently satisfying, but the kitchen truly excels in its preparation of pasta, like spaghetti alle vongole featuring meaty clams in a lemony garlic-wine sauce spiked with devilish chili peppers. For dessert, the torta della nonna is everything you dream it would be, layered with thick crema pasticcera and crowned with pignoli.

The lounge upstairs boasts a playful and flirty vibe, so stop by at any time.

■ 9960 S. Santa Monica Blvd.
(bet. Charleville Blvd. & Moreno Dr.)
☎ (310) 405-0155 — **WEB:** www.neranobh.com
■ Lunch & dinner daily　　　　**PRICE: $$$**

MAUDE 🏵

Contemporary • Elegant

🏵 ♿

Every quarter of the year, Maude finds its new culinary theme in a wine region. Whether focusing on Spain's Rioja or France's Burgundy, the menu is a creative exploration of the profound connection between food and drink. Ergo, its reputation for an impressive wine selection and adept pairings. Despite refocusing each season on a new area, its emphasis on viticulture and cuisine ensures success.

Chef Curtis Stone consistently showcases a serious yet delightful cuisine. Find evidence of this in the agnolotti filled with robiola rocchetta and finished in a rich butter-cream sauce or a play on the classic vitello tonnato donning shavings of dried veal shoulder. Meat is also king here, so if an image of perfectly roasted lamb with potatoes and nettles comes to mind, you're starting to get the picture of the Burgundian theme. Even straightforward dishes are emboldened here, like the assertive interpretation of pan con tomate.

Meanwhile, the dining room is intimate, elegant and overlooks an open, buzzy kitchen. While the latter is fun to peek into, it remains unobtrusive and peaceful throughout the meal. For dessert, guests may choose to retire into the lovely lounge located in the "wine loft."

■ 212 S. Beverly Dr. (bet. Charleville Blvd. & Gregory Way)
📞 (310) 859-3418 — **WEB:** www.mauderestaurant.com
■ Dinner Tue – Sat   **PRICE: $$$$**

NOZAWA BAR

Japanese • Minimalist

Nozawa Bar is an extraordinary little jewel box of a room and sushi counter, secreted away in the back of the Beverly Hills location of Sugarfish. Yet its menu, kitchen and overall spirit are totally independent of the local chain restaurant in which it is housed. Be sure to arrive on time, as each seating begins promptly.

Omakase is the sole dining option here, served as multiple courses of primarily nigiri as well as a few sashimi and handrolls. Each sequence centers on exceptionally pristine fish, most of which is caught in Japanese waters and exported straight to local markets. These nigiri are particularly distinctive thanks to a generous brush of nikiri and loosely packed rice, served just warm enough to contrast with and elevate the flavorful fish.

Chef Osamu Fujita may be a traditionalist, but the 24-course menu includes many novelties. Start with the bright, white and perfectly crunchy jellyfish dressed with ponzu. This might be followed by an impressive presentation of deliciously tender octopus, sliced into thin slivers for sashimi. Sushi highlights include the delicate halibut fin, ruby-red snapper cut before your eyes and a handroll of mountain yam, ume and shiso leaf.

■ 212 N. Cañon Dr. (bet. Clifton & Dayton Ways)
✆ (424) 216-6158 — **WEB:** www.nozawabar.com
■ Dinner Mon – Sat   **PRICE: $$$$**

SHU (SUSHI HOUSE UNICO) ᵡO

Fusion • Design

Find this beloved Italian-Japanese fusion restaurant between boutiques in an open-air mall. The small, well-appointed room is dark with shellacked wood as well as red-and-black motifs. All of this draws the eye towards that white-tiled wall where a line of itamae are hard at work in the open kitchen.

Owner Giacomino Drago has come to represent everything wonderful in cooking, thanks to his unique, personal touch. The menu features such forward-looking specials as vinegar-bathed halibut, topped with arugula and artichokes. Tempura is a high point, whether as soft-shell crabs or Kumamoto oysters, served in their shells with ponzu and truffle oil. Delightful handrolls might be stuffed with seared marinated tuna, wasabi, cucumber and crispy garlic with tamari.

◼ 2931 1/2 Beverly Glen Circle (at Beverly Glen Blvd.)
℘ (310) 474-2740 — **WEB:** www.giacominodrago.com
◼ Lunch Mon – Fri Dinner nightly   **PRICE: $$$**

SPAGO ᵡO

Californian • Historic

Since opening its doors in the 1980s, Spago has become an American institution that never seems to age. The stark white stucco exterior beckons diners into this iconic canteen, that's elegant in that inescapably Californian kind of way. The service team displays a certain gracious hospitality and attention to detail that can be increasingly hard to find these days.

The market-driven cuisine remains focused on the state's bounty with plenty of modern classics and perennial signatures. Imagine tuna tartare and smoked salmon pizza. Veal schnitzel, pounded flat and fried until golden, is another time-honored platter that just so happens to be the recipe of the chef's grandmother. Desserts, like the calamansi pavlova, also shine.

◼ 176 N. Cañon Dr. (bet. Clifton Way & Wilshire Blvd.)
℘ (310) 385-0880 — **WEB:** www.wolfgangpuck.com
◼ Lunch Tue – Sat Dinner nightly   **PRICE: $$$$**

SOMNI ❀❀

Contemporary • Design

Make your way past the stylish SLS Hotel lobby and through a set of discreet doors to arrive in a world enveloped by luxury—curved oak walls, polished marble and handsome leather seats all set the stage for a whimsical but utterly premium culinary experience. Colorful bull heads and perfectly calibrated lighting lend visual appeal to this elegantly neutral room. Tickets for dining must be purchased in advance as there are only two nightly seatings, but rest easy as the effort is completely worthy.

Here, members of José Andrés' brigade perform a veritable ballet and follow on the heels of Chef Aitor Zabala, whose dinner brings pure theater. His remarkable pedigree and passion surprise at every turn, so have no preconceptions of what a meal here entails. Instead, imagine a sensory experience where your fingers double as utensils. While some dishes appear deceptively simple, like a cool oyster topped with caviar or finely diced beef tartare, flavors run deep, with unparalleled ease. Your feast may reach its peak over the turbot wing lacquered with teriyaki or dry-aged strip loin emmolada.

Desserts, like a matcha ice cream donut, are especially memorable and display a mind-boggling attention to detail.

◼ 465 S. La Cienega Blvd. (bet. Colgate Ave. & Clifton Way)
☏ (310) 246-5543 — **WEB:** www.sbe.com/restaurants/locations/somni
◼ Dinner Tue – Sat   **PRICE: $$$$**

TEMPURA ENDO 🍴

Japanese • Minimalist

There are few restaurants in the nation dedicated to tempura, but Endo makes a legitimate case for this impossibly delicate and difficult technique. Its distinguished reputation in Japan has made inroads in LA, presenting the artistic style of cooking that is so much more than just "frying."

For a true introduction, go for the priciest of the three prix-fixes and experience scallops stuffed with caviar. Then indulge in cool appetizers, such as "wild mountain plants" with vinegary okra. The main attraction centers on a handmade copper cauldron heating a blend of sesame and vegetable oil, as well as their distinct wine-based batters (one for coating fish, another for vegetables). What emerges, from summery corn to uni wrapped in shiso, is pure joy.

▪ 9777 S. Santa Monica Blvd.
(bet. Linden Dr. & Wilshire Blvd.)
✆ (310) 274-2201 — **WEB:** www.beverlyhills-endo.com
▪ Dinner Tue – Sun   **PRICE: $$$$**

UMEDA 🍴

Japanese • Contemporary décor

♿ 🖐

Everything at Umeda is a bit more impressive and inventive than the rest of the pack; and in some ways, the omakase served here could belong to any of the area's high-end dining counters. Its interior seems to bestow a quiet glamour to everything and everyone—this is a welcoming and tranquil destination for dinner. At the dining room's entrance, find a visually stunning glass floor that appears suspended over flowing water. This feature is tailed by large panes that lend an open and airy feel.

The kitchen offers an array of menus, from a chef's tasting to a parade of supremely delicious sushi and sashimi. The udon is downright superb, brimming with noodles imported from Japan in a truffle-scented stock bobbing with jidori chicken tsukune.

▪ 6623 Melrose Ave. (at Citrus Ave.)
✆ (323) 965-8010 — **WEB:** www.umedarestaurant.com
▪ Dinner Mon – Sat   **PRICE: $$$$**

URASAWA

Japanese • Minimalist

Welcome to one of the most expensive dining experiences in the country that also happens to showcase some of the Pacific Ocean's best seafood.

The space is designed to be an oasis of tranquility, spotless and beautiful, leaving nothing to distract the eyes besides those floral arrangements and a polished cypress counter. And behind that stretch of wood, Chef Hiroyuki Urasawa can be seen handling each morsel of fish himself in a display of world-class skills and expertise. In this kitchen, every slice and movement seem to demonstrate his focus, dedication and efficiency. Some guests appreciate such extreme concentration; others might find that it makes the atmosphere seem cold or tense.

The chef serves every artfully arranged course on hand-crafted Japanese ceramics. These include a bowl of aromatic dashi with soft and nutty goma dofu, Hokkaido uni and a few decorative gold leaves, which manage to deck most dishes here. Other items that follow might unveil superlative sashimi, a live shrimp that is cut and char-grilled before your eyes as well as Wagyu beef shabu shabu. Eating sushi here is intense—from the opening piece of smooth otoro to the succulent and sweet tamago finale.

218 N. Rodeo Dr. (at Wilshire Blvd.)
(310) 247-8939 — **WEB:** N/A
Dinner Tue – Sat   PRICE: $$$$

GREATER
DOWNTOWN

BÄCO MERCAT 🍴

Spanish • Rustic

Lauded as the beating heart of Chef Josef Centeno's expanding LA empire, this lively room can feel dressed up or down depending on the occasion—a snack at the long bar, an intimate corner date or a group celebration at the communal tables. Oscillating between Spanish, Middle Eastern and Italian accents, this food is big on flavor, fun and ideal for sharing.

The menu centers around "bäcos" and "cocas"—types of flatbread sandwiches packed with quirky, yet satisfying fillings like oxtail hash, cheddar and horseradish yogurt. Small plates are also big stars here, from a creamy eggplant-fava dip with za'atar and mint, to buttermilk-fried quail over smoky and tart pea leaves. A dreamy disc of pistachio-and-crème fraiche cheesecake makes for a worthy finale.

- 408 S. Main St. (bet. 4th & Winston Sts.)
- (213) 687-8808 — **WEB:** www.bacomercat.com
- Lunch & dinner daily   PRICE: $$

BADMAASH 😃

Indian • Colorful

Come here, eat and decide for yourself what it means to be an Indian gastropub—know however that it will be a thoroughly delicious process. The skilled kitchen delivers each dish with flavor and fun through its use of authentic ingredients mingled with global inspiration. Find the clearest expression of Chef Pawan Mahendro's philosophy in the poutine, accompanied by masala-spiced potatoes with the perfect dab of gravy, mozzarella and chicken tikka. Some mains may feature a simpler pairing of appetizing flavors, like fried fish served with chutney. Other menu options just rely on standard favorites, like Southern fried chicken—traditional in look only but a head-spinner in flavors.

The bi-level dining room and tiny kitchen are as colorful as the cuisine.

- 108 W. 2nd St. (bet. Main & Spring Sts.)
- (213) 221-7466 — **WEB:** www.badmaashla.com
- Lunch & dinner daily   PRICE: $$

BAVEL ⵏⵔ

Middle Eastern · Trendy

After putting the Arts District on the culinary map with the perennially popular spot Bestia, Ori Menashe and Genevieve Gergis have returned with their equally buzzy sequel. Its whitewashed walls, well-stocked bar and impossible-to-score reservations mark it as the elder's compatriot, but this time, the focus is on Middle Eastern eats—from roasted meats to fresh-baked pita.

Speaking of which, a selection of wood-fired flatbreads make for appealing starters, with toppings like spicy lamb sausage, red onion and pine nuts. From there, it's on to inventive eggplant "escabeche" with walnuts and pomegranate molasses; or whole-grilled dorade slathered with chermoula. Desserts are memorable, especially the strawberry-sumac cheese pastry with labneh.

■ 500 Mateo St. (at 4th Pl.)
℘ (213) 232-4966 — **WEB:** www.baveldtla.com
■ Dinner nightly   PRICE: $$$

BEST GIRL ⵏⵔ

Contemporary · Design

This upscale spot in the Ace Hotel typifies the neighborhood's revival, with an open floor plan, mirrored walls, popular wines and ambitious food from a pedigreed and well-known kitchen team, starring Chef Michael Cimarusti. It also honors the area's history, taking its name from the first film shown in 1927 at the adjacent theater.

The menu reflects a few strong Italian overtones, as evidenced by the paccheri stuffed with bitter greens and layered with a cheesy béchamel. But you'll also find the freshest of seafood here complete with global influences—imagine black cod crudo with powdered nori and tortilla salt. Close out over coconut pandan pudding with mango and calamansi.

■ 927 S. Broadway (bet. 9th St. & Olympic Blvd.)
℘ (213) 235-9660 — **WEB:** www.bestgirldtla.com
■ Lunch & dinner daily   PRICE: $$$

BESTIA

Italian • Trendy

Remaining as hot and hip as ever, this is the kind of place you head to for rib-sticking pastas or a whole branzino fresh off the wood-burning grill. It all feels like a labor of love inside, thanks to the husband-and-wife team who make it their mission to bring delicious food to this neighborhood. The space itself is warehouse-sized, with a copper bar, booths that almost appear suspended and a red-domed oven firing in the corner.

The lobster crostino is justifiably popular, but also sample casarecce al pomodoro—pasta made from semolina and tossed in tomato sugo and ricotta. Desserts are equally enticing: don't miss the humbly named "coffee and donuts," served as spiced chestnut zeppole alongside excellent coffee gelato and a dollop of sweet whipped cream.

■ 2121 E. 7th Pl. (at Santa Fe Ave.)
℘ (213) 514-5724 — **WEB:** www.bestiala.com
■ Dinner nightly   PRICE: $$

BROKEN SPANISH

Mexican • Trendy

Broken Spanish bustles with a pre-performance and after-work crowd near the Staples Center. A communal table, kitchen counter, two dining rooms and humming sidewalk area offer a nice range of seating for groups of any size. Cement block walls and wood floors amplify the revelry.

The food is equally buzzy and modern, thanks to native Angeleno, Chef Ray Garcia, whose Mexican cooking delivers flavor-forward dishes like ribeye carne asada with salsa molcajete. Tender poached rabbit cooked with thin strips of nopales and meaty bacon brims with succulent juices, cradled in thick and chewy blue corn tortillas. Local ingredients and vibrant flavors come alive in small plates like roasted beets with zesty, earthy achiote salsa alongside thick tortillas for sopping.

■ 1050 S. Flower St. (at 11th St.)
℘ (213) 749-1460 — **WEB:** www.brokenspanish.com
■ Dinner nightly   PRICE: $$

CHOSUN GALBEE 🍴

Korean • Contemporary décor

♿ 🍴 🎬 💳

There are elements of reverence and seriousness to dining here, which is an asset for anyone seeking authentic Korean food. The warm servers all wear traditional garments to heighten the classic feel, while also donning earpieces in the upscale modern setting. The wait may seem long, but the food is worth it.

The menu, too, can seem extensive with familiar classics from the barbecue lineup, but these are then elevated by the kitchen's distinct care and skill. The sheer variety of banchan is a feat here. This is also the perfect place for large groups on the hunt for superbly tender meat to grill on the spot. Galbee junullk is a standout, presenting short ribs prepared with the house's own "secret" soy sauce, then seared before your eyes with onions and mushrooms.

🔲 3330 W. Olympic Blvd. (at Manhattan Pl.)
📞 (323) 734-3330 — **WEB:** www.chosungalbee.com
🔲 Lunch & dinner daily   PRICE: $$$

CHURCH & STATE 😊

French • Bistro

♿ 🍴

It's easy to forget that this locale, in the trendy Arts District on the edge of downtown, is actually the former Nabisco Bakery. The interior feels like a genuine French bistro, right down to the vintage counter, servers' accents and perhaps most importantly, those excellent baguettes.

The perfect way to start off the night is with an Absinthe cocktail before moving through a well-priced meal of soupe à l'oignon, steak frites or bouillabaisse, all made from carefully sourced ingredients. On the domestic front, find a delightful assortment of charcuterie such as chicken liver mousse, duck prosciutto and paté de campagne. Finish with a chocolate pot de crème, or maybe a selection of cheese from their chalkboard listing.

🔲 1850 Industrial St. (at Mateo St.)
📞 (213) 405-1434 — **WEB:** www.churchandstatebistro.com
🔲 Lunch Mon – Fri Dinner nightly   PRICE: $$

CORNER PLACE ⅋○
Korean • Simple

A largely Korean crowd has been keeping this corner spot in business for decades—a fact that speaks to its authenticity and fantastic cooking. It is fast, efficient and tidy, with gas-fueled tabletop grills and plenty of vents to keep the room smoke-free as guests gather around their searing meats.

Portions are generous, so one order of bulgogi, thinly sliced tenderloin marinated in sweet and garlicky soy sauce, will easily feed two. Of course, a wide range of kimchi arrive as an ideal complement to those meats—including cabbage, crisp white radishes and bitter soybeans. Combine that with a bowl of their refreshing, tangy and mouthwatering chilled noodle soup, dong chi mi gook su, and your decisions are done for the night.

▨ 2819 James M. Wood Blvd.
(bet. Vermont & Westmoreland Aves.)
✆ (213) 487-0968 — **WEB:** www.cornerplacerestaurant.com
▨ Lunch & dinner daily   PRICE: $$

DAMA ⅋○
Latin American • Design

 ♿ 🏬 🕯 🤞

Sultry, colorful and complete with a breezy Caribbean vibe, folks flock here to tuck into satisfying food. While starters like whipped white beans with crispy pork, cotija and pickled pearl onions are captivating, delve deeper into such unlikely items as a Latin take on panzanella, featuring tomatoes and garlic confit. And while a dry-aged ribeye is hard to beat on its own, it's especially good in build-your-own tacos with pickled sweet peppers and salsa verde.

Dama's feisty flavors play well off its chic old-Havana-style dining room, with plush leather sofas, massive wicker fans spinning overhead and colorful tile underfoot. The jaunty front patio is filled with plenty of greenery, while the glam central bar busily blends tropical cocktails to order.

▨ 612 E. 11th St. (bet. San Julian & San Pedro Sts.)
✆ (213) 741-0612 — **WEB:** www.damafashiondistrict.com
▨ Lunch & dinner daily   PRICE: $$$

DHA RAE OAK

Korean • *Family*

It's all about the duck—whole roasted in a clay pot—at this dining delight. And since the very best things take time, seat-of-the-pants types must know that this signature platter requires a bit of planning; order at least a day in advance. However, upon entering this Koreatown gem, one may look forward to being rewarded with a duck to dream about for weeks. Stuffed with chestnuts, sweet potatoes, rice and herbs, then wrapped and roasted for hours, the bronzed bird is plated before your eyes. A spicy dipping sauce and seasoned salt tailed by a light duck broth with greens simply transforms the dish into delectable goodness.

Bring a special somebody to partake in this festive experience, since it's impossible to finish on your own and food this good deserves to be shared.

■ 1106 Western Ave. (at 11th St.)
℘ (323) 733-2474 — **WEB:** N/A
■ Lunch & dinner daily   **PRICE: $$**

THE EXCHANGE ⑩○

Middle Eastern • *Rustic*

♿ 🚪 🛏 🐾

Named for the historic 32-foot-tall "Commercial Exchange" sign that marks its exterior, this watering hole defined by geometrically set glass panes and set inside the hip Freehand Hotel is an oasis of contemporary Middle Eastern cooking. Its bright and comfortable dining room is quite the looker, bursting with lush greenery, while wood paneling lends the space a 70s vibe.

Mirroring the striking setting, Chef/partner Alex Chang presents a splendid, wholesome and vibrant menu of this pan-regional cuisine. Opt for the salatim platter, a rotating trio of items like rich hummus with a dusting of piquant Syrian pepper; or shredded red cabbage with peanuts and dukkah. Simple desserts, including a warm dark chocolate chip cookie, are especially satisfying.

■ 416 W. 8th St. (at Olive St.)
℘ (213) 395-9531 — **WEB:** www.freehandhotels.com/los-angeles
■ Lunch & dinner daily   **PRICE: $$**

THE FACTORY KITCHEN

Italian • Chic

This "factory" is actually sleek, with cement columns, a modern bar and wide-open garage doors that enhance its lofty feel. However, the heart and soul of its kitchen is dedicated to traditional Northern Italian cuisine. This should come as no surprise, as Angelo Auriana and Matteo Ferdinandi are turning heads with their quickly expanding empire. Devotion to regionally specific flavors is clear in every bite, such as the focaccina calda di Recco al formaggio, layering shatteringly crisp dough between Crescenza cheese, tomato sauce and capers. Everything in the mandilli di seta is delightful, from the thick sheets of "handkerchief" pasta to the almond-basil pesto.

Desserts, including a Saracena espresso-soaked buckwheat tiramisu cake with toffee crunch, are ambitious.

▨ 1300 Factory Pl. Ste. 101 (bet. Alameada Ave. & Mateo St.)
✆ (213) 996-6000 — **WEB:** www.thefactorykitchen.com
▨ Lunch Mon – Fri Dinner nightly   **PRICE: $$**

GISH-BAC ¶○

Mexican • Simple

This family-style Mexican spot in Arlington Heights is known for its brilliant barbacoa, a signature of the owners' based on an old family recipe. While a few varieties are offered here, the goat enchilada marinated with spicy guajillo chile and served falling off the bone is unmissable. This recipe passed down through generations of Chef Maria Ramos' family is pure and delicious comfort.

That's no knock on Ramos' take on other specialties, including densely spiced moles, like the negro with pulled chicken in a tamal, or thin and crispy tlayudas topped with refried beans, quesillo and choice of meat. All of this pairs nicely with refreshing horchata with delightful additions of diced cantaloupe and cactus fruit sorbet.

▨ 4163 W. Washington Blvd.
(bet. Crenshaw Blvd. & Bronson Ave.)
✆ (323) 737-5050 — **WEB:** www.gishbac.com
▨ Lunch & dinner daily   **PRICE:** ⊜

GUELAGUETZA 🍴○

Mexican • *Family*

♿ � 🛵 💵

This distinct Oaxacan eatery, 20 years young, knows exactly what its culinary mission is—so much so that it is made abundantly clear in everything from its website address (ilovemole.com) to the orange façade that announces its presence from blocks away. Inside, pops of green, vinyl-covered tables and happy faces brighten the whimsical setting. A grill station fills the room with the scent of blistering peppers and more.

The tlayudas, enchiladas and pozole are all delightful, but it is their negro and rojo moles that are absolute favorites. Mole estofado is so complex that it is nearly impossible to pick out the ingredients creating such a rich and dark sauce, slathered onto chicken or pork. Everyone gets a taste of mole coloradito, drizzled over gratis chips.

■ 3014 W. Olympic Blvd. (at Irolo St.)
📞 (213) 427-0608 — **WEB:** www.ilovemole.com
■ Lunch & dinner daily   PRICE: $$

GUERRILLA TACOS 😀

Mexican • *Design*

After years on the road chased by adoring fans, this rock star taco truck has finally ditched its wheels and settled down permanently in the burgeoning Arts District. Its long lines, however, remain unchanged, thanks to Chef/owner Wes Avila, who's developed his very own style of haute Mexican cuisine after having played backup in myriad highbrow kitchens. Of course, the sleek space, with fun touches like table numbers made from spray paint bottles, perfectly matches his vibrant aesthetic.

Almost everything on this menu is a hit—from fish tacos with chipotle créma to taquitos stuffed with all the accoutrements of a loaded baked potato, then drizzled with tomatillo salsa. For a more unusual bite, try the pocho tacos, highlighting rich and gamey wild boar.

■ 2000 E. 7th St. (at Mateo St.)
📞 (213) 375-3300 — **WEB:** www.guerrillatacos.com
■ Lunch & dinner daily   PRICE: $$

GUISADOS ⊗

Mexican • Taqueria

&

Set on a busy corner with an unassuming façade, this may be a humble storefront, but it's all heart with an inimitable taste of home. The eldest in a small but growing group of locations, you'll be summoned to the counter here for a Styrofoam plate—but the braised meat with vegetables and handmade tortillas that fill it are the ultimate trophy.

This clean, airy and family-owned spot is open all day, so pop in when the mood strikes to sample their daily specials. Consult the chalkboards for the latest update, then snag a seat at one of the few tables with a view of the grill. Cochinita pibil, shredded pork with sweet achiote spice and creamy black beans, is the very picture of comfort, especially when bested by the warm and toasty tortillas.

■ 2100 East Caesar E. Chavez Ave. (at St. Louis St.)
℘ (323) 264-7201 — **WEB:** www.guisados.co
■ Lunch & dinner daily   **PRICE:** ⊗

GUSTO ⊗

Italian • Osteria

& ⊞ ⊕ ⊠

Packed since day one, this Cal-Ital moved into a larger space down the street so that it had room to grow (quite literally—check out the olive tree on the back patio). Comfy and homey, featuring dim lighting and a glassed-in wine display, it makes for a relaxed perch in which to relish a leisurely meal.

The menu hits all the standards, from meatballs to crispy squash blossoms along with a few other seasonal riffs, like a tomato panzanella with cucumber, watermelon and ricotta salata. But the real draw is their impressive selection of house-made pasta—including bucatini carbonara or tonnarelli with pomodoro, basil oil and a parmesan emulsion. Round things out with a slice of the popular coconut gelato pie, drizzled with chocolate sauce and toasted coconut.

■ 8022 W. 3rd St.
(bet. Crescent Heights Blvd. & Edinburgh Ave.)
℘ (213) 951-9800 — **WEB:** www.gusto-la.com
■ Dinner nightly   **PRICE:** $$$

HAYATO ✿

Japanese • Intimate

The entrance can be a bit tricky to locate within the newly transformed ROW DTLA, so look for the fluttering noren on the first-floor of building M2. Inside, a white cedar counter dominates the softly toned room and ensures that dining here is an intimate and engaging experience with Chef Brandon Hayato Go. This is the kind of place where celebrants and gourmands come to enjoy a culinary show. Many courses begin with ingredients artfully arranged in the back kitchen and handed to the chef on trays, then finished before your eyes and presented with detailed explanations.

The chef's nightly omakase presents an impressive parade of sashimi along with grilled, fried, steamed and simmered items. Seafood is sparkling beyond compare, especially the intense and focused presentation of a hollowed-out snow crab shell filled with seasoned rice, roe and tomalley. Morsels of tender abalone with small but mighty cubes of abalone gelée and a dab of liver sauce deliver flavors that are simultaneously pure and restrained. Everything seems to shine in a rice pot of grilled wild yellowtail and daikon, showered with slivered chives and served with pickles.

■ 1320 E. 7th St., Ste. 126 (at ROW DTLA)
℘ (213) 395-0607 — **WEB:** www.hayatorestaurant.com
■ Dinner Tue – Sat   **PRICE: $$$$**

HERE'S LOOKING AT YOU 🍴

Contemporary · Trendy

This whimsically named restaurant just outside of Koreatown seems to have captured the spotlight, and for good reason. Much of the attention is earned by the fact that the kitchen team previously worked together at beloved Animal. The dining room is decorated with antelope heads, heavy drapery and shelves of cookbooks for visual appeal.

Evenings should begin with a serious exploration of their cocktail program, reflecting the season through original creations or maybe just a classic Mai Tai. First-rate ingredients and impressive skill are clear in small plates like diced heirloom tomatoes set over crème fraîche, fragrant herbs and Chinese sausage crumbles. Head-on prawns are then deep-fried in their shells, rendering them wholly edible and quite delicious.

■ 3901 W. 6th St. (at Oxford Ave.)
☏ (213) 568-3573 — **WEB:** www.hereslookingatyoula.com
■ Lunch Sat – Sun Dinner nightly   **PRICE: $$**

HOCK + HOOF 🍴

Contemporary · Trendy

Courtesy of husband-and-wife chefs Kat Hu and Justin Yi, this culinary retreat may be in an area churning with change. However, its cuisine boasts consistency, drawing inspiration from the chefs' myriad trips to Southeast Asia and South America. Their concept is to weave Asian flavors into a global repertoire of dishes using, at times, classic French techniques. The result is a delightfully diverse menu, where Japanese tempura and Navajo fry bread sit side-by-side.

Inside, the white-walled dining room is stuffed with nearly as many leafy plants as it is eager patrons. The clean visual slate lets the couple's culinary imagination take center stage, from baby octopus with lollipop kale to chicken-liver mousse with Hawthorne berry gel.

■ 517 S. Spring St. (bet. 5th & 6th Sts.)
☏ (213) 279-9983 — **WEB:** www.hockandhoof.com
■ Lunch Sat – Sun Dinner nightly   **PRICE: $$$**

HOLBOX 😋
Mexican • Taqueria

Named for a tropical island off the Yucatán Peninsula, this cheery walk-up stall shines bright with seafood, whether that's a whole grilled branzino, an exemplary Baja-style fried rockfish taco or an electrically spiced scallop aguachile. Run by the second generation of the Cetina family, it skews a bit younger than sibling Chichen Itza, with a sleek look, an open kitchen and a slightly higher (though still gentle) price point.

Though it anchors the Mercado La Paloma, a market hall focused on affordability for first-time business owners, this stall does have a few splurges up its sleeve. The one worth splashing on is the addictive ceviche of spanking-fresh wild sheepshead fish, Santa Barbara sea urchin and pico de gallo on a crisp tostada.

◻ 3655 S. Grand Ave. (at Mercado La Paloma)
☏ (213) 986-9972 — **WEB:** www.holboxla.com
◻ Lunch & dinner Tue – Sun   PRICE: $$

JAFFA 😋
Israeli • Rustic

While its sandstone walls hint at the Holy Land, the plant-filled front patio is 100% LA; and however ancient seeming, this room soars with contemporary accents like jumbo windows, banquettes lined with textured fabric and an electric-blue pipework bar.

Chef/partner Anne Conness deftly blends Middle Eastern flavors with Israeli comfort food. Classic palates might not approve of sweet potatoes and cashew cream in hummus or even frozen yogurt with peach hamentashen, but they'd be hard-pressed to resist them. Nostalgic types will thrill to the clear chicken consommé with a light and fluffy matzoh ball. Though it may arrive on a fancy plate, the shawarma wrap has real soul.

◻ 8048 W. 3rd St.
(bet. Crescent Heights Blvd. & Edinburg Ave.)
☏ (323) 433-4978 — **WEB:** www.jaffa.la
◻ Lunch & dinner daily   PRICE: $$

JUN WON

Korean • Family

This beloved diner shines brighter than ever thanks to an upgrade to a more modern space set in the rear of a mall. Congenially run by a mother-and-son team, its soundtrack appropriately flits from traditional tunes to hip-hop, while Korean cooking shows can be seen on their TV screens.

Seafood dishes are the house specialty and the steamed cod—braised until it's all but melting in a spicy and salty broth—is the absolute winner. Also worthy of consideration: beautifully crisp, pan-fried whole sea trout; scallion pancakes stuffed with plump and juicy oysters; as well as spicy raw crab. Bring a group, since reservations are typically accepted for only five or more, and tuck into the banchan with a sip or two of soju as you wait for your food.

▨ 414 S. Western Ave. Unit B (at 4th St.)
𝒞 (213) 383-8855 — **WEB:** N/A
▨ Lunch & dinner Mon – Sat   PRICE: $$

LA BOUCHERIE ON 71

Steakhouse • Luxury

Few restaurants offer the same level of high drama and culinary appeal as the wonderful La Boucherie on 71. In fact, the InterContinental Los Angeles Downtown in which it is housed is the tallest building west of Chicago, so its 71st-floor dining room naturally boasts panoramic views of a stunning array of glass, steel and sky for miles.

Yet dining here is about much more than just the vistas, thanks to excellent steakhouse fare served with a heavy French accent, as well as seafood towers and choice of poisson. The menu focuses on succulent well-aged steaks offered with impressive accompaniments, like the cognac and green peppercorn sauce. Regulars know to seal their meals on a sweet note with macarons full of chocolatey coffee ganache.

▨ 900 Wilshire Blvd. (bet. Francisco & Figueroa Sts.)
𝒞 (213) 688-7777 — **WEB:** www.laboucheriedtla.com
▨ Lunch & dinner daily   PRICE: $$$$

LA CASITA MEXICANA 🍴

Mexican • Colorful

♿ 🛅

An LA original, this colorful room has been dispensing regional Mexican cooking for two decades. Along the way, Chef/owners Jaime Martin del Campo and Ramiro Arvizu have become culinary celebrities, earning slots on Telemundo and Univision. But the recipes they learned at the feet of their Jaliscan grandmothers endure, just like the classic mariachi tunes that play overhead.

The kitchen turns out a host of complex and festive family dishes that are menu musts—like chicken enchiladas smothered in a trio of rich moles (including the famed 45-ingredient mole negro). Poached fish in chipotle crema is intense, yet delicate; while a stuffed poblano chile en nogada is a riot of flavor—spicy pepper, rich ground beef, pecan cream and tart pomegranate seeds.

◻ 4030 E. Gage Ave. (bet. Corona & Riverside Aves.), Bell Gardens
☎ (323) 773-1898 — **WEB:** www.casitamex.com
◻ Lunch & dinner Tue – Sun   PRICE: $$

LANGER'S 😊

Deli • Historic

♿ 🛅

Pico Blvd. is lined with Jewish delis, but stray from the pack and make a beeline to MacArthur Park and Langer's, which has been ladling matzoh ball soup since 1947. And while it began life as a 12-seat counter, it's transformed over the years to a massive space decked out with that classic counter and booths.

Equally ample is the menu, with all of the requisite standards such as latkes, blintzes and chopped liver. Breakfast is served all day, but really, if you're here for the first time, opt for the hot pastrami sandwich. Sugar-cured, seasoned and smoked, then piled with cheese, sauerkraut and grilled between two slices of rye—it's the king of the castle. The only way to make this meal better is to end with a slice of sinfully rich cheesecake.

◻ 704 S. Alvarado St. (at 7th St.)
☎ (213) 483-8050 — **WEB:** www.langersdeli.com
◻ Lunch & dinner daily   PRICE: ⬭

LE COMPTOIR

Californian • Intimate

Find this tiny sparkler tucked inside the historic Hotel Normandie and helmed by Chef Gary Menes along with his talented team. The name, French for "counter," is a literal description of the space, which seats no more than ten guests before the stainless-steel kitchen, and features little more than a wine alcove to adorn the room. Such intimate seating means that the ambience depends primarily on the patrons, who are either uniformly quiet and contemplative or lively and interactive.

Dining here is a personal experience, emphasized by the fact that the chef is cooking and plating everything right before your eyes. Dishes turned out of this kitchen are innovative and handled with great care, with the chef focused almost entirely on vegetables—protein plays a subsidiary role here. Keeping that in mind, anticipate the likes of a savory carrot velouté or morsel of cured squash, both of which are as monumental as the supplemental grass-fed beef. Much of the produce arrives fresh from the chef's Long Beach garden.

An amazing accompaniment to this meal is the skillet toasted sourdough bread—it's made from a starter that may be older than some of the diners in the room.

■ 3606 W. 6th St. (at Normandie Ave.)
☏ (213) 290-0750 — **WEB:** www.lecomptoirla.com
■ Dinner Tue & Thu – Sat   **PRICE: $$$$**

MACCHERONI REPUBLIC 😊

Italian • Trattoria

With its tall mirrors, tiled walls and tin ceilings, this rustic Italian eatery is every inch the classic trattoria. Hidden in plain sight just across from Grand Central Market, it's a known quantity with the local office crowd, who fill the tightly packed tables at lunch. A few bites, and you'll be ready to pledge allegiance to the Republic, too.

The array of excellent handmade pastas is seemingly endless, from classic lasagna and osso buco-stuffed agnolotti to the "chef's favorite" passarelli in a tomato-rich tripe stew. But pry yourself away from the noodle nexus, and you'll be equally delighted by daily specials like octopus with lentils and roasted peppers. Be sure to finish with the buttery olive-oil cake, studded with blueberries and citrus.

■ 332 S. Broadway (bet. 3rd & 4th Sts.)
☏ (213) 346-9725 — **WEB:** www.maccheronirepublic.com
■ Lunch & dinner daily   **PRICE: $$**

MAJORDŌMO 😊

Asian • Fashionable

For years, New York has enjoyed Korean-American chef David Chang's hip, singular take on Asian cuisine—and now LA gets a taste of what all the buzz is about. Sequestered inside a former warehouse on the industrial fringe of Chinatown, reservations can be a challenge to land online, but gamblers can test their luck by trying for one of the few counter seats on a walk-in basis.

Is it worth the hype? You know it. Chinese bing bread, a pita-like offering, may be topped with spicy pulled lamb or smoked roe and egg. Then, vegetable-inspired market dishes like raw sugar snaps with horseradish share equal time with staples like Chang's legendary crispy pork belly, wrapped in tender leaves of Bibb lettuce along with green papaya salad and spicy homemade chili sauce.

■ 1725 Naud St. (near Wilhardt St.)
☏ (323) 545-4880 — **WEB:** www.majordomo.la
■ Lunch & dinner daily   **PRICE: $$**

MASTER HA ¶○

Korean • Simple

In a sea of more-is-more Koreatown restaurants with massive menus, Mister Ha stands out for its singular focus on a handful of dishes, namely marinated seafood and suhllungtang (or oxbone broth). Start with the remarkably fresh shrimp and crab, served plump and meaty after a light fermentation in miso. They're accompanied by an array of deliciously addictive banchan, including other more unusual kimchi like sesame-leaf.

From there, it's on to the soothing and restorative broth, which gets added heft from the addition of slippery, chewy noodles along with beautiful and tender slices of accompanying brisket. Ideal for a sick day (or a hangover), it is comfortingly bland—even though you can easily spice it up by plunking in some chili-infused daikon.

■ 1147 S. Western Ave. (at Country Club Dr.)
℘ (323) 998-0427 — **WEB:** www.masterhala.com
■ Lunch & dinner daily   **PRICE: $$**

MI LINDO NAYRIT MARISCOS 😊

Seafood • Family

 ♿ 🌲

This colorful, welcoming spot is the ideal respite for simple Mexican fare, focusing on the small region of Nayarit, located between the forested mountains of the Sierra Madre and Pacific Ocean. The name also hints at their focus on straightforward seafood. The semi-enclosed dining room is well appointed and cheerful, with a clear eye on regional traditions.

Ceviche de pescado is a zesty, textural feat, stocked with octopus and shrimp, set atop a tostada for delicious crunch. The caldo de siete mares is a deeply flavored and brothy feast of abalone, langoustine and much more. The number of signature items can seem overwhelming, but go with a group and be sure to get the molcajete al gusto and mi lindo Nayarit platter.

Sundays may even bring live music.

■ 1020 E. Florence Ave. (at Central Ave.)
℘ (323) 589-5109 — **WEB:** www.milindonayarit.com
■ Lunch & dinner daily   **PRICE: $$**

OFFICINE BRERA 🍴

Italian • Contemporary décor

With a nod to the Brera design district, the Milan neighborhood celebrated for its museums and furniture boutiques, this operation honors its namesake with an edgy space, warm décor and cooking specific to the Lombardia and Veneto regions. Servers are pleasant, informed and on point, thereby making the setting ideal for groups as well as solo diners.

Pastas like foiade ripiene, chicory and ricotta-stuffed tubes, are rendered ever so unique with foraged mushrooms, reflecting the tenets of the Cali-fresh philosophy of top produce with simple preparations. Equally worthy is sirloin carpaccio with Ligurian olive oil as well as lesser known specialties like bread dumplings (pisarei e verdure) tossed with beans, tomatoes and chili flakes. Desserts, too, follow suit.

▪ 1331 E. 6th St. (at Mill St.)
☏ (213) 553-8006 — **WEB:** www.officinebrera.com
▪ Lunch Mon – Fri Dinner nightly   **PRICE: $$$**

OKIBORU RAMEN 😊

Japanese • Contemporary décor

&

Set on the edge of Chinatown, this laboratory-like artisanal factory of ramen draws a crowd who come here solely to savor these handmade noodles in slowly simmered broths. Order at the register, then pull up a chair to watch the staff crafting these strands behind the glass-enclosed room.

This kitchen is reputed for presenting three styles of ramen as well as a handful of sides during the day. Come dinner though, the dish to beat is tsukemen, whereby the noodles are placed in neat nests on a silver tray for a quick dip in the rich and flavorful broth. Add to that the smoky and tender slices of pork, a perfectly creamy-centered soft boiled egg as well as a sheet of nori, and you have a pleasure-packed, slurp-worthy meal that is the very definition of umami.

▪ 635 N. Broadway (bet. Caesar E. Chavez Ave. & Ord St.)
☏ (213) 988-7212 — **WEB:** www.okiboru.com
▪ Lunch & dinner daily   **PRICE: ☜**

OLYMPIC CHEONGGUKJANG 🍴○

Korean • Simple

If Korean isn't in your linguistic arsenal, you'll need to pack a fluent friend for your journey to this well-regarded strip-mall spot, where the menu and the welcome aren't available in English. Don't be daunted though, as the food is worth it, with authentic takes on everything from boiled game hen stuffed with sticky rice to the namesake cheonggukjang—a thick stew made with intensely pungent fermented soybeans that are this nation's answer to Japanese natto.

For those who aren't ready to brave the beans, simpler dishes are still compelling, including a spicy seafood soup full of crab, shellfish and enoki mushrooms to a deep-fried whole fish. Of course, the banchan here is also a big draw, especially those spicy cucumbers or sweet, salty and dried anchovies.

■ 2528 W. Olympic Blvd. No. 104
(bet. Arapahoe & Hoover Sts.)
𝒞 (213) 480-1107 — **WEB:** N/A
■ Lunch & dinner daily   **PRICE: $$**

OPENAIRE 🍴○

Contemporary • Trendy

It's a new day at Koreatown's Line Hotel, where noted chef, Josiah Citrin, has updated the once Commissary space with his distinct touch. Showcasing a pitched glass roof, thicket of plants and plush seating, this room has retained its conservatory feel, but it's unquestionably an urban jungle, thanks to buzzy diners debating what to pick from the delightfully tempting menu.

Two winning selections include a meaty duck ragout tagliatelle with a dusting of pistachios and pecorino, and perfect Parker House rolls accompanied by an array of spreads, such as cashew-arugula pesto. A sumptuous stew of Caledonian shrimp and heirloom beans is an earthy delight, not unlike the brown butter-pear tart served with lemongrass ice cream.

■ 3515 Wilshire Blvd. (bet. Normandie & Ardmore Aves.)
𝒞 (213) 368-3065 — **WEB:** www.thelinehotel.com
■ Lunch & dinner daily   **PRICE: $$$**

ORSA & WINSTON ✻

Fusion • Fashionable

Small, sleek and stylish, this gleaming, trendy and serious destination features the culinary pyrotechnics from both the Mediterranean and Japan, married under the watchful eye of Chef Josef Centeno. Inside, the sophisticated room presents generously spaced tables and a small dining counter, set before a polished kitchen where the only colors are the red and orange flames.

Turned out of the kitchen, the multiple prix-fixe menu items may comprise of wide-ranging flavors, but they also showcase the beauty of local ingredients. Highlights include diver scallops served in their shells—with barely warmed and supremely tender Manila clams, lobster meat and roe—all of which release a powerhouse of sea flavors. Also sample the perfectly crisp soft-shell crab tempura, enhanced with sweet pumpkin and fermented chilies to tantalize the palate; or perfectly seared slices of guinea hen set atop smooth semolina. The Sonoma lamb T-bone accompanied by a rich Bordelaise sauce, rye porridge and peaches is dense, juicy and particularly delicious. Sensational desserts have featured the chef's tribute to almond roca candy.

Albeit casual and less ambitious, lunches are far more affordable.

■ 122 W. 4th St. (bet. Main & Spring Sts.)
☎ (213) 687-0300 — **WEB:** www.orsaandwinston.com
■ Lunch Tue – Sun Dinner Tue – Sat   **PRICE: $$$$**

OTIUM

Contemporary · Design

Chef Timothy Hollingsworth has another triumph on his hands with Otium. This stunning wood-and-glass building seems to soar above the park plaza below and features a lovely outdoor seating area. Inside, find an industrial-chic décor with a dramatic display kitchen. Vertical rooftop gardens support their farm-to-table ethos; ingredients are pristine; and the menu is brazenly eclectic.

To wit: a funnel cake with earthy beets, fennel ribbons and a smear of chamoy sounds like a fusion nightmare. But in truth, this extraordinarily planned dish is a success, not unlike the lamb loin paired with roasted tomatoes and mashed potatoes. A caramel-crowned parsnip-banana cake may sound simple but delivers a solid finish.

■ 222 S. Hope St. (bet. 2nd & 3rd Sts.)
☏ (213) 935-8500 — **WEB:** www.otiumla.com
■ Lunch Tue – Fri Dinner Tue – Sun   **PRICE: $$$**

PARK'S BBQ

Korean · Family

Lauded as one of the city's most cherished destinations for Korean barbecue, Park's has lured patrons for over a decade now. Its interior is simple and friendly servers warm up the vibe. Tables are equipped with grills, but you're not required to work too hard, as waiters appear at just the right time to flip or slice the meat. Pork, chicken and shrimp are on offer, but prime beef, as seen in mouthwatering bulgogi, is your best bet. While their pricier American Wagyu is always worth the splurge, the acclaimed garlic-soy-brown sugar marinade is ace with short ribs. Still, you may want to avoid too much of a good thing by balancing it with cuts of non-marinated meat.

Lunch specials are easier on the wallet, offer great variety and are very popular.

■ 955 S. Vermont Ave., Ste. G
(bet. San Marino St. & Olympic Blvd.)
☏ (213) 380-1717 — **WEB:** www.parksbbq.com
■ Lunch & dinner daily   **PRICE: $$**

PATINA 🍴

Contemporary • Elegant

Set in the iconic Walt Disney Concert Hall designed by architect Frank Gehry, and home of the LA Philharmonic, the sophisticated Patina makes its impression long before the food arrives. The sleek space is spacious but intimate, with glossy double-glass windows embracing the front of the room and soft lighting emanating from above. Colorful water glasses and beautiful artwork dot the soothing, neutral décor.

The menu is founded in contemporary French, but international flavors make their way into each show-stopping dish. The guest-composed, three-course dinner is especially popular, and might begin with a combination of excellent Dungeness crab laced with crème fraîche, crunchy apple batons and brunoised mango, topped with viola blossoms and yuzu gel.

■ 141 S. Grand Ave. (at 2nd St.)
✆ (213) 972-3331 — **WEB:** www.patinagroup.com
■ Dinner Tue – Sat   **PRICE: $$$$**

PREUX & PROPER 😊

Cajun • Tavern

Calorie-conscious, vegetable-venerating locals may not seem like the ideal audience for rich Cajun and Creole fare, but this downtown veteran has carved out a niche with its Louisiana spin on SoCal-chic plates. With wall-to-wall crowds nightly, risk happy hour sans reservations at your own peril. But know that this food is worth it, as it follows these contours: Southern influences with creative touches. The deep-dish biscuit dough "pizza" stuffed with barbecue pork, Tillamook cheddar and Paulie's pomegranate-habanero sauce is a crowd favorite, as is the cast-iron cornbread and Dungeness crab hushpuppies.

However, the kitchen also flaunts real range—roasted carrots and beets topped with jerk chickpeas promise to drive vegetarians senseless with pleasure.

■ 840 S. Spring St. (at Main St.)
✆ (213) 896-0090 — **WEB:** www.preuxandproper.com
■ Lunch Fri – Sun Dinner nightly   **PRICE: $$**

Q SUSHI ⌘

Japanese • Minimalist

Authenticity and tradition are paramount in this very special and extraordinary little sushiya, which is sure to leave guests stunned from the start. Outside, there is nothing more than a modest, narrow beige-tiled façade with an enigmatic "Q" hanging above the door. Inside, vintage Japanese masks, pottery and lithographs bring a certain soul and spirit to the space.

A comfy banquette may be inviting for small groups, but the best perches in the house are found at the ten-seat dining counter.

From the moment you walk in to the rapid succession of wonderful nigiri, everything here seems steeped in a sense of calm. This begins with Chef Hiroyuki Naruke, who gracefully prepares each course and thoughtfully serves each diner—virtually from his own hands. Edomae sushi arrives as an omakase of fine fish, while some meals commence with downright flawless amberjack sashimi mingled with onions and soy—each morsel is sliced, seasoned and set before your eye. Just as popular is an arrangement of nigiri beginning with Hokkaido scallops, then kohada, fatty tuna and so much more. The complete and sublime pleasure of dining here extends right to the custardy tamago, layering soft eggs and a savory shrimp purée.

▪ 521 W. 7th St. (bet. Grand Ave. & Olive St.)
📞 (213) 225-6285 — **WEB:** www.qsushila.com
▪ Lunch Tue – Fri Dinner Tue – Sat   **PRICE: $$$$**

QUARTERS BBQ 🍴

Korean • Trendy

&

There are so many specific types of barbecue to choose from along this bustling strip that it can be hard to ferret out the more desirable ones. But, the lines wrapping around this particular gem are a sure sign you've chosen well. This is a hip, industrial joint and if you try sneaking in for lunch or early dinner on the outdoor patio, you may even succeed in skirting the crowds.

The name reflects how the menu is organized (offering meats in quarter pound portions), thereby allowing diners to sample an array of deliciously marinated cuts. Kick things off with the spicy short rib fondue or kimchijeon. Then chase it down with one of the specialty ice-cold beers on tap. For dinner, opt for the beautifully marbled and perfectly succulent short ribs.

 3465 W. 6th St. (at Alexandria Ave.)
℘ (213) 365-8111 — **WEB:** www.quarterskbbq.com
 Lunch & dinner daily

PRICE: $$

REDBIRD 🍴

Contemporary • Trendy

🍸 & 🍴 🛋 🍽

This airy stunner, which occupies a former church in the heart of Downtown, flaunts an impressive open glass ceiling allowing diners to stargaze—and that's not even counting the occasional celebrity sighting. The boisterous atmosphere is beloved by the trendy patrons, who can be seen swapping small plates from perches at the two circular bars and eclectic sofa-stuffed lounge.

On the global menu, creative dishes sit side-by-side with more traditional treats like John Dory in a leek fondue strewn with pan-seared gnocchi and mushrooms. Save room for clever desserts like yuzu custard with basil oil and cucumber sorbet, or opt for another cocktail from the extensive list.

 114 E. 2nd St. (at Main St.)
℘ (213) 788-1191 — **WEB:** www.redbird.la
 Dinner nightly

PRICE: $$$$

ROCIO'S MEXICAN KITCHEN

Mexican · Colorful

Hanging on the wall of this stamp of an establishment is a T-shirt that reads, "Better than your grandmother's mole." If you aren't Mexican, the slogan definitely holds true, but if you are it probably still holds true. After all, they don't call Chef Rocio Camacho "The Goddess of Mole" for nothing. Her sauces are ace, served in a humble outpost.

Diners are greeted with a basket of warm chips laced with a myriad of moles that range from sweet and spicy to smoky. Best of the lot though is the classic mole Oaxaqueño, a 32-ingredient symphony of flavors. Coming in at a close second is the black-as-night huitlacoche sauce composed with "Mexican truffle." Poured over a square of seared mahi mahi, it would be as good even if served atop an old shoe.

■ 7891 Garfield Ave. (at Park Ln.), Bell Gardens
✆ (562) 659-7800 — **WEB:** N/A
■ Lunch & dinner daily   **PRICE:** ⬭

ROSSOBLU

Italian · Chic

You won't wander by this Italian standout or pop in on a whim, since this Fashion District restaurant is a bit of a trek. There's not much else in this area, but that's just fine because if you've made the trip to Rossoblu, you won't be disappointed. The setting—a capacious and glamorous industrial warehouse—may look and feel cutting edge, but there's nothing avant-garde about the food (thank goodness).

The cuisine pays tribute to quality ingredients with simple but well-executed cooking. Make no mistake, this isn't Mamma's Sunday pasta, but the kitchen excels in regional styles, including eggplant folded over a tomato sugo and olive oil, as well as tagliolini tossed with cuttlefish and English peas for a lovely ode to Emilia-Romagna.

■ 1124 San Julian St. (bet. 11th & 12th Sts.)
✆ (213) 749-1099 — **WEB:** www.rossoblula.com
■ Dinner Tue – Sun   **PRICE:** $$

SHIBUMI ❀

Japanese • Trendy

🍶 ♿

There may be no more pleasurable place to learn about kappo-style cuisine, which has only recently made inroads into the American dining scene, than this stellar Japanese dining counter. The latter is crafted from a centuries-old cypress tree, set before chefs grating wasabi and a backdrop of amber-hued whisky. While the décor feels minimalist, surrounded by an industrial edge of soaring concrete ceilings and exposed pipes, service is wonderfully engaging and attentive, with thorough explanations of each unique course.

À la carte is offered, but the multi-course kappo-style is the best way to experience this kitchen's creations. Dishes bring together a unique range of inspired Japanese flavors, but equal attention is given to texture and artistic presentations. Fixed menus here present a progression of courses selected by the chefs, which may include a few raw dishes.

Highlights reveal an innovative "true chicken teriyaki" that has been dried and rehydrated to render enticingly chewy results. A bowl of California rice with favas, peas and shiso makes for a delicious prelude to Holstein steak topped with spicy wasabi and diced pickled plum that's been aged for four years.

◼ 815 S. Hill St. (bet 8th & 9th Sts.)
☎ (323) 484-8915 — **WEB:** www.shibumidtla.com
◼ Dinner Tue – Sun

PRICE: $$$$

SHOJIN ۱O

Vegan • Intimate

&

In LA's competitive Japanese food scene, Shojin stands tall thanks to a menu that's delicious, complex and 100% vegan—not to mention further options for diners sensitive to garlic, onions and gluten. Though it's set on the third floor of the busy Little Tokyo Market Place, it has an appealingly sleek vibe, carefully decorated with fresh flowers and fine linens.

That care extends to the menu, which will make even omnivores sit up and take notice. Stuffed shiitake mushrooms are perfectly calibrated with miso, tamari and just a hint of smoke; while the soy-paper sushi roll encases a surprisingly hearty and satisfying mix of cucumber, shiso and seaweed. At the end, their pumpkin "cheesecake" is so blissfully creamy that it's hard to believe there is no dairy.

▦ 333 S. Alameda St., Ste 310 (bet. 3rd & 4th Sts.)
℘ (213) 617-0305 — **WEB:** www.theshojin.com
▦ Lunch Sat – Sun Dinner nightly   **PRICE: $$**

SIMONE ۱O

American • Contemporary décor

⅛ 🍸 & 🖵 🖐

Step inside Simone and you'll be wowed by this dominantly mid-century spot decked out with chrome accents, sleek doors and contemporary art. The space is buzzy, vast and features a veritable who's who of industry insiders, including an acclaimed mixologist and noted sommelier. But never mind all that, it is the highly anticipated cooking that's worthy of the chatter. In a kitchen lined with jars of pickles and fermentations, she deftly toes the line between pushing the envelope (employing new ingredients such as prity melons) and giving diners what they want (pork meatballs in parmesan brodo).

Her brilliance is in the details: pole beans bathed in tomatillo salsa and hit with a spicy-smoky aioli take a side dish and bring it center stage.

▦ 449 S. Hewitt St. (bet. 4th & 5th Sts.)
℘ (424) 433-3000 — **WEB:** www.simoneartsdistrict.com
▦ Dinner Tue – Sun   **PRICE: $$$**

SIXTH & MILL 😊

Italian • Contemporary décor

The most casual of the trio of Arts District spots from Matteo Ferdinandi and Chef Angelo Auriana (of Factory Place Hospitality Group), this budding pizzeria takes its pie-making very seriously. Its cornicione is perfectly blistered and chewy—whether on a Margherita with slices of salsiccia and broccoli rabe, or even grilled wild boar sausage infused with cumin and fennel. For outright indulgence, go for the montara with dough fried until crisp and piled with cherry tomatoes and mozzarella.

The concise menu is full of classics, including pastas like the al dente lardiata tossed in a tomato sauce with prosciutto and pecorino. Even a classic, like babà al rum, gets a twist here: pillowy-soft and boozy with vanilla liqueur.

■ 1335 E. 6th St. (bet. Mateo & Alameda Sts.)
℘ (213) 629-3000 — **WEB:** www.sixthandmill.com
■ Lunch & dinner daily   PRICE: $$

SOBAN 🍴

Korean • Simple

The vibe at this tiny haunt isn't much to speak of—it doesn't even have a liquor license. But if you take notice of the many framed reviews and accolades that serve as its sole décor, you'll realize you're in for a treat. Even amid tough Koreatown competition, Soban is known for its banchan. Featuring everything from traditional kimchi to sautéed eggplant, the selection is ever-changing and quite impressive.

Most diners opt for the house signatures, including ganjang gejang (raw crab pickled with soy, garlic and ginger) or galbi jjim, a sweet and tender braised short rib stew. But the menu holds innumerable other delights, like nakji bokkeum, soft and chewy baby octopus stir-fried with chili, garlic, leeks and served with sticky brown rice.

■ 4001 W. Olympic Blvd. (at Norton Ave.)
℘ (323) 936-9106 — **WEB:** N/A
■ Lunch & dinner daily   PRICE: $$

SOOT BULL JEEP 🍴

Korean • Simple

Forget the ubiquitous gas grills used at so many run-of-the-mill Korean spots. Low-key and very authentic Soot Bull Jeep elevates their barbecue game by gracing each table with the real charcoal deal for ideal searing and infusing their tender morsels of meat with a delicate char. It may add a bit more smoke to the experience, but it is well worth it and no one seems to mind, as the vibe is always vibrant.

Be sure to try their signature galbi, juicy and well-marbled, char-grilled to perfection with the help of the waitstaff, and served with their own special barbecue sauce. Pair your grilled meats with their array of delicious banchan including spicy spinach kimchi, fish cakes and fire-hot shredded daikon.

Free parking in the back is an added bonus.

◾ 3136 W. 8th St. (bet. Catalina St. & Kenmore Ave.)
℘ (213) 387-3865 — **WEB:** N/A
◾ Lunch & dinner daily   **PRICE: $$**

SOOWON GALBI 🍴

Korean • Family

&

Soowon Galbi is smack dab between a laundromat and a chicken shack, so this tidy little destination may not be a top pick for design divas. However, it is an authentic darling with two decades under its belt and always delivers when it comes to taste.

Pancakes, steamed eggs and banchan start things off, but like all good Korean barbecue joints, it's all about the charbroiled and gas-grilled meat. Soowon is a cattle town in South Korea, so know that the beef combo is an absolute winner, with a variety of cuts offering especially good value at lunch and hitting all the marks in terms of flavor and texture. Whether indulging in straightforward ribeye or garlicky soy-marinated galbi, each morsel is charred perfectly on the grill and will melt in your mouth.

◾ 856 S. Vermont Ave., Ste. B
(bet. Francis Ave. & James M. Wood Blvd.)
℘ (213) 365-9292 — **WEB:** N/A
◾ Lunch & dinner daily   **PRICE: $$**

SUSHI ENYA 🍴

Japanese • Neighborhood

For those who prefer their sushi with a splash of style, this may not be their cup of (green) tea. But, for true aficionados seeking substance in the form of top-quality fish, this is heaven, as the kitchen delivers an all-out omakase that doesn't pull any punches. It's a no-holds barred and seemingly no-expense spared wild romp through Japanese cuisine as envisioned by Chef Kimiyasu Enya. Expect things to begin with a bang—in the form of charred toro belly topped with tuna tartare—and take off from there. Courses oscillate between simple and dazzling, like bowls of dashi and still-bouncy giant clam with nori to such dramatic presentations as a smoke-filled cloche revealing tender cubes of duck breast. Caviar makes for a lovely, if lavish, supplement.

- 343 E. 1st St. (bet. Judge John Aiso & Alameda Sts.)
- ☏ (213) 626-3692 — **WEB:** www.sushienya.com
- Dinner nightly

PRICE: $$$

WATER GRILL 🍴

Seafood • Brasserie

&

Following a major renovation a few years ago, this darling brasserie feels more casual and comfortable than ever. Lunchtime is popular among suits discussing deals over gourmet sandwiches and salads, while dinner is more upscale. Service may have a misstep or two, but the vibe is always lively and animated. Subdued gray tones and a large, nautically themed picture set above the booths remind guests of the menu's theme. Start with a bite or two from their lovely selection of crudo, before moving on to unquestionably fresh wild fish, such as roasted Chilean sea bass. Americana desserts, like caramel bread pudding, are also a surprising highlight.

Parking is available next door, but don't forget to get your ticket validated by the hostess.

- 544 S. Grand Ave. (bet. 5th & 6th Sts.)
- ☏ (213) 891-0900 — **WEB:** www.watergrill.com
- Lunch & dinner daily

PRICE: $$$$

YONG SU SAN ⅋○

Korean • *Family*

 ♿

Specializing in the storied dishes that were once served to Korea's royals, this mini Seoul-based chain stands out from the K-town crowd. This is largely thanks to its hanbok-attired servers and warren of private rooms, featuring an expansive foyer with a counter and carved wooden seats with plush cushions. Most diners arrive in large groups to sample set menus that are available at various price levels. However, dining à la carte is a great option as well.

Those accustomed to the banchan will be astounded by the intricacy of bo ssam kimchi—a simple, warm and appetizing cabbage soup accompanied by a cold nest of pungent kimchi. This may be tailed by tang pyeong chae—savory mung bean jelly noodles tossed with sesame oil for a delicate palate-cleanser.

◼ 950 S. Vermont Ave. (at San Marino St.)
℘ (213) 388-3042 — **WEB:** www.yongsusanla.com
◼ Lunch & dinner daily   **PRICE: $$**

YXTA ⅋○

Mexican • *Rustic*

Tucked inside a small shopping center near the Arts District, this airy spot woos with an open kitchen and industrial look combining exposed ducts, brick walls and glass-block windows.

The menu goes on to please palates with favorites like chunky guacamole. Tostaditas de ceviche have just the right amount of crunch, heaped with citrus-marinated whitefish, diced cucumber, mango, avocado and slivered fresh chili for a zesty one-two punch. Enchiladas de mole arrive with generous chunks of roasted chicken and enveloped in a dark brown mole poblano that is sweet with ripe plantain and balanced by bitter chocolate and myriad other ingredients. Silky-smooth flan ends things nicely, especially with a shot of custard-rich rompope.

◼ 601 S. Central Ave. (at E. 6th St.)
℘ (213) 596-5579 — **WEB:** www.cocinasycalaveras.com
◼ Lunch Mon – Fri Dinner Mon – Sat   **PRICE: $$**

HOLLYWOOD

ABURIYA RAKU 😊

Japanese • Design

After a successful launch in Las Vegas, this swank and polished izakaya has made the jump to Los Angeles, where its signature robata skewers and ample sake list continue to thrill. The zen-like dining room, featuring plush banquettes and potted bamboo, has its own appeal, even though the prodigious late-night industry types prefer their seats in front of the open kitchen, where grill-masters work their magic.

Must-order items include juicy Kurobuta pork cheeks, tender enoki mushrooms wrapped in crisp bacon and meaty pork ribs brushed with teriyaki sauce, which arrive falling off the bone. But don't sleep on their appetizers—the silky house-made tofu is a delight and that decadent poached egg mixed with uni and salmon roe is a marvel of texture.

- 521 N. La Cienega Blvd. (bet. Melrose & Rosewood Aves.)
- (213) 308-9393 — **WEB:** N/A
- Lunch Mon – Fri Dinner Mon – Sat   **PRICE: $$**

A.O.C. 🍴◯

Mediterranean • Rustic

As the name (an acronym for French wines' regional certification) would suggest, this Mediterranean bijou lives up to its moniker with a serious book of Californian and European varietals. The vibe is casual and cozy, with rustic furniture, fireplaces and a charming brick patio adorned with olive trees.

From 5:00-7:00P.M., treat yourself to cocktails with focaccia and cheese pairings. Their focus on produce is clear in everything from a lunchtime farmer's salad to the peppery arugula that may garnish a fillet of Arctic char. Then proceed to small plates fired in the wood-burning oven or premium charcuterie. Desserts are beautifully executed, especially the bittersweet chocolate torte topped with coffee cream, medjool dates and candied hazelnuts.

- 8700 W. 3rd St. (bet. Arnaz Dr. & Hamel Rd.)
- (310) 859-9859 — **WEB:** www.aocwinebar.com
- Lunch & dinner daily   **PRICE: $$**

ANGELINI OSTERIA 🍴○

Italian • Osteria

The delicious cooking at this humble osteria has been drawing crowds for nearly two decades—and in a city that rolls out the red carpet for the hottest new thing, that's no small feat. This simple, authentic charmer is the real deal, right down to the red scarf-bedecked chef in the kitchen as well as those regulars sipping and supping on Italian wines and fresh pasta in the dining room.

Though the service brigade leans old school, their generous spirit defies the gruff stereotype. Menu favorites include expertly grilled calamari, linguini with sea urchin and a perfectly authentic tiramisu for dessert. On your way out, be sure to pop into the café next door for a jar or two of Chef Gino Angelini's sauce and bring the goodness home.

🔲 7313 Beverly Blvd. (at Poinsettia Pl.)
☏ (323) 297-0070 — **WEB:** www.angeliniosteria.com
🔲 Lunch Tue – Fri Dinner Tue – Sun   **PRICE: $$$**

ANIMAL 🍴○

Contemporary • Trendy

Animal may not be the youngest kid on the block, having recently celebrated a decade in operation, but still it remains enviably cool and inviting. Its plain walls, wood furnishings and large windows read simple but defer to the good-looking crowd who frequents the place. This might have something to do with the owners—a duo of culinary geniuses—who are also the brains behind other LA hot spots, namely Trois Mec and Son of a Gun.

Of course, the crowd might actually be here for the food, because it's that good. As the name suggests, the menu focuses on meat and seafood, like rabbit larb and hamachi tostada. Inspiration comes from around the world, with cooking styles as diverse as Mexican, Chinese and even Indian, which makes an appearance in tandoori octopus.

🔲 435 N. Fairfax Ave. (bet. Oakwood & Rosewood Aves.)
☏ (323) 782-9225 — **WEB:** www.animalrestaurant.com
🔲 Lunch Sat – Sun Dinner nightly   **PRICE: $$$**

AWASH ¶○

Ethiopian · Simple

Restaurant exteriors don't get much more unassuming than this terrific café's façade. And though the name, Awash, is printed clear as day on the brick outside, the barred entrance never really looks open. Having said that, grab a pal when dining here (these dishes are meant to be shared) and take a leap of faith—you won't regret it.

Just as the eponymous river is vital to those that live near its banks, this restaurant is an absolute standout for those craving authentic Ethiopian food. Vegans will rejoice at the vegetable-laden menu, while carnivores will delight in such savory entrées as the raw, minced beef kitfo tossed with spiced, melted butter; or the meaty tibs (a hearty stewed preparation) that can be scooped up with torn pieces of tangy injera.

■ 5990 1/2 W. Pico Blvd. (bet. Point View St. & Stearns Ave.)
℘ (323) 939-3233 — **WEB:** N/A
■ Lunch & dinner daily   **PRICE: $$**

BEAUTY & ESSEX ¶○

Contemporary · Chic

Break out your velvet smoking jacket and glide past the speakeasy-style pawn shop stocked with eye-catching items before heading upstairs to this A-lister lounge and ballroom-esque dining room, featuring dramatic chandeliers. With original outposts in New York and Las Vegas, this Hollywood beauty attracts a moneyed crowd that comes for glitter, glam and a bite or two. The staff is as cool and stylish as the décor and clientele.

The share-worthy menu runs the gamut from raw bar selections (oysters, ceviches) to tomato tartare toast points. Take your eyes off the crowd for a moment to nosh on lollipop sprouts or chile relleno empanadas. Tandoori-spiced chicken served fanned over curried cauliflower with romesco illustrates the kitchen's global skills.

■ 1516 Cahuenga Blvd. (at Selma Ave.)
℘ (323) 676-8880 — **WEB:** www.beautyandessexla.com
■ Dinner nightly   **PRICE: $$$**

CARLITOS GARDEL ¶○

Argentine • Romantic

This may be the land of big, glitzy steakhouses, but Carlitos Gardel offers guests something more refined and quiet, with juicy meats and empanadas that have people coming back again and again. The evening mood here is romantic, and often accompanied by live piano music. There are larger seating options for groups, but those tiny, close-knit tables are often occupied by celebrities, without the paparazzi in tow.

That said, big red wines, sharp knives and cutting boards laden with bone-in ribeye are sure to cover every available space. Start with a salad or crispy empanada with a side of chimichurri that's so good it's even available online for purchase. Sweet lovers rave about desserts, like a fluffy wedge of mascarpone tart with strawberry drizzle.

▦ 7963 Melrose Ave. (bet. Edinburgh & Hayworth Aves.)
℘ (323) 655-0891 — **WEB:** www.carlitosgardel.com
▦ Lunch Fri Dinner nightly   PRICE: $$$

THE CAT & FIDDLE ¶○

Gastropub • Pub

This mainstay English pub has reemerged in a space that oozes with family-run charm. Its fresh digs remain cozy and old school, with a dark wood bar, hanging lanterns and intimate booths. There's still however a bit of Cali-cool in this cat—Londoners only wish they could dine year-round on the patio, which is surrounded by palm trees.

Expats seeking the comforts of home will delight in the Scotch egg, encased in homemade sausage, fried golden brown and accompanied by Coleman's mustard. Steak and mushroom pie is textbook, chips are hand-cut and the Guinness is poured to perfection. Sticky toffee pudding makes for a subtly sweet finish. Despite the feline name, dogs are welcome here, with their own "doggie menu" offering treats like chicken jerky.

▦ 742 N. Highland Ave. (bet. Melrose & Waring Aves.)
℘ (323) 468-3800 — **WEB:** www.thecatandfiddle.com
▦ Lunch & dinner daily   PRICE: $$

CHATEAU HANARE ¶○

Japanese • Chic

Look for the noren marking an entrance hiding in plain sight to find this striking retreat. The name roughly translates to "cottage set apart," which makes sense as it operates in collaboration with Chateau Marmont, just one block away. Everything has a sort of Hollywood-cool feel—from the bare wood tables and disposable chopsticks to the strings of party lights and lanterns.

Choose from two kaiseki tastings as well as à la carte sushi and izakaya bites. An absolute favorite is the house-made tofu, scooped tableside and served warm with wari-joyu. Be sure to appreciate their dramatic opening presentation of uni on Japanese milk bread served under a cloche with cherry blossom smoke. Lighter appetites will love the trio of raw and marinated fish dishes.

▦ 8097 Selma Ave. (at Sunset Blvd.)
℘ (323) 963-5269 — **WEB:** www.hanarela.com
▦ Dinner nightly   **PRICE: $$$$**

CHI SPACCA ¶○

Italian • Intimate

The carnivorous heart of Nancy Silverton's "Mozzaplex" is as intimate and engaging as it is expensive—a place to splurge on date night with a special vintage and view of the bustling wood-fired oven and grill. The result is a modern Italian take on the old-school steakhouses of a bygone era, with the focaccia di recco and bistecca alla Fiorentina being some of their key indulgences.

Others may choose to feast upon the exquisite house charcuterie, from pistachio-crusted pork terrine to classic pancetta and speck. A perfectly grilled and boldly flavored lamb shoulder chop meets its match in oven-roasted cauliflower tossed with garlicky bagna cauda. If that's insufficient absolution, the dark and decadent cocoa nib-caramel tart should send you over the top.

▦ 6610 Melrose Ave. (at Highland Ave.)
℘ (323) 297-1133 — **WEB:** www.chispacca.com
▦ Dinner nightly   **PRICE: $$$$**

CONNIE & TED'S ¶○

Seafood · Design

It's set in the West Coast, but this new-school shack still has serious East Coast vibes—even if it does indeed source its sustainable, wild-caught seafood from both the Atlantic and Pacific. With an extensive raw bar, parking lot strewn with shells and a funky interior plastered with seafaring knickknacks, it's a fitting tribute to Chef Michael Cimarusti's New England origins.

Chowder is a must for a seafood spot and this particular one offers a tempting flight of three: creamy New England, tomato-based Manhattan and buttery Rhode Island. The lobster roll, packed with tail and claw meat, is a gem among solo diners, while chilled seafood platters and the oak-grilled fish are great for crowds. Don't forget to grab a bit of saltwater taffy on your way out.

■ 8171 Santa Monica Blvd. (at Havenhurst Dr.)
℘ (323) 848-2722 — **WEB:** www.connieandteds.com
■ Lunch Wed – Sun Dinner nightly   **PRICE: $$$**

THE DISTRICT BY HANNAH AN ¶○

Vietnamese · Exotic décor

The dining room at this upscale Vietnamese respite is a knockout—and so is the food from Chef Hannah An, of the family behind San Francisco favorites Thanh Long and Crustacean. With lush greenery, modern wood accents, elegant light fixtures and lacquered tables, this is definitely a place to see and be seen. The extensive menu accommodates the dietary restrictions of a celebrity clientele.

Those whose careers don't depend on calorie avoidance should opt for the An family's signature noodles bathed with garlic and butter, or the beautifully tender shaking beef with cubes of stir-fried filet mignon. On the lighter side, caramelized black cod in a clay pot is a top choice, as it allows some wiggle room for the excellent pear tarte Tatin.

■ 8722 W. 3rd St. (at Arnaz St.)
℘ (310) 278-2345 — **WEB:** www.thedistrictbyha.com
■ Lunch Sat – Sun Dinner nightly   **PRICE: $$$**

EVELEIGH

Californian • Rustic

There's something utterly charming about Eveleigh. Nestled inside a rustic building that once stood on an orchard—yes, they paved paradise—this delightfully bright and airy restaurant flaunts an attractive and clean elegance. The light shines on this gem, but don't worry since the open-air patio with a retractable roof is also equipped with heaters for those moments when the rays take a break.

This kitchen subscribes to the notion that simple, honest cooking is best; and with standouts like crushed peas and burrata or buttery pound cake topped with strawberries, you'll wholeheartedly agree. Spaghettini twirled with tender and delicious chunks of Dungeness crab is a straight-up success.

Less reliable is the service, which can be a bit lackadaisical.

- 8752 W. Sunset Blvd. (at Sherbourne Dr.)
- (424) 239-1630 — **WEB:** www.theeveleigh.com
- Lunch Sat – Sun Dinner nightly　　　　　　**PRICE: $$**

FIGARO BISTROT ᵀⓄ

French • Bistro

Cure your wanderlust by pulling on your striped mariniére, hopping on your wicker basket-topped bike and heading over to Paris by way of Figaro Bistrot. It's as close as you'll get to the City of Light in the City of Angels. This locally cherished lounge and boulangerie has France down pat. Smoky mirrors? Check. Zinc bar? You betcha. Sidewalk seating? Mais oui.

Try not to swoon as you walk past the enticing displays of macarons and tarts. The classic menu echoes the interior's oh-so faithful flair. Croque Madame, that golden brown marriage of ham and Gruyère topped with creamy béchamel sauce and a sunny side-up egg on bakery-fresh bread, is positively Proustian. Don't forget to pick up a few croissants or éclairs on the way out to extend the bonhomie.

- 1802 N. Vermont Ave. (bet. Melbourne & Russell Aves.)
- (323) 662-1587 — **WEB:** www.figarobistrot.com
- Lunch & dinner daily　　　　　　**PRICE: $$**

GENWA 🍴

Korean • Simple

&

Set slightly west of the Koreatown pack is a dining room that feels more polished and upscale than your typical Korean barbecue dining.

Their high-quality meats are deftly handled by the staff, who intensely marinate them for searing on the grill and then slicing right before your eyes. Servers are attentive and tend to your cuts regularly, ensuring that each morsel has just the right crust. The "Combo A" is a veritable feast for two hungry people—this head-spinning array includes a spicy kimchi soup, thinly sliced bulgogi with all the fixings and perhaps the most succulent galbi in town. The parade of banchan; steamed vegetable- and pork-filled mandu; as well as japchae are equally impressive and must be sampled to truly grasp the skills of this kitchen.

■ 5115 Wilshire Blvd. (at Mansfield Ave.)
℘ (323) 549-0760 — **WEB:** www.genwakoreanbbq.com
■ Lunch & dinner daily   **PRICE: $$**

GRACIAS MADRE 🍴

Vegan • Trendy

& 🛖

This plant-based darling set along Melrose Avenue may seem like a pretty place for young'uns, but it should not be underestimated. The space is an open, airy and beguiling combination of serape fabric banquettes, whitewashed walls and lofty ceilings. The patio is an even lovelier destination, surrounded by old shade trees, while a lengthy bar pours an aficionado's array of some 60 tequilas and 70 mezcals.

On the menu, explore Mexican cuisine through vegan items, like young coconut ceviche with house-made chips, pozole and grain bowls. The addictive tacos naturally feature top-quality tortillas, heaped with astoundingly delicious shredded jackfruit, lightly pickled cabbage and a drizzle of cashew crema. The prix-fixe lunch is of prodigious value.

■ 8905 Melrose Ave. (bet. Almont & La Peer Drs.)
℘ (323) 978-2170 — **WEB:** www.graciasmadreweho.com
■ Lunch & dinner daily   **PRICE: $$**

GWEN
Steakhouse • Chic

During the day, this enticingly arranged butcher shop sells humanely raised meats from local partner farms. By night, Gwen opens into a glowing dining room showcasing the same upscale à la carte and on its multi-course tasting. Named for their beloved grandmother, this collaboration between Chef Curtis Stone and his brother, Luke, conjures art deco glamour by way of crystal chandeliers and a roaring fireplace.

The kitchen yields Chef Stone's own red-blooded show of culinary skill, with such decadent mains as fire-roasted pork or grilled boneless short rib. Non-meat eaters can take heart in a lovely ocean trout or saffron cavatelli with a hint of shaved bottarga. For dessert, the pavlova offers a fantastic nod to the chef's Australian heritage.

■ 6600 Sunset Blvd. (at Seward St.)
 (323) 946-7513 — **WEB:** www.gwenla.com
■ Lunch Mon – Fri Dinner Mon – Sat   PRICE: $$$$

JAR ‖○
Contemporary • Elegant

Its name is displayed in elegant gold script on the red brick corner building, instantly setting the stage for this self-described "modern chophouse." The dining room seems timeless, outfitted in rich wood panels, thick white linens and dark spherical pendant lights for a flattering glow. Off to the side lies a comfortable bar and large semi-private table for groups.

The enticing menu highlights ingredient-driven starters and meat-based entrées, as well as a lengthy list of daily specials. But, this cooking relishes global flavors and creativity, so expect such inspired items as char siu pork chop or lemongrass jidori chicken to be cited along classic broiled steaks or pot roast. Sides continue in the same vein, with creamed corn or duck-fried rice.

■ 8225 Beverly Blvd. (at Harper Ave.)
 (323) 655-6566 — **WEB:** www.thejar.com
■ Dinner Tue – Sun   PRICE: $$$

LOS ANGELES ▶ HOLLYWOOD

371

JITLADA 😊
Thai • Cozy

Ignore the fact that Jitlada is located in a strip mall beneath a neon sign—the crowds prove that this skilled cadre of chefs knows what they're doing in the kitchen. The setting even has a touch of Hollywood; next to their framed awards and reviews, find illustrations by the Simpsons creator (and Jitlada super-fan)—Matt Groening.

The offerings are extensive, but certain dishes jump off the page. Be sure to sample bubbling-hot Taepo chicken curry, rich with coconut milk, brightly flavored with turmeric and tender morning glory stems. The range of "Spicy Thai Dipped Dishes" are equally delicious, particularly nam prik pla, vibrantly seasoned red snapper, ground with red chilies and served with the soothing tastes and textures of crunchy vegetables.

■ 5233 1/2 W. Sunset Blvd. (at Harvard Blvd.)
✆ (323) 667-9809 — **WEB:** www.jitladala.com
■ Lunch & dinner Tue – Sun   **PRICE: $$**

JON & VINNY'S 😊
Italian • Pizzeria

&. 🛋

Those namesake chefs, Jon Shook and Vinny Dotolo, bring serious talent and experience to this easygoing Italian-American café—they are in fact two of the Trois Mecs (with Ludo Lefebvre).

The slender room features a branded display of pizza boxes, counter seating and a wide-open kitchen with views of the wood-fired grill and blazing oven. And those chewy, tender pies boast a blistered crust with creative toppings, like the Roman Gladiator heaped high with meat. Another treat is the Salad Days, tastefully decked with thick tomato sauce beneath bits of crunchy gem lettuce, sungold tomatoes and shaved caciocavallo in a garlic dressing. House-made pastas of all strands and shapes are equally tempting, especially when bathed in their six-hour Bolognese.

■ 412 N. Fairfax Ave. (bet. Oakwood & Rosewood Aves.)
✆ (323) 334-3369 — **WEB:** www.jonandvinnys.com
■ Lunch & dinner daily   **PRICE: $$**

KALI ⟪⟫

Californian • Contemporary décor

Blending seamlessly into its surrounds, this modest storefront forms the very essence of neighborhood dining. Make your way inside to discover Chef Kevin Meehan's kitchen, whose credentials and locavore spirit are just as formidable as its eclectic wines and craft beers. The main room sports a restful, Scandinavian look that mixes caramel tones and leather banquettes with wood tables. Service has a fine-dining feel; and the mission of this kitchen is clear—wholly organic and sustainable cuisine.

A meat refrigerator displaying dry-aged ducks, steaks and even a whole pig's head is a natural conversation-starter and keeps all eyes on the food, which in turn lives up to its promise. Imagine a distinct spin on local flavors and of-the-moment techniques, like fermentation, preservation and deep charring to get a sense of what this place is about. Creativity also dominates each course, as seen in the barley risotto. Everything paired with the hanger steak, like buttermilk-garlic jus and porcini mushrooms with roasted potatoes, tastes like its perfect complement.

When considering its ingredient quality and chef's ability, it is quite apparent that a meal at Kali offers diners a stellar deal.

■ 5722 Melrose Ave. (bet. Larchmont & Lucerne Blvds.)
✆ (323) 871-4160 — **WEB:** www.kalirestaurant.com
■ Lunch Sun – Fri Dinner nightly   **PRICE: $$$**

KATANA 🍴

Japanese • Chic

Named for the sword of the samurai, this is a fashion-forward dining jewel catering to celebrities looking for a bit of glitz and glam. Thanks to its sexy interior and sleek-chic dress code, diners know to steer clear of shorts and flip-flops. The outdoor tables are some of the most sought after on the Sunset Strip.

This robata-yaki specializes in skewers of meat grilled over binchotan, flame-licked and infused with smoke. However, their fish and sushi offerings can be even more impressive. Start off with shiro maguro, lightly seared tuna sliced sashimi-style and fanned over crispy fried onions and ponzu. Crowds also appear to clamor for their raw hamachi topped with copious amounts of sautéed red and green chilies finished with a bit of sesame oil.

- 🟦 8439 W. Sunset Blvd. (at La Cienega Blvd.)
- ☎ (323) 650-8585 — **WEB:** www.katanala.com
- 🟦 Dinner nightly   PRICE: $$$

LA CEVICHERIA 😋

Latin American • Simple

Ceviche enthusiasts know that this petite, blue-walled restaurant is the place to go for the finest of raw fish. Though owners Carolina and Julio Orellana hail from Guatemala, their seafood-centric menu spans the map of Latin American flavors, with options ranging from shrimp sautéed in Caribbean-spiced coconut milk to fried Baja-style fish tacos, drizzled with spicy mayo.

The number-one draw, though, remains ceviche, particularly the "bloody clams" version. This maroon-tinted preparation has won them a legion of loyal devotees. If they're all sold out, the shrimp and octopus ceviche tostada, zesty with lime juice and topped with ripe avocado, is a worthy substitute. Savvy diners must save room for Carolina's expertly made tres leches cake.

- 🟦 3809 W. Pico Blvd. (bet. 5th & Norton Aves.)
- ☎ (323) 732-1253 — **WEB:** N/A
- 🟦 Lunch & dinner Wed – Sun   PRICE: 🆑

THE LITTLE DOOR 🍴◯

Mediterranean • *Romantic*

The name is a necessary clue: look for two rickety wooden doors to enter. This is literally hidden-in-plain-sight, since all that signals its presence is a diminutive blue-and-white plaque emblazoned with the street number. Don't be discouraged though, since it merely adds to the notion that you've stumbled upon a secret paradise. From the brick and cobblestone floors to deep blue walls and plentiful greenery, this «Little Door» gives the impression of dining outdoors. Of course, twinkling fairy lights and flickering candles make it impossibly romantic.

Ample portions and modest plating seem slightly out of place amid the splendor, but good cooking leads to harmonious results—as seen in the sea bass. Be sure to share a tarte Tatin with your sweetheart.

◾ 8164 W. 3rd St. (bet. Crescent Heights Blvd. & La Jolla Ave.)
✆ (323) 951-1210 — **WEB:** www.thelittledoor.com
◾ Dinner nightly   PRICE: $$$

LUCQUES 🍴◯

Mediterranean • *Rustic*

Hidden under a lush canopy of foliage, the woodsy, elegant vibe here will have you feeling like you've stepped into Napa for the night. This one-time carriage house boasts a cozy brick interior, with a blazing hearth and small bar where friends catch up over the legendary house martini. The covered garden patio, with its light-filtering, canvas roof and lush tangle of vines, is stunning.

The kitchen has maintained its impeccable reputation for nearly 20 years thanks to the graceful hand of Chef Suzanne Goin. Meals begin with an addictive bowl of almonds and the namesake olives. Then move on to mains like the market lettuce with roasted beets, a soft egg and creamy burrata; or morel mushroom lasagna tucked with an English pea purée and asparagus batons.

◾ 8474 Melrose Ave. (at La Cienega Blvd.)
✆ (323) 655-6277 — **WEB:** www.lucques.com
◾ Lunch Tue – Sat Dinner nightly   PRICE: $$$

LUV 2 EAT 🍴

Thai • Simple

If you crave authentic Southern Thai food, you'll love this homey restaurant, which draws crowds to an otherwise unremarkable setting on Sunset. Chefs Noree Pla and Fern Kaewtathip spare no detail in rendering the cuisine of their native Phuket, concocting dishes rarely seen on American menus, including tai pla (a fish organ curry) or jungle curry with chicken feet.

Even if you're not ready for such adventurous food, there's still a lot to enjoy here. Noodle soups are a specialty, with zeed (featuring a pho-like clear broth with three kinds of pork) being a standout. There's also the Southern Thai fried chicken with sticky rice as well as a yellow fish curry. Cool down the spice with a homemade pudding in flavors like Thai tea, durian or Ovaltine.

▧ 6660 W. Sunset Blvd., Ste. P
(bet. Cherokee & Las Palmas Aves.)
℘ (323) 498-5835 — **WEB:** www.luv2eatthai.com
▧ Lunch & dinner daily   PRICE: ⌬

MARINO 🍴

Italian • Osteria

⚘ ♿ 🍽

This family-run restaurant is now in its second generation, but Mario Jr. still shakes your hand and (if you're lucky) plants a peck on your cheek just like his father did. It's all part of the old-school charm of Marino, which has been open since the 70s.

While tradition reigns (note the fresh flowers on each table), this osteria isn't above pulling in some new influences. From the wine list, which balances Italian favorites with new world labels, to the dessert menu, where typical tiramisu and torta di ricotta mingle with farmer's market apple strudel, the kitchen seamlessly blends old and new. You'll never go wrong with classics, like pollo Parmigiana, lightly breaded and smothered in cheese. There's a reason some places stick around.

▧ 6001 Melrose Ave. (at Wilcox Ave.)
℘ (323) 466-8812 — **WEB:** www.marinorestaurant.com
▧ Lunch Mon – Fri Dinner Mon – Sat   PRICE: $$

MATSUMOTO

Japanese • Simple

Once home to Hirozen, helmed for 15 years by Osaka chef Naruki Matsumoto, this bright little space is today his own sushi-ya, serving a straightforward selection of maki and nigiri crafted from fish sourced straight from Japan. No detail is overlooked by the kitchen—from the fine-grained rice that's judiciously seasoned and served at the ideal temperature, to the expertly sliced fish paired with it.

Sushi is offered by the piece or as part of the omakase that lists each course with its respective price. Commence with a trio of red snapper, tender squid over shiso leaf and sliced sea scallop all sprinkled with lemon juice and sea salt. Grilled and fried appetizers round out this fine menu, but finish with a simple handroll of cool crabmeat.

- 8385 Beverly Blvd. (bet. Kings Rd. & Orlando Ave.)
- (323) 653-0470 — **WEB:** www.matsumoto-restaurant.com
- Lunch Mon – Fri Dinner Mon – Sat   **PRICE: $$$**

MEALS BY GENET

Ethiopian • Elegant

This specialty spot calls "Little Ethiopia" home, a bustling little strip filled with restaurants, coffee shops and thrift stores. The no-frills exterior and ambiguous name don't suggest much, but once inside, discover a contemporary space with whitewashed walls, artwork and—of course—stunningly good food that's meant to be enjoyed sans utensils.

These dishes are authentic and prepared with great care and attention; the menu ventures well past the region's best-known items. Don't miss the pan-fried freshwater trout, sumptuous chicken stew, and crumble-in-your-mouth teff cookies to close. Another delight is Hirutye's yebegsiga alitcha, a lamb preparation featuring luscious, slightly spicy berbere and awaze paired with spongy injera.

- 1053 S. Fairfax Ave. (bet. Olympic Blvd. & Whitworth Dr.)
- (323) 938-9304 — **WEB:** www.mealsbygenetla.com
- Dinner Thu – Sun   **PRICE: $$**

MERCADO LOS ANGELES

Mexican • *Family*

Don't dodge the valet or you'll likely miss nabbing a table at this ever-packed place where Sunday brunch involves a perpetual wait list. Mercado is loud and proud, so if you're planning to whisper sweet nothings to your companion, those heartfelt words will go unheard.

Margaritas and Mexican food go hand in hand, and the spicy cucumber margarita offered here is a sure thing. Opt for one of the many tequilas or mezcals for sipping while snacking, preferably on the dip duo of chunky guacamole and creamy choriqueso blended with spicy house chorizo, plus crispy and crunchy chips. This is not a street taco joint, so check the mirror for the specials, including a daily tamale. Top it off with Mercado's flan, served with a brandy-spiked rompope.

■ 7910 W. 3rd St. (at Fairfax Ave.)
✆ (323) 944-0947 — **WEB:** www.mercadorestaurant.com
■ Lunch Sat – Sun Dinner nightly   **PRICE: $$**

NIGHT + MARKET 🍴

Thai • *Colorful*

This original location is a bright pink local destination for reliable Thai cooking. The dining room is a pleasing amalgam of (fake) flowers, beaded curtains and string lights; a bar area lies beyond the colorful wall hangings.

Menu highlights unveil larb gai, a zesty tossup of minced chicken, ginger, cilantro, lime, rice powder and finely diced chilis. Continue along the spice route via the gaeng hanglay, a hearty Burmese-style curry infused with tamarind and pickled garlic. Close out with pad see ew, starring thin rice noodles sautéed with chicken, egg and Chinese broccoli—sambal served on the side makes this quite the house delight.

■ 9043 W. Sunset Blvd. (bet. Doheny Dr. & Hammond St.)
✆ (310) 275-9724 — **WEB:** www.nightmarketla.com
■ Lunch Tue – Thu Dinner Tue – Sun   **PRICE: $$**

NORAH

Contemporary · Chic

Norah boasts floor-to-ceiling windows and its gorgeous open and airy room is flooded with light. Handsome wood columns mix with sleek marble counters for a pale, ethereal setting that's as pretty to look at as the food is delicious. Guests line the two-sided marble cocktail bar to enjoy hand-crafted cocktails from a carefully curated menu.

Starters like the skillet cornbread with rosemary butter hint at the chef's Southern culinary influences, but the carte spans the globe to include everything from cauliflower tartare with tahini and chickpeas, to jasmine rice congee or squid ink tagliolini. Lighter appetites may opt for the winter squash tempura with black garlic aïoli; while hearty appetites devour uni butter-poached shrimp with smoked tomato.

- 8279 Santa Monica Blvd. (bet. Harper & Sweetzer Aves.)
- (310) 643-5853 — **WEB:** www.norahrestaurant.com
- Lunch Sat – Sun Dinner nightly　　　　　**PRICE: $$**

ODYS + PENELOPE

Contemporary · Chic

This slightly rustic yet enticing venture, brought to you by husband-and-wife team Quinn and Karen Hatfield, is a massive Fairfax charmer. Inside, lofty wood-beamed ceiling, exposed brick walls and open kitchen all combine to create a modern farmhouse vibe. Of course, happy hour at the long, inviting bar is always abuzz.

The menu showcases an American take on Brazilian churrascaria fare, including tri-tip, bacon-wrapped chicken thighs or maple-rosemary glazed ribs that arrive tender off the oak-fired brasero. On the other hand, vegetable sides flaunt a touch of Middle Eastern flavor and may reveal grilled brassicas piled over beet hummus and dusted with za'atar. The chocolate pie, with a rye crust and fudgy filling, makes a hearty finish.

- 127 S. La Brea Ave. (bet. 1st & 2nd Sts.)
- (323) 939-1033 — **WEB:** www.odysandpenelope.com
- Dinner nightly　　　　　**PRICE: $$$**

189 BY DOMINIQUE ANSEL ⅋○

Contemporary • Chic

♿ 🛋 🍷

An acclaimed NYC baker who rocketed to fame for inventing the Cronut, Dominique Ansel has crossed the country to debut his first full-service restaurant inside The Grove. Perched above his very own bustling ground-floor bakery, 189 is equal parts restrained and raucous, featuring a soothing white palette contrasted against a loud soundtrack.

While rooted in classic French technique, the cuisine is inventive and global. Brioche pull-apart rolls conceal a sweet elote filling flecked with spicy chili and cotija cheese, while seared hen-of-the-woods mushrooms sub for pasta in a rich cacio e pepe. Unsurprisingly, desserts are impressive—the "apple five ways," a deconstructed apple pie, is an elaborate confection with puff pastry, sorbet and meringue.

■ 189 The Grove Dr. (bet. 3rd St. & Beverly Blvd.)
☎ (323) 602-0096 — **WEB:** www.dominiqueansella.com
■ Lunch & dinner daily   PRICE: $$

PAPILLES 😊

French • Bistro

♿

Sure, its unassuming location just off the 101 makes it easy to drive right by, but boy what a mistake that would be. This darling is the real deal—quaint and cozy, complete with a pressed-tin ceiling, smoky glass fixtures and colorful tile floor. That wall lined with French vintages isn't just for show; take your pick and the waiter will pluck that bottle for your table as well.

The cooking features spot-on classics prepared with great care and little fuss. Highlights like plump frog legs drizzled in verdant pistou as well as the ever-so-slightly crisp red snapper sided by buttery potatoes and grilled romaine are delightful. For dessert, the vacherin with layers of tangy lemon meringue and berry ice cream, is textbook-perfect and oh-so-French.

■ 6221 Franklin Ave. (bet. Argyle & Vista Del Mar Aves.)
☎ (323) 871-2026 — **WEB:** www.papillesla.com
■ Dinner nightly   PRICE: $$

OSTERIA MOZZA 😣

Italian • Fashionable

A mega hit since opening over a decade ago, this Hollywood darling—sitting on a prominent corner of Melrose Avenue—continues to please with creative cocktails and delicious Italian cuisine. Its entrance is clearly marked outside the massive one-story building, though it is also home to Pizzeria Mozza, as well as a to-go option. The décor veers from typical osteria-style, thanks to handsome dark-wood paneling and a beautiful white marble counter. The front room is lively with music, while the back is quieter. A seat at the Mozza bar lets guests have a prime view of the antipasti being prepared.

This kitchen strives to show you around the corners of Italian cooking, so dive right in with the calf's brain ravioli with burro e limone. Bread is something of an obsession here—don't be shocked to see hungry diners tucking a slice of multigrain or two into their purses.The crispy chicken leg is pure and simple comfort food; and pastas are unsurprisingly phenomenal—try the orecchiette with sausage and Swiss chard. Other highpoints include the mozzarella menu, which should be explored with gusto, as should the very smart wine list.

Waits—for tables and again between courses—are to be expected.

■ 6602 Melrose Ave. (at Highland Ave.)
✆ (323) 297-0100 — **WEB:** www.osteriamozza.com
■ Dinner nightly   **PRICE: $$$**

PETIT TROIS

French • Bistro

Open and operating non-stop from noon until late night, this bijou is the casual sibling of Trois Mec next door. The narrow room is always full and the counter cramped, as four chefs display their skills before you, assembling such lovely dishes as pâté de campagne. And while the setting may not sound overly comfortable, there is a focus on service which makes every meal here a pleasant experience from start to finish.

The French hip-hop in the background eschews tradition, but the cooking does the exact opposite. This menu is a canon of bistro favorites, like garlicky escargot in melting butter, steak au poivre and what may be the city's best omelet. Save room to indulge in desserts like chocolate mousse or rice pudding with salted caramel sauce.

- 718 Highland Ave. (at Melrose Ave.)
- *(323) 468-8916 — **WEB:** www.petittrois.com
- Lunch & dinner daily   **PRICE: $$**

PETTY CASH

Mexican • Trendy

This place is all about Tom Petty, Johnny Cash and gussied-up Tijuana street food. Pictures of those namesake artists, a colorful dining room and great playlist also make this a fun place to dig into contemporary Mexican fare, with an eye on the humble taco. Plus, the tequila and mezcal selections are second to none.

The menu opens with shareable starters, like the gringa-style quesadilla with chili-rubbed smoked pork shoulder and jack cheese pressed between flour tortillas and drizzled with avocado crema. Don't forget to try the Baja fish tacos, filled with Negra Modelo beer-battered rockfish, crema, cabbage and pico de gallo. Their tacos, folded with house-made blue corn tortillas, may be a few dollars extra but are absolutely worth it.

- 7360 Beverly Blvd. (bet. Fuller & Martel Aves.)
- *(323) 933-5300 — **WEB:** www.pettycashtaqueria.com
- Lunch Fri – Sun Dinner nightly   **PRICE: $$**

PIZZERIA MOZZA 😊

Pizza • Trattoria

  ⛏

Mozza is at its essence a pizzeria, but so much more than a mere neighborhood haunt. Why, you might ask? It boasts the presence of Co-owner Nancy Silverton, whose culinary pedigree has foodies flocking to this Hollywood hottie. Adding to that, its sunny-yellow exterior and orange canopy set a Mediterranean scene.

Make your way into this bright room donning bare wood tables and skylights. Pizzas are far above average, beginning with that unmistakable cornicione—perfect spots of char that rim the crust and bring the flavor. Toppings are just as fanciful, highlighting goat cheese, leeks and bacon; or maybe squash blossom with burrata. Come dessert, Pastry Chef Dahlia Narvaez works her magic with scrumptious treats, like Meyer lemon and kumquat crostata.

◾ 641 N. Highland Ave. (at Melrose Ave.)
✆ (323) 297-0101 — **WEB:** www.pizzeriamozza.com
◾ Lunch & dinner daily   **PRICE: $$**

REPUBLIQUE 🍴

Mediterranean • Rustic

Republique welcomes guests to its warren of intimate dining areas with an abundant display of oysters, charcuterie and an ample bar. At the center and beneath a skylight, the fully open kitchen provides entertainment for a long communal table. Details are thoughtfully integrated—even the servers' aprons match the indigo wall color.

The cooking follows suit with a consistent show of talent, right from the first bite of their parmesan grissini. The menu goes on to explore the cuisine of Southern Europe through local Californian ingredients. Expect finely crafted cavatelli dressed in a simple springtime array of morels, trumpets and wild ramps; grilled octopus salad with Santa Barbara pistachios; or saffron mezze maniche with lamb ragout.

◾ 624 S. La Brea Ave. (bet. 6th St. & Wilshire Blvd.)
✆ (310) 362-6115 — **WEB:** www.republiquela.com
◾ Lunch & dinner daily   **PRICE: $$$$**

PROVIDENCE ✿✿

Seafood • Luxury

For over a decade, Providence has been at the forefront of LA's fine-dining scene. Little has changed here, which is a beautiful thing. The dining room is as formal as the suited staff, who are well-orchestrated and on the cooler side of attentive. Even just watching each course as it leaves the kitchen, artistically presented on bespoke plates, is a pleasure to the senses.

Each of the three tasting menus features the freshest and most sustainable seafood, often wild-caught from American waters. Chef Michael Cimarusti uses these ingredients deftly to craft his California cuisine inspired by the flavors and ideas of Asia and the Mediterranean. The sheer range of styles proves this kitchen's talent and technical know-how, using classic methods to pair seafood with rich sauces. The uni egg served in its shell with warm yolk and champagne beurre-blanc is—unsurprisingly—a luxurious signature. Meals here usually begin on a high note with a diverse selection of canapés, including the nasturtium leaf taco filled with sushi rice, arare crackers and sea beans; or pickled sardine crostini topped with coriander blossom.

Raspberry-rose semifreddo set atop lychee granité makes for a pristine palate-cleanser.

■ 5955 Melrose Ave. (at Cole Ave.)
☏ (323) 460-4170 — **WEB:** www.providencela.com
■ Lunch Fri Dinner nightly   **PRICE: $$$$**

RONAN 🍽️

Italian • Trendy

Aim for the two-story floral mural to find this Italian favorite with a dive bar-feel and plenty of LA style. Sit in the lovely patio, or head inside to the black marble bar. Other options include booths as well as an attractive communal table crafted from a varnished wood slab. Diners can expect to see pizza dough stretched, blenders whirring and the wood-fired oven crackling, all of which contribute to Ronan's swank allure.

Cute and quirky food descriptions make perusing the menu as entertaining as it is appetizing. Many are here just for the hand-tossed Neapolitan pizza—its thin-crust enticingly blistered beneath minimal ingredients. But the rest of the menu is just as divine, especially such bites as blanched asparagus with Fresno chilies and lemon aïoli.

▦ 7315 Melrose Ave. (bet. Fuller & Poinsettia Pl.)
☏ (323) 917-5100 — **WEB:** www.ronanla.com
▦ Dinner Wed – Mon   **PRICE: $$$**

ROSALINÉ 😊

Peruvian • Chic

From its servers sporting hibiscus-hued tops and orange kerchiefs to its upbeat Latin music, Rosaliné looks and feels like a happy place. Chef/owner Ricardo Zarate shows off his Peruvian roots at this local haunt, where an exhibition kitchen and light-filled greenhouse-style dining room vie for your attention.

The cooking also demands to be front and center. In addition to seafood, there are plenty of traditional meat-focused dishes, such as lomo saltado and adobo pork osso bucco. The comprehensive menu with an array of small plates and family-style items means that it pays to bring a friend who likes to share.

The one thing you won't need to bring however is extra cash, as tips here are politely declined thanks to a service charge added to all checks.

▦ 8479 Melrose Ave. (bet. La Cienege Blvd. & Melrose Alley)
☏ (323) 297-9500 — **WEB:** www.rosalinela.com
▦ Lunch Sun Dinner nightly   **PRICE: $$**

RUNNING GOOSE 🍴○
Latin American • Rustic

♿ ⛱ 🍸 🍽

Patrons enter this popular Hollywood restaurant through the small dining room, but most make a beeline straight for the cozy outdoor patio. In the evening, the inviting fire pit beckons; and by day, the flourishing gardens offer a scenic backdrop for the generous happy hour, which runs from noon to 6.00P.M. Weekend brunch features bottomless mimosas; and there are typically a dozen or so West Coast beers on tap, so sip away.

The menu is centered around LA's many Central-American influences, with a good dose of Californian flair. Diners should definitely try the tostadas, featuring deliciously unique fillings—one with burnt corn aïoli, charred sweet corn kernels, lime and basil; or another with carrot purée, queso fresco and celery leaves.

▪ 1620 N. Cahuenga Blvd.
(bet. Hollywood Blvd. & Selma Ave.)
℘ (323) 469-1080 — **WEB:** www.runninggoose.weebly.com
▪ Lunch & dinner daily   **PRICE: $$**

SON OF A GUN 😊
Seafood • Vintage

♿ ⛱ 🍽

Located among a fashionable string of shops and restaurants, find this bohemian delight for seafood-focused Californian fare.

Begin meals with a sample of wonderful small plates, like the shrimp toast sandwich with hoisin sauce, herbs and Sriracha mayo. Raw offerings are often prepared with innovative twists and unexpected pairings, such as hamachi carpaccio in a delicate galbi vinaigrette with Pink Lady apples, radish and microgreens. Also, be sure to sample the lobster roll, crusty yet buttery and generously laden with sweet meat bathed in celery-lemon aïoli; or the tuna melt, layering cheddar, tomato and crème fraîche over toasted rye. But the lunchtime favorite has nothing to do with the seas—their fried chicken sandwich is downright famous.

▪ 8370 W. 3rd St. (at Orlando Ave.)
℘ (323) 782-9033 — **WEB:** www.sonofagunrestaurant.com
▪ Lunch & dinner daily   **PRICE: $$**

SOREGASHI 🍴

Japanese • Minimalist

Though it's popular with the locals, Soregashi also lures fans from far and wide, and for good reason. This little sushiya is serious-minded without being seriously pricey, offering a welcome middle ground between those cheap maki factories and high-end omakase counter destinations.

The nigiri, from toro to tai (snapper), are of pristine quality; and the excellence of the fish belies its simplicity—even minced tuna with scallions or hamachi sashimi sing in the capable hands of these itamae. As if that isn't enough, they also do an excellent job with izakaya standbys, from house-made cold soba noodles to crispy octopus. The stir-fried Japanese eggplant with miso paste is a melt-in-your-mouth delight, tailed by soft, silken tofu with dashi gelée.

▨ 6775 Santa Monica Blvd. (at Highland Ave.)
✆ (323) 498-5060 — **WEB:** www.soregashi-la.com
▨ Lunch Tue – Fri Dinner Tue – Sat   PRICE: $$

SQIRL 😀

Californian • Trendy

Jessica Koslow's tale began in 2011 with a line of seasonal homemade jams and an ever-growing fan base for her sweet and savory offerings. Just a year later, Sqirl was born—and the rest, as they say, is history. Today, hordes fill this tiny gem, and Koslow—a success story straight out of a Hollywood script—has a cookbook as well as an expansion in the works.

Her no-frills café embodies southern California's current food philosophy—healthy indulgence. Think grain bowls filled with globe-spanning ingredients, often topped with an impeccably sourced egg; or the chef's signature ricotta toast, a buttery brioche sporting creamy ricotta and the jam that started it all. The latter is also available in such divine flavors as raspberry and Tahitian vanilla bean.

▨ 720 N. Virgil Ave. (at Marathon St.)
✆ (323) 284-8147 — **WEB:** www.sqirlla.com
▨ Lunch daily   PRICE: 👄

SUSHI GINZA ONODERA ⽊⽊

Japanese • Elegant

Sushi aficionados may have to look a little harder to discover this jewel box, hidden among a host of high-end boutiques. Sushi Ginza Onodera may have outposts around the world, but its fame has not diluted the exemplary quality of this cuisine. That said, it comes with a hefty price tag, though their strictly enforced no-tipping policy certainly helps. Notable attention is also given to the light-filled space, resplendent with Japanese elegance; and the knowledgeable staff is just as pleasing and impressive as the meal itself.

Fish of this caliber is not easy to find and the kitchen gives each morsel the painstaking care it deserves. Surprises and delights abound in the delirious array of courses, starting with an earthenware cup of chawanmushi topped with Italian caviar and a petal of uni. Some might feel guilty devouring squid in a matter of seconds after watching the exacting chefs take ten minutes to prepare it, but the experience is utterly memorable. The nigiri are a clear highlight here, revealing tiger shrimp with miso, sea perch seared for a hint of smoke as well as a duo of anago with sansho and yuzu zest.

The signature matcha- and coconut-panna cotta is a delectable finale.

▢ 609 N. La Cienega Blvd. (at Melrose Ave.)
✆ (323) 433-4817 — **WEB:** www.onodera-group.com
▢ Dinner Tue – Sun   **PRICE: $$$$**

SUSHI PARK ⅋O

Japanese • Simple

Tucked into a nondescript shopping center along Sunset Blvd., this modest spot takes a bit of work to find. Make your way to the discreet entrance on the second floor, and there you'll find the laws of the land: authentic, traditional sushi is the name of the game, so don't expect fancy preparations, tempura, teriyaki or even a California roll in sight. And takeaway? Forget about it.

What you will find, however, is a simple set-up that includes a ten-seat counter and half-dozen small tables; a direct, no-frills waitstaff; as well as some seriously solid food. Don't miss the albacore tuna sashimi, served with a side of soy sauce that's kissed with citrus. A long sushi serenade is next—by the time the check is dropped, you're guaranteed to part happy.

▪ 8539 Sunset Blvd., Ste. 20
(bet. Londonderry Pl. & Miller Dr.)
℘ (310) 652-0523 — **WEB:** N/A
▪ Lunch Tue – Fri Dinner Tue – Sat   **PRICE: $$$$**

TESSE ⅋O

French • Design

Tesse is French slang for charcuterie, and sure enough, you'll find an impressive lineup of terrines, rillettes and artisanal sausages at this stylish restaurant. And though the cured meats program is integral to its spirit, this kitchen spins out an array of contemporary dishes as well, with careful attention to classical details and masterful contemporary flourishes.

The chefs make daily treks to LA's various farmers' markets for seasonal produce. Blue crab simplissime marries whipped potato and tarragon with reduced crab stock and Cognac; while bone marrow—roasted over the wood fire—is tossed with bucatini, duck prosciutto and shallots for a rich and delightfully balanced plate. The carefully procured wine list offers numerous bottles by the glass.

▪ 8500 W. Sunset Blvd.
(bet. Alta Loma Rd. & La Cienega Blvd.)
℘ (310) 360-3866 — **WEB:** www.tesserestaurant.com
▪ Lunch Sat – Sun Dinner nightly   **PRICE: $$$**

THAI THING 😳

Thai · Contemporary décor

There's no shortage of good Thai food in LA, but this retreat separates itself from the rest with an easy-breezy vibe. Of course, the kitchen's devotion to bright, fresh flavors and (when possible) locally sourced ingredients certainly helps it along.

Dishes are cooked to order and your patience is duly rewarded. The genial staff takes evident pride in the food here, as they should—cooking techniques are exemplary and your best bet is to put yourself in the more-than-capable hands of the talented chef. Be sure to order the "Crispy Creamy Lime Chicken" to start, followed by the "Truly Crispy Rice Salad." The latter is a mélange of fried curry rice balls, cilantro, ginger, chili flakes, peanuts and ground pork, served with romaine lettuce for wrapping.

■ 6015 W. 3rd St. (at Vista St.)
℘ (323) 954-8424 — **WEB:** www.thethaithing.com
■ Lunch Thu – Sun Dinner nightly   **PRICE: $$**

THE TOWER BAR AND RESTAURANT 🍴

American · Historic

An art deco relic of the Great Depression and hailed as Los Angeles's first earthquake-proof structure—the Sunset Tower is a formidable home. Here, the maître'd is known as a local gatekeeper of sorts, and alone decides whether you are seated at a mauve banquette by the terrace or in the more boisterous and desirable bar. Service can be hit or miss.

Like the Hollywood legends that were rumored to stay upstairs, the menu offerings can seem old timey with deviled eggs and vegetables sticks. Yet they are prepared with skill and care, resulting in a perfectly juicy pork chop, well-seasoned and grilled until succulent, served with sautéed spinach and fingerling potatoes. Desserts are fun and may include a baked Alaska or make-your-own sundaes.

■ 8358 Sunset Blvd.
(bet. Crescent Heights & La Cienega Blvds.)
℘ (323) 654-7100 — **WEB:** www.sunsettowerhotel.com
■ Dinner nightly   **PRICE: $$$$**

TROIS MEC

Contemporary • Trendy

Fun, creative and consistently delicious, there is no doubt as to why this bijou is always shining. It should come as no surprise though, as the "Three Guys" for which the restaurant is named are Chefs Ludo Lefebvre, Jon Shook and Vinny Dotolo, all of whom are renowned for other hot spots like Petit Trois and Animal. In classic LA style, the cozy establishment is located in a modest space. But have faith in the fact that its contemporary décor combining cool stone with warm wood bears no resemblance to its former life as a pizza parlor. Service is knowledgeable, attentive and speedy with an audible "Bonjour!" as guests enter the room.

There is one nightly tasting menu that begins with canapés like savory madeleines or a radicchio spring roll set over black olive tapenade. The five larger dishes that follow may highlight an impeccably cooked lamb loin with yogurt and a dollop of mint pesto. Desserts are often reinterpreted French classics, as seen in the chestnut cream encased by shards of meringue, dusted with mushroom powder.

This cuisine is ambitious and every dish might not achieve its lofty goal, but that does not diminish the fact that dining here is a special and singular experience.

■ 716 N. Highland Ave. (at Melrose Ave.)
℘ (323) 484-8588 — **WEB:** www.troismec.com
■ Dinner Tue – Sat   **PRICE: $$$$**

TSUBAKI 😊
Japanese • Cozy

First things first: Tsubaki is not a sushiya. Barring a lovely plate of sashimi (kanpachi), the menu at this delicious Japanese gem is comprised of classic izakaya food. Think fluffy whipped miso tofu, topped with marinated cherry tomatoes and pickled scallion kimchi; Salmon Creek Farm pork shumai with braised bacon dashi; and tender grilled chicken "oysters" kicked up with yuzu kosho. Dishes are meant to be shared and paired with beer or sake. Beverage lovers will thrill to the excellent selection of local craft and distilled sake—where they'll also get to choose their own cups to enjoy these sips.

Reservations and use of the restaurant's valet are highly recommended, especially in the summer when nearby Dodger Stadium is stormed with traffic.

◼ 1356 Allison Ave. (at Sunset Blvd.)
✆ (213) 900-4900 — **WEB:** www.tsubakila.com
◼ Dinner Tue – Sun   PRICE: $$

VERNETTI ⅒
Italian • Intimate

This bright and attractive space, adorned with a few shelves of canned Italian tomatoes and bold red wines, is as simple and straightforward as its cooking. The sidewalk patio fills with people appreciating the graces of good weather and great food.

That dedication to simple pleasures begins with a house Caesar salad, composed of baby romaine lettuce tossed in a heady blend of garlic, capers and anchovies. Chef/owner Steve Vernetti's Calabrian roots are abundantly clear in dishes like rigatoni salsiccia mingling sweet peppers, sausage, sautéed rapini and those spicy namesake chilies. Ample portions of classics like osso bucco, chicken parmigiana or pan-roasted branzino ensure that no one leaves hungry. Come on weekends for brunch, which is wildly popular.

◼ 225 N. Larchmont Blvd. (bet. Beverly Blvd. & 3rd St.)
✆ (323) 798-5886 — **WEB:** www.vernetti.la
◼ Lunch & dinner Tue – Sun   PRICE: $$

WOLF 🍴○

Contemporary · Trendy

Wagon-wheel chandeliers and a Dali-esque funhouse mirror over the bar set the tone for this darling of food adventurers. Of course it's no surprise, as Chef Marcel Vigneron integrates French, Moroccan and modernism into his whimsical cuisine. Dishes are so inventively plated that some guests may forget to put their smart phones away and start eating.

It may share its kitchen with neighboring spot, Tacos Lobos, but this dining room is beloved for such playful compositions as roasted, dehydrated, pickled and flash-frozen beets with complements ranging from fresh berries to an icy-cold goat cheese "snow." Desserts showcase just what this kitchen can accomplish, through a blueberry soufflé with frozen cherry yogurt slipped into the center.

■ 7661 Melrose Ave. (bet. Spaulding & Stanley Aves.)
℘ (323) 424-7735 — **WEB:** www.wolfdiningla.com
■ Lunch Sat – Sun Dinner Tue – Sat   **PRICE: $$$**

The sun is out — let's eat alfresco! Look for 🛖.

NORTHEAST

ALIMENTO

Italian • Fashionable

Set amidst fashionable shops and eateries in a hipster neighborhood, this Italian-influenced restaurant's modern house with a much-talked-about terrace doubles as a headquarters for area denizens. The young, stylish staff is highly dedicated to delivering a pleasant experience without putting on any airs.

The menu is equally unpretentious, with a nice selection of not-so-small plates along with dishes designed for sharing. It's all about clean flavors and simple preparations here, with delicious braised lettuce bruschetta and smoked yellowtail collar. Pastas are rave-worthy; the salumi agnolotti dazzles with its smoky and salty flavors.

Wines from small producers in France and Italy, as well as organic and biodynamic labels, show attention to detail.

 1710 Silver Lake Blvd. (at Effie St.)
  (323) 928-2888 — **WEB:** www.alimentola.com
  Dinner Tue – Sun   **PRICE: $$$**

BOWERY BUNGALOW 😊

Middle Eastern • Rustic

A white picket fence and bit of greenery ensure that this Silver Lake cottage is instantly likeable. Inside, the rooms and wood-plank walls feel lived in, despite the restaurant's young age. The backyard is popular for festive occasions. Over in the kitchen, fine touches embellish the Middle Eastern cooking and infuse most items on the menu. Babaghanoush is rich and creamy, topped with startlingly spicy coal-roasted shishito peppers as well as wedges of hot pita. Meat skewers arrive sizzling on wood boards with dollops of spicy harissa and intense toum. And of course, that dark chocolate pot de crème makes for an ace finish.

Brunch is equally enjoyable here, featuring the likes of shakshuka with French feta or a traditional Lebanese breakfast platter.

  4156 Santa Monica Blvd. (bet. Del Mar & Myra Aves.)
  (323) 663-1500 — **WEB:** www.bowerybungalow.com
  Lunch Sat – Sun Dinner Tue – Sun   **PRICE: $$**

COSA BUONA 🍴○
Italian • Minimalist

♿ 🛏

Courtesy of the same owners behind the posh Alimento, this is a neighborhood pizza joint done right. Familiar items aside, the kitchen boasts a clear eye toward quality ingredients and careful presentations. For instance, hand-breaded mozzarella sticks with chunky marinara bring out the kid in all of us, while pizza reigns supreme at lunch and dinner. The latter features such adult inflections as fiery chilies alongside more typical trappings like pineapple on the Hawaiian. The stepmother Italian sub is addictive and not unlike the salads, which are far from a tag-along, highlighting large portions with tasty blends.

Desserts are somewhat limited but with a creatively rendered tiramisu and hefty wedge of cookies & cream semifreddo pie, who's complaining?

◾ 2100 W. Sunset Blvd. (at Alvarado St.)
✆ (213) 908-5211 — **WEB:** www.cosabuona.com
◾ Lunch Wed – Sun Dinner nightly   **PRICE: $$**

FREEDMAN'S 🍴○
Deli • Family

♿ 🛏

This is a Jewish deli with an old soul. Inside, the décor is classic bubbe, arranged with floral wallpaper, wood floors and marble-topped tables. There's even a vintage rotary phone mounted on the back wall that serves as a conversation piece or perhaps even a gentle reminder to call your mother already.

You will not leave hungry here—even the small matzoh ball soup feeds two. The house-made Toronto-style bagels are terrific at any time of day, while the heartwarming Reuben surely ranks as one of the city's top. Come dinner, start with a chopped liver spread with fried onions, trout roe popovers or potato latkes with sour cream. Then tuck into a comforting smoked fish platter or glazed brisket, which serves three or more at any given time.

◾ 2619 Sunset Blvd. (bet. Benton Way & Coronado St.)
✆ (213) 568-3754 — **WEB:** www.freedmansla.com
◾ Lunch Tue – Sun Dinner Tue – Sat   **PRICE:** ⬤

HIPPO 🍴

Italian • Family

 ♿ 🏠

The name comes from the building's former life as the Highland Park Post Office, but everything else here is Cal-Ital in spirit. The dining space is convivial and airy, with beamed ceilings and an open kitchen as its focal point. The vibe is as good for dates as it is for groups.

Complimentary bread is rarely as satisfying as their focaccia, with its crispy, salty crust and soft interior. Begin with a sampling of small plates, like hamachi crudo topped with dollops of Meyer lemon relish. Then move on to freshly made pasta, like tender purses of cappellacci filled with sweet corn and dressed in a sauce of butter, mushrooms and thyme. While a meal could end there, you'd be remiss not to order the wood-grilled game or cedar-smoked ocean trout.

◾ 5916 1/2 Figueroa St. (bet. Aves. 59 & 60)
☎ (323) 545-3536 — **WEB:** www.hipporestaurant.com
◾ Dinner Tue – Sun   **PRICE: $$**

KISMET 😀

Middle Eastern • Design

 ♿ 🛋

In that eternal quest for that great neighborhood restaurant, Kismet fits the bill. Of course, that only works when your 'hood is Los Feliz and said restaurant sports a mélange of Middle Eastern influences. This kitchen offers all-day dining, but with the shakshuka, or poached eggs in tomato stew, this isn't your pancake and French toast crowd.

Dishes hail from Israel, Turkey, Iran and elsewhere and create harmonies that make the United Nations green with envy. From barbari bread to chicken and pine nut pies wrapped in flaky phyllo, you'll be scraping your plate for crumbs. Freekeh fritters with "pickley green" sauce are like a carnival treat with an elevated international twist. Come hungry and armed with a crowd, since this food is best shared.

◾ 4648 Hollywood Blvd. (bet. Rodney Dr. & Vermont Ave.)
☎ (323) 409-0404 — **WEB:** www.kismetlosangeles.com
◾ Lunch & dinner daily   **PRICE: $$**

MA'AM SIR 🍴○

Filipino • Exotic décor

The name is inspired by the cheery Filipino greeting offered to travelers, and is a fitting introduction to this friendly and authentic outpost. The exterior proudly flies the flag of the nation, while the interior is adorned with a tasteful tropical theme comprised of banana leaf wallpaper, high ceilings dangling faux-vines and woven hemp light fixtures.

The kitchen focuses on their renditions of Filipino classics, like chicken adobo, lumpia and pork sisig. The uninitiated are sure to find the food here complex, interesting and consistently good. Purists may take issue with a few of the kitchen's creative choices, but no one is complaining about the deep flavors of their slow braises. Everything pairs nicely with beer and cocktails from the bar.

■ 4330 W. Sunset Blvd. (bet. Bates & Fountain Aves.)
✆ (323) 741-8371 — **WEB:** www.maamsirla.com
■ Lunch Sat – Sun Dinner Wed – Mon   **PRICE: $$**

MOMED ATWATER VILLAGE 🍴○

Middle Eastern • Mediterranean décor

The name, which is a blend of two words "modern" and "Mediterranean," perfectly describes this kitchen's focus on Middle Eastern cuisine. Inside, the dining room is casual yet cute with cocktails galore; it captures a certain breezy sophistication at the heart of the Atwater Crossing Arts District (there's a sib in Beverly Hills as well). But the best place to dine is outdoors on the sunny patio dotted with bare wood tables, wicker chairs and potted olive trees.

The menu reflects the flavors of Turkey, Morocco and beyond, beginning with crispy falafel over avocado hummus. Also try duck shawarma layering house-made lavash with duck confit, blistered tomatoes and black mission figs. Those tender momo chips are best dipped in their own garlicky hot sauce.

■ 3245 Casitas Ave. (bet. Fletcher Dr. & Tyburn St.)
✆ (323) 522-3488 — **WEB:** www.atmomed.com
■ Lunch & dinner daily   **PRICE: $$**

OTOÑO 🍴

Spanish • Tapas bar

&

Otoño offers one of the best "siesta hours" around. With excellent $3 tapas alongside a solid selection of Spanish beers and bargain-priced cocktails (artisanal gin and tonic, anyone?), you'll want to snag a seat between 4:00-6.00P.M. if you can. Pressed-tin panels, a colorful mural and exposed rafters give the space an eclectic vibe.

Modern California touches influence the tapas turned out of this kitchen, while larger dishes like braised octopus, smoked chicken thighs and paella options offer heartier fare if you're game. Don't miss the boquerones y mantequilla—a delicious little plate of fresh anchovies paired with roasted radishes and a terrific tuna and anchovy goat butter. Crema Catalana with wine-soaked blackberries is a light, boozy delight.

- 5715 N. Figueroa St. (bet. Aves. 57 & 58)
- ☎ (323) 474-6624 — **WEB:** www.otonorestaurant.com
- Dinner Tue – Sun   **PRICE: $$**

PARSNIP 🍴

Eastern European • Rustic

& 🏠

It's tiny here—as in there is seating for just four people indoors—but if the weather is nice and you have a hankering for some soul-soothing Romanian food, Parsnip is an ideal bet. Take a number, place your order and if you're lucky, grab a folding chair because these items are meant to be eaten sitting down.

Bulz dumplings filled with melted cheese, sauerkraut and red peppers are tangy and delicious; just as plachinta stuffed with potatoes and red chili is especially satisfying in all of its doughy goodness. Sarmale (cabbage rolls stuffed with beef, pork, rice and spices) toe the line between hearty and heavy, but if you prefer the classics, order the chicken paprikash or beef goulash. They come with that glorious dollop of sour cream, naturally.

- 5623 York Blvd. (bet. Ave. 56 & Nolden St.)
- ☎ (323) 739-0240 — **WEB:** www.parsnipcafe.com
- Dinner nightly   **PRICE:** 🍴

PINE & CRANE 😊
Asian • Trendy

Find this laid-back little café opposite the pedestrian plaza, Sunset Triangle. The dining room itself is triangular as well as hipster-friendly with a rustic blend of exposed brick, concrete floors and varnished wood tables.

As casual as the vibe may seem, this is a serious kitchen dedicated to Asian cuisine. Be sure to try their vegetarian variations on classics such as pork-free mapo tofu, daikon dumplings and daily specials like the lotus root or seaweed salad. However, the cooking truly shines with Taiwanese specialties. The three-cup jidori chicken is its own simmering feast in a clay pot of dark meat with equal parts soy, sesame oil and rice wine reduced to a deep brown glaze, then studded with chopped green onion, dried chilies and whole garlic.

■ 1521 Griffith Park Blvd. (bet. Edgecliffe Dr. & Maltman Ave.)
✆ (323) 668-1128 — **WEB:** www.pineandcrane.com
■ Lunch & dinner Wed – Mon   **PRICE:** 🍴

SALAZAR 😊
Mexican • Trendy

♿ 🏡 🛋 🍽

This breezy haven is at once pretty and edgy, thanks to its location in a former auto-body shop. The festive aura and fruit-laden lime trees practically command you to order a margarita. In a departure from the norm, the bar area is located inside, while the family-friendly dining room is outdoors. Windows overlooking the kitchen offer enticing views of the tortilla making. However delectable those may be, this kitchen's real specialty is mesquite grilling, from the meat that fills your tacos to the subtly charred sweet corn, cut from the cob and mixed with chili-spiked crema. The midday menu is comprised of smaller plates like tacos or chips coupled with roasted salsa vaquero.

Reservations are not accepted, so lines are just part of the fun.

■ 2490 Fletcher Dr. (at Ripple St.)
✆ N/A — **WEB:** www.salazarla.com
■ Lunch & dinner Tue – Sun   **PRICE:** $$

SAPP COFFEE SHOP 🍴○
Thai · Simple

If you're looking for a classic diner, this may not be your cup of tea. But for those who love hunting hidden culinary gems, there are few pleasures more profound than an 8:00A.M. bowl of Sapp's spicy, funky beef boat noodle soup, sprinkled with fried pork rinds and accompanied by a creamy, slushy iced coffee.

Aside from a few decorative altar shelves, the décor here is sparse, but rest assured as there's much vibrancy on the plate: fiery red chilies, bright-green jade noodles with spinach and golden-fried spring rolls filled with tender pork, crab and water chestnuts. Prices are so sound that you might even want to grab an afternoon snack on your way out—maybe those crispy rice cakes accompanied by a dipping sauce with pork, shrimp and peanuts?

■ 5183 Hollywood Blvd. (at Kingsley Dr.)
🕾 (323) 665-1035 — **WEB:** N/A
■ Lunch & dinner Thu – Tue   PRICE: 🍜

TROIS FAMILIA 🍴○
Fusion · Trendy

🅰 🛌

Only the power trio of Chefs Ludo Lefebvre, Jon Shook and Vinny Dotolo could make a unique take on French-Mexican food work here in LA. The prices are downright affordable when compared to their other restaurants, like Animal or Trois Mec. The décor is a simple mix of blue-and-white rattan chairs set around marble tables, with modern indie and 70's funk music keeping company with the eclectic aura.

While the concept may sound fusion, it is more of a classical French rendition of Mexican favorites. Double-decker tacos may be folded with brown-butter mashed potatoes, marinated carrots and crème fraîche. Since it started as a brunch spot before expanding to lunch and dinner, many dishes survived the transition. The churro French toast remains a revelation.

■ 3510 Sunset Blvd. (bet. Golden Gate & Maltman Aves.)
🕾 (323) 725-7800 — **WEB:** www.troisfamilia.com
■ Lunch & dinner daily   PRICE: 🍜

PASADENA

ADANA RESTAURANT 😳

Middle Eastern • Elegant

♿

Come with a group and order with abandon. The food here is so good that it will be hard to hold back. This dining room manages to be both modest and ornate, filled with large round tables covered in purple linen, alongside walls of gold-framed photos and murals. The vibe is so open and friendly that you might see cheese plates being enthusiastically shared among neighboring diners.

The cooking is as honest as the servers, who are happy to direct you on how to order best. Dolmeh and chicken kebabs with stewed sour cherries and an irresistible yogurt sauce are the kind of dishes one can imagine eating every day of the week. Fattoush made with crunchy vegetables, verdolagas and dressed in a lemony dressing sprinkled with sumac spells of garden goodness.

▪ 6918 San Fernando Rd. (bet. Elm & Spazier Aves.), Glendale
✆ (818) 843-6237 — **WEB:** www.adanamenu.com
▪ Lunch & dinner daily
PRICE: $$

ALEXANDER'S STEAKHOUSE 🍴

Steakhouse • Luxury

🐙 🍹 ♿ 🏮 🎪

This carnivorous delight is a stone's throw from City Hall and sports a smart appearance with black beams and glass walls. However, rest assured that this isn't your typical creamed spinach kind of spot. Instead, you'll find a refreshingly inventive menu scattered with Asian influences—ranging from hamachi shots, Sichuan steak rubs and wasabi-studded béarnaise. Whether you opt for the dry-aged tataki featuring lightly seared NY strip massaged with wasabi and tossed with scallions, or perfectly charred Kobe, quality is king in this kitchen. If Wagyu is what you want (and really, who doesn't?) order the seven-course tasting menu.

Also of note is the bar, which maintains a remarkable collection of wine, whiskey and Bourbon for enjoyably endless sipping.

▪ 111 N. Los Robles Ave. (bet. Union & Walnut Sts.)
✆ (626) 486-1111 — **WEB:** www.alexandurssteakhouse.com
▪ Dinner nightly
PRICE: $$$$

ARROYO CHOP HOUSE 🍴

Steakhouse • Rustic

This venerated spot subscribes to the belief that tradition trumps trend and judging by the crowds that collect here, they seem to be right on the money. In terms of décor, it's a classic steakhouse, with dark cherry wood walls and spacious booths. Piano tunes mixed in with the din of deal-making keeps the vibe celebratory at all times.

Start with a glass of wine from their lengthy list or sip on a cocktail. While some opt for standbys like sizzling steaks or barbecue shrimp with Cajun-spiced butter, others can't wait to skip ahead to the finale by way of the warm chocolate soufflé. Whatever you do, don't miss the garlic bread (for sopping up every drop of the spicy butter sauce) or sides—the creamed spinach and jalapeño-corn soufflé are clear winners.

■ 536 S. Arroyo Pkwy. (bet. California & Del Mar Blvds.)
☏ (626) 577-7463 — **WEB:** www.arroyochophouse.com
■ Dinner nightly

PRICE: $$$$

BOURBON STEAK 🍴

Steakhouse • Elegant

Everything you really need to know about this notable steakhouse is foretold within minutes of your arrival, when those complimentary duck-fat fries are placed on your table. They are pretty much perfect and very welcoming. Spend as much time savoring them as the lengthy Bourbon and wine lists, which flaunt a deep knowledge of top producers in Spain, Napa and Burgundy—all available at reasonable prices.

The most notable specialty may be the butter-poached steak, sporting a serious crust and cooked to order. However, the pot pie filled with two pounds of lobster meat in puff pastry ensures that flavors are thoroughly enjoyable. Sides are better than they need to be, so do not miss the black truffle mac and cheese or asparagus with preserved lemon gremolata.

■ 237 S. Brand Blvd. (at The Americana at Brand), Glendale
☏ (818) 839-4130 — **WEB:** www.michaelmina.net
■ Dinner nightly

PRICE: $$$$

FISHWIVES ¡🍴

American • Trendy

&

On the doorstop to Old Pasadena's shopping district, find this airy New England-inspired raw bar offering plump oysters, shrimp, lobsters and so much more. Its simple, straightforward but appetizing food—relying on little more than top quality ingredients—is a real treat for this neighborhood. The interior feels like a bright bistro, combining white brick accents, vibrant blue tiles and schools of decorative fish hanging on the walls.

Start off with a seafood sampler, like "The Fish" for instance, which comes with an array of delicious bivalves dressed with a ponzu-citrus pesto. The entire plate is assembled before your eyes at the raw bar, which underscores the beauty of having fish flown in daily. The lobster roll is a necessary treat here.

▪ 88 N. Fair Oaks Ave. (bet. Holly & Union Sts.)
𝒞 (626) 219-6199 — **WEB:** www.fishwives.com
▪ Lunch & dinner Tue – Sun   **PRICE: $$**

MAESTRO ¡🍴

Mexican • Elegant

& 🛖 ⌀

Maestro's location amidst Old Town Pasadena's national chains (The Cheesecake Factory, for instance) is a bit of a red herring as this upscale Mexican restaurant is anything but ordinary. Instead, discover a sexy, modern space with soft lighting and lofty ceilings (perfect for date night) along with an ambitious kitchen delivering ingredient-driven dishes.

The chef plates with an artist's eye, elevating even the most humble of items to a creative form—imagine the likes of tamale with its red and green swirls, a surefire hit on Instagram. Braised lamb shank with just a bit of heat is yet another standout, but save the best for last with a moist corn cake topped with sweet and salty caramel popcorn, huitlacoche ice cream and crème anglaise.

▪ 110 E. Union St. (bet. Historic Rte. 66 & Raymond Ave.)
𝒞 (626) 787-1512 — **WEB:** www.maestropasadena.com
▪ Lunch Sat – Sun Dinner Tue – Sun   **PRICE: $$$**

MINI KABOB

Middle Eastern • Simple

It really is all in the name at Mini Kabob, since this teeny-tiny shack is scarcely appointed with just three tables and no air-conditioning. Still, it's family run and has been going strong for 30-plus years. Why? The delicious food, no doubt.

Sidle up to the counter and take your pick. Everything is made in-house and cooked to order here, so don't expect a quick turnaround despite the brisk takeout business. Semi-smooth hummus topped with Syrian Aleppo pepper powder for a whisper of heat is a zesty opener, while the Egyptian-style falafel, made with green garlic, parsley and fava beans, revels in all its familiar glory. Naturally, kabobs are a must, and the charred bits of chicken thighs coupled with homemade garlic sauce are a sensory treat.

■ 313 1/2 Vine St. (bet. Central & Columbus Aves.), Glendale
℘ (818) 244-1343 — **WEB:** www.mini-kabob.com
■ Lunch & dinner daily   PRICE: ◔

OSAWA ⴵ○

Japanese • Simple

This restaurant is a utility player offering everything from lunch specials to sushi, but the real star here is the outstanding shabu shabu—available only at the counter, where iron cauldrons bubble with a variety of exceptional broths. Each is accompanied by a bowl of accoutrements, including several types of greens, two kinds of noodles, rice and tofu.

If soup isn't right for the season, opt for the crave-worthy sushi. Sample rich bluefin nigiri gently glazed with ponzu, or the off-menu battera (pressed rice with pickled mackerel)—a house favorite. Service is swift, with food arriving quickly to the counter or well-spaced tables. For those in a rush however, adjacent and fast-casual The Delicatessen by Osawa is definitely worth a visit.

■ 77 N. Raymond Ave. (bet. Holly & Union Sts.)
℘ (626) 683-1150 — **WEB:** www.theosawa.com
■ Lunch & dinner daily   PRICE: $$

PARKWAY GRILL ¶○

American • Elegant

Parkway Grill may be known to have ushered in the open kitchen and exposed brick phenomenon back in the 1980s; and while many of the servers have been here for decades as well, this Pasadena favorite never shows her age. In fact, it's always bustling with a convivial scene inside, but everyone stops in their tracks and heads swivel when that platter of whole fried ginger catfish makes its way through the dining room. This aromatic behemoth is definitely a trophy, but with its deliciously deep-fried crust and addictive yuzu-ponzu dipping sauce, it's by all means a golden one.

Regulars know to save room at the end for the crème brûlée Napoleon. This dessert may look a touch throwback but lingers on your taste buds for weeks to come.

▨ 510 S. Arroyo Pkwy. (bet. California Blvd. & Bellevue Dr.)
☏ (626) 795-1001 — **WEB:** www.theparkwaygrill.com
▨ Lunch Mon – Fri Dinner nightly   **PRICE: $$$$**

RAFFI'S PLACE ¶○

Middle Eastern • Family

There are places where you go for a tête-à-tête, and then there is Raffi's. This establishment promises a rollicking good time and its large open-air dining room simply adds to the good mood. Indeed, it is a favorite among friends dining en masse, so bring your best pals and settle in for some fun. You may even find yourself celebrating with the table next to you before too long—it's that sort of joint.

The kitchen focuses on Persian and Middle Eastern cooking and the portions match the size of the dining room (read: huge). Ghormeh sabzi, a bowl filled with tender beef chunks, kidney beans and spices, has a slightly sour, stick-to-your-ribs appeal; while charbroiled chicken, lamb and mahi mahi kebabs set atop fluffy rice are ever-satisfying standards.

▨ 211 E. Broadway (bet. Artsakh Ave. & Louise St.), Glendale
☏ (818) 240-7411 — **WEB:** www.raffisplace.com
▨ Lunch & dinner daily   **PRICE: $$**

THE RAYMOND ¶◯

American • Tavern

This longtime favorite may show a little age in its décor, but the food is as vibrant as ever thanks to the ministrations of an adept kitchen. Known for salads, sandwiches and strong vegetarian options like a gorgeous burnt carrot salad with avocado, this team can also turn out a top-notch burger—with lamb, feta, mint pesto and garlic aïoli. Other favorites include that old Raymond classic—tender chicken simmered in a curried chicken sauce and served with peanuts, raisins and coconut.

This "something for everyone" philosophy extends to the clientele—you're as likely to find millennials gossiping over cocktails at the 1886 Bar as you are boomers on date night, right by the crackling fireplace. Regulars know not to sleep on the easy-breezy lunch service.

■ 1250 S. Fair Oaks Ave. (at Railroad St.)
✆ (626) 441-3136 — **WEB:** www.theraymond.com
■ Lunch & dinner Tue – Sun

PRICE: $$

ROYCE ¶◯

Steakhouse • Luxury

Set inside The Langham Hotel, this dining room is a stunner thanks in large part to the work of bright spotlights, glass walls, plush chairs and banquettes, some of which overlook the lush grounds. Patrons may rest assured though that this isn't your typical stuffy operation, as the servers are warm and affable and the soundtrack is complete with cool rock and roll beats.

The kitchen knows its way around steakhouse classics, serving an array of favorites. Their beef may arrive fresh from Pennsylvania, Australia and even Japan—try the "global cut tasting" if you're curious. Sides like grilled broccolini doused with a cheddar-mornay sauce are a delicious play on flavors, while non-steak offerings from the land and sea are also noteworthy.

■ 1401 S. Oak Knoll Ave. (at The Langham Hotel)
✆ (626) 585-6410 — **WEB:** www.roycela.com
■ Dinner Tue – Sat

PRICE: $$$$

SALADANG 🍴◯

Thai • Neighborhood

&

Two Thai sister restaurants face each other in this pocket of southern Pasadena: Saladang, the original business opened in 1993; and Saladang Garden, a more recent offering from the same owner. Inside the original, you'll find a simple, industrial décor fitted out with exposed technical pipes and a smiling, attentive cadre of servers at the ready.

Even if some of the spices are toned down for an American audience, the food is mostly authentic and quite delicious. Prices are affordable, both for the set lunch (offered even on Sundays) and on the à la carte menu. Thai staples like tom yum soup, glass noodle salad and curries find new life here, as do house specialties like gai yang (barbecue chicken), crab pot and sizzling beef on spinach.

■ 363 S. Fair Oaks Ave. (bet. Bellevue & Waverly Drs.)
℘ (626) 793-8123 — **WEB:** www.saladang-pasadena.com
■ Lunch & dinner daily   **PRICE: $$**

SUSHI ICHI 🍴◯

Japanese • Simple

&

Its location in Arroyo Plaza, amid a nail salon, doughnut shop and pizza spot, should be the first hint that this sushiya is as modest as ever. But, don't let that be your judge as these itamae certainly know how to spin some serious culinary game. In fact, Chef Ichiro—who runs the show with his wife—began crafting sushi at the age of 18 in Tokyo, and his experience shines in every bite.

Quality fish is the one and only focus. Sea eel, shrimp and yellowtail are remarkably unctuous. Then halibut fin, salmon belly and barracuda are lightly torched to deliver a slight crunch before collapsing into a tender morsel. It all keeps coming until you cry mercy, so be sure to set a limit ahead of time or you'll be overwhelmed with a cavalcade of plates.

■ 633 S. Arroyo Pkwy. (bet. Pico & Fillmore Sts.)
℘ (626) 395-9977 — **WEB:** N/A
■ Lunch Thu – Fri Dinner Mon – Sat   **PRICE: $$$$**

UNION ¶○
Italian • Neighborhood

&

This original, chef-driven restaurant is truly something of note, set amidst quaint brick buildings near Old Pasadena. The design is simple: boxy with high ceilings, red brick and mason jars everywhere. Make reservations or go early, as Union's strong local following ensures that the tables are full soon after opening.

Carb-loading has never been more gratifying, as the kitchen kneads, extrudes and slices its way to pasta excellence. The squid ink lumache is carefully shaped like escargot. Then it's coated in butter with flecks of black truffle and set beneath a heaping pile of meaty Maine lobster for a bright and exciting dish. House-made spaghetti alla chitarra is a tease to the taste buds, slicked with a sweet and fiery tomato sauce.

■ 37 E. Union St. (bet. Fair Oaks & Raymond Aves.)
✆ (626) 795-5841 — **WEB:** www.unionpasadena.com
■ Dinner nightly   **PRICE: $$$**

© kitleong/Fotosearch LBRF/age fotostock

SAN GABRIEL VALLEY

BABITA MEXICUISINE 🍴○

Mexican • Cozy

&

While San Gabriel Valley is certainly known as a mecca of first-rate Asian food, this address offers another delicious reason to venture east of Los Angeles. This landmark Mexican restaurant has packed them in since 1999, cranking out authentic, flavor-forward, elegant food to crowds that just can't get enough. Inside the cozy dining space, you'll find a hospitable chef and warm, welcoming service staff.

You can't go wrong on the menu, but heat-seekers should try the chef's signature sautéed shrimp, a spicy, tail-on shrimp dish served with a chayote gratin and warm, fresh tortillas best dipped in creamy black beans. The tender Oaxacan mole chile relleno, featuring a knockout sweet-and-savory sauce complete with hints of chocolate, is a standout for good reason.

◾ 1823 S. San Gabriel Blvd. (at Norwood Pl.), San Gabriel
✆ (626) 288-7265 — **WEB:** www.babita-mexicuisine.com
◾ Dinner Tue – Sat   **PRICE: $$$**

BENTEN RAMEN 🍴○

Japanese • Minimalist

San Gabriel Valley lucked out as the first U.S. location for one of Tokyo's most popular ramen joints dating back to 1995. There's often a wait, but know that tables turn fast at this sleek restaurant, designed like a minimalist shoebox with concrete floors, high ceilings and largely blank walls.

The menu is just as abbreviated, offering only a few starters like takoyaki and yuzu potato salad alongside a handful of ramen options. As quickly as the kitchen works, diners know to get started right away while the broth is still hot and billowing clouds of steam. Dipping ramen (tsukemen) is the restaurant's claim to fame, but other bowls like hearty tonkatsu chock full of green onions, or spicy miso ramped up with habanero powder and chili oil, also delight.

◾ 821 W. Las Tunas Dr. (bet. Bridge St. & Mission Dr.), San Gabriel
✆ (626) 910-5075 — **WEB:** www.bentenramen.com
◾ Lunch & dinner Wed – Mon   **PRICE:** ෨

BISTRO NA'S ✿

Chinese · Luxury

  ♿ ⊡

Find the standout Bistro Na's in an ordinary shopping block, set just off Rosemead Blvd. Yes, its façade may appear rather sterile, but one foot inside this expansive room and you will be enveloped in warmth and cordiality. The gentle strains of soothing tunes, bright red and gold accents, as well as ample, well-accoutered tables segue smoothly into a classic and regal Chinese repast.

Proficient and accommodating, the staff is happy to steer diners through the menu—a veritable tome—and wine list. Dishes are then turned out in a judicious manner, unveiling such stellar presentations as sweet and tender shell-on shrimp seasoned with dried red chilies along with more inventive combinations like braised sea cucumber with beef tendon and scallions. Neatly trimmed and gently seared New Zealand lamb chops arrive with lightly fried onions for a divine coupling, and may warrant an order of the perfectly fluffy shrimp fried rice with egg and bonito.

Donning a joyous demeanor and buzzing with an appealing mix of diners, this elegant statesman in Temple City certainly feels like a special-occasion destination.

◼ 9055 Las Tunas Dr., Ste. 105 (at Camellia Sq.), Temple City
☎ (626) 286-1999 — **WEB:** www.bistronas.com
◼ Lunch & dinner daily   **PRICE: $$**

BORNEO KALIMANTAN CUISINE 🍴

Indonesian • *Simple*

You wouldn't expect to find such a homey respite in the center of downtown Alhambra, amid an outdoor shopping mecca with a bustling movie theater. And yet, nestled within is this tiny and focused kitchen named after an island situated between Indonesia and Singapore.

Diners start with skewers of chicken satay blanketed in a dark peanut sauce, before taking comfort in a big bowl of oxtail curry soup or a tangle of Hakka and Indo-style noodles. But true to form, the best dish here is the smallest—namely, the roti prata, which is a wheat flour-based pancake griddled until puff pastry-like perfection and served with a subtly sweet and spicy curry. It's the kind of dish you'll want to begin and even seal a meal with.

▦ 19 S. Garfield Ave. (at Main St.), Alhambra
☎ (626) 282-4477 —
WEB: www.borneokalimantancuisine.com
▦ Lunch & dinner daily   PRICE: 🍴

BURRITOS LA PALMA 😀

Mexican • *Simple*

If the word "burrito" conjures up images of hearty, newborn baby-sized bundles of deliciousness, this kitchen is here to alter your perception. Specializing in the slim, egg roll-shaped burritos of Mexico's Zacatecas region, this down-home duo of spots is all about the holy trinity of tortilla, meat and salsa—no cheese, beans (except in the veggie option) and definitely no lettuce.

But while these delicacies may not be "supersized," they are indeed superb. La Palma's single-minded focus on fillings presents some memorable bites, from tender, well-spiced beef birria to soul-satisfying carne deshebrada, studded with chunks of potato and green chile. You may want to pass on the fried flautas though—the magic is all in the soft handmade tortillas.

▦ 5120 N. Peck Rd. (bet. Cherrylee Dr. & Hemlock Sts.), El Monte
☎ (626) 350-8286 — **WEB:** www.burritoslapalma.net
▦ Lunch & dinner daily   PRICE: 🍴

CHENGDU IMPRESSION 😊

Chinese • Contemporary décor

&

This stateside location of a popular Asian chain is in fact a sleek and lovely Sichuan destination that prides itself on classic techniques. While ingredients may be imported from near and far, some items are made in-house (including the cured pork belly). An upstairs area is dedicated to gaiwan-cha, a traditional tea brewing method with roots in the Ming Dynasty.

Even those familiar with this region's spicy cuisine will likely find intriguing dishes to sample on the extensive menu. Think of Chengdu-style lettuce tossed in a vinegary dressing to pungent spicy chicken, gently poached in a broth and finished with a heavy dose of chilies and scallions. Don't miss the perfect meatball soup, a gingery consommé bobbing with delicate bites of pork.

▪ 21 E. Huntington Dr. (bet. Santa Anita & 1st Aves.), Arcadia
☏ (626) 462-9999 — **WEB:** www.chengduimpression.com
▪ Lunch & dinner daily   PRICE: $$

CHENGDU TASTE 😊

Chinese • Minimalist

&

With an eye-catching red-and-black design as well as a tome-like menu packed with tempting photos, it's clear that this operation commands your attention. It certainly succeeds in nabbing buzz, as it is a favorite of critics and foodies alike.

Dishing out fiery cuisine true to its Sichuan province namesake, it's difficult to find anything on the menu without the red chili symbol. This food is not intended for milquetoasts, so if you have a spice-loving pack of friends, round them up, as the sharing-minded food caters to groups. Sup on mapo tofu, cold noodles with garlic sauce or shrimp with a crispy rice crust before readying yourself for the tongue-numbing fish cooked with serrano chiles, cracked Sichuan peppercorns and a piquant chili oil.

▪ 828 W. Valley Blvd. (bet. 8th & 9th Sts.), Alhambra
☏ (626) 588-2284 — **WEB:** N/A
▪ Lunch & dinner daily   PRICE: $$

CHONGQING SPECIAL NOODLES ¶◯

Chinese · Simple

Made in-house, noodles at this special spot arrive in all sorts of preparations, each more delicious than the next. Think dan dan, a springy mix of strands slicked with chili oil, ground pork, peanuts and bok choy; or fragrant, boldly seasoned soups like spicy beef noodle.

Chili oil fans will want to order the Sichuan-style dumplings, packed with tiny bits of pork and sporting fiery little pools of red oil. Another highlight is the Sichuan classic, Chongqing chicken, featuring juicy little morsels of fried chicken tucked into a mound of dried red chilies. Fresh ripe cantaloupe arrive sat the end of each meal and is the perfect way to cool down your taste buds.

▦ 708 E. Las Tunas Dr. (bet. San Gabriel Blvd. & Pine St.),
San Gabriel
℘ (626) 347-1849 — **WEB:** N/A
▦ Lunch & dinner daily   **PRICE:** ⬤

CHUAN'S 😊

Chinese · Rustic

&. ⬚

With locations across China and one in Australia, Chuan's is the first U.S. outpost of the successful Ba Guo Bu Yi restaurant empire. The stylish interior is modern-meets-rustic and designed to resemble an updated imperial court, with sturdy tables, slinky tubes of lighting and a stage for musical performances.

Design interest aside, you're here for the fiery Sichuan cooking, which seems to pack more serious heat than its contemporaries. Mapo tofu—a soft pile of fresh cubes laced with dark chili oil—is deliciously savory thanks to an umami punch from fermented black beans. Don't miss the flavorful soups though, including braised duck with wood ear mushrooms and scallions; or even chicken and ginger infusing an intensely warming broth.

▦ 5807 Rosemead Blvd. (bet. Las Tunas & Hermosa Drs.),
Temple City
℘ (626) 677-6667 — **WEB:** www.joveusa.com
▦ Lunch & dinner daily   **PRICE:** $$

DAI HO 😊

Chinese • Simple

First things first: doors open at 11:30 A.M. here and close three and a half hours later. It's so small a window you know they'll pack the house. And indeed they do, with lines forming long before doors open at this popular Taiwanese restaurant.

Once inside, things move fast. A concise menu hangs above the cash register and you'll be pressed to order quickly. Three surefire hits include the fiery beef noodle soup (one of the best renditions in town); the sesame dry noodles; and the beef tripe and pork shank. The food comes quickly, before you even think to ask for water (tables are pre-set with steaming hot tea and Styrofoam cups). All said and done, you'll be out in 20 minutes—but talking about your meal for weeks to come.

▦ 9148 Las Tunas Dr. (at Loma Ave.), Temple City
☎ (626) 291-2295 — **WEB:** N/A
▦ Lunch Tue – Sun   **PRICE:** ⊜

DIN TAI FUNG ⑪○

Chinese • Family

♿ 🍴

There are multiple outposts of this dumpling and noodle nirvana scattered throughout LA, but this Arcadia location is the original. The place is always jammed and there is a line out the door on weekends. Din Tai Fung is a temple of dumplings. Should you need further proof, simply walk past the kitchen to spot the chefs, kitted out in surgical masks and white lab coats, sculpting these little beauties by hand.

You'll check off the items you desire on an order form, but be sure to include the pork soup dumplings, those impossibly thin-skinned wonders bobbing in flavorful broth are scented with scallion and ginger. Later, swap savory for sweet and taste the warm chocolate-filled mochi dumplings for a creative take on dessert.

▦ 1108 S. Baldwin Ave. (bet. Arcadia Ave. & Duarte Rd.), Arcadia
☎ (626) 574-7068 — **WEB:** www.dintaifungusa.com
▦ Lunch & dinner daily   **PRICE:** ⊜

DONGLAISHUN 😊
Chinese • Elegant

Pity the poor soul who arrives at DongLaiShun alone. This hot pot chain out of Beijing has a festive, high-energy appeal and from its mood to sheer quantity, it's best enjoyed with a group.

Select from the various soup bases, pick your proteins and vegetables and then sit around the steaming cauldrons as servers guide you on this steaming-hot ride. Lamb is the signature protein—there's even a chef slicing away at a station in the back—but handmade beef meatballs are popular too. The sauces, including the sweet and creamy sesame or the hot chili oil, up the ante. Large plates of meaty shiitake mushrooms, napa cabbage and noodles arrive last but leave a lasting impression.

Fret not about waste; the servers will gladly package it for later.

🍽 402 S. San Gabriel Blvd. (bet. Commercial Ave. & Broadway), San Gabriel
☎ (626) 766-1757 — **WEB:** N/A
🍽 Lunch & dinner daily   **PRICE: $$**

GOLDEN DELI 🍴
Vietnamese • Simple

One look at this extensive menu and you might find yourself overwhelmed with the dizzying number of options—from steaming bowls of pho and hearty portions of rice noodles to gut-busting meat and rice platters. But take a look around and you'll see why everyone is here—they've come for the cha giò. Indeed these Vietnamese egg rolls are like no other, stuffed with vegetables and deep fried until perfectly crispy and rightly charred. This dish has been a citywide star, ever since the restaurant opened its doors in 1981. This neighborhood gem has truly endured the test of time, and customers continue to storm the place as if it's brand new, with lines out the door from morning to night.

A second location in Temple City features a sleeker setting but smaller menu.

🍽 815 W. Las Tunas Dr. (bet. Bridge St. & Mission Dr.), San Gabriel
☎ (626) 308-0803 — **WEB:** www.goldendelirestaurant.com
🍽 Lunch & dinner Thu – Tue   **PRICE:** ⬮

GRAND HARBOR 😳

Chinese • Elegant

This dim sum stunner fills up fast despite its multiple private rooms and sea of tables, enough to fill a small village. Missing among the aisles are the usual roving caravan of carts since dishes here are made to order. Chandeliers, countless mirrors, chrome surfaces and pristine fish tanks set the stage for some of the area's finest seafood. Find servers dressed in black jackets and ties delivering in succession platters of har gow filled with shrimp, tender abalone dumplings wrapped in nori and slippery beef rice noodle rolls finished with soy. Come dinner time the focus swings to bigger items.

Specialties like sea cucumber, geoduck and lobster can add up quickly, so be sure to always inquire about the day's market price.

▓ 5733 Rosemead Blvd.
(bet. Muscatel Ave. & Rosemead Blvd.), Temple City
𝒞 (626) 280-2998 — **WEB:** N/A
▓ Lunch & dinner daily   **PRICE: $$**

HAIDILAO HOTPOT 🍴

Chinese • Family

Straight out of Sichuan comes this bustling hot pot chain, whose name means "fortune." Much like the Westfield Santa Anita Complex it calls home, the gorgeous restaurant is massive in scale, with tables in every direction and a dipping sauce buffet stretching down the center of the room.

Diners each have their own pot, so you can season your soup base to your liking (if your pot gets too fiery, for example, just remove those chilies and peppercorns). Raw ingredients, from premium beef and sweet shrimp to scallops and clams, are pristine in quality; the servers are friendly and equipped with iPads and earpieces. Ask them for help on your sauces, and they will likely put together something that's leagues better than what you had in mind.

▓ 400 S. Baldwin Ave. (at Huntington Dr.), Arcadia
𝒞 (626) 445-7232 — **WEB:** N/A
▓ Lunch & dinner daily   **PRICE: $$**

HUNAN MAO 🍴

Chinese • Simple

&

Often enough, guests enter this modest dining room to see a group of servers huddled around a table, prepping veggies and picking through a box of fire-red chilies. This is a prescient tableau for the blazingly hot cuisine that is to follow. The kitchen's Hunan specialties feature those very chilies across a range of dishes, with a delicious focus on fish. Don't miss the steamed fish head casserole—an enormous specimen of fresh "river fish" cooked until flaky and served with fiery peppers in a bright, herb-flecked broth. Mao braised pork is enticing in its clay pot of unctuous sauce that should be poured over every last grain of rice.

The menu is mostly pictures and waiters are friendly, so don't hesitate to ask for guidance.

▧ 8728 Valley Blvd. (bet. Garrett & Muscatel Aves.), Rosemead
℘ (626) 280-0588 — **WEB:** N/A
▧ Lunch & dinner daily　　　　　　　　**PRICE: $$**

LAOXI NOODLE HOUSE 😊

Chinese • Simple

The beauty of dining at this noodle house is that you don't have to guess what they're good at—the menu is brief, and everything you really need to know is in the name. But, their eight tables fill quickly so plan ahead.

This kitchen focuses entirely on slinging noodles inspired by the cuisine of China's famed Shanxi Province, so start with a chilled bowl of these gelatinous strands slathered with sesame-peanut sauce and the tingling heat of house-made chili oil. Then move on to the slender "wife special" noodles, with their springy, toothsome texture mixing with bits of crisped pork belly and fermented soy sauce. While dumplings are absolutely worth the order, also keep room for savoring some of the chef's special fried noodles.

▧ 600 Live Oak Ave. (at Hempstead Ave.), Arcadia
℘ (626) 348-2290 — **WEB:** N/A
▧ Lunch & dinner daily　　　　　　　　**PRICE:** ⊛

LONGO SEAFOOD

Chinese • Family

The parking lot is likely full and you may need to wait for a seat, but this tidy and efficient Cantonese parlor is large and more than capable of handling its crowds. The interior is filled with wood floors, upholstered chairs and large round tables. The full house may be lively, but service is always admirably delivered.

These steamed parcels of dim sum are offered on paper menus (there are no carts wheeling around) so check off what you'd like brought to your table. Everything is piping hot, freshly prepared and very enjoyable. Highlights include light and fluffy steamed buns filled with chicken and dried scallops, or ground white fish skewed with sugar cane stalks, deep fried to crunchy perfection. Rice noodle rolls with barbecued pork are a perennial favorite.

▧ 7540 Garver Ave. (bet. Jackson & New Aves.), Rosemead
☏ (626) 280-8188 — **WEB:** N/A
▧ Lunch & dinner daily   PRICE: $$

LUNASIA

Chinese • Elegant

Few kitchens can prepare a noodle roll quite like this local Alhambra favorite. Rice wrappers filled with gently cooked lobster meat and finished with a subtly sweet soy sauce arrive on a platter set with the lobster shell itself for a presentation that draws attention from all corners. Indeed, this kitchen puts a fine edge on the area's dim sum scene. There is not a single cart roaming this elegant dining room, which in turn is managed by a team of fast and friendly servers who will ensure that you never leave less than stuffed. Traditionalists will want to end with a rich egg tart, but for a more soothing finale, order the minced pork congee infused with soy, green onions and wonton chips.

The restaurant also runs a second location in Pasadena.

▧ 500 W. Main St. (at 5th St.), Alhambra
☏ (626) 308-3222 — **WEB:** N/A
▧ Lunch & dinner daily   PRICE: $$

MARISCOS JALISCO 😋

Mexican • Taqueria

When Raul Ortega started his taco truck in Boyle Heights back in 2001, he probably had no idea just how hard the city would fall for him. Today his Jalisco-inspired tacos have become a rite of passage, and he now runs a number of trucks around town, not to mention this modest but cherished spot in Pomona.

The menu is the same everywhere, limited to tostadas piled with various lime-kissed ceviches. Inside tip: opt for his signature fried shrimp taco tinged with spicy salsa and creamy avocado slices. It's an unequaled version, complete with a crunchy shell that collapses like tempura, as well as a rich and savory filling. First-time customers start with a single order, while regulars get right to business with a whole plate of them.

▦ 753 E. Holt Ave. (at Claremont Ave.), Pomona
☎ (909) 634-6808 — **WEB:** N/A
▦ Lunch & dinner Thu – Tue   PRICE: ⊜

MIAN 😋

Chinese • Friendly

Brace yourself, Angelenos. Tony Xu (of Chengdu Taste fame) has a veritable hit on his hands with this young'un (and its queues attest to that). The menu is dedicated to noodle soups and a smattering of appetizers, but trust us when we say there is beauty in that restraint.

Prepare to dig in to these sinus-clearing broths filled with endless tangles of noodles. The zing of peppercorn and the one-two punch of ma la enhance every dish. Sichuan cold noodles hit the mouth with a sweet heat, while the ziwei beef featuring a red broth flecked with those same peppercorns and chili flakes has a sweet-and-sour bitterness that is positively addictive. One bowl is plenty but order more to allow your palate to oscillate between various tastes.

▦ 301 W. Valley Blvd., Ste. 114 (bet. Abbot & Prospect Aves.), San Gabriel
☎ (626) 693-6888 — **WEB:** www.mian.us
▦ Lunch & dinner daily   PRICE: ⊜

NEWPORT SEAFOOD 🍴

Seafood • Family

&

This San Gabriel Valley spot is not of the salty old fisherman and oyster crackers ilk, but it's still a seafood fave, albeit one that imbues Chinese, Thai, Cambodian and Vietnamese flavors and cooking styles.

Begin with a hot and sour soup before moving on to seafood-studded chewy rice noodles. Salt and pepper crab drowned with sliced chilies, chopped scallions and golden fried garlic is a delicious deep-fried mess, but don't ignore the elephant—er, lobster—in the room, though. It's why everyone is here. This Newport special is wok-fried and tossed with spicy jalapeño, green onions and clarified butter. The plucky creature, served at a minimum four pounds and dripping with juices, is an undertaking worth ruining your best shirt.

▩ 518 W. Las Tunas Dr. (bet. Mission & St. Anita Sts.), San Gabriel
℘ (626) 289-5998 — **WEB:** www.newportseafood.com
▩ Lunch & dinner daily   **PRICE: $$**

SEA HARBOUR 😊

Chinese • Elegant

& ⊡ ✎

This highly regarded Cantonese restaurant could easily glide solely on its reputation, and yet, its devoted chefs bring the goods again and again. One of the first of its kind to offer dim sum à la carte, rather than by an actual cart, items arrive piping hot, fresh from the steamer. You really can't go wrong here, as each is more inventive than the next, flaunting ace flavor and wondrous texture. Bigger plates are all the rage at night—including sweet and sour pork, which finds elevation in this trusty kitchen's hands.

Anything with seafood is a sure bet, but don't miss the preserved salty egg bun with molten yolk. Families can be seen digging into steamed rice noodle rolls studded with bitter melon, or fried durian pastries oozing with the warm fruit.

▩ 3939 Rosemead Blvd. (at Nevada Ave.), Rosemead
℘ (626) 288-3939 — **WEB:** N/A
▩ Lunch & dinner daily   **PRICE: $$**

SHANGHAI NO. 1 😊

Chinese • Colorful

The menu here goes to epic lengths to present a thorough survey of Chinese regional cooking through photos and essays. Be sure to spend particular time on its many pages, especially those that begin with "Ten Great Privately Reserved Dishes." One visit here will surely lead to dozens more, with the goal of tasting as much as possible from the vast tome.

Their golden-brown Old Shanghai dumplings tucked with a tender pork filling don't appear until the back of the menu but deserve top billing. Also try clay pots brimming with the vibrant and complex flavors of house-made Chinese charcuterie, salted fish and perfect rice.

Crystal chandeliers, white carved seats and silk pillows lend a certain elegance to the dining room.

■ 250 Valley Blvd. (at Abbot Ave.),
San Gabriel
☏ (626) 282-1777 — **WEB:** www.shanghaino1seafood.com
■ Lunch & dinner daily   PRICE: $$

SICHUAN IMPRESSION 😊

Chinese • Rustic

ᕫ ᚛

Paradise for diners seeking a culinary adventure, this dining room flaunts a pleasing aura. Service is prompt and tables turn quickly, so those in a rush should come at lunch. It's no wonder that crowds are the norm at peak hour, as meals have been known to render palates smitten, thanks to the likes of fiery oils, funky offal and numbing chilies. Yet there is restraint, with ingredients enhanced by a none-too-over smoky heat.

From the menu's creative lingo to a host of familiar items, few will have tasted such bold and perfectly calibrated flavors. The "big mouth" ginger frog in a chili-soaked broth, for instance, is an extraordinary start; while mapo tofu, cold noodles and other myriad preparations go well beyond the usual renditions.

■ 1900 W. Valley Blvd. (at Ethel Ave.), Alhambra
☏ (626) 283-4622 — **WEB:** www.sichuanimpression.com
■ Lunch & dinner daily   PRICE: $$

XIANG YUAN GOURMET 🍴○

Chinese • Elegant

With its soaring ceilings, amply sized tables armed with lazy Susans and gold chairs, this is the quintessential banquet hall that's been serving freshly made dim sum for some time now. If that's not impressive enough, the menu, which can be overwhelming, includes items categorized into sections like congee, deep fried and buns. Servers may not be adept at explaining dishes in detail, but rest assured that portions are generous, making meals here a particular value.

Indulge in beautifully made classics like crystal shrimp har gow, tender spareribs in black bean sauce and sautéed chicken feet with a mouth-numbingly spicy blend of chili and ginger. Round out your feast with a sweet treat, like fried custardy bamboo paste.

◼ 9556 Las Tunas Dr. (bet. Primrose Ave. & Temple City Blvd.), Temple City

✆ (626) 286-6788 — **WEB:** N/A

◼ Lunch & dinner daily

PRICE: ⊛

SANTA
MONICA BAY

CASSIA
Asian • Contemporary décor

& ⛲ 🍽

Whether you're on date night or doodling with the kids, Cassia fits the bill. This neighborhood stunner nails that effortless easygoing restaurant vibe, albeit with a ramped-up style that marries winsome brasserie with chic urban loft.

Southeast Asian flavors mingle on the menu, which delivers enough variety to keep you coming back. From clay oven-baked breads and house-made charcuterie to an extensive raw bar, the kitchen impresses with bold offerings. Popular Vietnamese-inspired plates feature pork with vermicelli noodles alongside colonial mash-ups like chopped escargot with lemongrass butter. Those "sunbathing" prawns, charred and slathered with a pungent garlic and chili sauce, are a delight when spiked with the house hot sauce.

▓ 1314 7th St. (bet. Arizona Ave. & Santa Monica Blvd.), Santa Monica
✆ (310) 393-6699 — **WEB:** www.cassiala.com
▓ Dinner nightly   **PRICE: $$**

CHARCOAL VENICE 🍴
American • Contemporary décor

🍸 & 🛋

Chef/owner Josiah Citrin works his magic at this casually upscale grill, where nearly everything is cooked over the fire. Wafts of aromatic charred meat greet guests before they've even made it through the door. The menu may be inspired by a backyard barbecue, but the décor is a contemporary mix of concrete walls, beige booths and modern artwork.

Steaks come with ramekins of sauce like creamy and smoky choron, in addition to the trio of signature condiments on the table. However, this meat is too flavorful to really need anything. Diners may be here for the steaks, but those in the know also order the cabbage baked in embers, served with lemon-sumac yogurt.

The bar area is bustling and loud, thanks to the list of happy hour specials.

▓ 425 Washington Blvd. (at Clune Ave.), Venice
✆ (310) 751-6794 — **WEB:** www.charcoalvenice.com
▓ Lunch Sat – Sun Dinner nightly   **PRICE: $$$**

DIALOGUE 🏵

Contemporary • Trendy

Secreted away in The Gallery Food Hall (a remodeled food court), finding this tricky location can feel like an adventure, albeit a glorious one. Just exit the elevator on the second floor and head for the first door on the left. The small interior is bright and noisy, warmed up by the open kitchen as well as Chef Dave Beran's commentary and insights into his cooking. There may be banquettes, but a seat at the counter provides a necessary view into the action and preparation of intricate plates. The suited servers are well coordinated and flaunt a friendly demeanor.

The cooking exudes inspiration from start to finish. The kitchen is particularly adept in its delicately steamed nuggets of lobster with a dollop of béarnaise covered in nasturtium. An effort to show seasonal flavors can seem daring in a city not known for its autumn foliage. Yet this is handled with wit and talent, through a dish of "fallen leaves" served on a square "plate" of dried birch bark and arranged with fried sweetbreads.

Overall, this cuisine's vision and meticulous plating feels veritably unconfined, as it glides seamlessly from modernism to Japanese fare, with a wintry finale of coconut and chocolate pudding.

■ 1315 3rd St. Promenade, Ste. K
(bet. Arizona Ave. & Santa Monica Blvd.), Santa Monica
✆ N/A — **WEB:** www.dialoguerestaurant.com
■ Dinner Tue – Sat   PRICE: $$$$

CHINOIS ON MAIN ¶⚪

Asian • Exotic décor

&

A destination since 1983, this local darling has been welcoming guests as old friends to dine on their cuisine, which is a tad Asian, a touch Californian and a bit French. Little seems to have changed through the decades—it is busy, loud and served by an attentive staff. The location, amid boho-chic shops, remains a boon.

This kitchen shines by way of a number of signature items, like made-to-order garlic chicken spring rolls or Cantonese duck with plum sauce. The sizzling calamari salad is deliciously seasoned with hot chili paste and presented in a wonton cup over crisp vegetables. Many dishes are served family style, so don't hesitate to order half-portions when available. At the end, splurge on pleasing desserts like a warm chocolate fondant cake.

▨ 2709 Main St. (at Hill St.), Santa Monica
℘ (310) 392-9025 — **WEB:** www.wolfgangpuck.com
▨ Lunch Wed – Fri Dinner nightly   **PRICE: $$$**

FELIX ¶⚪

Italian • Cozy

This Venice Beach trattoria is run by Chef Evan Funke who studied pasta-making at the celebrated La Vecchia Scuola Bolognese. There may be other delicious and well-prepared menu items, but diners come here for the pastas, listed regionally and made in-house behind a glass-walled laboratorio. The proof of their skill lies in the rigatoni all'Amatriciana, a "del Centro" specialty of large, finely ridged tubes in a tomato sauce enriched by delicious guanciale and finished with Pecorino Romano. Wonderful pizzas hail from the wood-burning oven and their dessert crostata is made with equal care and talent.

The space is chic and homey with multiple dining sections that add to the overall sense of intimacy. Crowds can arrive early, making this something of a hot spot.

▨ 1023 Abbot Kinney Blvd. (at Broadway St.), Venice
℘ (424) 387-8622 — **WEB:** www.felixla.com
▨ Dinner nightly   **PRICE: $$**

GJELINA 🍴

Mediterranean • Fashionable

In its ten-year run, this buzzy restaurant has spawned a to-go counter, highly popular bakery and cookbook. The ambience is ceaselessly upbeat, resulting in a scene that is a major draw among pretty young things.

Brick floors and creeping vines fashion a picturesque, garden-like setting that is an idyllic match for their simply prepared Mediterranean menu of pizzas, vegetables and shared plates. Highlights include roasted artichoke hearts, imparted with a lovely smokiness, cooked until the edges are gently charred and centers deliciously creamy. House-made pastas—like nettle rigate tossed in a white wine sauce with morels, chicken hearts and ramps—tailed by a delicious date cake topped with a scoop of ginger gelato are exceptionally tasty.

■ 1429 Abbot Kinney Blvd. (at Milwood Ave.), Venice
℘ (310) 450-1429 — **WEB:** www.gjelina.com
■ Lunch & dinner daily   PRICE: $$

THE LOBSTER 🍴

Seafood • Brasserie

True to its name, this lovely perch overlooking the Santa Monica pier has earned its reputation for great American seafood, thanks to its focus on Maine lobsters and much more. Don't let its beachy location lure you into thinking that this is a tourist trap. Tightly spaced tables don't leave much room for privacy and the service seems focused on efficiency, but those expansive views and steaming seafood more than compensate.

Lobsters arrive at the height of temptation—find them beautifully steamed until the meat is so incredibly tender, rendering that side of melted butter all but superfluous. Hearty seared crab cakes have a crisp exterior and are generously filled with meat, served alongside peppery arugula, fennel salad and remoulade.

■ 1602 Ocean Ave. (at Colorado Ave.), Santa Monica
℘ (310) 458-9294 — **WEB:** www.thelobster.com
■ Lunch & dinner daily   PRICE: $$$

LUNETTA

Contemporary · Chic

Beneath a striped awning, this corner location is warm and elegant, with sleek leather banquettes, wood cabinetry and rustic woven chairs adorning the dark blue interior.

Chef Raphael Lunetta helms the kitchen, delivering dishes that have their roots from his time at JiRaffe. Imagine the likes of thick slices of an enticingly browned pork chop with wild rice and bacon. The dinner menu is an au courant list of impressive cooking, including crispy duck with quince or wood-grilled barbecue salmon. For dessert, try the rich, dense and burnt-sugar butterscotch pot de crème served in a coffee cup with a dollop of whipped cream.

In addition to Lunetta's contemporary food, their all-day café next door is a pleasant spot for coffee and pastries.

■ 2424 Pico Blvd. (at 25th St.), Santa Monica
℘ (310) 581-9888 — **WEB:** www.lunettasm.com
■ Dinner Tue – Sat   **PRICE: $$$**

MICHAEL'S

American · Elegant

After launching the careers of numerous renowned chefs—including Jonathan Waxman, Nancy Silverton and Sang Yoon—Michael's has earned the right to be considered an icon. Following its course of history, the recent arrival of an ambitious new chef means that fresh life has been brought into the kitchen. The dining room is a nostalgic and transporting oasis of potted plants, with woven chairs and simple tables to frame out the jungle's worth of greenery.

The cooking succeeds in creatively blending unique ingredients, as seen in the petite quail marinated with turmeric and coconut milk, then grilled for smoky-sweet flavor. A side of branzino is cooked to tender exactness beneath a shatteringly crisp skin and accompanied by black butter sabayon.

■ 1147 3rd St. (bet. California Ave. & Wilshire Blvd.), Santa Monica
℘ (310) 451-0843 — **WEB:** www.michaelssantamonica.com
■ Lunch & dinner Mon – Sat   **PRICE: $$$**

MTN
Fusion • Trendy

Chef Travis Lett of Gjelina and Gjusta turns away from the Mediterranean to focus on izakaya food with a local California spin at MTN. Outside, its timber-clad façade boldly stands out and could not look hipper in its Abbot Kinney location. The interior is loud but fun, with sound bouncing off the rough-hewn wooden walls, tall tables and dark counters. Behind the bar, a brightly lit kitchen offers a peek of the action, visible through its glass wall.

The menu focuses on hearty grilled items, like charred sweet potatoes with miso butter. Ramen is another highlight, served as a choice of five different noodle soups including jidori chicken or yuzu. Other creative snacks include a hand roll stuffed with barbecue pork and fermented chili sauce.

■ 1305 Abbot Kinney Blvd. (at Santa Clara Ave.), Venice
℘ (424) 465-3313 — **WEB:** www.mtnvenice.com
■ Lunch Mon – Fri Dinner nightly   **PRICE: $$**

PLANT FOOD + WINE
Vegan • Minimalist

Plant-based chef and lifestyle guru Matthew Kenney successfully brings the vision of pure food and fine wine to the West Coast by way of Plantlab—a lifestyle brand replete with cookbooks, wellness retreats and a plant-based cooking school. Unsurprisingly, his Venice restaurant offers a taste of all that deliciously wholesome and gorgeous vegan goodness with vibrant, complex and beautifully plated dishes.

This serene and contemplative space is the perfect backdrop for his bright and flavorful cuisine—and with such prime access to the Santa Monica farmer's market, the quality of ingredients is all but guaranteed. Heirloom tomato- and zucchini-lasagna finds next-level palatability thanks to a wonderful macadamia nut "ricotta" and sundried tomato sauce.

■ 1009 Abbot Kinney Blvd.
(bet. Broadway St. & Brooks Ave.), Venice
℘ (310) 450-1009 — **WEB:** www.matthewkenneycuisine.com
■ Lunch & dinner daily   **PRICE: $$**

PUNTA CABRAS

Mexican • Contemporary décor

The exterior may be white, but inside, this dining room is a riot of hot pink, vibrant yellow and blue tables that add to the fun and festive atmosphere. Piñata heads are hung on the wall like hunting trophies.

A three-course prix-fixe lunch and happy hour specials both offer bargains, but the Cal-Mex cooking is so good that most people will happily pay full price any time of day. Those excellent house-made tortillas are slightly thick and perfect for their range of fillings. Try a plate of tacos stuffed with fried cod and cabbage slaw or tender short ribs with pickled onions and cheese crumbles, as well as sides like a warm corn salad and salsa. Creative starters feature a shaved cauliflower ceviche with cashew crema and sweet-spicy pineapple salsa.

■ 930 Broadway (at 9th Ct.), Santa Monica
✆ (310) 917-2244 — **WEB:** www.puntacabras.com
■ Lunch & dinner daily   **PRICE: $$**

Share the journey with us!
🐦 @MichelinGuideCA
📷 @MichelinInspectors

435

RUSTIC CANYON ⁕

Californian • Chic

⚭ ♿ 🥾

Chef Jeremy Fox's seasonal kitchen and wine bar already has the feeling of a timeless institution. The dining room and lounge are toasty and relaxed with an unpretentious neighborhood vibe, thanks to the boisterous local crowd. A large picture window overlooking the street brightens the dark wood tables and cushioned banquettes.

The market-inspired menu is proudly crammed with the names of local farmers, reminding guests of the humble ingredients at the base of each sophisticated composition. The kitchen's versatility and range of talent is clear from the first bite of green beans in shallot vinaigrette with a delectable heap of shaved cheese. Heavily embellished or more ambitious dishes are just as pleasing—especially the unexpected combination of earthy-sweet beets, grains and berries all held in perfect balance. The aromatic pozole verde is wonderfully tangy and refreshing, loaded with Hope Ranch mussels, hominy and fried tortilla strips. Much of this elevated farm-to-table menu is designed for sharing.

Breads and desserts are a formidable treat here, so be sure to try the bread au chocolat made with chunks of caramelized brioche, or ice cream in flavors like pea, mint and macadamia.

◾ 1119 Wilshire Blvd. (at 11th Ct.), Santa Monica
℘ (310) 393-7050 — **WEB:** www.rusticcanyonrestaurant.com
◾ Dinner nightly   **PRICE: $$$**

SOUTH BAY

AMOR Y TACOS

Mexican • Colorful

&

Yet another in the wave of Mexican-American LA chefs transforming the cuisine, Thomas Ortega brings his fine-dining drill to bear on this vibrant offering in his native Cerritos. Here he fuses his specific style of the city's Mexican cuisine, like handmade tortillas and spicy salsas, with an American twist. Look for that Coca-Cola glaze on his pork belly or the sprinkle of Doritos on chilaquiles, not to mention such luxurious accents as truffles.

It's hard to miss with any of Chef Ortega's tacos, which range from light and crisp beer-battered cod with smoky salsa de arbol to gloriously tender and charred al pastor. And that fried "calamari famoso," bright and peppery with onions and cilantro? It's the ideal partner for a spicy michelada.

■ 13333 South St. (at Carmenita Rd.), Cerritos
℘ (562) 860-2667 — **WEB:** www.amorytacos.com
■ Lunch & dinner daily   PRICE: $$

THE ARTHUR J 🍴

Steakhouse • Vintage

🍸 &

Dimly lit and swanky with mid-century modern furnishings, this Manhattan Beach steakhouse feels as though it is from another era. In fact, Mad Men could shoot a reunion here without changing a single Scotch glass. The pricey menu is at odds with its beachy surrounds, making this retreat ideal for corporate diners and dressed-up duos.

The carte is built around a variety of different cuts and grades of meats—such as angus, Wagyu, prime and the uber-natural "never ever" beef—all cooked here over a wood-fired grill. Steaks arrive with a choice of one sauce, but be prepared to pay for individual sides, toppings and Parker House rolls. Desserts are a particular treat so indulge in fun takes on classic American layer cakes, sundaes and cherries jubilee.

■ 903 Manhattan Ave. (at 9th Pl.), Manhattan Beach
℘ (310) 878-9620 — **WEB:** www.thearthurj.com
■ Dinner nightly   PRICE: $$$$

AYARA THAI CUISINE ☺

Thai · Simple

&

Unless you're heading to LAX, the location may seem out of the way, but know that eating here is always worth the trek. It's a family spot that is known for Thai recipes that have been passed down and updated with the freshest local ingredients. The space is simple yet no one seems to mind—expect crowds during peak times. The kitchen excels in cooking flavorful dishes that might begin with a spicy beef salad, loaded with juicy grilled tri-tip over cabbage slaw dressed with lime and fish sauce. Their rich curries are an absolute highlight of any meal, especially the khao soi with coconut, free-range chicken, noodles and eyewatering heat.

The excellent and affordable lunch set is offered until 4:00 P.M. and includes a starter, entrée and drink.

■ 6245 W. 87th St. (at Sepulveda Eastway)
℘ (310) 410-8848 — **WEB:** www.ayarathai.com
■ Lunch & dinner daily   PRICE: ⊜

BARAN'S 2239 ☺

Californian · Bistro

🍺 &

This lovely little bistro is tucked into an unassuming mall a few blocks from the beach, giving it that ideal neighborhood feel and easy seaside vibe. Natural wood and serene colors run the length of the space, which features a large communal farmhouse table in the middle of the room.

The friendly Baran brothers can usually be found on site, doing their best to make sure every patron feels welcome. The kitchen turns out a seasonal menu that's constantly evolving but may include a filet of beef with a sumptuous black garlic-Sichuan sauce, chili broccoli and pickled shiitakes. Desserts like mini buttery bundt cakes are paired with ginger-blueberry sorbet and apricot coulis for a refreshing treat. Sip as you go with a choice from over 40 craft beers.

■ 502 Pacific Coast Hwy (bet. 5th & 6th Sts.), Hermosa Beach
℘ (424) 247-8468 — **WEB:** www.barans2239.com
■ Dinner Tue – Sun   PRICE: $$

CONI'SEAFOOD

Mexican • Family

This local treasure has been earning accolades since it first opened in 1987. Today it continues to flourish as a family affair, as the founder's daughter is running the show.

The front dining room is welcoming, but the large and enclosed back patio is really the place to be—pleasantly green and breezy with ceiling fans, hanging plants and potted palms. It's the perfect setting for relishing the kitchen's Nayarit-style cooking that showcases shrimp and fish imported from Sinaloa. Those shrimp appear again and again, perhaps breaded and fried in tacos, or sautéed head-on in a bright red sauce of roasted chilies and beer. Enjoy their fish fried, cooked whole or even inside heaping bowls of ceviche with bracing, lemony flavors and a basket of chips.

◼ 3544 W. Imperial Hwy. (bet. Cherry & Yukon Aves.), Inglewood
☏ (310) 672-2339 — **WEB:** www.coniseafood.com
◼ Lunch & dinner daily

PRICE: $$

FISHING WITH DYNAMITE ⫴○

Seafood • Rustic

This tight and warm seafood spot is located just down the block from the ocean. Inside, it's decidedly beachy, flooded with sunlight and colors that make it feel cozy even when it's loud and busy.

Raw bar dishes comprise half the menu, which lists different types of oysters, clams and lobsters that can be ordered as set platters or individually. The rest of the carte offers a selection of "old school" classics like gumbo, crab cakes and New England clam chowder revealing huge, meaty unshelled bivalves with chunks of bacon and potatoes. Adventurous palates will take pleasure in the "new school" fare—perhaps grilled octopus with saffron and chorizo, yellowtail tacos or rockfish ceviche with pluots. Desserts are generously portioned and genuinely desirable.

◼ 1148 Manhattan Ave. (at 12th St.), Manhattan Beach
☏ (310) 893-6299 — **WEB:** www.eatfwd.com
◼ Lunch & dinner daily

PRICE: $$

LOVE & SALT

Italian · *Contemporary décor*

Everything is fresh and fun at this favored spot, thanks to a solid and passionate staff who serve Cal-Ital cuisine. A laid-back vibe and superb drinks that mix everything from herbs and fruits to veggies and shrubs ensure that everyone is having a good time. The heart of the dining room is a large communal table, set amid old timey barstools and Edison bulbs to glorify the city's cool and hip feel.

The entire menu is built around pizzas, roasted meats and vegetables emerging from a wood-fired oven. Some may dive into a mini lamb "Reuben" on toasted rye with pickled peppers, tomato aïoli and oozing fontina, while others save room to sample seasonal antipasti and homemade pasta—think pappardelle with a slow-cooked and deeply flavored lamb Bolognese.

■ 317 Manhattan Beach Blvd. (bet. Highland Ave. & Morningside Dr.), Manhattan Beach
☏ (310) 545-5252 — **WEB:** www.loveandsaltla.com
■ Lunch Sat – Sun Dinner nightly   **PRICE: $$**

MANHATTAN BEACH POST

International · *Family*

Big and buzzing with excitement over Chef/co-owner David LeFevre's creations, this is a fun and casual place that has something for everyone, just a stone's throw from Manhattan Beach Pier. The food is a proud foray into just about every global cuisine—from pork chili chimichangas and bibimbap to Scotch eggs—but always with clear Californian flair. Their bacon-cheddar buttermilk biscuits are so good that they don't even need the maple butter that accompanies them.

Everything revolves around gathering, conversing and sharing; portions are small so plan your ordering as a group to explore a majority of the menu. Weekends can veer towards loud and crowded with plenty of young families in tow, so this isn't a place for anyone with a yen for calm.

■ 1142 Manhattan Ave. (at Center Pl.), Manhattan Beach
☏ (310) 545-5405 — **WEB:** www.eatmbpost.com
■ Lunch Fri – Sun Dinner nightly   **PRICE: $$**

MAR'SEL ⅊○

American · Elegant

At the end of the Palos Verdes Peninsula, find a windy road that meanders through the plush grounds of the Terranea Resort. Beautiful herb gardens are planted along the sidewalk leading you to Mar'sel's main entrance. Inside, breathtaking ocean views and a roaring fireplace in the dining room take the chill off the evening breeze. A sense of opulence pervades everything here, including the superb service.

Meals commence with a warm homemade English muffin that may have its own cult following. Every dish looks beautiful and well made, especially those cubes of supremely tender Wagyu beef short ribs, with celery prepared four different ways. For dessert, caramel pot de crème is the house specialty, with ganache, cocoa nibs and flecks of sea salt.

100 Terranea Way (off Palos Verdes Dr.),
Rancho Palo Verdes
☎ (310) 265-2836 — **WEB:** www.terranea.com
Lunch Sun Dinner nightly   **PRICE: $$$$**

Remember, stars ✿
are awarded for cuisine only! Elements
such as service and décor are not a factor.

VENTURA BOULEVARD

ASANEBO

Japanese • *Regional décor*

With its spare design, fire-glazed stone pottery and even Hello Kitty dolls doubling as décor, everything about Asanebo's look is appealing. There is certainly no dearth of sushi restaurants in this city, but this well-regarded favorite has been at it for more than two decades. Three omakase options open the menu, which then expands to an impressive, if somewhat dizzying five pages filled with everything from maki, house signature dishes and an entire page dedicated to desserts. With so many decisions, it's best to stick to the daily specials, though do keep a close watch on the prices, which climb slowly but steadily.

While the items may pander a bit to the Western palate and aren't known for razzle-dazzle, they remains a standby for good reason.

■ 11941 Ventura Blvd. (bet. Carpenter & Radford Aves.), Studio City
☎ (818) 760-3348 — **WEB:** www.asanebo-restaurant.com
■ Lunch Tue – Fri Dinner Tue – Sun　　　**PRICE: $$$$**

THE BELLWETHER

Californian • *Fashionable*

Studio City has its fair share of gastropubs, but this beauté looms large not only for its cooking, but the enticing buzz from its lively crowd. Big, bright and rustic, with closely spaced tables and lots of counter seating, it's a packed spot that's equally cherished for a quick bite and craft cocktail as it is for a multi-course, multi-drink affair.

The menu reads global, with myriad enticing options for sampling. Begin with the likes of delicately battered tempura cauliflower glazed with Thai chili, basil and lime; or charred octopus with yogurt and preserved lemon. Vietnamese braised pork ribs cooked to fall-off-the-bone softness and accompanied by a fiery sambal sauce is a standout entrée, while a pear upside-down cake makes for a pleasing finale.

■ 13251 Ventura Blvd. (at Longridge Ave.), Studio City
☎ (818) 285-8184 — **WEB:** www.thebellwetherla.com
■ Lunch Sat – Sun Dinner nightly　　　**PRICE: $$$**

KATSU-YA 😳

Japanese • Simple

 ♿

This is the original spot that spawned a little chain of LA restaurants serving Japanese food with a spicy twist. It remains a treasure among the entertainment industry crowd looking to grab a quick bento box for lunch. The ambience is unpretentious, cooking is vibrant and the value for your money is excellent. However, be prepared for a wait at peak times.

Start with the bigeye tuna sashimi, topped with spinach judiciously dressed in ponzu sauce. The chef's special maki are a highlight, especially the very popular Robert Roll, combining spicy tuna, shrimp and sweet crab meat topped with slices of spicy mayo-seasoned avocado, all wrapped up in soy paper. The shrimp tempura is particularly delicious, lightly crisp, yet still firm and tasty.

◼ 11680 Ventura Blvd. (at Colfax Ave.), Studio City
☎ (818) 985-6976 — **WEB:** www.katsu-yagroup.com
◼ Lunch Mon – Sat Dinner nightly   **PRICE: $$**

KAZU SUSHI 🍴

Japanese • Simple

♿

Since 1989, this tiny spot on what is commonly known was "Sushi Row" has been serving top-quality fish with minimal fuss, in delicious accordance with tradition. The décor is stark, with a few abstract black-and-white paintings, small tables and posters of seafood displayed behind the counter.

Lunches are a great time to partake in a rapid sampling of their ten-course omakase, while dinners get more complex both in pricing and cuisine. The menu goes on to offer other dining options, like à la carte sushi, assorted combinations and chirashi bowls. Trust in their seasonal recommendations, especially the bigeye sea perch, nodoguro, of which the chef is a particular fan. Finally, be sure to sample from the carefully selected list of Japanese beers and sake.

◼ 11440 Ventura Blvd. (at Ridgemoor Dr.), Studio City
☎ (818) 763-4836 — **WEB:** www.kazusushi818.com
◼ Lunch Mon – Fri Dinner Mon – Sat   **PRICE: $$**

KIWAMI BY KATSU-YA ¶○

Japanese • Minimalist

With a Studio City location just a stone's throw from CBS and the Art Director's Guild, it is no wonder that mealtimes here are jammed with entertainment industry types making pitches or talking Pilates. Settle into one of their two sushi bars—the smaller one in the back features a reservation-preferred omakase, often prepared by the adept cadre of chefs.

Those looking for a simpler meal will find plenty of other creative and colorful offerings. One of the most popular at lunch is the kiwami (which translates as "ultimate") tray featuring many of their signatures, including spicy tuna on crisped rice cakes, salmon sashimi with avocado and onion as well as a baked crab roll. Fans of innovative maki will enjoy the lengthy selection offered here.

■ 11920 Ventura Blvd.
(bet. Carpenter Ave. & Laurel Canyon Blvd.), Studio City
✆ (818) 763-3910 — **WEB:** www.katsu-yagroup.com
■ Lunch Mon – Fri Dinner nightly   **PRICE: $$**

MISTRAL ¶○

French • Bistro

Named for the seasonal winds of Southern France, this local bijou has been transporting diners straight from Sherman Oaks to Lyon for the past 30 years. Inside, find crystal chandeliers, polished brass and red walls to complement the authentic cuisine. The main room features a convivial atmosphere, pleasant din of conversation and tables of four to six diners, making it a welcoming destination among groups.

Begin with gratis blue-cheese puffs, before moving on to the likes of sizzling platters of plump, tender and garlic-buttery escargot à la Bourgogne, nestled into their shells. For dessert, the bread pudding and chocolate soufflé are wonderful and fulfilling, but must be ordered at the beginning of your meal as they require time to bake.

■ 13422 Ventura Blvd. (bet. Dixie Canyon & Greenbush Aves.), Sherman Oaks
✆ (818) 981-6650 — **WEB:** www.mistralrestaurant.com
■ Lunch Tue – Fri Dinner Tue – Sun   **PRICE: $$$**

SADDLE PEAK LODGE ⑪○

American • Historic

Hollywood knows how to tell a really good story, but it might want to look in its own backyard for a little inspiration, since this lovely mountain respite undoubtedly has some anecdotes to spill. The place exudes old-world glam—focus on the word old—with a century of history behind it. This log cabin once drew Tinsel Town's finest, including Charlie Chaplin, Clark Gable and the Rat Pack, while today it lures a newly seasoned crowd.

If the hunting trophies on the walls didn't tip you off, this kitchen is best known for its wild game mains, including elk, emu and buffalo (don't worry, there's also chicken and fish for those feeling less adventurous). Tuck in to the perfectly cooked elk with bacon-and-onion jam or opt for the trio to expand your palate.

■ 419 Cold Canyon Rd. (at Piuma Rd.), Calabasas
℘ (818) 222-3888 — **WEB:** www.saddlepeaklodge.com
■ Lunch Sun Dinner nightly   **PRICE: $$$$**

SCRATCH BAR & KITCHEN ⑪○

Contemporary • Rustic

Located on the second floor of a shopping complex in The Valley, this young and contemporary looker is a perfect place to eat, drink and make merry. There is no formal service staff—wait for one of the chefs to greet you and suggest a seat at the dining counter. Behind it, a wood-burning stove and occasional flames from the kitchen become all the more enticing in the dim lighting.

The menu is comprised of a lengthy tasting that generally features dishes of one to three bites, and often cooked with fire. Other innovative offerings include crisply fried kale set over beet mustard, salmon roe and finished with grated parmesan. Strips of sliced cuttlefish are tender and almost noodle-like in a bowl filled with piquant cilantro leche de tigre.

■ 16101 Ventura Blvd. (at Woodley Ave.), Encino
℘ (818) 646-6085 — **WEB:** www.scratchbarla.com
■ Dinner Wed – Sun   **PRICE: $$$$**

SHIN SUSHI ✿

Japanese • Contemporary décor

Set in a nondescript shopping center, this highly pedigreed settler has managed to keep a low profile. But discerning locals know a great master when they see one, and Taketoshi Azumi is indeed the real deal. The chef has worked for two decades at top spots on both coasts and comes from a family of sushi connoisseurs. In fact, Shin is named for the Tokyo restaurant run by his late father, whose former sign now hangs behind the counter.

Despite its pedigree, the vibe is affable and laid-back. Tables fill with as many diners ordering lunch combos as the omakase, and the friendly chef engages each customer as he slices their fish to order. His approach to shari is singular and highly personal, with a dense texture and mild flavor from sake lees vinegar. It makes a delicate base for some of the more unusual nigiri around, like a tiny bundle of Japanese chives tied with crispy nori and topped with bonito. Then look forward to the very rare and lightly torched snow trout, which is a marvel thanks to its smoky outer layer giving way to melting richness.

Finally, all the luxurious standards are perfectly executed here, including Santa Barbara uni, Hokkaido scallops and first-rate fatty tuna.

🔲 16573 Ventura Blvd. (bet. Rubio & Hayvenhurst Aves.), Encino
✆ (818) 616-4148 — **WEB:** N/A
🔲 Dinner Tue – Sat   **PRICE: $$$**

SUSHI BAR ⍾○

Asian • Intimate

Advance planning is a must for this sushi speakeasy, which admits just 24 guests per night (in three seatings of eight). Tucked behind sister tavern, Woodley Proper, the hidden dining room feels like a portal to the past, with a candlelit wooden bar and nostalgic Japanese jazz on the stereo. Just two itamae and a bartender run the show, serving you and a few neighbors.

Though its vibe is old-school, the nigiri is anything but, featuring such creative ingredients as bone marrow, pineapple, sturgeon caviar and quinoa. Inspiration comes from everywhere, as in scallops bathed in a spicy and complex Peruvian leche de tigre, while LA-Japanese mashup charcoal mochi may cap the meal. Order up a couple of the top-notch cocktails to truly savor the ride.

◼ 16101 Ventura Blvd., Ste. 242 (at Encino Place), Encino
℘ (818) 906-9775 — **WEB:** www.woodleyproper.com
◼ Dinner Wed – Sun   **PRICE: $$$$**

SUSHI IKI ⍾○

Japanese • Simple

This is a place for purists, where guests are warned with a pleasant smile that California rolls and other such frivolity will not be served here. Dining in the presence of Chef Eddie Okamoto means that only good things will follow, including an in-depth discussion of Hokkaido's ice plankton or the fish you just ate that lived deep underwater and was so rich in omega-3 (read: fat) because it could hardly move.

Sushi may go on to include slices of Japanese yellowtail toro—briny, smooth and shining. The chef's special selection though features the likes of golden eye snapper resting on shiso over rice, dabbed with yuzu kosho; or live shrimp swiftly cut, topped with roe and served with the tempura-fried head. The omakase is pricey but always worth it.

◼ 18663 Ventura Blvd. (at Yolanda Ave.), Tarzana
℘ (818) 343-3470 — **WEB:** N/A
◼ Lunch Tue – Fri Dinner Tue – Sun   **PRICE: $$$**

SUSHI YOTSUYA

Japanese • Simple

&

For nearly 20 years, guests have known to "trust the chef," just as the entryway sign encourages them to do. Once inside, know that the counter is reserved strictly for omakase, which is a great way to dine here. Chef Masa Matsumoto is serious about selecting the 20 or more varieties of fish that he may showcase in his fixed menu, but is always a humble and upbeat host. And every diner here is treated like a regular.

Expect to sample myriad shellfish, mollusks and roe in the parade of dishes set before you. Begin with a range of tuna, from deep-red maguro to mild bonito. Also try interesting varieties of ono, pompano and barracuda. Each item is served on warm rice and dressed sparingly, because little embellishment is needed to make it a delightful bite.

▓ 18760 Ventura Blvd. (at Burbank Blvd.), Tarzana
☎ (818) 708-9675 — **WEB:** N/A
▓ Lunch Tue – Fri Dinner Tue – Sun   **PRICE: $$$**

Look for the symbol 🥐
for a brilliant breakfast to
start your day off right.

WESTSIDE

ALTA ADAMS 🍴

Southern • Contemporary décor

This is the kind of homey and comforting spot that anyone would be glad to have in their neighborhood, but would just as happily drive to find. Generous portions make it a favorite for family-style and group dining. The lovely back patio is draped with string lights and vines, fashioning a perfect backdrop for evenings alfresco. The cooking is soulful and comforting, starting with a plate of golden-fried black-eyed pea fritters with a garlicky green herb sauce for dipping. Their fried chicken is decadent, served juicy with a wickedly spicy hot sauce and caramelized sweet potatoes. Buttery coconut cake for dessert is pure, old-fashioned bliss.

The kitchen may only be open for dinner, but try the coffee shop next door for daytime visits.

 5359 W. Adams Blvd. (at Burnside Ave.)
📞 (323) 571-4999 — **WEB:** www.altaadams.com
■ Dinner nightly   PRICE: $$

DESTROYER 🍴

Contemporary • Trendy

The architecturally intriguing Hayden Tract district is the perfect backdrop for this adventurous little beau, brought to you by Jordan Kahn (of Vespertine). Those unfamiliar with the aesthetic might find this highly functional space too minimal, but every detail returns your attention to the food.

Each plate is a complex composition of flavors that are bound to delight and surprise. Begin with such harmonious starters as English peas cooked to varying degrees to emphasize a range of textures, coated in almond cream and topped with gooseberry slivers as well as a layer of feathery-light cream "snow." Chicken confit is hidden beneath a flurry of accoutrements that steal the spotlight, including aged cheese, toasted hazelnuts, yuzu and so much more.

■ 3578 Hayden Ave. (at Steller Dr.), Culver City
📞 (310) 360-3860 — **WEB:** www.destroyer.la
■ Lunch daily   PRICE: $$

453

FATHER'S OFFICE

Gastropub · Simple

This may appear to be a counter-service, first-come first-serve sort of joint for grabbing a bite, but Chef Sang Yoon has turned this—and the humble burger—into so much more. Made with dry-aged beef, caramelized onions and bacon compote, the elevated wares found in this kitchen are treasured as one of the country's first (and perhaps finest) craft burgers. The market-driven menu goes on to include items that one would not expect from a pub—imagine an heirloom tomato salad with Persian cucumbers dressed in a sweetened basil-goat's yogurt sauce; or even grilled skewers of deliciously spiced Sonoma lamb.

Housed in the historic Helms Bakery district, this Culver City location is more modern and comfortable than the Santa Monica original.

▦ 3229 Helms Ave. (bet. Venice & Washington Blvds.), Culver City

𝒫 (310) 736-2224 — **WEB:** www.fathersoffice.com

▦ Lunch Fri – Sun Dinner nightly   PRICE: $$

FLAME ⑩

Persian · Family

Sitting inside this pleasant dining room feels remarkably secluded, with its smoked glass windows (to obscure the noise and traffic outside), heavy brocade drapery and walls lined with polished stone. Towards the rear of the space, a tanor oven churns out hot flatbreads to welcome diners as soon as they arrive.

The cuisine offers specialties that focus on salads, grilled meats and slowly simmered stews enriched with dried lime and pomegranate. Start with the soulful classic ash reshteh, thick with beans, broken strands of pasta and finished with a drizzle of kashk (fermented whey). A wedge of the hearty tahchin is a treat, layering saffron-yellow basmati rice with creamy yogurt, chunks of white meat chicken and baked until golden brown.

▦ 1442 Westwood Blvd. (bet. Ohio & Wilkins Aves.)

𝒫 (310) 470-3399 — **WEB:** www.flamepersiancuisine.com

▦ Lunch & dinner daily   PRICE: $$

HINOKI & THE BIRD ¶○

Asian • Contemporary décor

Somehow, this stunning hideaway flies under the radar, as it remains tucked inside the Century Woods complex. Though the city seems to be on its way to becoming a cultural and culinary center, patrons here seem content to keep this restaurant a secret. A clear thread of Japanese subtlety runs through the décor, anchored by a long cedar bar and open kitchen, which churns out surprisingly good food.

Signature dishes flaunt modern creativity, often with hinoki wood playing a central role. Highlights include a tranche of pristine white sea bass in a complex duck broth, surrounded by gently wilted greens. A wonderful rendition of black pepper-crab rice foregoes authenticity by adding tart pickled eggplant for a lovely balance of salty, sweet and spicy flavors.

🔲 10 W. Century Dr. (bet. Constellation & Olympic Blvds.)
🖋 (310) 552-1200 — **WEB:** www.hinokiandthebird.com
🔲 Lunch & dinner daily   **PRICE: $$$**

KIRIKO ¶○

Japanese • Minimalist

One bite of a glistening piece of sashimi at this Westside gem and it will come as no surprise that Chef/owner Ken Namba was raised in the environs of Japan's famous Tsukiji fish market. Namba isn't content with the classics, and sashimi here will include varieties the likes of which many have never sampled before.

Whether you order sushi and sashimi à la carte or select one of three omakase menus, don't expect tradition, as Kiriko likes to play with your food with flavor enhancements and distinctive presentations. While some hit the mark—the Dungeness crab salad deconstructed in a martini glass elicits audible approval from diners—others swing and miss with a heavy-handed approach. Still, this chef has been at it since 1999 so he's no flash in the pan.

🔲 11301 W. Olympic Blvd. (at Sawtelle Blvd.)
🖋 (310) 478-7769 — **WEB:** N/A
🔲 Lunch Tue – Fri Dinner Tue – Sun   **PRICE: $$$**

KATO 🕸

Asian • Trendy

This small dining room looks spare but is in fact warm and lively, with a casual team of servers effectively managing each table and proving themselves knowledgeable and passionate about the cooking here. The cuisine is contemporary Asian but not strictly so; and is deftly prepared by California native, Chef Jon Yao—who trained under Chef Daniel Patterson at Coi. Naturally, his work in this kitchen is unique, with dishes that are at once simple and complex, playful and serious. In sum, this is a restaurant that showcases an ambitious young chef who is unafraid to change the menu in accordance with the day's produce or his own whim. The results leave the door open to greatness and maybe a bit of quirk.

With only one carte on offer, guests may look forward to offerings that feature fine local products at the hands of a very impressive kitchen. The judicious use of deeply flavored sauces and charred elements are repeated showstoppers. Memorable dishes include cold somen in a tomato-shoyu broth with clams and chrysanthemum petals; or grilled abalone with house XO sauce.

Homemade yuzu lemonade or refreshing strawberry sodas are some of the creative quenchers at this alcohol-free spot.

■ 11925 Santa Monica Blvd. (at Brockton Ave.)
✆ (424) 535-3041 — **WEB:** www.katorestaurant.com
■ Dinner Tue – Sat   **PRICE: $$$**

LUKSHON ⅏○

Asian • Simple

♿ ☕

This modern, upscale bistro arrives courtesy of Sang Yoon, the culinary genius behind the pioneering burger gastropub, Father's Office. The interior is sleek, smart and contemporary – the perfect backdrop to Yoon's bright, bold culinary style. A seat facing the open kitchen is one of the best in the house, bringing the heat in more ways than one.

The eclectic menu spans the Eastern hemisphere, from the Sichuan province of China to Vietnam, Malaysia and even India. Only a talented kitchen could pull off such a wide-spanning menu with integrity, and the team at Lukshon does it seamlessly. Chinese eggplant is paired with spiced tomato sambal and a cool yogurt raita; while steamed sea bream is complete with "black bean ghee" and pea shoots.

▦ 3239 Helms Ave. (bet. Venice & Washington Blvds.), Culver City
☎ (310) 202-6808 — **WEB:** www.lukshon.com
▦ Lunch Tue – Fri Dinner Tue – Sat   PRICE: $$

MAYURA ⅏○

Indian • Simple

Tucked away near the behemoth Sony Pictures lies this oasis of South Indian food. The simple interior of this local gem is fitted with bright purple chairs, colorful roses and booths lining the wall. But really, you're here for the food, which specializes in flavors from Kerala, a state set on the southwestern tip of the Indian peninsula. The lunch buffet is a popular way to sample various items, including rasam vada—a deep-fried lentil donut served with spicy and tangy rasam.

Be sure to save room though for the divine ghee roast dosa, as this tall, triangular and crisp creation served with sambar and chutney is mighty impressive even as it floats out of the kitchen. Simmering with spices, Kerala chicken curry will have you returning in no time.

▦ 10406 Venice Blvd. (bet. Mentone & Motor Aves.), Culver City
☎ (310) 559-9644 — **WEB:** www.mayurala.com
▦ Lunch & dinner Tue – Sun   PRICE: ⊷

MEIZHOU DONGPO 😳

Chinese • Elegant

 ♿ 🀄

Find wonderful Sichuan cuisine at this unexpected location, set inside the upscale Westfield Mall Century City. The lofty ceiling hangs calligraphy brushes and modern fixtures over the room's gold screens, blue silks and black lacquer accents; a buzzy bar and display kitchen augment the room's ambience.

Each dish is described and prepared with professionalism and care. Some, like the whole pork hock lodged in a sea of red chili oil, may be humble pleasures but are served with refinement, as the server pulls the tender flesh from the bone tableside for the guests. Thick and slippery dan dan noodles are twirled with rich and spicy minced pork balanced with the bracing flavors of scallion. The fish fillet is a classic rendition and makes for a fine finish.

🔲 10250 Santa Monica Blvd. (at Westfield Mall Century City)
📞 (310) 788-0120 — **WEB:** N/A
🔲 Lunch & dinner daily   **PRICE: $$**

MONTE ALBAN 🍴

Mexican • Family

 ♿ 🍽

Its environs may be modest, but the décor inside this rustic gem is colorful, featuring floor-to-ceiling murals, brick arches and high-backed wooden seats. All of this combined sets an authentic backdrop for delving into their menu of carefully crafted Oaxacan cuisine.

Showcasing an array of delicacies from tamales to tlayudas, regulars may start with molote, masa dumplings filled with potatoes, chorizo and fried until golden. The house-made mole is a revelation of 32 ingredients, from almonds and chiles to chocolate, which combine to create a deep, rich and complex sauce perfect for smothering on chicken and soaking in fresh tortillas. Portions are ample, but try to save room for the subtle and seasonal pumpkin flan that arrives dripping with caramel.

🔲 11929 Santa Monica Blvd. (at Brockton Ave.)
📞 (310) 444-7736 — **WEB:** www.montealbanrestaurante.com
🔲 Lunch & dinner daily   **PRICE: $$**

MORI SUSHI ✿

Japanese • Minimalist

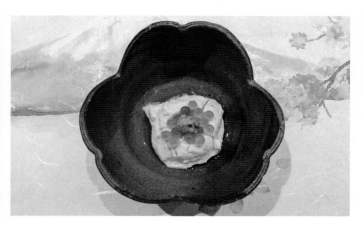

Perfectionists will thrill to a meal at this Westside sushiya, where everything from the homemade tofu to the kitchen's selection of seasonal fish is nothing short of exquisite. Everything inside the dining room is finely calibrated to highlight the wizardry behind the ubiquitous bar—soft lighting, white walls, wood accents and handcrafted ceramics. Even the wine and sake list is restrained, with each varietal specifically chosen to complement the fish.

Despite such delicacy, Mori is far from stuffy. This ship is steady with Chef Masanori "Maru" Nagano at the helm, explaining the provenance of each bite of the nigiri and omakase. A majority of the selection is flown in directly from Japan—with a few worthy exceptions, including the luscious Santa Barbara uni. The tasting might start with a dollop of creamy tofu brushed with soy sauce and a dab of wasabi, before progressing into wonderful bites of seared madai and lightly torched baby barracuda. Nigiri are ever-changing but may showcase sweet shrimp; rich and tart kohada; or outstanding buri.

A cooling scoop of buckwheat ice cream serves as the final memento, but really, it's the savory eats that will linger on for weeks to come.

■ 11500 W. Pico Blvd. (at Gateway Blvd.)
☏ (310) 479-3939 — **WEB:** www.morisushila.com
■ Dinner Mon – Sat   **PRICE: $$$$**

N/NAKA ❀ ❀
Contemporary • Chic

Los Angeles-born chef, Niki Nakayama, is a proud pioneer in the modern kaiseki tradition, yet she's humble enough to remain a constant in her dining room, checking in on each guest to ensure their every comfort. In this way, the much-lauded restaurant feels utterly personal, as though for this moment in time, you are the only diner that matters.

Set in an attractive and neutral-toned dining room, the space holds a devoted, almost cult-like reverence. It makes sense: guests don't want to miss a morsel of Chef Nakayama's genius. Her clever creations are delightfully unbound by Japanese tradition; instead, she rather inventively works within the spirit of it.

A nightly tasting menu might begin with a small glass of apple sake, followed by pristine scallop tartare coupled with sanbaizu gelée, carrot purée, toasted sunflower seeds and crispy carrot chips. From there, tiny yet exquisite dishes pour forth, including simply grilled branzino paired with rich Santa Barbara sea urchin, shiitake mushrooms and ponzu; or a tender lobster dumpling with king crab bobbing in dashi. Al dente spaghettini with abalone slices, pickled cod roe and black truffle is a personification of the chef's unique style.

■ 3455 S. Overland Ave. (at Lawler St.)
✆ (310) 836-6252 — **WEB:** www.n-naka.com
■ Dinner Wed – Sat   **PRICE: $$$$**

PIZZANA

Italian • Contemporary décor

Every pizza at this area darling begins with a nod to Neapolitan tradition: start with the perfect dough and bake it into a crust that remains crisp and light right through the middle. This careful process and that almighty oven shipped from Italy can be observed with longing through the glass-walled kitchen. The dining room also conjures the homeland through Mediterranean-blue murals and furnishings.

To top that crust, many pizzas go on to include premium ingredients like San Marzano tomatoes and fior di latte, which arrives several times a week from Italy. Alternatively, deck your pie with a more creative and locally minded blend of embellishments. A choice of appetizers, gourmet salads and luscious desserts rounds out the menu.

■ 11712 San Vicente Blvd. (at Barrington Ave.)
✆ (310) 481-7108 — **WEB:** www.pizzana.com
■ Lunch & dinner daily   PRICE: $$

POST & BEAM

American • Chic

This impressive Baldwin Hills location brings together LA celebrity chef, Govind Armstrong, with restaurateur Brad Johnson. It derives its name from the style of mid-century architecture that can be found within this thoughtfully designed room, outfitted with a dining counter facing the open kitchen, lively bar and plenty of windows. The tan stucco exterior is a welcoming combination of dark wood beams, citrus trees and a patio bounded by greenery.

The cooking focuses on American comfort food, like shrimp and grits; but also find wood-grilled salmon with curried lentils. While brunch brings buttermilk waffles topped with fried chicken, desserts showcase a wedge of light and fluffy sweet potato pie topped with candied pecans and cinnamon whipped cream.

■ 3767 W. Santa Rosalia Dr. (bet. Marlton Ave. & Stocker St.)
✆ (323) 299-5599 — **WEB:** www.postandbeamla.com
■ Lunch Sat – Sun Dinner Tue – Sun   PRICE: $$

SHAHERZAD ⅓○

Persian • Elegant

Since 1982, Shaherzad has been the established choice among this neighborhood's myriad Persian dining options. Inside, the room is a pretty combination of cream walls, blue furnishings and metallic accents. Larger tables attract groups of well-dressed ladies during lunch.

Everyone is welcomed with a basket of hot flatbread, served right from the oven on display through a glass wall. The menu goes on to list just about anything that a fan of Iranian cooking could wish for, including platters of crunchy salads, sizzling skewers of meat and an array of succulent stews. Kebabs are served with rice, but for a small charge you can upgrade to pilafs with wonderful combinations of sweet and savory flavors—like sour cherries and sautéed onion.

▨ 1422 Westwood Blvd. (bet. Ohio & Wilkins Aves.)
✆ (310) 470-3242 — **WEB:** N/A
▨ Lunch & dinner daily   **PRICE: $$**

Avoid the search for
parking. Look for valet ▨.

SHUNJI ✿

Japanese • Simple

Behind this notable counter is a chef whose experience runs deep. Japanese-born sushi maestro—Shunji Nakao—previously flashed his knife at Nobu Matsuhisa's eponymous 1980's spot. He is also known for his work at Asanebo, which he opened with his brother in the 90's.

While the menu here does offer à la carte, it is the omakase that is far and away the best option. The itamae will ask how much you'd like to eat, and so begins this memorable meal. After soups such as miso with special seaweed, the precise slicing and crafting of each morsel commences. This may include red snapper with salt and lemon or halibut with yuzu zest, tailed by live prawnswhere the tail becomes sushi dolloped with shrimp roe and the head disappears into the kitchen for frying. Then comes the parade of pieces brushed with nikiri, like lean tuna and bluefin toro. Finally, that shrimp head re-emerges to finish your meal with a beautiful bit of crunch.

Although this revered refuge is housed in a curious-looking circular building, just off Highway 10, guests arrive expecting serious sushi. Of course, that's exactly what they get, though the atmosphere remains low-key with just a small bar and handful of tables.

🔲 12244 W. Pico Blvd. (at Wellesley Ave.)
℘ (310) 826-4737 — **WEB:** www.shunji-ns.com
🔲 Lunch Tue – Fri Dinner Tue – Sat   PRICE: $$$$

VESPERTINE ❀ ❀

Contemporary · Design

❀ ⛄ ♿ 🖐

Dining at Vespertine is trippy, unsettling and out of the ordinary. Here, Chef Jordan Kahn executes his singular vision by preparing a cuisine that takes diners on a sensory, albeit futuristic, journey. If that doesn't conjure up a host of dramatic images, its monastic soundtrack will certainly do the trick. The result is a unique experience, which commences on the open-air rooftop where guests are presented with a welcome cocktail and canapés, before being escorted downstairs to the somewhat severe dining room.

Following suit, highly professional servers deliver this specific narrative. The chef has not forgotten his background at The French Laundry or Alinea, and uses it to build something wholly unexpected. Fans wait with bated breath for a highly conceptual meal that can last for hours and may not be for everyone. But these stunning plates are unforgettable, like Hokkaido sea scallop with yuzu broth and smoked bone marrow; mussels with celery, sweet plantains and topped with duck fat emulsion; or Dungeness crab with crisped duck skin and egg yolk.

After innovative desserts such as cucumber cream with redwood leaf granita, sojourn to the garden for some superb mignardises.

🟦 3599 Hayden Ave. (bet. Steller & Warner Drs.), Culver City
📞 (323) 320-4023 — **WEB:** www.vespertine.la
🟦 Dinner Tue – Sat   **PRICE: $$$$**

ORANGE COUNTY

ORANGE COUNTY

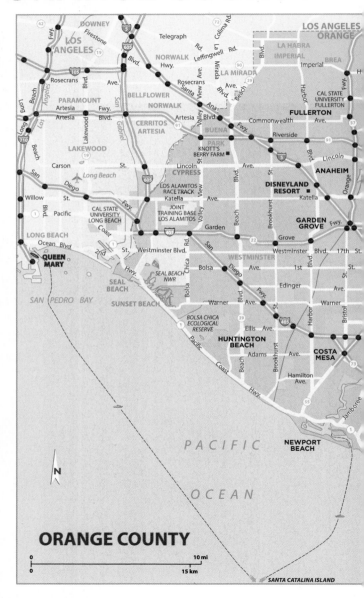

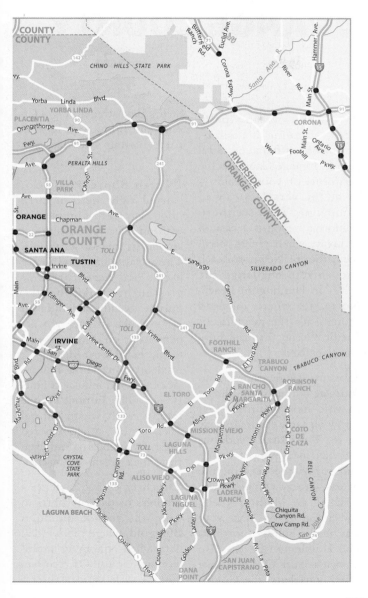

EATING IN...
ORANGE COUNTY

With its swaying palm trees, stunning mansions, oceanfront cliffs and beautiful people, Orange County is the California of your dreams—or at the very least an ad campaign. This southern California region is a bastion of luxury, where yachts bob in the harbor of Newport Beach and surfers challenge the waves in Huntington Beach. No matter where you land though, it's the magnificent Pacific Ocean that will have you transfixed.

Unsurprisingly, there is no shortage of waterfront dining in this neat county—just throw on some shades to truly fit in. **The Dock** overlooks the bay in Newport Beach and forms the very picture of easy-breezy, complete with a whiff of Mediterranean and SoCal flavor. Make your way just a smidge north to find Huntington Beach. Also known as Surf City, it is quite often considered the Golden

State's best stretch of golden sand and brims with retreats for refueling after hanging ten.

North Shore Poke Co. started right here in 2012 (though its reach is impressive, with an East Coast outpost among its newest locations). These salty hair-don't-care locals are here for their glistening poke bowls, pristine sashimi and fulfilling tacos. While six-pack abs are perpetually on display around town, that doesn't mean O.C. residents don't know how to kick back and indulge a little. In fact, **The Funnel House** tempts with warm funnel cake dusted with powdered sugar, fresh churros and even custom ice cream sandwiches.

Beach types may pull on a sundress or pair of shorts to enjoy the seaside dining at **Bluegold**, where the seafood is matched only by its drool-worthy views. Of course, nothing seals the deal after a

perfect day in the sun quite like a scoop of creamy gelato, and **Mangiamo Gelato Caffe** is one of this county's favorites.

It's not just hot at the beach though—Santa Ana's downtown is appealingly buzzy with its **4th Street Market** as the nerve center. Come for a little shopping and a whole lot of eating. Serving juices, coffees and baked goods in the morning, this bazaar comes to life during meal times, when grazers can nibble on Asian-Latin dishes, Vietnamese comfort food and fried chicken. For an edgier take on brunch (think: purple pancakes with coconut syrup), settle in at **Chapter One: the modern local**. Further south, Aliso Viejo's **Namaste** is an all-vegetarian spot with an Indian street food menu; while Anaheim's landmark **Packing House**, dating back to 1919 makes it name as a hub for diverse dining. Once home to a citrus packing facility, today it's filled with food stalls, restaurants, bars and live entertainment.

BLUEFIN 🍽

Japanese • Contemporary décor

🍸 🍶 ♿

After years of training under the renowned Nobu Matsuhisa, Chef/owner Takashi Abe brings a contemporary style and flair to every presentation that he sets before your eyes. This dovetails nicely with the bright dining room's clean and sleek décor. His loyal following ensures that the place is typically packed.

The food turned out of this kitchen is always delicious and proudly untraditional, served with more pomp and ceremony than typical sushiyas. Start with a beautiful bluefin toro tartare with garlicky soy, topped with caviar and set over a bowl of crushed ice. Sushi and sashimi are consistently excellent. In addition to the omakase and sushi-only selection, find a full slate of well-known, imported fish available à la carte, small plates and tempura.

▪ 7952 E. Pacific Coast Hwy. (at Crystal Cove Promenade), Newport Beach
📞 (949) 715-7373 — **WEB:** www.bluefinbyabe.com
▪ Lunch & dinner daily   PRICE: $$$

EL MERCADO MODERN CUISINE 🍽

Mexican • Chic

♿ 🍴 🛋

This restaurant strives to be a culinary microcosm of the distinctive regions of Mexico. On the outside, it may seem like a plain-Jane sort of space, but in fact bustles with passersby, shoppers and residents from around the way. Inside, bursts of color from the artwork make everything seem beautiful, cool and welcoming.

Serving a contemporary take on this nation's regional cuisine in Santa Ana is certainly no small feat, but this kitchen delivers wonderful flavors, compositions and quality through a range of dishes. Highlights include the sensational enchilada verde, combining perfectly stewed dark meat chicken bathed with a tangy tomatillo salsa verde and wrapped in blue corn tortillas. Save room for dessert to indulge in their coconut sorbet.

▪ 301 N. Spurgeon St. (bet. 3rd & 4th Sts.), Santa Ana
📞 (714) 338-2446 — **WEB:** www.mercadomodern.com
▪ Lunch Sun Dinner Tue – Sat   PRICE: $$

GABBI'S MEXICAN KITCHEN 😊

Mexican • *Traditional décor*

 ♿

The cooks at Gabbi's understand the essence of great Mexican food, which it has been delivering for many years. Trust in their skills and do not be dismayed with the menu line reading "substitutions are graciously declined." Yet many dishes offer a spin on traditions, such as the citrus-tinged achiote pork that tops the creamy black beans and puffed corn tortillas in panuchos de Yucatán. Tacos are a signature for good reason, and two per order encourages guests to explore their range of tortillas and fillings.

This delightful kitchen also makes the most of its idyllic setting, amid dozens of antique shops with an open front that spills onto the street. The interior is bright and warm, with plenty of tequila bottles lining the backlit shelves.

◼ 141 S. Glassell St. (bet. Almond & Chapman Aves.), Orange
☎ (714) 633-3038 — **WEB:** www.gabbipatrick.com
◼ Lunch & dinner daily   **PRICE: $$**

GARLIC & CHIVES 😊

Vietnamese • *Family*

 ♿

This local hot spot is housed in the Mall of Fortune, which is a suitably lofty name for such a local yet ornate treasure. Expect to be greeted by a line out the door; inside, find a giant sparkling chandelier as well as a clipboard with several names ahead of the free space to jot down your own. Don't worry—that queue moves quickly and you'll be slurping up glass noodles in no time.

Go with a group and order a feast, as prices are reasonable and the menu has much more to offer than one or two people can possibly explore. Fresh, clean flavors are at the forefront of grilled pork spring rolls full of herbs, vermicelli and fried garnishes for irresistible crunch. Unsurprisingly, the soft tofu with garlic and chives is a hearty, well-loved signature dish.

◼ 9892 Westminster Ave., Ste. 311 (at Brookhurst St.), Garden Grove
☎ (714) 591-5196 — **WEB:** www.garlicandchives.com
◼ Lunch & dinner Thu – Tue   **PRICE: ⛶**

HANA RE ❀

Japanese • Intimate

This Orange County sushi spot's scene is intimate, interesting and absolutely worth seeking out. The small, simple space seats ten at the dining counter, which in turn offers a fun, front-seat view of the buzzy kitchen and is far more preferable than the two tables in an auxiliary room. There is a happy sort of vibe here, ensuring that everyone is chatting by the end of their meal.

Behind that ubiquitous bar, Chef Atsushi Yokoyama is a one-man show, lending artistry to the feast without getting caught up in the pomp or fuss. The superlative sashimi and nigiri stand tall and are never overwrought. The freshness of this seafood is center stage when the chef presents live Santa Barbara prawns—you may even find yourself reaching for the camera to capture the swift knife skills and morsels of that sweet and slightly quivering tail meat. Cooked dishes are just as interesting, such as a trio of small bites including deep-fried Japanese river crab arranged to look as though it is climbing onto a stack of baby corn and anago tempura.

In-the-know patrons set aside three hours, as the omakase of cooked and raw items is the best dining option, with a few supplements added as nightly specials.

▦ 2390 Bristol St. (at Randolph Ave.), Costa Mesa
✆ (714) 545-2800 — **WEB:** www.hanaresushi.com
▦ Dinner Tue – Sat   **PRICE: $$$$**

HIRO NORI RAMEN 😊

Japanese • Simple

This eatery is located in a quiet complex, just steps away from an office park-dense area of Irvine. The diminutive gray interior is accented with wood slats, a vertical garden and plate-glass windows that overlook the gathering crowds waiting for your seat.

Everyone is here for the deliciously concise menu, offering rice bowls, and of course, their signature noodles. Those three types of ramen arrive in a choice of shoyu or vegan broth made with sesame and miso. Specialties include the tonkatsu, which showcases a bowl of wonderfully flavorful pork bone broth so rich that it seems almost milky, stocked with thin, flat noodles made by the chefs. This is finished with slabs of char siu and perhaps a dollop of zesty chili-garlic sauce.

▨ 2222 Michelson Dr., Ste. 234
(bet. Dupont Dr. & Von Karman Ave.), Irvine
☏ (949) 536-5800 — **WEB:** www.hironoricraftramen.com
▨ Lunch & dinner daily   **PRICE:** 🍜

IKKO 🍴

Japanese • Minimalist

"We do not serve American-style rolls." Just beyond the entrance, that's what the sign says at Ikko, a library-quiet retreat that prides itself on sushi and a sort of freestyle Japanese cuisine.

Despite the sense of hush, cave-like vibe, small size of its counter and smattering of tables, there is a surprising conviviality among the diners here as they nibble on an array of delicious options—ranging from multiple omakase menus to traditional à la carte. A board lists the dozen or so fish that have arrived as specials that day. Every item is sure to make the most of such immensely fresh seafood. Highlights include a slice of fatty otoro; red snapper topped with a tangle of sweet onions; chicken grunt hit with wasabi; and a perfect bite of firm hamachi.

▨ 735 Baker St. (at Randolph Ave.), Costa Mesa
☏ (714) 556-7822 — **WEB:** N/A
▨ Lunch Mon – Fri Dinner nightly   **PRICE:** $$$

IRENIA ¶❍

Filipino • Simple

Named for Chef Ryan Garlito's grandmother and muse, Irenia is a casual hipster hangout and local treasure for Filipino staples. The chef's tenure at Taco Maria shows in the careful presentations, with plates that command a serious Instagram following.

Adding to its group-friendly nature, the menu is widely appealing and prices are reasonable. Start with lumpia, Filipino egg rolls, served golden brown and steaming hot from the fryer. Filled with pork and vegetables, these crispy bites are accompanied by a wonderfully spicy vinegar dipping sauce to cut the richness. Don't miss out on dessert though, including halo halo, served as a tall glass of macerated fruit, coconut jelly and shaved ice topped with lightly sweetened purple yam milk.

■ 400 N. Broadway (at 4th St.), Santa Ana
✆ (657) 245-3466 — **WEB:** www.ireniarestaurant.com
■ Dinner Tue – Sat   **PRICE:** ⌖

JAVIER'S ¶❍

Mexican • Elegant

⌖ ⌖ ⌖ ⌖ ⌖

Views of the sun setting through the arches, columns and Moorish lanterns conjure a magical scene that is probably enough to draw crowds, who might consider lingering here until the sun rises again. Should your eyes move away from the vista, you'll find that the space is enormous and undeniably elegant. There may be no finer place for ceviche with a side of ocean breeze.

The comforting menu displays a dedication to sourcing seasonal ingredients from local farms. Each dish tastes as it should—prepared with care and precision. There is also a focus on familiar plates sprinkled with just the right bit of heat. Be sure to save room for their excellent relleno de picadillo, crafted with pasilla chilies stuffed with beef and floating in a delicious tomato sauce.

■ 7832 E. Pacific Coast Hwy. (at Crystal Cove Promenade), Newport Beach
✆ (949) 494-1239 — **WEB:** www.javiers-cantina.com
■ Lunch & dinner daily   **PRICE:** $$

J. ZHOU ⑪

Chinese • Elegant

♿ ⛲ 🍴 🖐

Bigger is better in O.C., and even by the standards of the huge open-air shopping mall that surrounds it, this dim sum palace is quite simply massive. Decked out with white tablecloths, traditional artwork and a plethora of chandeliers, it's a cart-free favorite for luxurious daily lunches—perhaps with a bottle or two from the high-end wine cellar.

Choosing the best items from the equally oversized menu can be tough. Plump, glistening dumplings in varieties like shrimp and chive or crispy seaweed are a must, and may be accompanied by the "golden scallion pie," a sesame-studded bun stuffed with scallions and pork. If you're still not sure what the fuss is about with congee, J. Zhou's, packed with tender shrimp and flaky fish, will make you a convert.

🔲 2601 Park Ave. (at the District at Tustin Legacy), Tustin
📞 (714) 258-8833 — **WEB:** www.jzhouorientalcuisine.net
🔲 Lunch & dinner daily   **PRICE: $$**

LSXO 😀

Vietnamese • Chic

Across from beautiful Huntington Beach, find this not-so-secret speakeasy tucked inside its parent restaurant, Bluegold. But the difference is palpable—LSXO is a bit cooler, louder and has a more defined personality. A trio of house-made condiments tops each table, with umami-rich fish sauce in place of salt, spice-infused oil as your pepper and a bottle of hot sauce as your furnace. Experiment with all three on refreshing noodle dishes like banh tam bi twirled with shredded pork, pickled vegetables and coconut milk. Other tantalizing mains may reveal shaky shaky beef, drizzled with burnt-butter soy sauce and set over garlic-tomato fried rice.

Getting a seat here can be tough, but good food makes this so much more than just a scene.

🔲 21016 Pacific Coast Hwy., Ste. D200 (at 1st St.),
Huntington Beach
📞 (714) 374-0083 — **WEB:** www.dinebluegold.com
🔲 Lunch & dinner daily   **PRICE: $$**

MARCHÉ MODERNE ᵗᐧO

French • Fashionable

Look for the off-center signature "M" to mark this spot. Here, Chefs/owners Florent and Amelia Marneau are back to delivering their signature French cuisine, with an eye on the contemporary palate of their southern Californian clientele. This is a stunning, elegant and sumptuous establishment that feels and tastes familiar yet original. The cooking follows suit from the glassed-in kitchen with soft globe lighting to the fire engine-red Berkel that's ready to slice their superb charcuterie.

Fans of this kitchen may recognize some of its signature dishes, including Amelia's chopped salad, featuring a touch of kale, julienned Little Gem, French feta, cucumber and celery. Luscious caviar with lacy crêpes, chives and sour cream is another menu standby.

■ 7862 E. Pacific Coast Hwy. (at Crystal Cove Promenade), Newport Beach
℘ (714) 434-7900 — **WEB:** www.marchemoderne.net
■ Lunch & dinner daily   **PRICE: $$$**

MIX MIX KITCHEN & BAR ☺

Contemporary • Trendy

This low-key downtown spot features two distinct dining areas: a light-filled bar and its wall lined with upscale spirits, as well as a more subdued dining room.

Chef/owner Ross Pangilinan delights everyone with his surprising, subtle and often ingenious spin on Filipino fare. That means that every dish seems contemporary and true to its southern California location, but the kitchen always returns to hints and touches of the chef's background. Sample adobo-style pork cheeks or tamarind-kissed soups. The tropical verrine—presenting a modern version of the traditional dessert halo halo—has mouthwatering layers of coconut panna cotta, tropical fruit and passion fruit gelée.

The best way to appreciate this kitchen is through the luxe prix-fixe.

■ 300 N. Main St. (at 3rd St.), Santa Ana
℘ (714) 836-5158 — **WEB:** www.mixmixkitchenbar.com
■ Lunch & dinner daily   **PRICE: $$**

OHSHIMA ¶O

Japanese • Minimalist

Within this banal strip of countless shops, look for the place with the line out front, before the door has even opened. Once inside, take a seat at one of the dozen places along the sushi bar, where the chef's omakase is served at bargain prices. A handful of tables along the back welcome larger parties. Reservations are strongly recommended and the house policies are strict: call precisely one week in advance, places are held for 15 minutes and meals will last no more than two hours.

The freshness and superb quality of the rice and fish, from soy-glazed amberjack to scallops with grated yuzu, make all of this worth it. The omakase is only sushi, but cooked specials include salmon quiche, fried chicken cartilage and slow-cooked beef tongue.

▓ 1956 N. Tustin St. (bet. Briardale & Meats Aves.), Orange
☏ (714) 998-0098 — **WEB:** www.ohshimasushi.com
▓ Lunch Tue – Fri Dinner Mon – Sat   PRICE: $$$

OOTORO ¶O

Japanese • Contemporary décor

Good things come in threes, and this third outpost of the burgeoning chain is indeed very good. Corporate types from the nearby office parks flock here seeking serenity, and sushi, of course.

Categorized by fish type, the menu makes it easy to pick and choose from the different families, but relinquish the reins and surrender to the omakase of sensational nigiri. The chefs treat you with great care and will advise when to dab soy sauce on their creations. Live abalone, trios of tuna, duos of salmon (one torched and the other garnished with kombu), seared shima aji and eel drizzled with unagi sauce plus sesame seeds—it's all quite enticing. A5 Wagyu followed by a cup of clam miso soup is the last hurrah and delivers a satisfying finale.

▓ 2222 Michelson Dr. (bet. Dupont Dr. & Von Karman Ave.), Irvine
☏ (949) 222-0688 — **WEB:** www.ootorosushi.com
▓ Lunch & dinner Tue – Sat   PRICE: $$$

THE RANCH 🍴○
Steakhouse • Rustic

🕸 ♿ ⛭

Big, dark and macho, this handsome stallion is located next to The Saloon at the foot of the Extron office building, all of which share the same owner. There may not be many cowboys in these parts, but there are plenty of decorative elements and music they'd covet here.

The menu is of course meat-centric, but also focuses on seasonal vegetables grown on their own farm. Here, a caprese salad is taken to creative peaks when their garden offers more than 90 heirloom varietals. Also sample crisp popovers served with sweet homemade tomato jam. The prime rib is ultra-tender with jus, horseradish sauce and a cast-iron skillet bubbling with cheese-topped scalloped potatoes. Top off the repast with such comforting desserts as a pecan tart with vanilla ice cream.

▪ 1025 E. Ball Rd. (bet. East & Lewis Sts.), Anaheim
☏ (714) 817-4200 — **WEB:** www.theranch.com
▪ Dinner nightly   PRICE: $$$

SHUNKA 🍴○
Japanese • Simple

♿

Aside from the framed samurai swords and black dragon painting, it's clear that this minimally dressed sushiya subscribes to the whisper-don't-scream school of thought. That spirit extends to the menu, where there is no sign of fusion. Surely that is why a largely Japanese clientele packs this place. Sushi is available à la carte, but the seasonal omakase features fish served in rapid-fire succession. Hirame, with a touch of freshly grated yuzu zest, is a delicious start. Then it's grouper with pickled daikon, which may be tailed by velvety kanpachi or shima aji with a dab of minced ginger. Spice heads will devour the red snapper with stir-fried shishito peppers.

In keeping with its no fuss-attitude, they don't take reservations, so be sure to plan ahead.

▪ 369 E. 17th St., Ste. 17 (at Tustin Ave.), Costa Mesa
☏ (949) 631-9854 — **WEB:** N/A
▪ Lunch & dinner daily   PRICE: $$

SUMMIT HOUSE RESTAURANT ᵀᵎO

Steakhouse • Elegant

&. ⟷ ⌂

Driving up to this «house» feels like you're entering a country club, which is a fair reflection of the restaurant's menu and model. No surprise though that said English-style manor easily doubles as a wedding venue. The classic feel extends to the interior, with a stone fireplace, exposed wood beams and—naturally—a player tickling the ivories. Opt for a seat by the window for an ace city view from the hills.

Prime rib—cut into a choice of three sizes—is the go-to entrée here. Their rendition is homey, well-executed and comforting with sides of creamed spinach, Yorkshire pudding and jus poured tableside. Desserts are generous enough for two and focus on steakhouse classics, like apple tart à la mode with caramel sauce, whipped cream and vanilla ice cream.

▉ 2000 E. Bastanchury Rd. (at State College Blvd.), Fullerton
🕿 (714) 671-4111 — **WEB:** www.summithouse.com
▉ Lunch Tue – Fri Dinner nightly   **PRICE: $$$**

VACA ᵀᎥO

Spanish • Tapas bar

&. 🛖 ⌂

Courtesy of Chef Amar Santana, this cool and rustic tapas bar offers consistently pleasing food and an extensive list of sherries and Spanish wines amid a quirky setting (the banquettes are decorated with jokes). In addition to the beautiful bar area, guests can choose to sit in two outdoor areas or the main dining room with views into the semi-open kitchen.

The lunchtime prix-fixe is a great deal, though it would mean skipping their wonderful array of tapas and paellas. Standouts include the bikini sandwich, layering cured jamón Ibérico, Manchego cheese and a bit of truffle oil into pretty little piping-hot grilled sandwiches. Croquettes de pollo tucked with shredded white meat are perfectly seasoned and fried to a golden crisp.

▉ 695 Town Center Dr., Ste. 170 (at Bristol St.), Costa Mesa
🕿 (714) 463-6060 — **WEB:** www.vacarestaurant.com
▉ Lunch Mon – Fri Dinner nightly   **PRICE: $$$**

TACO MARÍA ✿

Mexican · Minimalist

 ♿ 🍴 🛌

Nestled within an upscale galleria called The OC Mix, this simply appointed but highly desirable darling boasts some of the best and most refined tacos in town. Brought to you by the intensely creative chef, Carlos Salgado, lunch service may primarily focus on elevated tacos. But in truth, this kitchen shines through its prix-fixe dinner—complete with other culinary interpretations from the chef's Mexican heritage, as well as top-notch produce sourcing and techniques honed during his fine-dining training. Following suit, the clued-up staff excels in every way.

Centered around a sleek open kitchen and counter, a petite patio as well as a few tables offer supplemental seating in the dining room. Here, diners may look forward to such deeply intricate dishes as a carrot and masa tamal drizzled with mole Amarillo; or sea scallops gratinados with Chihuahua cheese and squid ink breadcrumbs. Even a simple potato cake is dressed to the nines with an hoja santa-anchovy salsa and a touch of caviar.

Beef birria is the evening's showstopper. Simmered in a blend of coffee, roasted chiles and cumin, it arrives with blue corn tortillas, chili oil as well as guacamole—and is quite simply, muy bueno!

🔲 3313 Hyland Blvd. Ste. C21 (at Sunflower Ave.), Costa Mesa
☎ (714) 538-8444 — **WEB:** www.tacomaria.com
🔲 Lunch Tue – Sun Dinner Tue – Sat   **PRICE: $$$**

SAN DIEGO

SAN DIEGO

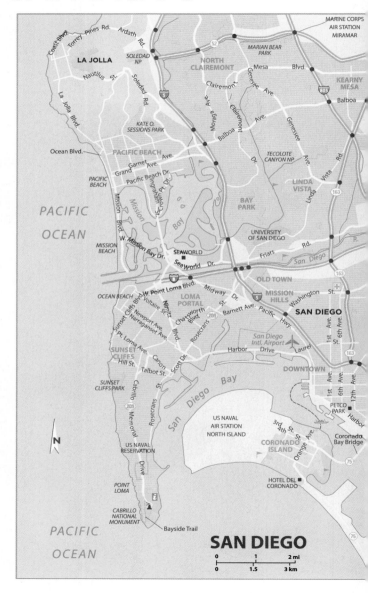

SAN DIEGO

0	1	2 mi
0	1.5	3 km

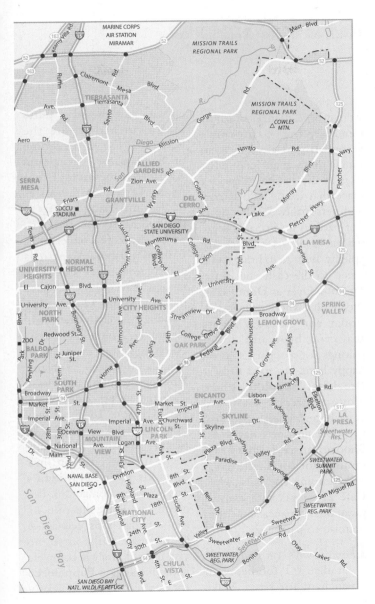

EATING IN...
SAN DIEGO

It may have 70 miles of sandy beaches, but California's second largest city offers so much more than just sunny days at the seaside. This is a place that teems with energy and personality. Waking up is not hard to do in San Diego, where breakfast choices are aplenty. Be sure to bring some green to the cash-only **Rose Donuts**. Over at **Donut Bar**, the menu changes daily—with Friday and Saturday nights featuring beer and donut pairings for a sugary spin on happy hour. It's hard to beat **Breakfast Republic**, where S'mores French toast and egg-shaped chairs promise to boost anyone's daybreak. **Snooze: an AM eatery** is a standby for breakfast, lunch and morning cocktails; while **Café 21** tempts with unusual variations on pancakes—from tiramisu to Japanese.

Downtown's Little Italy is a paradise for foodies with a penchant for pasta. Wake up with an espresso at **Caffe Italia**, tucked inside the Pensione Hotel, or come on Sundays for a wonderful waffle-bar brunch. From its basket-encased bottles of Chianti dangling from the ceiling to the red-and-white checkered tablecloths, **Filippi's Pizza Grotto** is classic red-sauce cooking. Lasagna lovers however may head to **Mona Lisa Italian Foods**, a family-owned deli/restaurant, which also boasts everything from manicotti to Marsala. Meanwhile, **Davanti Enoteca's** menu flaunts a Tuscany-meets-Napa flair, and **Civico 1845** serves up a modern approach to mama's favorites—including vegan-friendly hits—on their open-air patio. **Napizza's** crust may be Roman, but this green-minded collection of artisan pizza shops feels classic Californian. Of course, no visit to Little Italy is complete without a stop at **Pappalecco** for outrageously good gelato-

stuffed croissants or cookie sandwiches. The Gaslamp Quarter is where Victorian-era structures sit side by side with some of the most popular restaurants and bars around. Speaking of which, **Mariscos El Pulpo** plates up Mexican-style seafood along with the namesake octopus. Not far from Petco Park, **Tin Fish** is a casual stop for tacos, just as **Mezé Greek Fusion** has a funky menu of Greek and American eats. If burgers float your boat, then kitschy-chic **Hodad's** is your best bet. In Mission Valley,

try the Bobbie at **Capriotti's Sandwich Shop**. San Diego city's myriad global cuisines mean you can take your pick from Asian restaurants lining Convoy Street. Old Town, appropriately named, is widely considered the birthplace of California and marks the first Spanish settlement in the western U.S. Vibrant and festive, this 12-acre expanse is the ideal place for Mexican plates. Case in point: rural and lively **Cafe Coyote**, with traditional south-of-the-border cuisine and a notable selection of tequilas.

ADDISON

Contemporary • Luxury

Among other luxuries, an evening at the Addison is like wrapping yourself in culinary excellence. A lengthy drive through the exquisite grounds of the Fairmont Grand Del Mar resort sets the scene. Inside this much-celebrated space, arched ceilings stretch overhead, while a roaring fireplace sends light dancing off the marble. Glossy windows overlook the golf course greens, and guests settle in for one of San Diego's most coveted meals.

Critically acclaimed Chef William Bradley spins out one long dinner every evening, which is brought to you at the hands of gracious, polished and effortless servers. His French-influenced compositions are downright gorgeous, brightened up with a touch of southern California sparkle—and every resulting morsel is nothing short of revelatory.

Guests can choose from a four-course menu (with multiple options available in each section); or a far more involved tasting that's left entirely to the chef's discretion. The latter is the favorite by far and may highlight an heirloom pumpkin velouté with crispy shallots and toasted rye crumbs; while a plump, perfectly cooked Hokkaido scallop arrives with silky cauliflower purée, osetra caviar and savory brown butter foam.

■ 5200 Grand Del Mar Way
☎ (858) 314-1900 — **WEB:** www.addisondelmar.com
■ Dinner Tue – Sat   **PRICE: $$$$**

A.R. VALENTIEN 🍴○

Contemporary • Cozy

♿ 🪑 🛋️

Every element of this setting seems to exude a California-casual meets country-club vibe. Inside, choose from one of the Craftsman post-and-beam dining rooms, warm with amber lanterns and stained-glass light fixtures; or simply head outside to dine on the patio overlooking the pool and 18th hole of Torrey Pines Golf Course.

The city's unending growing season means that there is a boundless harvest of local ingredients to inspire this kitchen. Begin with Dungeness crab flan surrounded by watercress, Belgian endive and roasted grapes, drizzled with tangy balsamic dressing. Then, indulge in elevated comfort foods like chicken under a brick, set over Tuscan kale and cannellini beans in tomato sauce. The brûléed lemon sabayon tart is above par and pure joy.

▪ 11480 N. Torrey Pines Rd. (at Callan Rd.), La Jolla
☎ (858) 777-6635 — **WEB:** www.lodgetorreypines.com
▪ Lunch & dinner daily   **PRICE: $$$**

BORN & RAISED 🍴○

Steakhouse • Vintage

🍸 🍺 ♿ 🪑 ☐

If Frank Sinatra broke bread with Tupac, they'd probably meet at Born & Raised. No expense was spared making this wildly polished, upscale steakhouse that resembles a mid-century, art deco dream lined with black-and-white photos of old-school rap legends, like Eazy-E. There is a glassed-in meat cutting room in the back; and a lovely, open-air rooftop bar overlooking Little Italy.

Waiters dressed in tuxedos and Converse shoes drift between tables, pushing nostalgic tableside carts where they whip up starters on the spot or pour a drink to order. Certainly, you're here for the impeccably cooked steaks, but don't miss the tartare, prepared tableside with quail egg, capers and cornichons (to name just a few embellishments) and served with herbed aïoli.

▪ 1909 India St. (at Fir St.)
☎ (619) 202-4577 — **WEB:** www.bornandraisedsteak.com
▪ Dinner nightly   **PRICE: $$$$**

CALIFORNIA MODERN 🍴◐

Contemporary · Trendy

🎴 🍸 ♿ 🛋 🤝

Find this fine-dining treasure on the lower level of George's at the Cove. Their more casual dining options are upstairs on levels two and three. Not only is this the most sophisticated kitchen in the building, but it rises well above the surrounding neighborhood eateries. It is a place to enjoy a quiet, romantic meal prepared by a chef who takes extra steps to make everything special. Crisp linen-covered tables by the windows are coveted by all—request one when making your reservation.

Choose from two different prix-fixe menus or go à la carte, but don't miss their stunning and smartly composed take on beef tartare. Other highlights include an eye-catching and deeply flavorful lasagna layered with ricotta, huitlacoche and maitake mushrooms.

▪ 1250 Prospect St. (bet. Cave St. & Ivanhoe Ave.), La Jolla
℘ (858) 454-4244 — **WEB:** www.georgesatthecove.com
▪ Dinner nightly   **PRICE: $$$**

CAMPFIRE 😊

Contemporary · Rustic

🍸 ♿ 🏕 🛋 🛋

You won't be gathering in a circle, but there is something heartwarming and enticing about Campfire. It could be the World War II-era Quonset metal hut that anchors the space, the teepee or the custom-built 12-foot wood-burning hearth. Whatever it is, it exudes that cool glamping vibe. Imagine servers in gingham shirts offering DIY s'mores, thermoses doubling as water pitchers and even the check issued in a field notebook—this spot takes its campy theme quite seriously.

The kitchen is no joke either. From zesty ceviche and charred pumpkin drizzled with a vibrant chimichurri to tagliatelle topped with chorizo, egg and queso fresco, this cooking smacks of Chef Andrew Bachelier's fine-dining pedigree and his Mexican roots.

▪ 2725 State St. (near Beech Ave.), Carlsbad
℘ (760) 637-5121 — **WEB:** www.thisiscampfire.com
▪ Lunch Tue – Sun Dinner nightly   **PRICE: $$**

CATANIA ¡¡○

Italian • Trendy

In the historic heart of La Jolla, find this cool and hip retreat on the top floor of the Plaza Center. The artfully designed dining room features sunny Mediterranean colors and ceramic tiles. A large, elegant terrace offers panoramic coastline views.

Come early for their aperitivo (cocktails and snacks), but make sure you stay to explore this kitchen's modern twists. Start with a daily salad special, featuring lovely flavors like beet chips and butternut squash, crowned by ahi tuna crudo with poppy seeds and basil leaves. Then dive into a Neapolitan-style pizza from the wood-burning oven, or decadent pastas such as orecchiette mingled with slow-braised duck ragù accented by tomato coulis, porcini mushrooms and freshly grated parmesan.

■ 7863 Girard Ave. (at Wall St.), La Jolla
✆ (858) 551-5105 — **WEB:** www.cataniasd.com
■ Lunch & dinner daily

PRICE: $$

CLOAK & PETAL ¡¡○

Japanese • Chic

It's in the heart of Little Italy, but you won't hear any old crooners at this temple of Japanese haute cuisine. Instead, you'll find old-school rap on the soundtrack and graffiti art installations on the walls. And then there's the bar, flanked by two faux-cherry trees in full bloom.

The fresh-spirited menu brims with shareable plates such as blistered shishito peppers and crispy chicken karaage. Entrées include duck breast with golden tomato confit, miso-glazed black cod or even Wagyu grilled tableside on a yakitori. The sashimi is straight-up sublime, but it's the envelope-pushing items that make the most impact. Contemporary maki, including the 30th & University roll with minced crab, scallops and seared Wagyu, are a hit among the hungry hordes.

■ 1953 India St. (bet. Fir & Grape Sts.)
✆ (619) 501-5505 — **WEB:** www.cloakandpetal.com
■ Dinner nightly

PRICE: $$$

COWBOY STAR ¶○

Steakhouse • Rustic

This handsome "star" sports a Western flair with its hide-covered chairs and candle chandeliers, yet meat is the true monarch at this butcher shop and restaurant. You could pick up choice cuts to grill at home, but with an exhibition kitchen helmed by Chef Victor Jimenez, why miss out on all of the fun?

Ingredients are curated with great care here and the meat is sourced from the nation's leading purveyors. Buttery Wagyu beef is seasoned and cooked without fuss, but packed with flavor. Sauces, such as the brandy peppercorn, are well worth the investment for a few extra bucks. Steakhouse standbys include Caesar salad, while the rich and dark chocolate chip-bread pudding veers from the traditional slice of cheesecake for a decadent detour.

◾ 640 10th Ave. (bet. G & Market Sts.)
✆ (619) 450-5880 — **WEB:** www.cowboystarsd.com
◾ Lunch Tue – Fri Dinner nightly　　　　　**PRICE: $$$$**

CRACK SHACK ¶○

American • Family

Loud and proudly serving "all day chicken and eggs," this shack indeed lives up to its name. The dining area is almost entirely outside, so the planes flying overhead can't be ignored and neither can the enthusiastic crowds, who seem to compete with that level of noise.

Many come here for the fried chicken, but chicken sandwiches on bakery-fresh brioche, potato rolls or English muffins are heartwarmingly delicious. Pickled-brined and deep-fried chicken oysters (tender knobs of meat from the back) are the essence of what every nugget dreams of becoming. Simple but tasty homemade desserts like cookies and soft-serve ice cream complete the scene. Beer and bocce—beneath the watchful gaze of a larger-than-life rooster—is almost as much fun as the food.

◾ 2266 Kettner Blvd. (at Juniper St.)
✆ (619) 795-3299 — **WEB:** www.crackshack.com
◾ Lunch & dinner daily　　　　　**PRICE:** ⬡

CRAFT & COMMERCE ¶❍

American • Vintage

🍸 🍺 ♿ 🏠 🛋 ✋

Channel your best Ernest Hemingway before entering this place, designed to the hilt and a feast for the eyes with its library-meets-hunting lodge look. From its mounted trophies to the taxidermy specimens on loan from the Natural History Museum, this may not be the wisest pick for your PETA-supporting pal, but it definitely appeals to the trendy set.

The kitchen perfects contemporary comfort food and wood-fired dishes are a big deal. Flames work their magic on grilled oysters, smoked Duroc pork tenderloin with red mole as well as boar sausage with gnocchi. Even Brussels sprouts are amped up with thick chunks of rich pork belly. Finally, get a spoon for the cornbread, which is best eaten from its skillet with a dollop of honey-thyme butter.

▨ 675 W. Beech St. (at Kettner Blvd.)
✆ (619) 269-2202 — **WEB:** www.craft-commerce.com
▨ Lunch Sat – Sun Dinner nightly   **PRICE: $$**

CUCINA SORELLA 😊

Italian • Osteria

🍸 ♿ 🏠

Classy but casual, this Italian restaurant and wine shop is a Kensington neighborhood stalwart. You won't need to noodle over the menu, as the kitchen's forte is pasta. Grab a seat at the famous counter and watch them turn out orders by hand.

Begin with a plate of crispy fried potato gnocchi tots with house-made ketchup. Then take your pick from a spectrum of seasonal creations, such as tagliatelle with pistachio pesto, peas and pickled celery. But that's not all—gnocchetti Sardi tossed with spicy pork sausage, broccoli rabe and tomato in a sage- and brown butter-sauce is the very essence of comfort. While carbs rule the roost here, this kitchen also delivers other hits like octopus a la plancha served with grapes and soppressata for a zesty mix.

▨ 4055 Adams Ave. (at Terrace Dr.)
✆ (619) 281-4014 — **WEB:** www.urbankitchengroup.com
▨ Dinner Tue – Sun   **PRICE: $$**

CUCINA URBANA ☺

Italian • Osteria

Cucina Urbana, like the other siblings in the Urban Kitchen Group family, is an amiable place that promises a good time. It's casual, festive and draws regulars who flock here for their daily deals (Meatball Mondays are a favorite) and happy hour specials.

Snacks are also aplenty. One sniff and you know truffle fries are big, but there's also chicken liver pâté and black garlic hummus with crusty bread as a ride along. Ribeye carpaccio is thinly sliced and ruby red; grilled octopus tentacle with speck, cashews, lemon yogurt and salsa verde is another winner. Neapolitan pizzas like the spicy guanciale with marinated tomato, smoked cheddar, béchamel and spicy Fresno chilies is far from traditional, while creative pastas won't let you down.

▪ 505 Laurel St. (at 5th Ave.)
℘ (619) 239-2222 — **WEB:** www.urbankitchengroup.com
▪ Lunch Tue – Fri Dinner nightly   PRICE: $$

EL JARDÍN ☺

Mexican • Contemporary décor

Snapshots of Claudette Zepeda-Wilkins' travels across Mexico line the walls of this spot, offering a peek into the people and places that inspire this talented chef's contemporary cuisine. A dinner in her capable hands might unveil Michoacán carnitas, elegantly paired with avocado mousse and nopales salad; or mahi mahi birria and barbacoa lamb shank.

If you're here for their popular brunch, don't miss out on the chilaquiles divorciados. It's a two-flavor combination of delicious chilaquiles with sunny-side up eggs, pickled onions and cotija cheese—and you'll want to add those tender beef cheeks. Regardless of when you go, don't forget to get a side of the house salsa, a creative blend of macadamia nuts with olive oil and chile de árbol.

▪ 2885 Perry St. (at Truxton Rd.)
℘ (619) 795-2322 — **WEB:** www.eljardinrestaurantbar.com
▪ Lunch Sat – Sun Dinner nightly   PRICE: $$

THE FISHERY ᵢⵏ◯

Seafood • Family

&

Nestled within a restored mid-century warehouse in North Pacific Beach, The Fishery is exactly what it claims. As if you needed further proof, there's even a premier seafood market housed at its center.

You would be hard-pressed to find fish fresher than the selection offered here and the open kitchen does wonders with this market-driven menu overseen by these talented chefs, who let the quality product shine bright. Think—ahi tuna poke prepped with just a hint of soy sauce, sesame seeds and chili. Stuffed with crisp-fried cod fillets, rice, beans, guacamole and served with homemade chips, the cod burrito makes a hearty and hefty meal—just right for the many surfers who come here after tackling the waves at nearby Tourmaline Canyon Surfing Park.

▇ 5040 Cass St. (at Opal St.)
℘ (858) 272-9985 — **WEB:** www.thefishery.com
▇ Lunch & dinner daily   **PRICE: $$**

GREAT MAPLE ᵢⵏ◯

American • Family

& ⛺ 📺 🛏

Take the classic 50s diner, add a little swagger and you get Great Maple. It is one of four outlets statewide, but this particular location is always buzzing. Be warned though as parking and counter seats are coveted, so plan ahead.

Three-course chef dinners on Mondays; burger and beer nights on Wednesdays; and prime rib Fridays are popular, but it's also great at brunch. Fruity Pebbles pancakes, lolliwaffles on a stick and maple-bacon donuts are sweet-tooth satisfiers. Late night? Sip a Bloody Mary and tuck in to the brisket popover, a fluffy base with tender smoked meat, poached eggs and béarnaise that will cure what ails you. Seasonal dessert pies are all the rage—including the Valencia orange cream with a pistachio- and brown butter-shortbread crust.

▇ 1451 Washington St. (at Lincoln Ave.)
℘ (619) 255-2282 — **WEB:** www.thegreatmaple.com
▇ Lunch & dinner daily   **PRICE:** ⬤⬤

HERB & WOOD 🍴

Californian • Design

It's relatively new to restaurant-rich Little Italy, but this establishment has gained a loyal following since opening in 2016. The former warehouse could lean cavernous but its barrel-vaulted ceilings and funky artwork exude a distinct Parisian bohemian warmth. The whole place is set aglow and everyone, including the staff, wants to be here.

Its wide-ranging menu runs the gamut—from rustic, wood-fired dishes including grilled trumpet mushrooms and pizzas, to more refined plates like venison over buttermilk polenta. The PB&C, a chocolate-whiskey cake with peanut butter mousse and rich milk chocolate gelato, absolutely hits the spot.

If on the run, head to their connected all-day eatery—a good bet for lunch and Wednesday trivia nights.

▪ 2210 Kettner Blvd. (at Ivy St.)
☏ (619) 955-8495 — **WEB:** www.herbandwood.com
▪ Lunch Sun Dinner nightly   **PRICE: $$$**

IRONSIDE FISH & OYSTER 🍴

Seafood • Design

Few locations are more dedicated to their theme than this seafood-centric restaurant, with its garage doors thrown open to welcome a salty breeze. The building itself is a gussied-up warehouse topped with the quote, "A rising tide lifts all boats." Inside, the maritime-themed décor unveils brass portholes, octopus-like sconces and anchor-shaped bar hooks for purses.

The cooking is just as true to the seas and their fishermen, who are specifically named on the menu. Diners may start with rock fish ceviche with citrus, coconut milk, turmeric and a hint of habanero—it's just right for scooping up with house-made sweet potato chips. The thresher shark lunch plate is wonderfully mild, topped with a dollop of puttanesca relish and creamy slaw.

▪ 1654 India St. (bet. Cedar & Date Sts.)
☏ (619) 269-3033 — **WEB:** www.ironsidefishandoyster.com
▪ Lunch & dinner daily   **PRICE: $$**

JUNIPER & IVY

Californian • Trendy

Set within a 1920s warehouse, this fire-hot spot from celebrity chef Richard Blais boasts of rustic charm (imagine redwood beams and tan leather furnishings). Whether perched at the bar or in the dining room, the mood is always convivial.

Equally upbeat is the menu, which leaves no stone unturned in its quest for often kooky inspiration. Start with a spicy tuna handroll before tucking into pumpkin curry. From persimmon caprese with whipped burrata to cocoa powder-tinted bucatini with wild boar sausage, this kitchen is unafraid to mix and match with spectacular results. An upmarket version of a "Yodel" is delicious entertainment; and if you don't crack a smile after pouring hot chocolate over the frozen chocolate cylinder, well then, you cannot be saved.

■ 2228 Kettner Blvd. (bet. Ivy & Juniper Sts.)

☏ (619) 269-9036 — **WEB:** www.juniperandivy.com

■ Dinner nightly   **PRICE: $$**

KETTNER EXCHANGE

Contemporary • Rustic

Hip, laid-back and a model of design, this indoor-outdoor space is at once many things. Inside, relax with a creative cocktail and bowl of lemon-Dijon popcorn while contemplating the entryway's reflective blue-glass ceiling, the two-way fireplace and that nest of driftwood hanging from an upper floor. If in the mood for a clubbier scene, head to the rooftop cabana, complete with wet bars, TVs and self-service beer taps—just remember to reserve well in advance.

The menu presents dishes from around the globe, such as "ribbons" of bigeye tuna tangled with sliced avocado and much more in a flavorful makrut lime- and soy-marinade. Of course, those plump and tender duck meatballs are an instant classic, set over cheesy grits and smothered in tomato sauce.

■ 2001 Kettner Blvd. (at Grape St.)

☏ (619) 255-2001 — **WEB:** www.kettnerexchange.com

■ Lunch Sat – Sun Dinner nightly   **PRICE: $$**

LAS CUATRO MILPAS 🍴○

Mexican • Taqueria

This legacy restaurant is packed with loyal patrons who drive miles out of their way for a tamale or taco. It's old-school for sure (the Estudillo family has been running it since 1933), so if you're the type who likes to substitute this for that, you'll be laughed out of here. Instead, grab a tray and move along the queue where you'll barely have time to read the menu—located just above the ladies rolling and frying tacos.

But while you're expected to order at lightning speed (grumbles from diners are part of the charm), the food comes out equally fast. Dishes are simple and sumptuous, like chorizo with rice and beans as well as tacos filled with chicken or pork. Don't miss the hot sauce at the end of the line—it's what takes these eats to the next level.

 1875 Logan Ave. (bet. Beardsley St. & Cesar Chavez Pkwy.)
☎ (619) 234-4460 — **WEB:** N/A
◼ Lunch Mon – Sat   **PRICE:** ⌾

LOLA 55 😊

Mexican • Trendy

There may be plenty of taquerias around town, but this East Village gem is of a slightly different breed. The airy space, with its high ceilings, concrete floors and a full bar with lounge, reads über-cool. However, it's more than just about good looks—their tacos are what draw the crowds. The variations on offer here lean more sophisticated with creative combinations such as baby carrot adobada and squash blossom relleno. Ribeye carne asada cooked to order on the mesquite wood-burning grill or achiote-rubbed pork belly with grilled pineapple are just some of the winners. Posole verde is comfort in a bowl, while fried masa disks are plain delectable.

Remember to save room for the Mexican mole-chocolate ice cream and addictively crunchy churros.

◼ 1290 F St. (at 13th St.)
☎ (619) 542-9155 — **WEB:** www.lola55.com
◼ Lunch & dinner daily   **PRICE:** ⌾

LUCHA LIBRE

Mexican • Taqueria

This is a kitschy shrine to the masked warriors hailing from south of the border. Its walls are covered with evocative artwork, depicting everyone from wrestlers to world leaders graced by those trademark wrestling guises.

The entire space just exudes tons of fun but you'll need a wrestler-sized appetite to tackle its seriously good food. Tacos filled with steak and seafood are incredibly heartwarming, with a secret chipotle sauce adding just the right amount of heat. But, their burritos are for true competitors—bursting at the seams, these beasts are big, fat and quite delicious. Don't miss the champion fries though, smothered with melted jack cheese, sour cream, guacamole, beans and queso for a nacho-like, gut-busting experience.

◼ 1810 W. Washington St. (at San Diego Ave.)

✆ (619) 296-8226 — **WEB:** www.tacosmackdown.com

◼ Lunch & dinner daily   PRICE: ⊜

MAESTOSO

Italian • Trattoria

Remember the cronut? Well, move along because it's time to meet the pinsa. This focaccia-pizza mashup comes courtesy of Marco Maestoso and is crispy and bubbly on the outside; soft and fluffy inside. Take your pick, but La Mortazza with fresh burrata, mortadella and crumbled pistachios is a great start. In addition to such cutting-edge items, this adept kitchen also doles out nonna-approved Roman classics. Aside from their fresh pastas, opt for the passaggi—an inventive Italian take on dim sum that invites diners to pick small plates from carts rolled around by cooks. While the octopus carpaccio is a sure bet, pace yourself, as these wheels keep turning.

For a hot ticket to the heart of it all, nab a seat at the counter facing the open kitchen.

◼ 1040 University Ave. Ste. B101
(bet. 10th Ave. & Vermont St.)

✆ (619) 642-0777 — **WEB:** www.maestoso.com

◼ Lunch Sat – Sun Dinner Wed – Mon   PRICE: $$

MARINE ROOM ⒑○

French • Romantic

The Marine Room lures a well-heeled crowd to its sleek environs. Set within a luxury beach resort in the exclusive La Jolla enclave, it feels every bit the posh club. It's also a romantic spot to celebrate a special date, thanks to those dramatic sea views at sundown—when a spectrum of colors light up the sky. Land a table at high tide, when the waves come crashing against their westward-facing windows, for a truly enchanting experience.

The suggestion of jackets for gentlemen isn't the only nod to tradition; the kitchen trots out classics like surf and turf as well as a Caesar salad prepared guéridon style. Some items steer a bit too ambitious; while others, like the trio of lobster, ahi tuna and Kona kampachi, benefit from a deft hand.

■ 2000 Spindrift Dr. (at Paseo Dorado), La Jolla
℘ (855) 923-8057 — **WEB:** www.marineroom.com
■ Dinner nightly   **PRICE: $$$$**

MARKET RESTAURANT + BAR ⒑○

International • Romantic

Chef/owner Carl Schroeder is a La Jolla native with an encyclopedic knowledge of the region's bounty. He's been celebrating every locally sourced ingredient for over a decade now in this kitchen, and his repertoire of creative cooking continues to draw patrons for both special occasions as well as date night. The dark and seductive décor manages to be elegant without a hint of pretense, but one glance at the parking lot and you know that this spot is favored by a moneyed lot.

Sushi is well-loved here, but it would be a shame to miss the chef's creative and internationally influenced dishes. For instance, blue cheese soufflé with anise-orange marmalade shows off a European bent, while miso-glazed cod with shrimp dumplings is resoundingly Asian.

■ 3702 Via De La Valle (at De La Valle Pl.), Del Mar
℘ (858) 523-0007 — **WEB:** www.marketdelmar.com
■ Dinner nightly   **PRICE: $$$**

MILLE FLEURS

European • Romantic

Set in the quaint village of Rancho Santa Fe, Mille Fleurs has been a longtime—over 30 years—haunt among locals celebrating special occasions. Its elegant piano bar is often filled with well-dressed visitors in town to watch the Del Mar races, while the courtyard patio strung with lights makes for a romantic setting, especially when watching the fireworks.

French and German influences like spätzle and Wiener schnitzel make their appearance on this market-driven menu. In fact, the chef makes a beeline for tradition with mains like lobster bisque and Dover sole. Even dessert veers classic, with straightforward and delicious selections like apple strudel.

Five- and seven-course menus with wine pairings are also on offer and quite popular.

6009 Paseo Delicias (at Avenida De Acacias),
Rancho Santa Fe
(858) 756-3085 — **WEB:** www.millefleurs.com
Lunch Thu – Fri Dinner nightly   PRICE: $$$$

NINE-TEN

Contemporary • Elegant

There may be no better way to end a day of watching the seals and surf than tucking into a plate of Jamaican jerk pork belly at Nine-Ten. Located in the century-old Grande Colonial Hotel, this dining room and patio is more cozy and casual than grand, populated by folks who keep their shades on through dinner. Naturally. During lunch, the front sidewalk and back area overlooking the pool are divine.

Many patrons put themselves at "the mercy of the chef," which is their quirky way of offering a chef's tasting. Others may explore the menu filled with seared salmon, served over braised fennel and Romano beans in an aromatic lobster broth. The kitchen reaches its peak with desserts like strawberry-almond cake layered with mousse and fresh berries.

910 Prospect St. (at Jenner St.), La Jolla
(858) 964-5400 — **WEB:** www.nine-ten.com
Lunch & dinner daily   PRICE: $$$

NOLITA HALL ᵀⅼ◯

Pizza • Rustic

Nolita Hall brings new meaning to "flights" of beer, as it is directly in the flight path of the San Diego International Airport. This amiable hot spot doesn't waste time with superficial changes; instead, they play it up with a board announcing the origin city of all planes in flight. It's just one sign that this destination, where TVs show sports and shuffleboards await competition, is all about having a good time.

Wood-fired Neapolitan pizzas take center stage and are the perfect chaser to the 20-something, mostly local beers on tap. The Y Tu Brute salad is a delicious take on the Caesar, while charred sugar snap peas and baby carrots go to show that this kitchen is full of surprises. Just hold on tight to that brew when a Boeing rumbles overhead.

■ 2305 India St. (at Juniper St.)
℘ (619) 255-8000 — **WEB:** www.nolitahall.com
■ Lunch Wed – Sun Dinner nightly   **PRICE: $$**

OSCAR'S MEXICAN SEAFOOD ᵀⅼ◯

Mexican • Taqueria

This south-of-the-border spot seems straight out of central casting for a classic surfer snack shack. Laid-back and breezy, it's set just blocks from the beach so you won't need to brush the sand off your feet to eat here. That is if you can find a perch inside, as the counter offers very limited seating. Whether in or out, dine at all times on seafood-centric Mexican food, where tacos take center stage with familiar renditions like crispy fish and shrimp, as well as more unusual selections including grilled octopus and adobo-marinated tuna. Feeling hungrier than usual? Upgrade any taco to a burrito for an extra buck, or stop by mid-afternoon for happy hour and 99-cent treats.

One of five outposts in the region, most of these guys accept cash only.

■ 703 Turquoise St. (bet. La Jolla Blvd. & Wrelton Dr.)
℘ (858) 488-6392 — **WEB:** www.oscarsmexicanseafood.com
■ Lunch & dinner daily   **PRICE:**

PUESTO

Mexican • Family

Colorful, festive and beachy, this is La Jolla cove's beloved home for fast-casual Mexican cooking. There may be other Puesto locations, but this one seems to outshine the pack. The cuisine here has a restrained heat that emphasizes the fresh, bright flavors of Mexico, beginning with the pure pleasure from thin, crisp chips and fire-roasted salsa. Come on Taco Tuesdays when prices are slashed to explore their array of tasty fillings, many of which show artisanal flair through market-sourced grilled fish, garlicky mushrooms or zucchini and cactus. The exhibition kitchen also cranks out snacks like mezcal-pickled watermelon alongside heartier plates of seafood and enchiladas.

Arrive during happy hour to fully understand their mastery of the margarita.

- 1026 Wall St. (at La Jolla Cove), La Jolla
- (858) 454-1260 — **WEB:** www.eatpuesto.com
- Lunch & dinner daily   PRICE: 🍜

SOLARE 😊

Italian • Osteria

It's just steps from the Liberty Public Market in the NTC Promenade, but one step inside this elegant and chic arena where a warm apricot and sienna color scheme dominates, and you'll instantly feel like you're in Italy.

This masterful kitchen wants to feed you and they'll feed you very well indeed. Find proof of this in their crave-worthy creations—ranging from antipasti and salads to pastas and pizzas. Opt for a tasting menu and you'll select the number of courses (the kitchen determines the dishes you'll sample). Everything is made in house and with great care taken over each composition. Venison carpaccio with balsamic vinegar and Grana Padano foam is perfecto, not unlike the pappardelle with an exemplary and rich crumbled pork sausage sugo.

- 2820 Roosevelt Rd. (at Historic Decatur Rd.)
- (619) 270-9670 — **WEB:** www.solarelounge.com
- Lunch Tue – Sat Dinner nightly   PRICE: $$

SPICY CITY ⁑○

Chinese • Simple

&

Spicy Sichuan dishes are the name of the game at this spot, where the staff isn't prone to small talk or smiles but regulars don't seem to mind a bit. The food is solid and the portions are monstrous, leaving you with delicious leftovers for days.

The menu is littered with colorful pictures of noodles, preserved chilies, steaming hot pots, sizzling platters, casseroles and crispy rice-crusted dishes. In other words, there's something for everyone and it's all made to order. Eggplant with garlic sauce is divine and even simple stir-fried string beans will have your palate tingling. Keep an eye out for specials scribbled on construction paper at the entrance; if you want the fish head, tell them when you enter, as it takes at least 40 minutes to prepare.

◼ 4690 Convoy St. (bet. Engineer & Opportunity Rds.)
✆ (858) 278-1818 — **WEB:** N/A
◼ Lunch & dinner daily   PRICE: ⌾

TACOS EL GORDO ⁑○

Mexican • Taqueria

&

Look for the telltale sign of this taqueria—that smoky gray exterior with hot pink trim—and you'll know you've arrived at a local hot spot. Another sign? The throngs of people queued up at the Tijuana-style counter service-only joint.

It's serious business inside, where there are different lines and windows depending on what you want, but those in the know make a beeline for the sweet and spicy adobado pork tacos. Feel your taste buds tingle as taqueros slice hunks of spicy meat from massive spit-roasted cones of crimson adobada. Then grab a tray and stacks of napkins, as food this good doesn't come without a mess. Unique cuts are on offer here, including tripe, pork cheek, tongue and brain. Mulas, vampiras and quesadillas round out the selection.

◼ 556 Broadway (bet. H & I Sts.), Chula Vista
✆ (619) 691-8848 — **WEB:** www.tacoselgordobc.com
◼ Lunch & dinner daily   PRICE: ⌾

THE TACO STAND

Mexican • *Taqueria*

One of three locations, this family-run taqueria is inspired by the taco stands located just an hour away in Tijuana, but the name might as well refer to what you'll be doing here. That's right, you'll be doing a lot of standing around, as the lines are long. Pack your patience and a watchful eye to ensure someone doesn't snag your meal from the counter. The aggression is warranted, as the tacos, burritos and elote with mayo, parmesan and chili powder are all deliciously messy. The marinated pork in the al pastor taco is pure bliss; grilled mahi mahi is appetizing; and flame-grilled nopales are just right for vegetarians.

The California burrito, bursting with fire-grilled Angus beef steak with cheese and French fries, is a thing of beauty.

■ 621 Pearl St. (bet. Culver St. & Draper Ave.), La Jolla
✆ (858) 551-6666 — **WEB:** www.letstaco.com
■ Lunch & dinner daily   PRICE: 🍴

INDEXES

STARRED RESTAURANTS ✿

✿✿✿

Atelier Crenn	San Francisco	**134**
Benu	San Francisco	**193**
French Laundry (The)	Wine Country	**35**
Manresa	South Bay	**270**
Quince	San Francisco	**178**
Restaurant at Meadowood (The)	Wine Country	**43**
SingleThread	Wine Country	**58**

✿✿

Acquerello	San Francisco	**165**
Baumé	South Bay	**264**
Californios	San Francisco	**150**
Campton Place	San Francisco	**122**
Coi	San Francisco	**168**
Commis	East Bay	**218**
Lazy Bear	San Francisco	**157**
n/naka	Los Angeles	**460**
Providence	Los Angeles	**384**
Saison	San Francisco	**204**
Somni	Los Angeles	**327**
Sushi Ginza Onodera	Los Angeles	**388**
Urasawa	Los Angeles	**329**
Vespertine	Los Angeles	**464**

✿

Addison	San Diego	**490**
Al's Place	San Francisco	**148**
Angler	San Francisco	**191**
Aster	San Francisco	**149**
Auberge du Soleil	Wine Country	**27**
Aubergine	Monterey	**289**
Bar Crenn	San Francisco	**135**

BIB GOURMAND 😊

D

E – F

G – H

I – J

K

R - S

T - V

W - Y - Z

RESTAURANTS BY CUISINE

AFGHAN

Kabul ⊺○	Peninsula	**241**

AMERICAN

Ad Hoc ⊺○	Wine Country	**25**
Archetype ⊺○	Wine Country	**26**
Bacon & Butter ⊺○	Sacramento	**70**
Birdsong ❀	San Francisco	**194**
Buckeye Roadhouse ⊺○	Marin	**85**
Chalkboard ⊛	Wine Country	**49**
Charcoal Venice ⊺○	Los Angeles	**429**
Cockscomb ⊺○	San Francisco	**195**
Compline ⊺○	Wine Country	**32**
Crack Shack ⊺○	San Diego	**494**
Craft & Commerce ⊺○	San Diego	**495**
Dry Creek Kitchen ⊺○	Wine Country	**50**
Ella ⊺○	Sacramento	**72**
Evangeline ⊺○	Wine Country	**33**
Fishwives ⊺○	Los Angeles	**405**
Goose & Gander ⊺○	Wine Country	**34**
Grange ⊺○	Sacramento	**73**
Great Maple ⊺○	San Diego	**497**
Homestead ⊺○	East Bay	**222**
Mar'sel ⊺○	Los Angeles	**443**
Michael's ⊺○	Los Angeles	**433**
Monti's ⊺○	Wine Country	**54**
Mulvaney's B&L ⊺○	Sacramento	**76**
Mustards Grill ⊺○	Wine Country	**40**
Nick's Next Door ⊺○	South Bay	**273**
Outerlands ⊺○	San Francisco	**185**
Pacific's Edge ⊺○	Monterey	**293**
Parkway Grill ⊺○	Los Angeles	**407**
Pearl 6101 ⊺○	San Francisco	**186**
Post & Beam ⊺○	Los Angeles	**461**
Prospect ⊺○	San Francisco	**203**
Raymond (The) ⊺○	Los Angeles	**408**

CALIFORNIAN

Al's Place ✿	San Francisco	**148**
Aster ✿	San Francisco	**149**
Auberge du Soleil ✿	Wine Country	**27**
Backyard ⊛	Wine Country	**47**
Baran's 2239 ⊛	Los Angeles	**440**
Barbareño ⓘ	Santa Barbara	**304**
Barndiva ⓘ	Wine Country	**47**
Barrel House Tavern ⓘ	Marin	**84**
Bellwether (The) ⓘ	Los Angeles	**445**
Boulevard ⓘ	San Francisco	**192**
Brix ⓘ	Wine Country	**28**
Cafe La Haye ⓘ	Wine Country	**48**
Camper ⓘ	Peninsula	**239**
Central Kitchen ⓘ	San Francisco	**147**
Charter Oak (The) ⓘ	Wine Country	**31**
Chez Panisse ⓘ	East Bay	**216**
Eveleigh ⊛	Los Angeles	**369**
Farmhouse Inn & Restaurant ✿	Wine Country	**51**
Farmstead ⊛	Wine Country	**33**
fig café (the) ⓘ	Wine Country	**60**
Frances ⓘ	San Francisco	**106**
Gardenias ⓘ	San Francisco	**138**
Gather ⓘ	East Bay	**221**
Glen Ellen Star ⊛	Wine Country	**52**
Harbor House ✿	Wine Country	**53**
Harvest Table ⓘ	Wine Country	**36**
Herb & Wood ⓘ	San Diego	**498**
Jardinière ⓘ	San Francisco	**107**
John Ash & Co. ⓘ	Wine Country	**54**
Juniper & Ivy ⊛	San Diego	**499**
Kali ✿	Los Angeles	**373**
Lark (The) ⓘ	Santa Barbara	**306**
Le Comptoir ✿	Los Angeles	**345**
Localis ⓘ	Sacramento	**73**
Lord Stanley ✿	San Francisco	**175**
Lucia ⓘ	Monterey	**292**
Navio ⓘ	Peninsula	**243**
Nightbird ⓘ	San Francisco	**109**
Nopa ⓘ	San Francisco	**109**
Octavia ✿	San Francisco	**140**
Progress (The) ✿	San Francisco	**111**
Range Life ⓘ	East Bay	**227**
Rivoli ⓘ	East Bay	**227**
RT Rotisserie ⓘ	San Francisco	**114**
Rustic Canyon ✿	Los Angeles	**436**

CONTEMPORARY

KOREAN

LATIN AMERICAN

MEDITERRANEAN

MEXICAN

Lucha Libre ⭘	San Diego	501
Luna Mexican Kitchen ⭑	South Bay	272
Maestro ⭘	Los Angeles	405
Mariscos Jalisco ⭑	Los Angeles	423
Mayahuel ⭘	Sacramento	75
Mercado Los Angeles ⭑	Los Angeles	378
Monte Alban ⭘	Los Angeles	458
Nido ⭘	East Bay	226
Nopalito ⭑	San Francisco	110
Oscar's Mexican Seafood ⭘	San Diego	504
Papito ⭘	San Francisco	158
Petty Cash ⭘	Los Angeles	382
Playa ⭑	Marin	91
Puesto ⭘	San Diego	505
Punta Cabras ⭑	Los Angeles	435
Rocio's Mexican Kitchen ⭑	Los Angeles	355
Salazar ⭑	Los Angeles	400
Taco María ✿	Orange County	482
Tacos el Gordo ⭘	San Diego	506
Tacos Sinaloa ⭘	East Bay	229
Taco Stand (The) ⭘	San Diego	507
Tacubaya ⭘	East Bay	229
Yxta ⭘	Los Angeles	361
Zócalo ⭘	Sacramento	77

MIDDLE EASTERN

Adana Restaurant ⭑	Los Angeles	403
Bavel ⭘	Los Angeles	332
Bowery Bungalow ⭑	Los Angeles	395
DishDash ⭘	South Bay	267
Dyafa ⭑	East Bay	220
Exchange (The) ⭘	Los Angeles	336
Kismet ⭑	Los Angeles	397
Mini Kabob ⭘	Los Angeles	406
Momed Atwater Village ⭘	Los Angeles	398
Raffi's Place ⭘	Los Angeles	407

MOROCCAN

Khamsa ⭘	San Francisco	155
Mourad ✿	San Francisco	200

NEPALI

Yeti ⭘	Wine Country	61

PERSIAN

Flame ᴵⁱ◯	Los Angeles	454
Shaherzad ᴵⁱ◯	Los Angeles	462
Shalizaar ᴵⁱ◯	Peninsula	249

PERUVIAN

La Costanera ᴵⁱ◯	Peninsula	242
Rosaliné ⊕	Los Angeles	385

PIZZA

Bar Bocce ᴵⁱ◯	Marin	84
Cafe Reyes ᴵⁱ◯	Marin	86
Casey's Pizza ᴵⁱ◯	San Francisco	147
Del Popolo ⊕	San Francisco	123
Nolita Hall ᴵⁱ◯	San Diego	504
Pazzo ᴵⁱ◯	Peninsula	246
Pizzeria Mozza ⊕	Los Angeles	383
Pizzetta 211 ᴵⁱ◯	San Francisco	186
Vesta ⊕	Peninsula	252
Zero Zero ⊕	San Francisco	206

PORTUGUESE

Adega ᴵⁱ◯	South Bay	262
Uma Casa ᴵⁱ◯	San Francisco	117

PUERTO RICAN

Sol Food ᴵⁱ◯	Marin	93

SCANDINAVIAN

Stockhome ⊕	Wine Country	59

SEAFOOD

Anchor Oyster Bar ⊕	San Francisco	103
Bar Crudo ᴵⁱ◯	San Francisco	104
Connie & Ted's ᴵⁱ◯	Los Angeles	368
Fishery (The) ᴵⁱ◯	San Diego	497
Fishing with Dynamite ᴵⁱ◯	Los Angeles	441
Hog Island Oyster Co. ᴵⁱ◯	San Francisco	124
Ironside Fish & Oyster ᴵⁱ◯	San Diego	498
Lobster (The) ᴵⁱ◯	Los Angeles	432
Mi Lindo Nayrit Mariscos ⊕	Los Angeles	347
Monterey's Fish House ᴵⁱ◯	Monterey	292
New England Lobster Eatery ᴵⁱ◯	Peninsula	245
Newport Seafood ᴵⁱ◯	Los Angeles	424

SOUTHERN

SPANISH

SRI LANKAN

STEAKHOUSE

THAI

Ayara Thai Cuisine	Los Angeles	440
Farmhouse Kitchen Thai	San Francisco	153
Funky Elephant	East Bay	221
Jitlada	Los Angeles	372
Kin Khao	San Francisco	125
Luv 2 Eat	Los Angeles	376
Night + Market	Los Angeles	378
Saladang	Los Angeles	409
Sapp Coffee Shop	Los Angeles	401
Sweet Basil	Peninsula	250
Thai House	East Bay	230
Thai Thing	Los Angeles	390

VEGAN

Gracias Madre	San Francisco	154
Gracias Madre	Los Angeles	370
Mesa Verde	Santa Barbara	308
Millennium	East Bay	225
Plant Food + Wine	Los Angeles	434
Shizen	San Francisco	161
Shojin	Los Angeles	357

VEGETARIAN

Greens	San Francisco	139
Mother	Sacramento	76

VIETNAMESE

District by Hannah An (The)	Los Angeles	368
Garlic & Chives	Orange County	473
Golden Deli	Los Angeles	419
Khai	San Francisco	198
Lau Hai San	South Bay	269
LSXO	Orange County	477
Slanted Door (The)	San Francisco	129
Tamarine	South Bay	277
Thiên Long	South Bay	277

ALPHABETICAL LIST OF RESTAURANTS

A

N

ALPHABETICAL LIST OF RESTAURANTS

YOUR OPINION IS IMPORTANT TO US

What did you think of this product?

satisfaction.michelin.com

Please go to **satisfaction.michelin.com** to offer your opinion to help us better meet your expectations.

CREDITS

MICHELIN TRAVEL PARTNER

Société par actions simplifiées au capital de 15 044 940 €
27 Cours de L'Île Seguin - 92100 Boulogne Billancourt (France)
R.C.S. Nanterre 433 677 721

© 2019 Michelin Travel Partner - All rights reserved
Legal Deposit : 03-2019
Printed in Canada - 03-2019
Printed on paper from sustainably managed forests

Impression et Finition : Transcontinental (Canada)